PEAK PURSUITS

PEAK PURSUITS

THE EMERGENCE OF
MOUNTAINEERING IN THE
NINETEENTH CENTURY

Caroline Schaumann

Yale
UNIVERSITY PRESS

New Haven & London

Yale University Press books may be purchased in
quantity for educational, business, or promotional use.
For information, please e-mail sales.press@yale.edu
(U.S. office) or sales@yaleup.co.uk (U.K. office).

Set in MT Baskerville and MT Bulmer types
by Integrated Publishing Solutions.
Printed in the United States of America.

ISBN 978-0-300-23194-6 (hardcover : alk. paper)
Library of Congress Control Number: 2019953858
A catalogue record for this book is available from the British Library.

This paper meets the requirements of ANSI/NISO Z39.48-1992
(Permanence of Paper).

10 9 8 7 6 5 4 3 2 1

For Bruce and Matilda

CONTENTS

ACKNOWLEDGMENTS

Putting the final touches on the manuscript, I realize my hesitation to send off a complete version and to be done with this book at last. For the past decade, this project has occupied and accompanied me as a steady and trusted friend like no other, during a formative and eventful life period. Engaging with the idiosyncrasies and complexities of early mountaineers, scientists, and humanists provided purpose, passion, direction, focus, and distraction. But these pages are also a testament to past and current relationships: the inspiration and critique of friends and colleagues and the support of programs and organizations have developed into an remarkable and effective network that forms a solid base behind every page.

My colleagues in the Department of German Studies at Emory University, in particular Peter Höyng and Hiram Maxim (and more recently Paul Buchholz), supported this book from its earliest days even though it was a good bit removed from the traditional field of German literature. They not only provided enriching conversations and reassurance but also backed me on generous research leaves to ensure time for research and writing. The Center for Faculty Development and Excellence at Emory University, especially Allison Adams, buttressed the project in several crucial ways: the center's manifoldly excellent program informed the book's proposal and framework and helped me to establish contact with publishers. In addition, the Scholarly Writing and Publishing Award and the Emory Public Scholarship Advancement Fund made it possible to find and fund an editor and to cover fees for illustrations and the book cover.

Other fellowships afforded one of the most precious and cherished resources, which is time. The Alexander von Humboldt Foundation's steady support over the past decade enabled multiple research stays in Berlin and was thus instrumental in the various stages of the manuscript. What is more, as a fellow for Experienced Researchers, I was able to get to know and work with Ottmar Ette and his incredible team of researchers at Potsdam and in Berlin. In particular I want to thank Tobias Kraft, Julian Drews, Julia Maier, and Cettina Rapisarda for welcoming me into their circle and sharing their exceeding expertise on Alexander von Humboldt. Ottmar Ette at the University of Potsdam is one of the most incredible mentors I had the privilege of working with. I continue to be amazed by the enthusiasm, vigor, and encouragement he exudes, and I look forward to our continued collaboration. The German Academic Exchange Service (DAAD) provided funding through the Faculty Research Visiting Grant that also aided my research in Berlin.

Back at Emory, the indomitable Sander Gilman, over many lunch conversations, guided the emergence and evolution of this book. For the expertise, time, and effort he put into the manuscript, my sincerest thanks. The interdisciplinary Anthropocene reading group on campus offered an inspiring forum to discuss historical and contemporary texts and test out ideas. I wish to thank Shaunna Donaher, Eri Saikawa, and Lance Gunderson from environmental sciences; David Lynne from chemistry; Lynne Huffer from women, gender, and sexuality studies; and Karen Stolley from Spanish for their input and inspirational ideas.

Over the years, many people read parts of the manuscript and gave immensely valuable feedback. In particular, I am indebted to Bruce Willey, Cecilia Cancellaro, Katie van Heest, Colin Fisher, Jim Walker, Peter Mark, and Ulrike Guthrie for their much-treasured editing and helpful suggestions. I also fondly remember conversations with colleagues whose feedback shaped various ideas of the book. Here Sean Ireton, Heather Sullivan, Harald Höbusch, Hubert Zapf, Evi Zemanek, Gabriele Dürbeck, Christina

Frei, Gundolf Graml, Christoph Mauch, and Stewart Weaver deserve mention. Catherine Hollis freely sent me a copy of her wonderful book on Leslie Stephen. The three interdisciplinary "Thinking Mountains" summits I was able to attend in 2012, 2015, and 2018 likewise inspired much fruitful conversation and impetus.

Navigating the contracting and permissions process was greatly aided by Sarah McKee, senior associate director for publishing at the Bill and Carol Fox Center for Humanistic Inquiry; and Lisa Macklin, director of Research, Engagement, and Scholarly Communications at Emory. And the much-dreaded task of securing permissions for images became surprisingly easy and pleasant thanks to Melanie Kowalski, who offered hands-on help.

I want to thank especially the two peer reviewers of the manuscript whose detailed suggestions, helpful ideas, and expert references exceeded all my expectations and made the revision process exhilarating and satisfying. My editors at Yale University Press, Sarah Miller, Ash Lago, and initially Erica Hanson, were a dream to work with: encouraging, prompt, and reliable, and offering expert advice and much practical guidance, as well. Phillip King and William G. Henry provided superb assistance with copyediting and stylistic improvements, and Alexa Selph indispensable index work.

As we embark on yet another hotter summer in California, I grow wary of the extreme weather that marks our time and foreshadows the disasters to come. Admittedly with a sense of nostalgia, I feel gratitude for my time spent in the mountains and the deserts, always amplified by the presence of friends and family. I would like to thank my climbing partners far and near, David Trac, Ha Ngo, Shauna Murray, and Mary Devore, who made sure I had a rope to tie into. Papa and Mama, even though it must have been hard for you to watch me leave Germany at age twenty-two, study literature in the United States, embark on rock climbing, and eventually start a (mostly) English-speaking family, you supported my decisions despite them seeming often illogical and sometimes painful. This book is dedicated to my husband, Bruce Willey, whose boundless love and caring flexibility continue to amaze me, and our daughter Matilda, who, true to her name, strength in battle, is a shining beam of courage and hope. May the mountains continue to offer us a place on this planet Earth.

PEAK PURSUITS

INTRODUCTION

ENCOUNTERS WITH ROCK AND ICE

BETWEEN SCIENCE AND SUBLIMITY

The mood aboard the frigate *Pizarro* in June 1799 was one of excited anticipation. After six years of preparation for what turned into a five-year journey to South America, Alexander von Humboldt (1769–1859) and his travel companion, the French botanist and physician Aimé Bonpland (1773–1858), were finally about to drop anchor at their first stopover, the island of Tenerife, where Humboldt was said to have spent "the most enjoyable days of my life."[1] In his travel diary, Humboldt recorded the long-awaited vista of the Canary Islands and in particular its highest volcano, Mount Teide:

Despite the blue sky, the horizon was so hazy that we only saw the Island Gran Canaria in the evening, 5 hrs on June 18, and the Punta de Anbaga by daybreak the next day, June 19, but not Pic [de Teide]. The latter only became visible for a few minutes when we already had arrived at the mole of Saint Croix. But those few minutes bestowed a grand and surprising view. The morning was damp and cloudy. The solar disk was not yet visible to us, when suddenly the thick clouds clinging to the mountains west over the town toward the lagoon burst. Through this opening, the sky appeared in delightful blueness, and in the midst of this blueness, Pic de Teide in its entire majesty appeared, as if it didn't belong to this earth, and as if a glimpse into a foreign world had been opened. Only the last 2,000 feet of the crater were visible, up to the point where a second cone is piled onto the first one. The black, fuzzy clouds framing the picture contrasted most beautifully with the reddish light poured out in abundance by the first rays of sun. The broader the cloud masses scattered, the more slender and pronounced the shape of the enormous cone appeared. Its white, pumice-covered sides deceived us, as it did some other travelers. We took them for snow and glaciers reflecting the sunrays.[2]

Pico de Teide (3,718 m/12,198 ft.), the highest mountain of the Canary Islands and once thought to be the highest mountain in the world, revealed itself as the primary object of desire, symbolizing and epitomizing what Humboldt was about to encounter.[3] Framed by a curtain of clouds opening and closing as if onstage, the mountain granted its onlookers only temporary glimpses of the spectacle of nature. While Teide offered a first preview into "a foreign world," both imposing and elusive, Humboldt initially approached and conceptualized this new environment with a decidedly old-world mind-set. In this way, he first described the sight of Teide from a distance like a picture (*Bild*). His description bears the classic markers of the sublime, when grandness, suddenness, and formidableness converge to overwhelm the senses, causing an intense inner experience.

Viewing mountains from afar, however, was ultimately unsatisfying to Humboldt, and Mount Teide became the first of many volcanoes he set foot on along his journey, whether they were high or low in elevation, active or extinct. Humboldt ascended the mountain on June 21, 1799, along with a group of guides and officials, among them the French vice-consul and the secretary of the French consulate. After camping overnight under rock outcrops, Humboldt reached the summit the following day and descended into the crater. Various representations of his ascent testify to the mixture of excitement, gratification, fear, and fantasy he must have experienced. He first mentioned the undertaking in a letter to his brother: "June 23, evening. Last night I returned from the Pic. What a sight! What a pleasure! We advanced deep into the crater; perhaps further than any other naturalist."[4]

This brief depiction establishes a number of themes that return time and again in the description of his other climbs: superlative claims and exclamations denoting amazement and speechlessness, and pleasure about the undertaking's success in the face of challenges. Humboldt is filled with pride of having advanced further, farther, deeper, and higher than anyone before: he refers to the results of his measurements ("I made very important mineralogical observations here") and emphasizes the physical dimensions of his experience: "The storm began to roar fiercely around the summit; we had to peg ourselves firmly at the crater's rim. Like thunder the air rioted in the chasms, and a cloud cover divorced us from the world of the living. We climbed down the cone, utterly alone above the mist, like a ship at sea."[5] These material encounters with wind, cold, and thunder, and the resulting physical fatigue, anxiety, and isolation, form an increasingly important subtext in Humboldt's accounts of volcanic ascents. During his subsequent major mountain ascents in today's Ecuador, he recorded exhaustion, shortness of breath, bleeding, thirst, nausea, and coldness. He was overcome by fear and subject to fantasies, visions, and hallucinations. While Humboldt initially framed mountains in the European vernacular of the sublime and sought to ascend them in the name of science, the intimate encounter with rock and ice—though often far from pleasurable—decidedly unsettled theoretical constructs.

In his later, more detailed published description of the ascent in the *Personal Narrative,* Humboldt expanded on this new approach, promoting the climb in the following words: "An expedition to the summit of the volcano of Tenerife is interesting not solely on account of the great number of phenomena which are the objects of scientific research; it has still greater attractions from the picturesque beauties which it lays open to those who are feelingly alive to the majesty of nature. It is a difficult task to describe the sensations, which are the more forcible inasmuch as they have something undefined, produced by the immensity of the space as well as by the vastness, the novelty, and the multitude of the objects amidst which we find ourselves transported."[6] The passage offers one of the most lucid explanations of Humboldt's mountain quests. With a nod to scientific research, Humboldt emphasizes the even greater aesthetic value of the climb, not in a merely visual sense but accessible to those "feelingly alive to the majesty of nature." Expanding sublime reflection by its embodied dimension, Humboldt verily jumps into a sensual experience. It is here—where the scientist becomes dumbfounded, where the Enlightenment meets Romanticism, and sublime awe gives way to phenomenological perception—that the customary categories of definition, whether as the celebrated naturalist, explorer, or humanist, do not do Humboldt justice. While it comes as no surprise that the actual climbing experience upset a theoretical assessment of the mountain, the many unexpected turns and tensions arising from intense physical efforts in unfamiliar lands with different partners and groups deserve more careful and sustained attention.

What is more, Humboldt's keen sense of the afflictions and limitations of his body, as well as his unceasing enthusiasm for climbing to heights thought humanly impossible and his incessant drive to convey his experiences on paper (in experimental form and often unfinished), informed a generation of scientists and mountaineers and helped to establish the tropes in which mountaineering has since been articulated and communicated. Over the course of the nineteenth century, science, poetics, and embodiment became mutually constitutive in the evolution of mountaineering. That is, enlightened men felt the mountain in its full material force and grappled with their own physical ineptitude before processing their ascents intellectually and drawing some greater meaning from them. Their emotional and social experiences also influenced their attitudes toward mountains and the scientific, political, and social beliefs they projected onto them. Therefore the emerging elite mountaineering culture was one of profound ambivalence, contradiction, and paradox. Rather than documenting the history of Alpinism, recounting the ascents of peaks, or giving a portrayal of the most renowned climbers, this book presents a kind of Humboldtian history of mountaineering in the long nineteenth century (circa 1789–1914), when both scientific progress and aesthetic reverence became available through the embodied experience of the mountaineer.

Our current age of the Anthropocene, the era of climate change, species extinction, and global pollution, arguably demands such an approach. Along with other scholars, Christophe Bonneuil and Jean-Baptiste Fressoz have defined the central premise (and promise) of the Anthropocene as follows: "The Anthropocene challenges certain distinctions that were formerly deemed fundamental to the modern West: human exceptionalism and the ontological break between the human being as *subject* of entitlement and the *object* of nature."[7] As the science of environmental degradation is being studied, debated, and debased, we need not only new aesthetic mod-

4

els for a post-sublime environment but passionate involvement that reflects our inherent physical dependency on this earth. Whereas in the nineteenth century men were awestruck at the prospect and danger of exploring seemingly infinite mountain ranges, nowadays they are measured and mapped, often frequented, and even more excessively consumed as two-dimensional images in pictures and screen savers—and yet the mountains as we know them are severely threatened. In this way—as the damage done to our environment is greater than ever—our position of vulnerability has not changed.

In the face of an ever-warming climate, destructive fires, devastating floods, and melting glaciers, believing that life can continue as we know it seems hopelessly naive, and resigning ourselves to apathy likewise ignores the challenges at hand. Jonathan Franzen recently pointed out some middle ground in navigating these extremes: "Keep doing the right thing for the planet, yes, but also keep trying to save what you love specifically—a community, an institution, a wild place, a species that's in trouble—and take heart in your small successes. Any good thing you do now is arguably a hedge against the hotter future, but the really meaningful thing is that it's good today. As long as you have something to love, you have something to hope for."[8]

In a more hopeful vein, the promise of physical contact remains, as proven by the increasing popularity of climbing inside and outside. In their continual defiance of and deference to gravity, climbers are not only in direct contact with the elemental forces of the earth but also firsthand witnesses to its changes. We touch rock, step on ice, and breathe thin air, with plans and aspirations always dependent on the weather, and we suffer from melting mountain glaciers and increasing rockfall. In this sense, climbing mountains is a creative and performative undertaking, an example of what Stacy Alaimo has called transcorporeal interchanges.[9] Recent theories of material ecocriticism allow us to conceptualize mountaineering as an intimate exchange between the human and more-than-human world. Such theories are rooted in the approach of Maurice Merleau-Ponty, who sharpened Edmund Husserl's introduction of phenomenology as a turn to things themselves by focusing on the interaction between body and environment in his notion of perception. In contrast to the Cartesian subject-object split, Merleau-Ponty stressed the knowledge emerging from the living and sensing body: "I am all that I see, I am an intersubjective field, not despite my body and historical situation, but, on the contrary, by being this body and this situation, and through them, all the rest."[10] The immediate, reciprocal interchange between the material world and the perceiving body is the fundamental basis of every experience and empirical observation. Mountaineering then becomes a creative act of perceiving the world with one's hands and feet.

As a new geologic era with a yet-to-be-formed stratigraphic layer and a fiercely debated starting date, the Anthropocene brings to the fore previous ruminations on geologic epochs and deep time. This understanding of cyclical rather than linear time teaches us that we cannot take nature for granted, as it is continually evolving, with mountains expanding and shrinking. Humboldt and other scientist-mountaineers set out to discover stories embedded in stone and ice about the earth, its history, and future, becoming overtaken with pleasure and challenge along the way. Rather than pursuing the single-minded goal of summiting, they stumbled along mountain slopes and dropped into craters. Before the twentieth century's race to claim the highest mountains in the world for a particular nation, nineteenth-century climbers adopted a less summit-driven approach, frequently downplaying the actual act of reaching the top of a mountain. Often this humbleness was born from hubris and disappointment: in the face of a dynamic, powerful, and ever-changing environment, mountains became the sites where fantasies of conquest met disillusionment, and visions of male heroism, time and again, culminated in frustration and fright.

Nowadays, climbing Mount Everest has become attainable by anyone with reasonable fitness and disposable income. At the same time, we have seen an important development in recent climbing in relinquishing the primacy of the summit position in favor of the challenge of a given route, whether on rock, ice, or even plastic. "The ambiance of a crag, the view from the summit, and the uniqueness of a handhold are all part of the climbing experience," the contemporary climber (and multiple Everest summiteer) Conrad Anker recently wrote.[11] The narratives of nineteenth-century mountaineering, originating in an age of empires and fossil-fueled industrialization, cannot give us guidance on how to cope with the disappearing glaciers and changing mountains. They do, however, model the pleasures of climbing beyond the summit position, acknowledge cyclical geologic time on a changing earth, and exemplify the rewards and pitfalls of an intense entanglement and interaction with rocks, cliffs, and ice.

In antiquity and throughout the Renaissance, mountains held special importance to Western civilizations because of their rich deposits of metal and coal. After the publication of Georg Bauer's (Latinized to Georgius Agricola) authoritative treatise *De re metallica* (1556), which located precious metal mines in mountains, mining in continental Europe dramatically increased in the sixteenth and seventeenth centuries, fueling British industrialization in the eighteenth century.[12] At the same time, mountains became sites believed to hold answers to questions concerning the origin of the earth. In an inventive and comprehensive move, the English clergyman Thomas Burnet (1635–1715) attempted to reconcile modern scientific inquiries with the church's teaching. Significantly, Burnet's theories were inspired by direct experience when he crossed the Alps via the Simplon Pass on a three-year grand tour in 1671 and determined that the "wild, vast, and undigested Heaps of Stone" he saw could not have been devised by God himself.[13] In *Telluris theoria sacra* (published in two parts in 1681 and 1689, translated into English in 1684 and 1690 as *Sacred Theory of the Earth*), Burnet revolutionized scientific ideas of the day by claiming that the earth was initially egg shaped and covered by a thin crust that developed during the chaos of creation when "the heaviest and grossest parts would sink down towards the middle" (54), forming a solid core, while the oily parts above water mixed with heavier particles of the air to form a fertile slime that eventually dried into a surface shell. Burnet concluded that this once-perfect earth, "smooth, regular, and uniform; without Mountains and without a Sea" (60), was destroyed forever when God demanded punishment for man's sins and cracked the frame of the earth, its liquid erupting from beneath in a universal deluge and forming mountains, continents, and oceans. Merging scripture (both the Old and New Testament), scientific theories (astronomy and geology), and classical philosophy (Plato and Augustine) in inventive and suspenseful prose, Burnet was undeniably fascinated, if not obsessed, with mountains, which he regarded as "ruines of a broken World" (115), offering both evidence of deep time and man's destructive behavior.

7

Continuing the tropes of enormity and power, the paradigm of the sublime combined terror with awe, providing a much-cited rationale and vocabulary of mountain travel. Stemming from the Latin *sublimis, sub* meaning "up to," and *limin* meaning a "threshold," the term originally denoted an (often religious or transcendental) experience found at the limit of reason and expression, outside the bounds of conventional understanding. Among the first to stake out distinctly different realms of the beautiful and the sublime was Edmund Burke (1729–97) in his treatise *A Philosophical Enquiry into the Origin of Our Ideas of the Sublime and Beautiful* (1757). Working empirically, on the basis of personal experience, anecdotal evidence, literary examples, and generally held notions, Burke reasoned that the overcoming of pain, the "delightful horror" he termed sublime, constitutes the strongest emotion our mind is capable of, since pain and danger are inherently more powerful than pleasure.[14] Sublimity and power thus go hand in hand: to Burke, an object over which we have power is not sublime, but a force against which we feel powerless excites our passions and fears (59–65). The distinctly gendered implications of this juxtaposition cannot be overlooked: whereas the sublime signifies a heroic potency that, according to Burke, "produces a sort of swelling and triumph that is extremely grateful to the human mind" (46), women are relegated to the realm of domestic beauty and compassionate love.

By extension, theories of the sublime severed the thinking mind from the material world, making the body markedly absent in Western discourses on mountains, and also served to distinguish aesthetic from scientific concerns. Following up on Burke's theses, Immanuel Kant (1724–1804), in *Beobachtungen über das Gefühl des Schönen und Erhabenen* (1764, *Observations on the Feeling of the Beautiful and Sublime*), articulated both beauty and the sublime as an inner, subjective feeling. Kant posited that the sublime helps to develop moral character: when confronted with natural objects of immense magnitude (such as volcanoes, rock cliffs, hurricanes, waterfalls, or oceans), objects that we cannot comprehend and that threaten the self with feelings of annihilation, our reason enables us to confront the unimaginable and infinite. The sublime encounter is thus a mindful experience, both painful and pleasurable, and it is our ability to accept (via logic) the inadequacy of imagination that provides a sense of moral vocation.[15] By turning away from external reality, Kant defined the sublime as a moment in which the mind, through the faculty of reason, precisely transcends the world of experience. Friedrich Schiller (1759–1805) refined this aspect even further by proposing that man can realize his own freedom and independence from the laws of nature only when reflecting in relative safety on the chaos of nature. This intrinsically intellectual rather than sensuous experience denies that material reality has dominion over us: "Thus the sublime opens to us a road to overstep [literally, 'affords us an exit from'] the limits of the world of sense [literally, 'sensuality'], in which the feeling of the beautiful would forever imprison us."[16]

Denoting an increasing independence from a religious framework, definitions of the sublime ultimately celebrated the Western sovereign, rational subject. At the same time, the experience (and mastering) of uncontrollable nature became tied to sites of leisure such as Alpine resorts, long exclusive to the male upper and middle classes. Along with its gendered bent, such elitism was part and parcel of the sublime impetus: if novelty, surprise, and astonishment are all necessary ingredients for such experience, then the sublime loses its sublimity when it becomes the staple fare of everyday life. This culturally specific paradigm of the sublime offered a ready model to approach mountain ranges in the New World and significantly determined the ways in which Western explorers approached and perceived the Andean cordilleras. Accordingly, the framework of sublime exceptionalism resonates in many nineteenth-century mountaineering texts, though the sublime also deteriorated into an often-empty cliché and prompted significant reworkings.

Criticizing Kant and others for their overreliance on categories of rational understanding, Merleau-Ponty advocated a "plunge into the world instead of surveying it."[17] According to Merleau-Ponty, nature should be studied not as a separate object but as part of a circuit in which our bodies and minds are implicated, in a movement of perceiving and perceived. An experience then becomes an ongoing event engaging the senses, a reciprocal intercorporeal activity. More recently, Onno Oerlemans's notion of the "material sublime," developed in *Romanticism and the Materiality of Nature* (2002), explicated (and revised) the sublime process as an innate and material interaction between two dynamic bodies rather than an aesthetic consumption of an object or inward act of reflection. Oerlemans specifically suggests that Romantic travel, a mental and physical exploit that involved putting oneself in a different environment, transcends an idealized and escapist aestheticization of the landscape. In a similar vein, Alan McNee has expanded the notion of the "haptic sublime," a term coined by the philosopher Max Dessoir and used by the art historian Alois Riegl in 1901 to refer to a physical sense of proprioception. Similar to the material sublime, the haptic sublime adds an element of physicality to a new mountain aesthetic, emphasizing that mountaineers were in close and physical contact with the sublime object.[18]

By privileging a confrontation with wild and powerful places over experiencing beauty at home, the discourse of sublimity became inscribed into mountaineering from its very beginning. Humboldt and his fellow nineteenth-century mountaineers all employ the sublime vocabulary, but at the same time, their narratives contest, contradict, or intervene in such models. When trudging up slopes, battling storms, putting up tents, cooking and melting water, and even when eating, drinking, peeing, sleeping, and getting dressed, they hardly remained at a safe remove and aesthetic distance from dangerous places but rather experienced a web of greater dynamic forces, though still in relative privilege and comfort. Their often frightful and destabilizing experiences outside established frames of reference not only made familiar narratives of male triumph untenable but redefined aesthetic ideals, scholarly objectives, and social encounters in unusual and ambiguous terms. In this way, the beginnings of mountaineering, so intimately tied to intellectual principles, became a richly physical pursuit.

If sublimity offered an aesthetic framework, science provided the initial rationale that put Humboldt and other naturalists into the mountains. The Swiss botanist and geologist Horace-Bénédict de Saussure (1740–99) was among the first to research geography's central questions on-site, in the Alps. In the first volume of his landmark *Voyages dans les Alpes* (1779–96), he suggested: "The physical student, like the Geologist, finds on the high mountains worthy objects of admiration and study. These great chains, the tops of which pierce into the upper regions of the atmosphere, seem to be the workshop of nature and the reservoirs whence she draws the benefits and the disasters she spreads over our earth."[19] Pointing to the dual undertaking of aesthetic appreciation and scientific study, Saussure assigned special significance to mountains as an object of consideration. His words cleverly play off the age-old assumption that being in the mountains meant being closer to God so as to emphasize the importance of science rather than a Creator. Other nineteenth-century mountain climbers also incorporated metaphors of a heavenly journey to justify their endeavors and preempt criticism for feats rivaling Christ's ascent into the heavens.[20] After Saussure had identified mountains as a key area for scientific research, Humboldt (intimately acquainted with Saussure's work) followed up on his suggestion by heading to the Andean peaks.

Both Saussure and Humboldt engaged in one of the greatest scientific controversies of the time, the Neptunism versus Plutonism (or volcanism) debate. It was inaugurated by Humboldt's mentor, Abraham Gottlob Werner (1749–1817), who taught geognosy (the study of the earth's structure, an early form of geology) at the Freiberg Mountain Academy and whose ancestors had been involved in Saxon mining for over three hundred years. Werner famously posited that all rocks on earth had formed in layers by sedimentation in the oceans. His popular Neptunian theory did not question theology and was widely supported in the eighteenth century.[21] Conversely, the Scottish naturalist James Hutton (1726–97) theorized that over millions of years, sediments were continually deposited on the seabed, solidified, uplifted, and tilted through massive volcanic heat at the earth's core, only to become eroded again and eventually submerged once more. This Plutonist theory demonstrating the volcanic origin of rocks put Hutton in long-standing conflict with Werner's model and also challenged the biblical dating of the earth at six thousand years old. Following Werner, Saussure's *Voyages* sought to provide—sometimes far-fetched—evidence for Werner's Neptunist model, suggesting that Alpine valleys had formed when the floods receded and drained into the oceans. Humboldt also initially followed Werner's theories, but already during his stay on the Canary Islands and more fully during his research on the slopes of the Andean volcanoes, he came to doubt the theory that volcanoes were minor, localized phenomena, as Werner had claimed.[22]

In the wake of the Neptunist-Plutonist debate, major scientific shifts took place during the nineteenth century: both geography and geology came to be recognized as scientific disciplines, with British, French, and German geologic societies inaugurated, and geographic societies founded in major cities.[23] To geologists, mountains still provided the keys to the earth's history, but nineteenth-century meteorologists also believed they shaped weather and cyclones.[24] Thanks to the arrival of the telegraph—a significant development in meteorology for relaying observations—numerous weather-observation stations were established on mountaintops. As the list of the world's highest mountains grew steadily, new areas of research now included the atmosphere, air pressure, and altitude sickness. The new emphasis on dynamic and interactive models in the earth sciences caused scientists to move their indoor laboratories to outdoor sites, often placing them in the mountains. In what Saussure called the "workshop" or "laboratory of nature" (*laboratoire de la nature*), place and object of scientific inquiry became identical, so that scientists immersed themselves in their surroundings while trying to analyze them. This new approach of analytic field science that soon shaped both science and mountaineering required adaptation, flexibility, and coping strategies in the mountainous environment, taking into consideration weather, terrain, food, companionship, physical fitness, and state of mind, and making scientists acutely aware of the physical dimensions of their work.[25]

While new geographical and geological theories put scientists on mountain slopes to study plants, rocks, glaciers, and the weather, philosophers and naturalists such as Friedrich Schelling advocated—in contrast to what they took to be reductionist and perfunctory Enlightenment science—an understanding of nature as a whole rather than its mechanical parts. By studying nature and man's connection to it, Romantic scientists were especially interested in the "new" science of biology, as well as natural forces such as magnetism, galvanism, and meteorology. Fossil finds enabled the French naturalist and zoologist Georges Cuvier (1769–1832) to inaugurate the fields of anatomy and paleontology by establishing that the earth was composed of succeeding stratigraphic layers whose age could be determined by the fossils they contained. Cuvier was also among the first to suggest that large, now-extinct reptiles and mammals once roamed the earth in prehistoric times. In his groundbreaking *Principles of Geology* (three volumes, 1830–33), Sir Charles Lyell (1797–1875) challenged this catastrophic theory while expanding on Hutton's theses to develop the concept of uniformitarianism, stressing gradual geological forces that occurred throughout history and are ongoing today. In contrast to biblical models, Lyell argued that humans had no influence on the earth's development, proposing the term *Holocene* ("recent epoch") for the warm era beginning after the last ice age, then thought to coincide with the emergence of humans. Another major shift in geology did not occur until the late 1960s, when observations of seafloor spreading and continental drift led to the gradual acceptance of plate tectonics. In the wake of these discoveries, ocean floors supplanted mountains as the center of scientific interest in the twentieth century, a shift also mirrored in meteorology when satellites and space probes replaced weather stations and observatories on mountaintops.

Most studies have treated artistic, scientific, and touristic interests in mountains as separate research areas, but more recently scholars have begun to question a neatly divided, threefold process in which artists first waxed poetic in sublime reverence, scientists then analytically unlocked the mountainous environment, and finally tourists flocked to the newly developed and examined mountainscapes.[26] In the wake of post-colonial studies, scholars laid an important historical and archival foundation by elucidating the cultural, political, and economic context of scientific exploration and mountaineering.[27] In the past decade especially, our understanding of mountaineering has been sharpened significantly: Bernard Debarbieux and Gilles Rudaz's *The Mountain: A Political History from the Enlightenment to the Present* (2015) and Peter H. Hansen's *The Summits of Modern Man: Mountaineering After the Enlightenment* (2013) identify mountaineering within the political configurations of the Enlightenment but at the same time question a one-directional or linear development, as Hansen elucidates: "Mountaineering did not emerge 'after' enlightenment—they arrived together. Mountaineering and modernity mutually constituted one another in the eighteenth century and have continued to do so."[28] In addition, Tait Keller's *Apostles of the Alps: Mountaineering and Nation Building in Germany and Austria* (2017), Wade Davis's *Into the Silence: The Great War, Mallory, and the Conquest of Everest* (2011), and Maurice Isserman and Stewart Weaver's *Fallen Giants: A History of Himalayan Mountaineering from the Age of Empire to the Age of Extremes* (2008) emphasize the role of empire and nation building in the Alps and Himalaya, respectively.[29] Other books have offered a critique of mountaineering from a gendered perspective. While an abundance of important analyses have assessed the history of mountaineering in comprehensive arguments about modernity, imperialism, and masculinity, this book endeavors to complement the field by offering nuanced inquiries into individual mountain climbers that tend to complicate larger frameworks. Deriving from my approach as a literary scholar, my work comprises analyses of primary texts to illuminate the ambiguities and complexities of early mountain climbing. It focuses especially on the complex interplay of body and mind that can become lost in overarching historical arguments. If Richard White, a historian of the American West, cautioned against a post-modernist critique that "neglects this physical, tangible world, a world of substantial bodies, and trivializes our experience in it," the following chapters elucidate the multifaceted representations of particular mountain moments in their material dimensions.[30]

The celebrated naturalist, scientist, and humanist Alexander von Humboldt (1769–1859) is the most prominent case in point. Humboldt embarked on his legendary research trip to the Spanish colonies in the Americas in 1799. Unlike previous forays to the New World, Humboldt's five-year expedition to the Canary Islands, Venezuela, Cuba, Colombia, Ecuador, Peru, Mexico, and the United States was independently financed and not tethered to any immediate colonial, national, economic, or political aims. Rather, Humboldt's wanderlust, driven by a scientific quest as well as the desire to escape his restrictive Prussian environment, with no clear-cut agenda or predetermined travel route, was steeped in the Romantic ideal of traveling. As part of his research on vegetation zones and volcanism, Humboldt ascended several volcanoes, including Pico de Teide on Tenerife (1799); Silla de Caracas in Venezuela (1800); the imposing Ecuadorian volcanoes Antisana, Pichincha, Cotopaxi, Tungurahua, and Chimborazo (1802); and El Jorullo in Mexico (1803). These climbs, completed with small groups of various explorers and local guides, all without mountaineering boots, suitable attire, or technical equipment, exemplify a trial-and-error approach to climbing. Although Humboldt did not often reach the peaks' summits and was forced to turn around on Antisana, Cotopaxi, Tungurahua, and Chimborazo, his mountain feats still remain impressive.

Recent scholarship has shown a renewed upsurge of interest in Humboldt. Aaron Sachs (2006), Laura Dassow Walls (2009), and Andrea Wulf (2015) have all heralded Humboldt as an early environmentalist, "a visionary, a thinker far ahead of his time" who deeply influenced North American naturalists.[31] Meanwhile in Germany there has been consistent and thorough scholarship, greatly aided by the Berlin State Library's acquisition of the diaries in 2013 and culminating in numerous publications, exhibits, and conferences in the "Humboldt Year 2019" marking the 250th anniversary of his birth. Humboldt's far-reaching influence on emerging mountaineering discourses, however, continues to be underestimated. Predictably, Humboldt's journey galvanized young males to aspire to similar expeditions: Louis Agassiz sought to join Humboldt on his excursion to Russia; James David Forbes hoped to write a narrative similar to Humboldt's travelogue; John Muir declared, "How intensely I desire to be a Humboldt!" planning to follow in Humboldt's footsteps by venturing to South America; and Edward Whymper in Ecuador finally claimed the summits that Humboldt had unsuccessfully attempted.[32] But Humboldt's influence reached far beyond these immediate desires of emulation. Early mountaineers in the Alps such as Alfred Wills, Leslie Stephen, and John Tyndall were intimately familiar with Humboldt's texts and frequently referred to his measurements. Furthermore, they shaped their own narratives according to some of the traditions Humboldt helped to establish, merging scientific observation, aesthetic reflection, a keen sense of the body, and some degree of self-effacing reflection. To expand on the body of research on Humboldt and his counterparts in the nineteenth century, we must look at the moments when scientists became mountaineers, portraying their endeavors in narrative accounts.

Stunned and confounded by the climbing experience, Humboldt searched for new forms of representation—he experimented, variously, with text, drawings, maps, graphs, diagrams, and even photography.[33] His published travel descriptions, with their scientific details and laboriously detailed lithographs, shaped the conventions of scientific documentation, nature writing, and landscape painting and offered an educated audience a proverbial compass and narrative on how to read and see the New World. They also inspired generations of young men to escape from a seemingly mapped-out life to go abroad with scientific and exploratory aims. This book's first part, "From Europe to the Americas: Alexander von Humboldt," considers Humboldt's evolving language over the course of nine major mountain ascents that he describes in detail in his diary and other publications. With bold claims about the interconnectedness of geographical and biological forces and vast conclusions emerging from comparative, intercontinental analysis, Humboldt pioneered modern geography and influenced an entire generation of scientists who adopted his style of research travel. If Humboldt's project of studying the interconnectedness and interaction of natural forces is indebted to the Romantic paradigm, he also insisted on detailed analysis and precise measurements. Chapter 1, "The Vicissitudes of Humboldt's Mountain Moments," argues that Humboldt not only merged these opposing approaches but also experienced the dissolution of categories altogether when faced with extreme conditions high in the mountains. Thus Humboldt slowly departed from paradigms such as the European sublime and scientific enlightenment, admitting to becoming intoxicated with unknown heights, and boasting with altitudes and first ascents.

Delving deeper into Humboldt's multilayered style, chapter 2, "The Drama of Ascent," traces Humboldt's language as it oscillates between superlatives and negation, amazement and protest, exaggeration and humility, detailed measurement and silence. Rather than offering one complete and coherent narrative, Humboldt presents us with a multitude of representations of his mountain climbs in his travel diary, letters, and published travelogues and pictorial atlases, attesting to a multifaceted, shifting, and often inconsistent discourse. If Humboldt himself recognized incongruities in his works, he attributed them to the overall uneasiness of his mind. "Filled with restlessness and agitation, I never rejoice about what has been accomplished and am only happy when I endeavor something new, namely three things at once. In this emotional state of moral restlessness, sequitur to a nomadic life, one must search for the main causes of the great imperfection of my works."[34] What Humboldt dismisses as a weakness, however, contributes to the contemporary fascination, relevance, and timeliness of his oeuvre.

The book's second part, "Alpine Adventures," elucidates in six chapters the evolution of Alpine climbing in the mid-1800s, examining the ways in which Humboldtian writing and science, the Romantic sublime, and bodily sensations and disruptions shaped perceptions and representations of European forays to Alpine summits. Chapter 3, "The Alps: A Brief History," presents a brief overview of the history of Alpine development from antiquity to the present, with special consideration of British tourism in the Alps. Chapter 4, "Horace-Bénédict de Saussure's Quest for Mont Blanc," revisits the late eighteenth century to trace the steps of the aforementioned Swiss naturalist, who is widely credited as the father of Alpinism. After handing a generous reward to the first person to ascend Mont Blanc, Saussure finally reached the summit himself the following year in 1787 and, overcome with exhaustion and plagued by nausea, famously commented: "I was like a gourmet invited to a superb banquet whose utter revulsion prevented him from enjoying it."[35] His four-volume *Voyages dans les Alpes* delineated scientific observations and ecstatic descriptions of his travels but also betrayed moments of disillusionment, even irritation. Saussure never ventured as far as Humboldt: firmly rooted in a European intellectual and privileged perspective, he mostly remained in the lowlands and did not question conventional scientific paradigms, and his texts—following aesthetic traditions—hailed the Alpine sublime and idealized mountain peasants. Yet beyond the nods to conventions, the discerning reader finds inventive, sometimes radical, insights. Saussure created an entirely new model of depicting a mountain's summit perspective, introduced influential observations on glaciers and glacial movement, and visibly became obsessed with climbing Mont Blanc even though the mountain held no scientific value for him. Thus it comes as no surprise that Humboldt read Saussure's entire works before embarking on his trip, frequently referenced Saussure in his own publications, and credited Saussure's accomplishment whenever possible.

Mountaineering did not explode after Mont Blanc had been climbed. On the contrary, Philipp Felsch reports only six ascents of Mont Blanc by 1815, partly due to the Napoleonic Wars and partly because of the frightful reports by those who had scaled the mountain.[36] Even by 1854, ascents of Mont Blanc had merely increased to forty-five. In the meantime, however, glacier scientists had become progressively curious about the Alps and had begun to climb peaks in the process. The Swiss geologist and zoologist Louis Agassiz (1807–73) was among the first to publicly suggest that glaciers covered large parts of the earth during an "ice age." Agassiz's career began in Germany and was initially supported by Humboldt and Cuvier, but his ideas about glaciers met fierce resistance, sending him to the Alps in 1838 to prove his hypotheses. Agassiz spent a large part of the next five years refining his theories, a time during which he also completed harrowing ascents of the Jungfrau, Siedelhorn, and Wetterhorn. The chair of natural philosophy at Edinburgh University, James David Forbes (1809–68), met Agassiz in 1841 and accompanied him on the Jungfrau. Chapter 5, "Icecapades: James David Forbes and Louis Agassiz," takes the climb as a point of departure to delineate how the two glaciologists, while embattled in bitter controversy, fueled a passion for ice and snow that prominently figured in the public imagination. Agassiz's *Études sur les glaciers* (1840), with its accompanying atlas of thirty-two plates stunningly arranged with intricate overlays, stirred sublime awe and scientific curiosity. Forbes, in contrast, fashioned his *Travels Through the Alps of Savoy* (1843) in format and style after Saussure's *Voyages* for both scientists and mountaineers as a reference that bolstered his scientific reputation, described his journeys in Romantic terms, and offered actual climbing advice and methodologies. Both works divulge their authors' infatuation with glaciers as a highly dynamic, volatile, and agentic environment.

Turning to the so-called Golden Age of Mountaineering, chapters 6 through 8 critically assess the contested discourses of Alpinism in the years between 1854 and 1865 at the intersection of science, Romanticism, athleticism, and escapism. Chapter 6, "The Selling of the Alps and the Beginning of the 'Golden Age': Albert Smith and Alfred Wills," juxtaposes Albert Smith's fortieth ascent of Mont Blanc in an extravagant guided caravan equipped with luxuries from champagne to cognac to chocolate in August 1851 with Alfred Wills's September 1854 Wetterhorn ascent, commonly regarded as the beginning of the sport in the Golden Age. While the style of both ascents was decidedly different (though both were accomplished with the help of guides), their wide-ranging effects on the emergence of the sport proved similar. Smith's wildly successful London Piccadilly show *The Ascent of Mont Blanc* (1852) and book of the same title (1853) arguably had a greater effect on Alpine development than the spiritual writings and mountaineering accomplishments to date, and Wills's subsequent *Wanderings Among the High Alps* (1856) espoused mountaineering as an activity worthwhile in itself while hailing time in the mountains as restorative of health. In this way, both texts foreshadowed many developments to come, such as an emergent militarization and nationalization of the sport, a more prominent gender discourse, and the ensuing competition in the first ascent of the Matterhorn.

In his emphasis on competitive sportsmanship, hard-edged fortitude, and harrowing exploits, the wood engraver Edward Whymper (1840–1911) can be seen as an embodiment of Victorian masculinity. With little interest in climbing peaks that had been scaled before, Whymper became obsessed with being the first person to climb the Matterhorn, and after seven attempts his team finally succeeded in "conquering" the mountain on July 14, 1865, albeit with great loss when four of the team's seven members fell to their deaths during the descent. Chapter 7, "Poetic Science and Competitive Vigor: John Tyndall and Edward Whymper," looks at Whymper's best-selling *Scrambles Amongst the Alps* (1871) not only as a response to the ensuing controversy but also as a departure from the aesthetic and scientific concerns that marked previous texts. Yet a closer analysis reveals that Whymper's book is unmistakably shaped by Humboldt's discourse, prefaced by literary quotes, and brimming with references to Saussure, Agassiz, Forbes, Tyndall, and Stephen. Far more knowledgeable than he is given credit for, Whymper engages nineteenth-century traditions while pointing ahead to the nationally tinged race for first ascents in the twentieth century. In contrast, the profusely productive Irish physicist John Tyndall (1822–93), Whymper's contemporary and rival, also climbed with competitive vigor but praised challenges in the mountains as mental and physical recovery from his work in London. Recently, Tyndall's work gained renewed importance, as he was the first to prove the trapping of heat by CO_2 in the atmosphere (the greenhouse effect), publishing his findings starting in 1859.[37] By imbuing mountaineering with a spiritual dimension, Tyndall's writings prefigured those of Muir and lastingly shaped the representation and consumption of the sport. In this vein, Tyndall invents a language that, furthering Humboldt's vocabulary, infuses scientific observation with a passionate, poetic plea. But whereas Humboldt, Saussure, and Forbes keenly perceived physical sensations as interrupting measurement or worship, Tyndall boldly imbues the very categories of science and aesthetics with an inherent material dimension, dwelling on climbers' material entanglement in a dynamic earth that by its very nature entails suffering, helplessness, and loss of control.

Chapter 8, "The Making of Modern Climbing: Leslie Stephen," analyzes Stephen's seminal *The Playground of Europe*, published in the same year as Whymper's and Tyndall's books, as a foundational text of modern climbing. Stephen's work grapples not only with the aftermath of the Matterhorn disaster but also with the fact that all major Alpine peaks had been scaled by 1865, highlighting the need for a new rationale and philosophy of mountaineering. The answer, according to Stephen's philosophical and sometimes humorous reflections, is to move emphasis from a particular mountain to one's own faculties, finding challenge and pleasure in the activity of climbing rather than the conquest of first ascents. The explosion of high-altitude mountaineering, but also small-scale bouldering, and the growing popularity of rock climbing—now officially approved for the 2020 Olympic Games in Tokyo—in the wake of the opening of climbing gyms all over the world lends contemporary currency to Stephen's thoughts.

The book's third and final part, "Exploring the American West," investigates how European notions of mountaineering carried over to North America. Through Humboldt's influence on Frederic Edwin Church, Albert Bierstadt, and Thomas Moran, among others, European discourses had already merged with New World landscape aesthetics. Initially seen in the framework of the European Alps, the mountains of the American West were increasingly delineated as a manifestly separate space, shaped by the frontier experience rather than by European models. This development went hand in hand with a burgeoning travel industry: if 30,000 people had traveled from Omaha to San Francisco in 1871, the number rose to 75,000 by 1875, and 100,000 by the turn of the century.[38] North American writers and editors actively promoted this trend. The Massachusetts newspaper editor Samuel Bowles, in his tellingly titled book *The Switzerland of America* (1869), heralded the West's natural wonders—which came within travelers' reach after the completion of the Pacific Railroad—as nothing short of alpine beauty. The railroad not only facilitated travel and brought tourists to the western states but also greatly accelerated silver and coal mining. At the vanguard of the West's increased industrialization, the pioneer North American mountaineers Clarence King (1842–1901) and John Muir (1838–1914) celebrated the beauty of the Sierra Nevada as a uniquely American range, albeit in very different ways.

Chapter 9, "Transcontinental Shifts: Clarence King's Representation of the American West," explores the impact of European mountaineering discourses on Clarence King. Like some of his European counterparts, King came to the mountains to escape the confines of a Victorian society, but his representations of risks taken in the mountains helped create a distinctly American image of the explorer. King's *Mountaineering in the Sierra Nevada* (1872) mythologized the exploration of the West during a period in which some Americans began to worry that the frontier would disappear. While King himself would eventually transition from mountaineer to a businessman and mining consultant, his book ingeniously mixed European tradition with a more freshly acquired discourse more typical of the "blood and thunder" pulp novels of the day, in a curious mix of objective description and unfettered imagination. Yet despite the image of virile heroism that King harbored in his written texts as well as photographs of his expeditions, much ambiguity remains at play, divulging insecurities about masculinity, racial identity, science, and conquest.

When the Scottish immigrant John Muir first came to the Sierra Nevada in 1868, he, like King, quickly became enthralled with its granite domes and cliffs, alpine lakes, sequoias, and pine trees. Fittingly, Muir merges and expands all previous mountaineering pursuits, including scientific discovery, spiritual quest, physical challenge, and solitude, coming full circle from Humboldt to Forbes, Tyndall, Stephen, and King. Promoting places like Yosemite as a pristine, quintessentially "American"—that is, white American—wilderness that could offer solace to city dwellers, Muir paved the way for the touristic and capitalistic exploitation of "wilderness," facilitating the expulsion and extermination of Native American populations in the process. Chapter 10, "The Solitary Mountaineer: John Muir," investigates Muir's texts against the backdrop of privileged notions of exclusivity regarding race, gender, and class but also seeks to highlight Muir's astute environmental and political critique, as well as his passionate and sensual delving into a more-than-human world.

European and American forays to alpine summits began with the search for plants and minerals and the study of geology and glaciers. Yet many scientists became engrossed in the physical act of climbing itself, captivated by the views from above and fueled by the prospects of scaling summits. The tensions arising from the intersections of scientific and aesthetic interests, a material and metaphysical dimension, and gender and class have riddled these writers' depictions with a host of contradictions: inspired by idealized Romantic notions of nature, early mountaineers idealized their endeavors as sublime and spiritual experiences, all the while deliberately measuring and calculating what they saw. In the name of science, these men advanced to what they perceived as terra incognita, fashioning the mountains as a refuge from an increasingly industrialized western Europe. At the same time, their expeditions relied much on modern society's advancements in wealth, leisure time, and infrastructure, which in turn paved the way for further commercial exploitation of the mountains by the production of maps, climbing guides, and mountaineering equipment. Their intense focus on the body emerged precisely at a time when innovations in technology enabled an increasing independence from physical labor and hardship at the dawn of the Industrial Revolution, often thought to be the advent of the Anthropocene. With the help of steel manufacturing and steam power, when coal-fueled trains transported people throughout Europe and eventually across North America, the pioneers of climbing explored areas of cold and desolation, pushing their bodies into ever-increasing heights previously labeled inaccessible. Yet the early mountaineers remained caught in an unresolved tension between the struggle for emancipation from nature and precisely the desire to be at nature's whim. Other tensions concerned gender roles: though celebrated as triumphant adventurers and icons of masculinity at home, many explorers climbed mountains precisely to escape the inflexible gender roles of their societies.

In a mixture of sublimity, science, and sensibility, nineteenth-century mountaineering narratives responded to a rapidly advancing mechanized and modernized world and became highly marketable to a growing and interested middle class. Their inherent tensions reveal much about Victorian values and subcultures, leisure, sport, and the middle class: they both affirm and question a drive to conquer nature while also acknowledging a dynamic, if not agentic, environment.[39] They uphold hegemonic masculinities to legitimize men's dominant position, but also include (self) mockery and failure, highlighting differing and individualized responses.[40] They model curiosity in the face of geologic change and celebrate science in passionate, sometimes exalted, language. They draw attention to the occasional pain and inherent pleasure that arrives from experiencing our corporeal connection with the world, whether by encountering the miseries of altitude sickness, the jubilation of reaching a summit, or the satisfaction one feels when touching rock. In the Anthropocene, when mountain glaciers are shrinking by the year, when, as part of the great acceleration of a heating planet, the human imprint is destroying the earth as we know it, and when even science and the very facts of environmental destruction are under threat, we need reminders of mountain pleasures, wonder, and passion more than ever.

PART I
FROM EUROPE TO THE AMERICAS
Alexander von Humboldt

CHAPTER 1

THE VICISSITUDES OF HUMBOLDT'S
MOUNTAIN MOMENTS

The Meaning of Mountains

Mountains stand at the beginning of Humboldt's five-year journey and have become one of its most recognizable, lasting symbols. In Humboldt's oeuvre, mountains embody remarkable extremes and paradoxes. When Humboldt scaled the heights of the Andes, he was actually interested in the earth's depths, viewing the interiors of volcanoes as an opportunity to obtain firsthand glimpses into previous stages of the earth's crust. Meanwhile the physical challenges and demands of climbing continually diverted his mind from theoretical tasks. In contrast to the tropical heat so typical of the equator, on the Andean peaks Humboldt faced freezing cold, and then again tormenting heat when descending into a crater. The view from the mountaintop or his high point—if there was one to be had—could be grand but also frightening. At high altitude and dizzied by the sulfurous stench emanating from fumaroles, Humboldt was periodically subject to hallucinations and came to doubt the reality of his perceptions. What started out as a narrative of mountain triumph thus disintegrated into fragments, silence, and resignation, when Humboldt became stunned up high, and acute physical realities and bodily sensations complicated both aesthetic and scientific reasoning. As indicated by Humboldt's indefatigable quest for new modes of representation, the established textual categories were not sufficient to adequately illustrate his experiences and sensations.

Mountains were a constant thread throughout Humboldt's life. Already by his twenties, he had amassed considerable expertise in geology, mineralogy, and mining, having spent eight months of intensive coursework at the renowned Freiberg Mountain Academy in Saxony before accepting a position as mining inspector at the Prussian Department of Mines in 1792.[1] Humboldt climbed mountains wherever he went, whether on his trips throughout Europe, on the American journey, the later Siberian expedition, or in old age his "Potsdam Chimborazo," the 88 m (288 ft.) Brauhaus Mountain near his home. In the first half of his life, he was particularly drawn to the Andean Cordillera, then thought to be the highest mountain range in the world and thus a particular object of aesthetic wonder and scientific curiosity.

While two centuries of colonial history had both expanded and exploited the territories of the New World, scientific expeditions did not begin until the eighteenth century, when in the wake of James Cook's voyages and the spirit of Western Enlightenment, scientific interest in the lands beyond Europe was rising and often replacing local systems of knowledge. After the botanist Joseph Banks (1743–1820) withdrew from Cook's second expedition to the Pacific, Cook appointed the German naturalists Johann Reinhold Forster (1729–98) and his son Georg (1754–94), whose *A Voyage Round the World* (1777) ignited modern travel literature by combining trip reports, scientific data, and observations on flora and fauna with ethnographic descriptions and philosophical remarks. Humboldt befriended the young revolutionary, joining Forster on a trip through the Netherlands, England, and France and crediting him with the beginning of scientific travel: "Through him began a new era of scientific voyages, the aim of which was to arrive at a knowledge of the comparative history and geography of different countries."[2]

Attempts to map the New World had already begun some decades previously. In 1736, the French Académie Royale des Sciences sent the astronomers Charles-Marie de La Condamine and Pierre Bouguer on an expedition led by Louis Godin to Quito, then in the Viceroyalty of Peru, to measure the arc of the meridian and settle a long-standing debate about whether the earth was elongated along its polar axis (as Cassini claimed) or flattened at the poles (as Newton claimed).[3] The Spanish government assigned the Spanish naval officers Jorge Juan and Antonio de Ulloa to the geodesic expedition, which, in the years between 1736 and 1743, worked in two teams using triangulation, barometer readings, and gravity measurements. From 1743 to 1744, La Condamine sailed up the Amazon, mapping the river and collecting observations before heading back to France.[4] After their return, the expedition's members, entangled in internal quarrels and disputes, published separate accounts in French and Spanish about their scientific results and the natural world and peoples along the Amazon. For its blending of science and adventure, La Condamine's *Relation abrégée d'un voyage fait dans l'intérieur de l'Amérique méridionale* (1745) became the most popular of these volumes and also influenced Humboldt's account. Another Spanish expedition, headed by José Solano and José Iturriaga (1749–67), explored rivers, mountains, and other natural phenomena in Venezuela. Excited by these findings, Johann Gottfried von Herder endowed the new discipline of field geography with instrumental importance, declaring in his *Ideas for the Philosophy of History of Humanity* (*Ideen zur Philosophie der Geschichte der Menschheit*, 1784): "It would be highly gratifying, had we a map of mountains, or a mountain atlas, in which these pillars of the Earth were laid down and depicted with every circumstance that the history of man requires. . . . ; what a beautiful and instructive *physical geography of the Earth* would the inquirer into the history and natural philosophy of man have before him at one view!"[5] Humboldt happily heeded this call, citing Herder's words as stimulus for his own thinking. In preparation for his journey, Humboldt measured each hill that stood in his way. He studied astronomy, anatomy, and botany. He performed galvanic experiments on frogs, lizards, mice, and himself, hoping to prove the "life energy" of all animate beings.[6] He repeatedly read the works of Horace-Bénédict de Saussure.[7] He sought contact with major naturalists of his time, creating a vast communicative network.

In Germany, Humboldt felt marginalized, and despite his jovial and sociable nature, he remained an outsider owing to his rejection of conventional expectations such as a steady job and a family. Writing in 1792 to Carl Freiesleben, a friend and fellow student at the Freiberg Mountain

Academy, Humboldt bemoaned his privileged upbringing in Berlin: "Here in Tegel I spent the larger part of this unhappy life, among people who loved me and wanted the best for me and to whom I still didn't connect with any emotion, in thousand-fold restraint, in self-deprecating loneliness, in circumstances in which I was forced into constant disguise, sacrifices."[8] The revelation can be read as a hint as to Humboldt's homosexuality, his difficulties in disguising his affections, and the beginning of his desire for faraway places. In another document not intended for publication, an autobiographical sketch in his diary that Humboldt tellingly completed from afar while staying in Santa Fé de Bogotá in August 1801, he elaborated:

> My young soul, abused for eighteen years in my father's house and constrained in meager sandy soil smolders and glows brilliantly if—left to its own freedoms—it suddenly absorbs a world of things. . . . I felt constricted, short of breath. An indeterminate quest for faraway, unknown worlds, everything that powerfully moved my imagination, the danger of the sea, the wish to master adventures and transpose myself from an ordinary and commonplace existence to a magical world, tantalized me back then. I disdained everything connected to my father; I was disgusted by all the leisure of domestic life and a refined world. I lived in a world of ideas that pulled me away from the real one.[9]

Humboldt's dreams of travel thus reflected an attempt to free himself from predetermined roles and quiet his bouts of anxiety and depression. The extensive inheritance after the early death of his apparently rather cold and distant mother in 1796 made it possible to realize such dreams. While his older brother Wilhelm rose to become a respected philosopher and linguist, diplomat, and eventual founder of the Humboldt University in Berlin, Alexander broke with militaristic Prussia, aristocratic family roles, a predetermined professional career, and heterosexual gender roles. Mountains provided him with the opportunity to escape the constraints of civilization while also affording the company of close male friends.

Humboldt first embarked on a research trip to northern Italy and the Swiss and French Alps in 1795, during which he met Saussure in Geneva, and planned to visit the European volcanoes Vesuvius, Stromboli, and Etna in 1797, but the Napoleonic Wars that raged in Italy hindered this trip. He then turned his attention to the New World, praising its vast, overwhelming nature in general and its mountains in particular. In his unfettered enthusiasm, he raved in the introduction to his *Personal Narrative of Travels to the Equinoctial Regions,* the published report of the first part of his American journey: "Many years have elapsed since I quitted Europe, to explore the interior of the New Continent. Devoted from my earliest youth to the study of nature, feeling with enthusiasm the wild beauties of a country guarded by mountains and shaded by ancient forests, I experienced in my travels enjoyments which have amply compensated for the privations inseparable from a laborious and often agitated life."[10] Humboldt consequently climbed every major peak along his way, beginning with Pico de Teide on Tenerife, Silla de Caracas in Venezuela, Puracé in Colombia, and the major Ecuadorian peaks Antisana, Pichincha, Cotopaxi, Tungurahua, and Chimborazo, before moving on to El Jorullo in Mexico.

To Humboldt, mountains were microcosms of the earth in that the peaks' altitude resembled the earth's latitude. Thus, if one climbs up a mountain, one encounters the same vegetation and climatic zones as in the earth's latitudinal zones. The higher one climbs, the farther from the equator. In this way, the study of plants, animals, and inhabitants of mountain regions became vital to advances in botany, geography, geology, meteorology, and geomagnetism, furthering our general knowledge of the earth. Humboldt approached mountains equipped with barometer, thermometer, sextant, chronometer (to measure the longitude of his position), theodolite (to measure horizontal and vertical angles for surveying), inclinometer (to measure the slope), hygrometer (to measure the moisture content of the atmosphere), and cyanometer (to measure the color intensity or "blueness" of the sky)—all in all, about fifty instruments crafted specifically for the American journey. Even though he more often than not failed to reach the summit, he was able to climb to heights never reached before (first on Antisana and later on Chimborazo). More importantly, he was among the first to detail altitude sickness, which he correctly attributed to a lack of oxygen owing to the lessening air pressure and its effects on the body. His accomplishments, especially given the lack of equipment, remain impressive.

While considerable scholarship has focused on Humboldt's descriptions of his Chimborazo climb[11]—both Andrea Wulf's best-selling *The Invention of Nature: Alexander von Humboldt's New World* (2015) and Aaron Sachs's previous *The Humboldt Current* (2006) open with Humboldt on Chimborazo—

his other climbing feats have not yet received distinct scholarly attention.[12] In fact, reasonable confusion seems to persist in scholarship regarding the specifics of Humboldt's mountain achievements, possibly because he never recounted these climbs in the more well-known and widely translated *Personal Narrative*.[13] Humboldt, however, meticulously recorded all his ascents in his diaries, representing them as climactic episodes of his journey and crafting a dramatic narrative marked by sublime aesthetics, scientific reasoning, flights of the imagination, and material intervention. He thereby established and modeled a complex and malleable discourse of climbing that continued in nineteenth-century mountaineering narratives.

Colonial Interventions

Throughout Humboldt's American journey, mountains also became sites where contradictory discourses intersected and colonialist imperatives intervened with Humboldt's desire for equality. By creating a contrast between fertile nature and Western civilization, Humboldt participated in the colonial imperialism of his century, as Mary Louise Pratt has forcefully argued. To Pratt, "Alexander von Humboldt reinvented South America first and foremost as nature. Not the accessible, collectible, recognizable, categorizable nature of the Linnaeans, however, but a dramatic, extraordinary nature, a spectacle capable of overwhelming human knowledge and understanding."[14] Humboldt was firmly embedded in the western European tradition of exploring, mapping, and naming the territories of the New World. Inhabitants of the Andean regions had long climbed and dwelled in its mountains, as evidenced by relics, ruins, and figures, but did not endeavor to climb peaks in the name of science or aesthetics. Viewing the natural environment as complementary to the built environment, the Inka often integrated rock outcrops into stone walls or designed structures around crags, such as Machu Picchu. In *A Culture of Stone: Inka Perspectives on Rock*, Carolyn Dean fittingly observes: "In the South American Andes, in the fifteenth and early sixteenth centuries, the Inka (Inca) framed, carved, sat on, built with, revered, fed, clothed, and talked to certain rocks."[15]

Like any other European explorer of his time, Humboldt approached the New World with a firm belief in Western superiority, heralding European achievements in the arts and sciences as universally relevant and age-

less. And though Humboldt repeatedly criticized the tangible effects of colonial exploitation, he also benefited from and furthered colonialist power
structures, both voluntarily and involuntarily. For instance, Humboldt's
maps of Mexico were used by the United States for imperialist expansion,
and his discovery of guano as a highly effective fertilizer sparked an unprecedented European guano-import boom that led to the devastating exploitation of Chile and Peru and the Chincha Islands War (also known
as the guano wars) between Spain and its former colonies of Peru and
Chile in 1864 to 1866. At the same time, Humboldt had sharp and sour
words about colonialism and slavery: "In this relation of my travels I feel
no desire to dwell on pictures of individual suffering—evils which are frequent wherever there are masters and slaves, civilized Europeans living
with people in a state of barbarism, and priests exercising the plenitude of
arbitrary power over men ignorant and without defence" (*Personal Narrative*,
348). He not only voiced his critique of colonialism but also put it into
practice, such as in his well-known refusal to let himself be carried by other
humans.[16]

Humboldt was also keenly aware that the brittle Spanish regime would
not exist much longer. Mourning the loss of friends and colleagues as well
as acknowledging persisting tensions, Humboldt admitted that the *Personal
Narrative* "pourtrays the state of the greater part of the Spanish colonies
at the beginning of the 19th century" (xxii), an unstable world on the eve
of a widespread revolution. Even when the colonial empire broke apart—
beginning with the Mexican War of Independence and other uprisings
in 1810 and concluding with Simón Bolívar's victory in 1824 over the last
Spanish powers in Peru—social inequality persisted. Decades-long wars of
independence had stalled economic development and enabled aggressive
new powers such as the United States to take hold of the world's markets.
Humboldt's *Personal Narrative* chronicled his trip in light of these later developments.

Recent publications tend to revise Pratt's one-sided assessments, pointing instead to Humboldt's willingness to be formed and changed by his
environment.[17] Heralding Humboldt as an exception to dominant modes
of thinking, Aaron Sachs comes to a conclusion that directly clashes with
Pratt's stance: "In the end, Humboldt stands out as an important exception
to the European colonial paradigm. He was no doubt a man of his time,

but he also achieved enough distance from his society, both literally and figuratively, to transcend many of its prejudices. Indeed, the post-colonial critics themselves are deeply indebted to Humboldt's critique of Western hypocrisy."[18] That Humboldt was an exception in this sense becomes especially evident in the mountains, when outside the bounds of society, a frightful and often destabilizing experience made familiar narratives of male conquest and Western superiority untenable. Looking at Chimborazo specifically, Christiana Borchart de Moreno and Segundo E. Moreno Yánez point to Humboldt's pivotal role in establishing the volcano as Ecuador's national symbol.[19] Faced with the enormity of the Andean volcanoes, Humboldt revised established aesthetic discourses and questioned human dominance over nature. Pointing to the vast influence of the Mexican and South American Enlightenment on Humboldt, the historian Jorge Cañizares-Esguerra credits Humboldt with bringing scientific discourses of the global South and global North into conversation and laments that this important history of ideas is omitted in Wulf's influential biography. While much scholarship has painstakingly traced Humboldt's reciprocal influence on European and North American thinkers, a similar study examining his vast network of Spanish and criollo naturalists, whose names are often erased from the history of scientific exploration, remains outstanding.[20]

Representations

The different texts in which Humboldt documented his ascents—his travel diaries, letters, pictorial representations, and the *Personal Narrative*—are genres that have significant differences in origin, purpose, readership, and style. Though incomplete and fragmentary, the diaries and letters offer a lively and colorful glimpse into Humboldt's spontaneous reactions during his trip, while the *Personal Narrative*, which is similarly incomplete, provides a more straightforward perspective from a distance in time. Yet on closer scrutiny the distinctions and overlaps prove more complex. Humboldt consciously fashioned his diary as a document for posterity in case he should not return from his journey (which he assumed to be a probable scenario).[21] The diaries that exist are likely based on previous notes and drafts that Humboldt rephrased in precise, readable writing, complemented by numerous drawings and furnished with occasional directives for publication.[22] Rather than keeping a traditional diary that provided a daily overview of occurrences and encounters, Humboldt used his diaries as a medium to store information, measurements, observations, and analyses while he was in the field, often taking different notebooks for different disciplines. On his overland journeys, he only continued his diary during prolonged stays in cities or other resting points where he had the chance to summarize the previous excursions; on his river and sea journeys, however, he more consistently kept a diary, often writing while holding the book in his lap, as in the famous portrait by Friedrich Georg Weitsch.[23]

Humboldt's travel diaries not only formed the basis for his ensuing published travel reports but continued to function as a reference work: he unbound them for the purpose of amassing new notes, references, and quotes from letters, pasting paper slips into the existing pages. At the same time, Humboldt cut parts of pages to paste them somewhere else or send them to someone else altogether. Recently, scholars have described Humboldt's work methods and continued changes as a never ceasing movement characterizing Humboldt's life, his science, and writing.[24] Toward the end of his life, Humboldt had his—unsorted—diaries bound in nine leather volumes, and spelled out in his will that they were to be made accessible to other scientists at the Berlin Observatory. With respect to the latter two-thirds of the American journey, including the ascents of Ecuadorian volcanoes not covered in the *Personal Narrative*, the diaries serve as the primary and essential documents for reconstruction and analysis.

As was the case with the diaries, Humboldt's letters (many of which have been lost or destroyed) describe his travel routes and explorations in detail, giving a portrayal of the landscapes and people he encountered—though Humboldt later burned any letters that would expose too many details about his private life. Since these letters would be the only surviving written documents should the diaries be lost or destroyed, Humboldt likewise crafted his letters for potential publication. He meticulously recorded his measurements, gave directives for publication in the margins, and occasionally duplicated descriptions from the diary. Depending on the addressee, the letters were composed in German, French, Spanish, or English.

The first publication to emerge after the American journey, Humboldt and Bonpland's *Essay on the Geography of Plants* (1807, *Essai sur la géographie des*

Portrait of Alexander von Humboldt, 1806,
by Friedrich Georg Weitsch (1758–1828) (Wikimedia)

plantes), featured an elaborate color profile of Chimborazo and Cotopaxi, with detailed information on the vegetation, atmosphere, and rocks in the margins and the accompanying essay. Humboldt's second publication after the American expedition, *Views of Nature* (1808, published in German as *Ansichten der Natur*), provided readers with a new view of a particular landscape or cultural artifact in a twofold structure of main text and footnotes (whereby the notes, continually changed and complemented, often exceed in length and body the information of the main text). Aiming at "a far-reaching overview of Nature, proof of the cooperation of forces"—that is, a complete vision transcending mere description or empirical analysis and giving as much emphasis to aesthetic and moral concerns as to science—Humboldt sought to create a sturdy bridge between natural sciences and the humanities.[25] Significantly, the original edition did not contain a single image, obliging readers to produce their own imagery of the natural phenomena described.[26] Humboldt detailed his own insights or "views" of nature but more importantly encouraged his readers to turn inward to gain "views" that can be attained through reflection, emotion, and creative imagination. Accordingly, he explicated: "Natural philosophy transcends a mere description of Nature. It does not consist in a sterile accumulation of facts. It is the privilege of the curious and active mind of humanity to occasionally drift out of the present and into the darkness of prehistory, to gain a sense of what cannot yet be clearly discerned, and thus to take delight in the ancient myths of geognosy in their many recurring forms."[27] Within this general contemplation about the earth's formation, volcanoes take on particular importance, as they provide access into the depths of craters, imparting views into the earth's past. Whereas the volume did not single out any mountain ascent, it contained an all-important chapter, "Concerning the Structure and Action of Volcanoes in Various Regions of the Earth." As "intermediary earth-springs," volcanoes and their erupting lava to Humboldt constitute a rare connection between the inner and outer spheres of the earth, offering insights that culminate in "opened communication between the interior and exterior parts."[28]

In Paris in the years between 1810 and 1813, preceding the publication of the *Personal Narrative*, Humboldt had busied himself with preparing the pictorial account *Vues des Cordillères et monumens des peuples indigènes de l'Amérique* (*Views of the Cordilleras and Monuments of the Indigenous Peoples of the Americas*). *Views of the Cordilleras* included sixty-nine images and sixty-two essays on both natural scenes and human artifacts, "intended to represent a few of the grand scenes which nature presents in the lofty chain of the Andes, and at the same time to throw some light on the ancient civilization of the Americans" (*Personal Narrative*, xvii). Most of the illustrations were based on Humboldt's own drawings in the field; some derive from other scientists. With great care and cost, Humboldt arranged for the production of twenty-four colored, one partly colored, five sepia, and thirty-nine black-and-white plates, produced by renowned artists in several European cities. As a naturalist who viewed his science as art and his art as science, he sought to convey both scientific detail and artistic impression. Of the joint large-scale project to document and evaluate the American journey together with Aimé Bonpland, the *Personal Narrative* (though published later) covered volumes 1 to 3, and *Views of the Cordilleras* volumes 4 and 5, of the eventual twenty-nine volumes.[29]

Humboldt's much-anticipated *Personal Narrative,* published in French as *Relation historique du voyage aux régions équinoxiales du nouveau continent* between 1814 and 1825 and comprising three volumes and twenty-nine chapters, is a multifaceted travelogue that combines autobiographical narration, aesthetic description, scientific inquiry, and political statements. The narrative inexplicably ends after Humboldt's departure from Cuba and arrival in Cartagena in today's Colombia on April 20, 1801, the day before his trip up the Río Magdalena.[30] Thus almost two-thirds of the trip's description, including Humboldt's explorations in Colombia, Ecuador, and Peru, his longer stay in Mexico City, and the return trip through Veracruz, Havana, and Philadelphia, remain missing. The enormous cost and work involved—Humboldt's oeuvre was said to be the most expensive travelogue ever published by a private person, and it bankrupted at least one publisher—difficulties with the publisher, and other commitments may have contributed to Humboldt's decision not to complete the narrative.[31] Yet at least until 1836 he harbored plans to issue a fourth volume that would have included his most impressive mountain ascents, though considering his previous narration, the outstanding events would have required approximately six volumes.[32] In contrast to the diary, the *Personal Narrative* offers a complex mixture of report and analysis interspersed with flashbacks and flash-forwards, since Humboldt continually related his experiences to other events during his trip and evaluated his measurements and observations in light of the research completed after his return to Paris. In accordance with his understanding of nature as spatial, dynamic, and fluid, Humboldt thus processed the impressions of his journey in different media and artistic forms, using data, text, and image.[33] While these modes complement one another, at times they remain in an unresolved tension, mirroring nature itself.

The Curtain Opens: Pico de Teide

In the case of Teide, many sources available now allow for a fruitful comparison of diverging descriptions in the letters, the diary, the published travel report, and the pictorial account. In the diary, Humboldt's first view of Teide, presented as if a curtain opened onstage, harks back to well-established descriptions of the sublime. The resulting process of reflection, which, according to Burke's and Kant's logic of the sublime, leads to a realization of human insignificance vis-à-vis the vastness of the universe, is also evoked in Humboldt's depiction. "As friendly and beautiful as this view is insofar as nature directly grants it immediately, it is given something austere and formidable which is added by our imagination. The island seems so small against the colossus, which it serves as a footing. . . . The wind was howling in the clouds that enclosed the high cone, they crowded closer, and the curtain closed just as quickly as it had unexpectedly opened to us."[34] In keeping with the customary narratology of the sublime, a carefully constructed narrative arc—using words such as "austere," "formidable," and "unexpectedly" as counterpoints to beauty—lends his description tension and drama.[35] Preceded by a lengthy explanation as to why travelers at sea cannot see mountains from afar, Humboldt's view of Teide occupies a much more prominent space in the travel diary than in the published description of the *Personal Narrative*, where it is simply termed a "magnificent spectacle" (45–46).[36]

Concerning the ascent, however, only a short diary fragment is preserved, along with some subsequent notes that Humboldt made in French while in Mexico City and Philadelphia (1803 and 1804), where he studied the history of the Canary Islands.[37] Conversely, Humboldt depicted the ascent, summit experience, and descent of Teide in various letters and described them in depth in the *Personal Narrative* (60–87), giving evidence of the profound impact the experience had on him.[38] Yet according to the *Personal Narrative*, neither ascent nor descent transpires to be an enjoyable encounter with mountaineering. The climb is arduous, and the party endures a cold night bivouacked on the rocks without tents or blankets. Even the indefatigable Humboldt repeats the word "suffered" to characterize the difficulties caused by exertion, dust, cold, wind, heat, and smoke. From the summit they are able to discern the ocean, coast, and inhabited villages of

Tenerife and even see the islands Palma, Gomera, and Gran Canaria when the clouds lift, but they wait "in vain" (83) for a rewarding view of the entire archipelago. Finally a "cold and violent wind" (86) forces the party to seek shelter at the base of the crater. On the descent, the travelers find themselves unwillingly rolling down the loose ash slope. These unexpected difficulties disrupt scientific measurement and aesthetic awe.

But as he did in his letter to Wilhelm, Humboldt again boasts of his achievements. He insists that he has "never passed a night on a point so elevated" (67), goes on to declare that "no traveller, furnished with instruments, had as yet taken such an observation" (69–71), and concludes, "Of all the volcanoes which I have visited, that of Jorullo, in Mexico, is the only one that is more difficult to climb than the Peak, because the whole mountain is covered with loose ashes" (73–74). At the same time, Humboldt is stricken by the area's lonesomeness. During the ascent and on the summit, he finds "perfect solitude" (66) and writes that "no insect fluttered in the air" (85), an observation he also makes in his accounts on Chimborazo. Toward the end of his description, Humboldt gleefully elevates his ascent in superlative terms while downplaying the value of its narration: "When a traveler attempts to describe the loftiest summits of the globe, the cataracts of the great rivers, the tortuous valleys of the Andes, he incurs the danger of fatiguing his readers by the monotonous expression of his admiration" (80). The statement is rendered ironic by the fact that most contemporary and current audiences were, and continue to be, engrossed by Humboldt's tales of adventure and awe but became bored by his scientific excursuses and extensive footnotes. Humboldt repeatedly employs comparisons to places he visited after his return to Europe, such as Chamonix and the volcanoes Aetna and Vesuvius, the latter of whose eruption he witnessed in August 1805. At the same time, he jumps ahead to his experiences on Chimborazo, Antisana, and Jorullo, so that the ascent of Teide turns into a key moment and a crucial transition.[39]

Although Teide was not strictly part of his trip to the Americas, *Views of the Cordilleras* includes a plate and accompanying essay on the volcano. The brief essay focuses on the composition of the rock and the history of eruptions, and Humboldt only indirectly mentions his ascent by referring to the drawing he crafted at the rim. The plate based on this drawing, however, exceeds the essay in drama and charm. Uncharacteristically for the volume,

View of the interior of the crater of Teide, from *Vues des Cordillères*, 1813, plate 54 (Drawing by Hans Konrad Escher von der Linth, provided by the Zentralbibliothek Zurich)

it neither depicts the volcano from below nor shows the view from the top but reveals three people at the crater's rim: two explorers—Humboldt and Bonpland—staring into the abyss, with a third person still climbing an impossibly steep and loose slope while carefully reaching for rocks at the rim. Revealing a barren, otherworldly landscape of bizarre formations and spikes of cooled lava, the illustration corresponds more fittingly to Humboldt's later description in the *Personal Narrative* of the "vastness, the novelty, and the multitude of the objects, amidst which we find ourselves transported" than to the accompanying scientific essay. At the same time, the image both expands and contradicts the published account of the climb: we see the explorers only from the back, and since they are looking down, not up, we are denied their vista and cannot see what they discover at the bottom of the crater. In typical fashion, Humboldt's partial panorama of the mountain and its ascent leaves much to his readers' and viewers' imaginations.

Apparently Humboldt's stay in the Canary Islands left a persuasive, lasting impression, though the naturalist only spent a few days there. Humboldt vowed to return and in the *Personal Narrative* even voiced his preference for the Canarian landscape over tropical South America—but his plans never materialized. Teide was Humboldt's first successful climb at altitude; it also confirmed the value of his elaborate instruments and substantiated his scientific methods in the field.[40] Passing through various vegetation zones whose equivalent he later found in the Andes, Humboldt began to develop his concept of global climatology. Thus Teide embodies a seminal mountain ascent against which all his ensuing attempts are measured. In the *Personal Narrative,* Humboldt's emphasis on hardship and success frames the even grander and more difficult adventures to come, lending the volume a powerful foreboding. During each subsequent attempt on an Andean peak, Humboldt would invoke his Teide experience, wavering between grandiosity and humbleness, conquest and failure. Such incommensurability is arguably fundamental to Europe's experience of the New World in general.[41] In this way, the description of the Teide climb becomes the blueprint for the narration of his most famous ascent on Chimborazo while also hinting at the complex colonial power dynamics in which he intervened. As the Canary Islands served as a prototype for Spanish exploration and colonialism from the late fifteenth century onward, Teide symbolized Humboldt's departure from the Old World and a transition to the New, marking the beginning of a mountaineering discourse that fused science, aesthetics, physical immersion, and personal inspiration.

Disillusioning Difficulties: Silla de Caracas

After the exhilarating success of the Teide climb, Humboldt found himself in viscerally harsh conditions on Silla de Caracas. The New World could be punishing, to a degree he had not experienced before. Disappointment and uncertainty rise to the fore in all of Humboldt's accounts of South American peaks but especially overshadow the Silla climb. Yet it is little known that these texts—in their vacillation between pride of the accomplishment and recognition of the failure—serve as the founding documents of mountaineering. Humboldt's distinctive voice found its wellspring in the descriptions of suffering, hardship, and frustration that have become a staple of any mountaineering or extreme-sport narrative. To trace the emergence of this discourse, we will have to take into account Humboldt's published descriptions and illustrations in the *Personal Narrative,* essays, and the pictorial atlas *Views of the Cordilleras,* as well as initially unpublished letters and diary descriptions, often our only sources of information.

On July 16, 1799, two months after starting the journey from Madrid and a month after visiting the Canary Islands, Humboldt and Bonpland arrived in Cumaná, Venezuela, their place of residence for the following four months. During local excursions, they ascended several lower peaks in relative comfort—"camping" at a house on the mountain slope—and without major difficulties or hardships. Reveling in the picturesque beauty, Humboldt compared the scenery to the Swiss Alps, and his descriptions overflow with details about flora and rock composition, the results of his measurements, and aesthetic marvel. Yet when Humboldt faced the discomfort of his next mountain expedition to Silla de Caracas on January 1 and 2, 1800, such awe quickly dissipated. Humboldt and Bonpland arrived in Caracas in late November 1799, moving into an empty house for the following two months, and attempted to plan the expedition to Silla according to the weather, a strategy that proved to be difficult: "uncertainty, since almost never two consecutive days are clear, whether one should decide on a clear or a cloudy day."[42] The expedition comprised eighteen people, among them the Capuchin missionary Francisco de Andújar, two guides, and around a dozen slaves. At 2,640 m/8,622 ft., Silla de Caracas was a lower peak of the Ávila massif along the Venezuelan coast, but the ascent indicated some of the challenges and inconveniences of mountaineering in the tropics.

In his diary, Humboldt devotes a lengthy and detailed description to the successful first ascent, which remains the only cohesive narration during his stay in Caracas. Rather than sublime and scientific reflection, the account is overshadowed by physical displeasure and brims with negative superlatives and petty accusations: "For the last 11 years I have climbed mountains throughout all of Europe—but I never suffered so much simply because of poor outfitting and false information regarding the distance to the summit, because of waiting for others."[43] Humboldt has a host of other complaints. Already on the morning of January 1, the first day of the new century, he feels "resentment because of the lost, sleepless night," because he and Bonpland had waited for a Jupiter lunar eclipse they missed owing to a miscalculation.[44] He goes on to reject the food offered as "pigs' grub" and grumbles about timid porters, thirst, and sore feet.[45] He gives us no grand depiction of the summit experience, only a quick remark about the elusive yet expansive vista, affording a view of Caracas and its surroundings to the south and the Atlantic Ocean to the north, "but in these moments a grand and wide-ranging view." He then adds a sentence about the practical (and imperialist) value of his ascent: "My height measurement [of Silla's summit] can serve for the Mexican bay, so ships may consequently determine by the angle of elevation their distance from the coast, because Silla is discernible from far away in the sea because of its saddle forma-tion."[46] Humboldt's joy seems limited to the successful measurement on the summit and the prospect of leaving it as soon as possible, though the descent, in part completed barefoot, turned into an equally painful and toilsome affair: "Joyous about the observations and about having accom-plished our purpose, we plucked up our courage to descend still that same evening. . . . We descended more on our butts and hands than on our feet."[47]

In all its wretchedness and torment, Humboldt's diary depiction becomes a decisive moment in the overall evolution of his climbing accounts in that it begins to outline the manifold mental, material, and bodily aspects. Here we find no overarching crafted narrative arc, and fragmentary impressions prevail, often interrupted by physical suffering, as in the following passage: "With deliberation and vigor one endures anything. But the feet still hurt very much, and from 1:30 to 10 p.m. we were without a drop of water or wine."[48] In the face of the ascent's hardship, Humboldt's diary lends a voice to acute bodily sensations and suffering while pondering the resulting mental processes:

> These fantasies [and] conjectures absorbed me at altitude, and because they always afflict the geognost at altitude, this kind of furor soothes the pain of the endured discomforts. The thinking man becomes exhilarated on the top of the mountains, and, comparing his state with that of the mob accompa-nying him, he becomes aware that the moral-intellectual stimulus has a more sthenic effect than any food and drink. The imagination is a balsam full of miraculous healing powers that nature bestowed to suffering humans as in-separable companions, and it heals the wounds of the physical organism as well as the deep wounds punched by reason, one's own and others'.[49]

Despite his bigoted undertones distinguishing the enlightened man from the "mob," Humboldt identifies imagination as a key component when scaling heights. He recognizes that altitude causes not only physical but psychological afflictions, presenting the interplay of body and mind as in-herently valuable rather than pure whimsy.[50]

View of the Silla de Caracas, from *Vues des Cordillères*,
1813, supplement, plate 68 (Internet Archive)

In contrast to the unsentimental account of adverse conditions and general misery in the diary, other descriptions of his Silla climb diverge sharply. Humboldt mentioned the ascent in several letters, but his remarks remain limited to the measurements undertaken, notes on vegetation, and brief references to his successful summit.[51] In *Views of the Cordilleras* (plate LXVIII), he included a picturesque drawing of an explorer sitting in a meadow (Humboldt himself, inserted by the illustrator), sketching a steep, heavily vegetated mountain on the opposite side. The brief elaboration (four sentences) leaves out more than it reveals: "This granitic mountain, very difficult to scale because its slope is covered in a thick turf, has an absolute height of over thirteen hundred fifty toises."[52]

The *Personal Narrative*, however, offers a thoroughly reworked account that even begins with a different date of the climb, namely, January 2, 1800. The extensive (some twenty-five pages) description focuses mainly on measurements by thermometer, barometer, electrometer, cyanometer, and hygrometer.[53] Humboldt repeats some of the details from the diary, such as the fact that no one had scaled the mountain before, the missed sleep owing to a miscalculation, the difficulty in timing the weather, and the particular steepness of the climb. He also mentions uncooperative guides and companions and missing provisions, but whereas the diary had repeatedly poked fun at the Capuchin missionary, the *Personal Narrative* partly blames the slaves.[54] Yet Humboldt has omitted physical suffering from the text, and the narrative instead emphasizes pleasant scenery ("Nothing can be more picturesque" [418]), an exceptional view from the summit ("the eye ranged over a vast extent of country" [431]), and skilled climbing ("this part of the way is not dangerous, provided the traveller carefully examines the stability of each fragment of rock on which he places his foot" [431]). The description of the summit alone comprises some six pages, in which Humboldt declares himself "satisfied with the success of our journey" (437). Finally, the narrative concludes in sublime awe with the descent at night: "The noise of the cascades gave this nocturnal scene a grand and wild character" (438). In this published version, Humboldt markedly concealed his anger and softened the annoyed tone of the diary. As the *Personal Narrative* sets different priorities, beautifying and whitewashing the experience of the ascent compared to the diary, mountaineering aesthetics and firsthand experience remain in an unresolved tension.

The Silla account in the *Personal Narrative* also gives Humboldt the opportunity for a more comprehensive, comparative narrative. In this vein, he compares the vegetation to Switzerland, relates his views from the top of Teide and Pichincha, and determines the angle of the slope compared to Mont Blanc. In addition, he mentions "those measurements which elevate the mountains of Himalaya above all the colossal Cordilleras" (439), an observation that reveals Humboldt's keen interest in and intimate knowledge about geographical debates about mountains. In 1810 the British surveyor Lieutenant William Webb had fixed Dhaulagiri from four measuring points at 8,187 m/26,862 ft., though his findings were generally dismissed in Europe.[55] Only in the 1830s, some fifteen years after Humboldt's publication, would the Great Trigonometric Survey of India under George Everest measure the mountains known today as Everest, K2, and Kanchenjunga, settling the question.

The *Personal Narrative* gives us additional indicators of Humboldt's interest in mountains and mountain climbing: in his account of Silla, he mentions that in light of the climb's steepness, he felt "the want for cramp-irons, or sticks shod with iron" (419). Such a statement reveals Humboldt as an avid follower of the evolution of mountaineering. While three- or four-point iron-pronged shoes designed for travel on snow and ice were developed by hunters as early as the sixteenth century and illustrated in woodcuts such as *Theuerdank* (1517), ten-point crampons did not emerge until the late nineteenth century. Alpenstocks, or long sticks tipped with iron, were already more widely used for the purpose of scaling mountains and eventually evolved and shortened into the modern and specialized ice ax we know today. In his treatise on Alpine travel, *De Alpibus commentarius* (1574), Josias Simler had mentioned the use of alpenstock, crampons, and rope. Since Humboldt did not use any of these terms in his diaries, he presumably familiarized himself with Alpine mountaineering techniques after his return when he embarked on more extensive explorations in the Alps.

In keeping with his view of a dynamic and changing nature, Humboldt processed his impressions and measurements in different genres and artistic forms, taking advantage of text, illustration, and data. These media convey information about his journey from different viewpoints and analytical perspectives that sometimes remain in unresolved conflict. Humboldt was duly proud of his altitude achievements but continually questioned the mountaineering quest, and his various depictions radiate gratification, irritation, doubt, and discomfort. From letters, the diary, and the published travel reports and pictorial representations—manifold sources that complement and sometimes contradict one another, as in the discordant depictions of the Silla climb and diverging descriptions of Teide—we can piece together the evolution of a mountaineering discourse that adopts original narrative strategies and rhetorical devices while underscoring the endeavor's overall ambivalence.

CHAPTER 2

THE DRAMA OF ASCENT

Higher than Anyone Before: Humboldt on Antisana

"We had such a clear day that we were able to move higher than any human on this earth has climbed before. I determined the altitude and amplitude of several geographic points, I recorded the layout of the entire volcano, I measured its highest summit geodetically, I analyzed the air at 2,773 toises [5,404 m/17,729 ft.], I carried the cyanometer and the inclination compass to an altitude to which never before an instrument was carried."[1] Full of enthusiasm, Humboldt eagerly divulges information of his altitude record and successful measurements—not Mount Chimborazo but Antisana, the fourth-highest peak in Ecuador, roughly one hundred miles northeast, now measured at 5,753 m/18,875 ft. In the following diary pages, Humboldt repeats his altitude feats three more times, reveling in pride about his climbing experience. Exhausted from the arduous ascent and blinded by the intense light, Humboldt and his companions decided to descend when "a very steep snowbank hindered us from venturing any higher. We cut some steps in the snow in order to climb a few toises higher, but since we saw that it was very dangerous to follow them with the instruments, we abandoned this plan."[2]

Although he failed to reach the summit, Humboldt's Antisana climb on March 16, 1802, was indeed impressive: he established a new altitude record and detailed the physical effects of high altitude while successfully testing his instruments in severe weather, on a mountain even today rarely climbed because of its technical difficulty, numerous crevasses, and unstable weather. At the same time, the mountain introduced Humboldt and his companions to the difficulties of high-altitude mountaineering: as he did later on Chimborazo, Humboldt failed to reach the top, and his claim to have reached an altitude of just three hundred meters below the summit remains unconfirmed. The Antisana climb therefore turned into an important precursor to Chimborazo, both in its success and in its failure. Yet it did not garner much public attention. Just three months later on Mount Chimborazo, Humboldt surpassed his own altitude record, so that the Antisana climb remained overshadowed by the Chimborazo experience.

In the *Personal Narrative* and *Views of the Cordilleras,* Humboldt refers only briefly to Antisana, mostly in conjunction with other volcanoes that he ascended; and in letters, any mention of the mountain is in passing and merely informative. Yet the rich and dense description in the diary shows how Humboldt wrestled with pride, failure, fear, and illusion, all the while refining his narrative craft. Over the course of his mountain ascents, Humboldt departed from the aesthetic framework of the sublime to make room for diverging observations and sensations and in the process created a language of mountaineering that bears witness to human limitations, uncertainty, and helplessness.

The exploration of some of the highest mountains in the world, specifically the volcanoes of the Andean Cordillera, was an integral if underpublicized aspect of Humboldt's trip to the Americas. After reaching Bogotá in Colombia, Humboldt traveled to Quito, Ecuador, and devoted the next eight months to exploring and climbing the surrounding high peaks. In his diary, he revealed his general strategy as follows: "Upon my arrival in the province of Quito, I resolved to seek out the great *nevados* [snow-capped mountains] one after the other in order to conduct mineralogical examinations, to collect Alpine plants, to gather atmospheric air at a great height, and to determine the magnetic inclination."[3] Humboldt apparently considered a separate study of volcanoes, contemplating in the preface to the *Personal Narrative* "a work devoted wholly to the description of the volcanos of Peru and New Spain" (xiii). In the end, however, he opted for a chrono-logical description of his trip even though he never completed his story: the *Personal Narrative* breaks off in April 1801, before Humboldt reached Quito and completed his major mountain ascents. A published description of his Antisana climb therefore remains missing, as do accounts of almost all his ascents in Ecuador and Mexico.[4]

Since we have no comprehensive analytical perspective available in pub-lished form, Humboldt's diary descriptions of his climbs of the Ecuadorian volcanoes, written in German and French, become all the more important. They have become fully available only recently: beginning in 1958, the di-aries were kept at the Alexander von Humboldt Research Center at the Berlin Academy of Sciences and Humanities in East Berlin, where in the following decades they were transcribed, sorted, and published in select excerpts. Only after 2013, when the Prussian Cultural Heritage Founda-tion purchased the diaries, have they been digitized page by page, though a typed and searchable transcribed version is still outstanding. To date, no English translation is available. Owing to issues of access and translation, Humboldt's mountain ascents, aside from his attempt on Mount Chimbo-razo, have received relatively little attention in scholarship. Although a large body of works exists on Humboldt's aesthetic principles and scientific achievements, his minute attention to the body and its limits in interaction with the mountain landscape has likewise eluded scholarly attention.[5] To fully appreciate Humboldt's changing perspectives, including the fear, suf-fering, and failure that begin to inform his narrative once he set foot on a mountain, we must pay particular attention to his diary descriptions of mountain ascents. Against the backdrop of Humboldt's few published mountain depictions, the English translations of pertinent diary passages provided here allow us to focus on the peculiar contradictions and com-plexities in his texts.

In his extensive diary passages on Antisana, Humboldt begins with a lengthy description of the views, terming the mountain's location in sub-lime fashion "very romantic."[6] Already on the approach, however, concrete physical reality interrupts the aesthetic experience and demands Hum-boldt's attention: "The wind picked up so heavily on that ridge that once one set foot on the ground to collect some plants or examine rocks it was almost impossible to mount the mule again. It took effort to keep straight."[7]

Different from his exasperations on Silla, however, on Antisana Humboldt discerns his afflictions with unceasing curiosity, and his tangible descriptions of the effects at altitude serve to exemplify and further the existing knowledge of altitude sickness. "I am used to rush[ing] untroubled and without strain in full stride from one signal to the other, even if they are 800–1,000 toises [1,559–1,949 m/5,114–6,394 ft.] apart from each other, . . . ; in the plains of Antisana I could not walk 70 toises [136 m/447 ft.] without losing my breath and feeling strong chest pains. Even the animals here have difficulties in breathing."[8] Humboldt finds his breathing increasingly labored and suffers from chest and heart pains, pressure and fluid filling his lungs, and bloodshot eyes. He correctly identifies these symptoms as precursors to dangerous high-altitude pulmonary edema, concluding, "After these experiences I believe that when ascending to 2,900 or 3,000 toises [5,650 or 5,850 m/18,536 or 19,192 ft.], one could run the danger of spitting blood and seeing all lung vessels dangerously burst."[9] Humboldt here augments the known afflictions of high altitude first outlined as early as the sixteenth century by the Jesuit priest José de Acosta, who likewise found his condition worsening when he ascended to high altitudes in the Andes.[10] Expanding on these descriptions, Humboldt, like Saussure before him, attributes his afflictions to the decreasing pressure at altitude. "Since the counter pressure of the atmosphere is diminished by a ratio of 28:15, the small vessels which have the thinnest fascia burst; we all had the white of our eyes full of blood, clotted by the discharge of blood from the small arteries of this body part. We all felt ill and almost suffocated. How curious it is when the extremes of physics and morality intersect."[11] Importantly, to Humboldt these bodily afflictions are inherently connected to the climber's state of mind, which explains his holistic curiosity about the climbing process.

Antisana also marked the first climb with the young Creole Carlos Montúfar, son of the provincial governor Marqués de Selva-Alegre, whom Humboldt befriended in Quito. While staying at Selva-Alegre's home in Quito and his estate in Chillo, Humboldt apparently became quite taken with the twenty-two-year-old, and Montúfar accompanied the expedition for the remainder of its duration at Humboldt's expense, even living with Humboldt after his return to Paris. This meant that Humboldt rejected other contenders for his companionship, such as the promising young naturalist Francisco José de Caldas (1768–1816), even though Caldas came with a recommendation from South America's best-known botanist, José Celestino Mutis. Caldas complained bitterly, questioning Humboldt's reputation and moral code in a letter to Mutis.[12] Why precisely Humboldt chose the young and inexperienced Montúfar over the more qualified and eager Caldas is left to speculation, which indeed was fueled by rumors that he and Montúfar entertained a relationship. While scholarship has stubbornly refuted the stigma of Humboldt's homosexuality and continues to "uncover" Humboldt's supposed romances with women, queer studies have since outed Humboldt, opening the closet door for deeper, more open-minded examinations of Humboldt's relationships with men.[13]

The fact remains that Montúfar has often been diminished in scholarship if not written out of the journey altogether, though Humboldt's diary suggests great intimacy between Humboldt and Montúfar.[14] As the recent collection *The Complete Drawings,* edited by Ottmar Ette and Julia Maier, shows, Humboldt even allowed Montúfar to practice his drawing skills in his diary.[15] Moreover, extended passages in the diary, especially those that take place in mountainous terrain, are devoted to Montúfar. On their first overnight stop on Antisana, for instance, Humboldt describes a torturous night trying to soothe Montúfar's suffering from wind and altitude. "I lay in the same bed with Carlos Montúfar, the second son of the Marqués de Selva-Alegre, with whom we lived in greatest intimacy since our arrival in Quito. He was a young officer full of kindness and of such ease to learn everything that signals true talent. . . . The poor man had stomach and chest pains, an intestinal colic. . . . Because of lack of light, we went to bed at 7 o'clock at night. How long this night seemed . . . and how agonizing. Several times I offered to get up and have a warm foot bath prepared for my friend. He always resisted because the wind blew and howled like on the open sea."[16]

While these lines reflect the quality of nineteenth-century intimate same-sex friendships, they also show how the bonds between men intensify in the mountains regardless of sexual inclinations. At a safe remove from civilization and the confines of bourgeois society, male relationships become characterized by ambiguity, as we will see in other nineteenth-century mountaineering tales—for instance, in the case of Clarence King, who also describes nights with travel companions in the mountains at close quarters.

The point here is not to pass judgment on Humboldt's actions or catego-
rize his inclinations; rather, highlighting ambiguous passages will allow for
multiple readings. While Humboldt depicts Montúfar with great affection,
he also uses him as a subject for study to observe and diagnose the effects
of altitude sickness. Maintaining that his companion had a much harder
time on the mountain than he himself, Humboldt asserts, "Mister Carlos
Montúfar, a young man in rude health who accompanied us in the most
exhausting endeavors in the mountains, threw much blood from his
mouth."[17] A later description on Chimborazo likewise draws attention to
Montúfar's greater afflictions at altitude.

During the ascent, the sun is unbearable, the light blinding, the wind
excruciating. Despite these challenges, the narrative is characterized by
triumph. Humboldt and his team climb "above the line of eternal snow,
higher than any mortal before," before turning around at a very steep slope,
pleasantly surprised at the altitude their instruments indicate.[18] While
Humboldt climbed Antisana in the name of science, the all-encompassing
physical and mental effort not only overrides efforts of instrumentalizing
the body but more importantly demonstrates that the physical experience
cannot be separated from aesthetic and moral concerns. In light of their
prodigious effort, Humboldt doubts that one could climb much higher,
and he develops a somewhat eccentric theory for ascending to the top of
Mount Chimborazo: "One might think that—if a government demanded
it—one could gradually and with patience advance to the summit of Chimborazo by building houses in the snow every 150 toises [292 m/959 ft.],
where fire and food supplies would be stored. These shelters would allow
for a connection with the inhabited region. One could seek refuge from
one to the other in case one could not hold out in the highest one."[19]

By recognizing that one cannot stay at high altitudes for a long time, and
returning to lower-lying camps is mandatory, Humboldt imagines and
anticipates the era of reconnaissance climbing in the twentieth century,
in which climbers acclimatized in gradual, graduated steps. His proposed
method of ascent therefore does not seem so strange when considering the
ensuing Himalayan expeditions, organized in similar siege style. Even his
measurements turn out to be surprisingly accurate: to facilitate appropriate acclimatization, today's experts advise that one should not gain more
than one thousand feet of elevation per day once at high altitudes.[20] In the

progression of his Andean climbs, Humboldt outlined some modern prac-
tices of high-altitude mountaineering, such as crampons (as we saw in the
depiction of the Silla climb) and a deliberate style of ascent, facilitated by
multiple camps. His scientific observations on the bodily responses to altitude were also largely on the right track. Most importantly, in the diary he
pioneered a climbing narrative that gave voice to success and failure, pleasure and misery, measurement and aesthetic marvel, bodily afflictions and
the mind's flights of fancy.

Humboldt's achievements become all the more remarkable when we consider that Antisana's first ascent was not accomplished until March 1880,
when Edward Whymper, on his quest to claim first ascents, followed in
Humboldt's footsteps, climbing Cotopaxi, Antisana, and Pichincha, among
other peaks. Whymper considered Antisana the most difficult of all Ecuadorian volcanoes, and his first attempt ended in retreat when the party navigated several crevasses while roped up but had to turn around at a large
cleft two hundred feet deep and sixty feet wide. For Whymper, the final
push to the summit three days later on March 10, 1880, remained uncli-
mactic: "At last we could perceive no tendency to rise or fall in any direction, and came upon a nearly level plain of snow, lost in mist on all sides.
This was the summit."[21]

The Picture-Perfect Cone: Cotopaxi

When Humboldt attempted to climb Cotopaxi (5,897 m/19,347 ft.) a few
weeks later on April 28, 1802, between his various ascents of Pichincha,
these mixed emotions came to bear once more, and he freely embellished
on the beauty and danger of the volcano. Cotopaxi embodied another set
of contradictions: On one hand, Humboldt described the mountain as
"a perfect cone, the most beautiful of the *nevados*, because of its even form
and immaculate snow cover, unbroken by protruding rocks."[22] Likely for
this reason, Humboldt chose to include Cotopaxi in his color profile in
Geography of Plants, picturing it right behind Chimborazo, though in reality
the two volcanoes lie roughly a hundred miles apart. On the other hand,
the ascent proved disappointing, as the team could not advance to a higher
altitude than on Antisana and probably only reached an elevation of about
4,500 m/14,763 ft. when chasms below the actual cone prohibited further

progress. In his diary, Humboldt sums up, not without irony: "It seems impossible to reach Cotopaxi's crater, even if the king would have mountain huts built of which I spoke about on the occasion of the excursion to Antisana."[23] With upward progress halted, Humboldt resorted to hunting, stating laconically: "We spent the rest of the day hunting deer, of which there are many and large ones. I saw no difference to European deer."[24] Hunting indeed was a significant activity for Alpine mountaineers, climbers and guides alike, and at times compensated for climbing disappointments (as likewise for John Tyndall's failure on the Matterhorn).

With Cotopaxi's depiction in the pictorial atlas *Views of the Cordilleras,* Humboldt finds an altogether different answer to his climbing failure. Cotopaxi is the first of six volcanoes described, with an illustration of the entire peak, as well as a more detailed image of the upper cone, embedded in an essay that offers more in-depth information. Humboldt emphasizes again the beauty and evenness of the cone: "The shape of Cotopaxi is the most beautiful and most regular of all the colossal peaks in the upper Andes. It is a perfect cone that, cloaked in an enormous layer of snow, shines dazzlingly at sunset and stands out delightfully against the azure sky."[25] The picture-perfect image he describes finds its equivalent in the drawing of an exaggeratedly steep, uniform, white cone contrasting with the cloudless sky in the background. While the essay describes at great length the appearance of the peak and the history of its eruptions, comparing Cotopaxi to Teide, it downplays the actual ascent. Humboldt mentions the difficulties encountered only in passing, once more declaring it impossible to gain the rim of the crater. Instead the essay reveals Humboldt's imagination and artistic latitude: reflecting on his own drawing, he admits that he added smoke rising from the cone, even though he did not observe any. In fact, according to the diary, Cotopaxi rarely emits any smoke at all: "We did not see even a trace of smoke rising from the crater. Those who live nearby the volcano say that they never have seen any smoke, except during times of eruption."[26] Despite this better knowledge, Humboldt thus added smoke in his drawing as if to fulfill his own wishes for enhancement. What is more, Humboldt also added a plume of smoke rising from Cotopaxi in the tableau of the *Geography of Plants,* one of the most influential images of the journey. The meticulous scientist apparently had no qualms about embellishing the image for the sake of dramatization. Perhaps unknowingly,

Humboldt here invents another mountaineering convention. Feeding both his own and his readers' imagination, he begins to beef up a depiction in case the actual experience does not deliver.

Looking into the Abyss: Pichincha

The three ascents of different peaks of Pichincha during April and May 1802 gave Humboldt another opportunity to build his narrative craft, with dizziness and outright disorientation presenting rich fodder for story and drama. While not as high as Antisana, Pichincha is more remote and forces climbers to cross several gorges, which presented many challenges for Humboldt's party. On April 14, 1802, Humboldt, Bonpland, Montúfar, and three others embarked on an arduous hike to the more accessible, crater-less Guagua Pichincha peak (4,784 m/15,696 ft.). Humboldt mistakenly took this for the lower peak and began a grueling climb of the cone ("one makes three steps forward and two backward") in freezing cold.[27] On top, he completed his measurements with thermometer, barometer, and electrometer, awed by the views: "The steep slopes on the side of Pomasqui offer a magnificent spectacle. What destruction, what chaotic disorder, especially on the side toward the ocean! How this volcano was manhandled!"[28] Humboldt determines the boiling temperature of water, measures electricity, and conducts triangulation. But physical sensations disrupt aesthetic and scientific pursuits: feeling miserable because of exhaustion, cold, lack of food and sleep, he becomes dizzy when breathing the vapors from the boiling water, and his condition worsens on the descent. "I was alone. The dizziness increased. I saw yellow. My courage did not leave me. I gathered my last strength. Once arrived at the cliff's apex, I passed out. The others saw me outstretched on the ground. They gave me wine. This caused me to regain my consciousness."[29]

Humboldt's straightforward, unadorned description here mirrors the bluntness and suddenness of the material intervention and cleverly reflects what is happening by switching the subject of the sentences from "I" to the others. He then drily remarks that on Silla de Caracas, they hiked even longer distances without rest, concluding, "Thus it was apparently the carbon emission rather than exhaustion that caused this incident. I remounted the horse and did not feel any further effects."[30]

After the ascent of Cotopaxi, Humboldt returned to Pichincha, determined to reach Rucu Pichincha peak (4,698 m / 15,413 ft.) on May 26, 1802. According to the diary, he insisted that Bonpland and Montúfar not come along, ostensibly to spare them the misery of an outing that Humboldt acknowledged he was undertaking out of pure "stubbornness."[31] Instead Humboldt put together a group of Spanish locals and Indios, choosing a gentler line of ascent to avoid the slopes where he had previously fallen unconscious. Nevertheless, when faced with the steepness of the climb, all companions except Pedro de Urquinaona y Pardo and the Indio Philippe Aldas stayed behind. The depiction in Humboldt's diary reads much like a dramatic mountaineering tale, with a meticulous description of the ascent, the dangers encountered, and accidents survived, along with an accompanying drawing tracing and analyzing his footsteps. Presumably following La Condamine's line of ascent from 1742, the party climbed an ever-steepening snow slope, using rock outcrops as handholds. After Aldas broke through the snow, his legs dangling over what Humboldt presumed to be a crevasse, they turned around, carefully trying to avoid the snow and instead following rock slabs toward the crater. Humboldt maintains, wryly, "We boosted each other's courage, proof that one is scared," but insisted on continuing the ascent so that their effort would not be in vain: "On the other hand [there is] the thought to have endured so much to no avail, the thought to leave Quito without witnessing the greatest spectacle that nature offers."[32]

Fashioning Pichincha's crater into the "greatest spectacle" he had seen echoes Humboldt's dramatic description of the Teide ascent. Yet Humboldt's diary description of Pichincha expands much beyond sublime awe. With its narrative tension, details of the particular technique of ascent, emphasis on fear and courage, and references to Saussure's scaling of Mont Blanc, the account resonates in later descriptions by Tyndall, Whymper, King, and Muir, among others. Once more, Humboldt lets his mind run wild: on the steep slope, he imagines himself falling and rolling down a couple hundred meters, crashing against rocks along the way. And when crossing a tenuous snow bridge above the crater, he finds himself "trembling in fright," picturing a fall into the chasm: "We would have fallen 200 toises [389 m / 1,278 ft.] deep into the most inflamed part of the crater, and no one in Quito would have known what had become of us, if not for our tracks in the snow."[33] Yet Humboldt is simultaneously fascinated with the void and, once on secure footing, begins "to test the danger from which we were safe" by throwing a rock into the crater and watching it slice through the thin snow cover.[34] The climbers gape into the abyss, spellbound:

> No language has words to express what we saw. An almost circular oval, a bit elongated from the northeast to the southeast, the interior of a receptacle whose walls are vertically cut and black as ink, while the edges are covered with snow up to the ridge of the precipice. To our right we saw high mountains rise from the bottom of the crater to the northeast. Our eyes rested on the top of several peaks in the form of enormous stalactites. They too are black and their surface seems more slagged because it is shinier than those of the crater's edges. What depth may be the foot, the base of these peaks whose tops seem to lie at least 80 toises [155 m/511 ft.] below us? Mr. La Condamine compared this place very fittingly with the chaos of poets. We seemed to look into a devastated world, without hope of ever serving as a habitation for living creatures. I have never seen anything in this world that gave me a deeper but simultaneously also more unpleasant impression. Again I see myself dangling above this ghastly void. The bleak, sorrow-announcing color, the immensity of the masses, and especially the indistinguishableness in the distinction of the objects, this mystical veil of the vapors that enshrouds one area while baring another—all this enlivens the imagination and challenges it like a song of Pope's Lost Paradise.[35]

Although Humboldt apparently confused John Milton and Alexander Pope, his depiction appropriately harks back to the pre-modern *Paradise Lost* (1667) in its emotive language and horrific visions. Despite the realistic description of the geologic formations in the beginning, Humboldt's narrative soon turns to impressions and associations. Inside the mountaintop, chasms gape, consisting of more peaks and voids, reversing the familiar sense of top and bottom. Overwhelmed by the depth, darkness, and intensity of the abyss, Humboldt links it to a hell of mythical proportions, all the while admitting his fascination with the spectacle. A central element of the experience is its amorphousness and fleetingness: since the view is constantly changing, the eyes cannot fixate on objects, and the mind cannot trust reality. Yet Humboldt continually reflects his thought and writing process, bemoaning the very lack of language to represent his experiences. These figures of speech—the indescribability of experience, the immensity of top and bottom, the frightful fantasy of falling—resume and expand earlier climbing descriptions and return in the account of Humboldt's attempt on Chimborazo. Notably, on Pichincha, Humboldt provides us with a by now familiar mountaineering narrative of overcoming obstacles, but instead of promising triumph or conquest, the summit offers a glimpse into the abyss.

In another recurring aspect of his mountaineering descriptions, Humboldt employs irony and wit. When Urquinaona cannot make the last steps to the summit, Humboldt sends Aldas back to search for him, waiting on the summit. He remarks, understatedly: "I remained alone. This was not the most pleasant moment in my life."[36] Rather than sublime triumph, the mountaintop evokes loneliness and fright. The descent proves difficult as well: soon darkness falls, and the men stumble down the mountain, lost and exhausted. Yet even here Humboldt maintains his sense of humor and calculation, passing the time by counting the number of each person's falls: "In less than three hours Don Vincente Aguirre who walked behind me counted 123 falls for me; for the Indio walking in front of me I counted 34 falls. This means that the agility of an Indio to a White corresponds to 34:123."[37] The witty remark mocks and counteracts colonial stereotyping and even pokes fun at Humboldt's own fanatical measurements.

On a third climb just two days later with the same line of ascent, Humboldt remained more in control. This time the party again included Aguirre and Aldas, but also Bonpland and Montúfar, who wanted to see the crater for themselves. Humboldt's brief description focuses on the various measurements undertaken, concluding with remarks on the tremors that he believes make Pichincha an even more active volcano than before his first ascent.

In *Views of the Cordilleras,* Humboldt includes an illustration of the various peaks of Pichincha, along with a brief characterization in the accompanying essay. The image depicts three explorers and another group of two in the plains below the mountain, looking up and pointing to its top. The people, however, are dwarfed by the snow and rock formations towering over them, lending the illustration a sublime quality that contrasts the narrative that Humboldt gave in his diary. Here, as in the previous example of Cotopaxi, the aesthetic rendering of the mountain remains in tension with the climbing narrative. Adding to the multiplicity of Humboldt's oeuvre, both representations proved highly influential, the former for his contemporaries' aesthetic consumption of the new world and its wonders, the latter for an emerging climbing narrative over the course of the nineteenth century.

Chimborazo: The Ascent to Record Heights

On June 23, 1802, we find Humboldt and his companions, Carlos Montúfar and Aimé Bonpland, and a Mestizo farmer from San Juan faltering up the slopes of Mount Chimborazo in Ecuador, which at 6,268 m/20,565 ft. was thought to be the highest mountain in the world. Just four days earlier, they had attempted to ascend the Tungurahua volcano (5,023 m/16,480 ft.) but turned around at an impassable wall, in pouring rain. On Chimborazo, heavy snow had fallen the night before, and the day was foggy and dark. The mountain was only visible when the swirling clouds lifted momentarily. The large party of a dozen locals and guides started on mules and horses, but the animals sank up to their flanks in the freshly fallen snow. The men left the mules behind and pressed onward amid fog and snowdrifts for another thousand feet at an excruciatingly slow pace, repeatedly stopping to determine the altitude and angle of slope. At 15,600 feet, as their path turned ever more narrow and steep, the remaining locals refused to go any farther, despite Humboldt's pleas and threats to continue. This left only four people to lug the sextant, thermometer, and barometer up the mountain. With bloodshot eyes, bleeding gums and noses, and frozen and skinned hands, the climbers pushed on until an impassable cleft, more than four hundred feet deep and sixty feet wide, hindered further progress. Despite the cold and his nausea, Humboldt managed to unpack the mercury barometer to measure the air pressure and temperature, estimating that they had climbed to only a little more than a thousand feet below the summit (Whymper's later estimates, however, placed Humboldt considerably lower). He collected a wide array of rocks as the party began an equally toilsome descent, hurrying down the mountain in a thick mist that soon turned into pounding hail.

The ascent of Chimborazo was meant to be the crowning achievement of Humboldt's Andean ascents and his American journey as a whole. Humboldt himself emphasizes that the expedition was carefully timed on the third anniversary of his ascent of Pico de Teide to conclude the series of climbs near Quito. Yet the culmination of Humboldt's climbing exploits ultimately embodied failure, since the team was not able to advance to the summit. Though the exact altitude of Humboldt's ascent is debated and likely lower than he had estimated, his feat set a new altitude record that remained in place until 1831, when Jean Baptiste Boussingault was able to advance higher on the mountain, though he likewise failed to reach the summit.[38] Not until eight decades later, in 1880, did Edward Whymper, the successful Matterhorn contender, climb to the top of Chimborazo and subsequently bag the first ascent of Antisana on the same trip.

The Janus-faced nature of the ascent, exemplifying both success and failure, extended to Humboldt's depictions of the climb. Humboldt featured the mountain in his *Essay on the Geography of Plants* (*Essai sur la géographie des plantes,* 1807), the first published work of the American journey, which he admittedly wrote in large part "in the very presence of the objects I was going to describe, at the foot of the Chimborazo."[39] As its focal point, the essay presented a highly inventive and influential color profile of Chimborazo titled "Geography of Equatorial Plants: Physical Tableau of the Andes and the Neighboring Countries" (*Géographie des plantes equinoxiales: Tableau physique des Andes et pays voisins*). Inspired by Humboldt's previous work in mining and his familiarity with mining profiles, the tableau revealed a cross section of Chimborazo viewed from the south. As the name implies, Humboldt sought to fuse image and text to provide scientific detail in an aesthetically pleasing form. The image of Chimborazo is highly exaggerated; in the essay, Humboldt bemoaned the tension between aesthetics and precision, elucidating that if it was depicted according to scale, the mountain would have appeared ridiculously small. He also gave himself artistic latitude by depicting Cotopaxi next to Chimborazo, though in reality the two volcanoes lie roughly one hundred miles apart.

Despite the liberal artistic embellishment, image and text strive to convey a multiplicity of scientific factual measurements: on the right, the mountain's cross section is filled with the names of plant species occurring at that elevation, giving insight into the various vegetation zones drawn into the image on the left (the vertical axis of the figure remains to scale). In the brown part below sea level, Humboldt inserted the names of fungi, mosses, and algae that he had known since his mining days at Freiberg. In the sky,

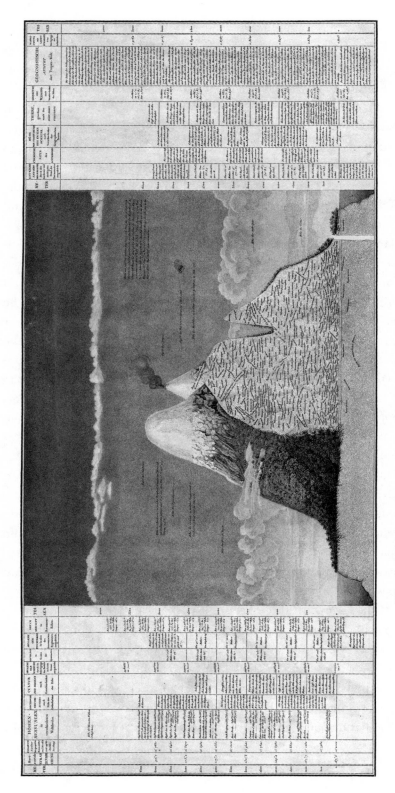

"Physical Tableau of the Andes and the Neighboring Countries" (*Tableau physique des Andes et pays voisins*), 1807 (Provided by the Zentralbibliothek Zurich)

he inserted reference points from a western European perspective: the height of Mont Blanc, Vesuvius, and Teide, Gay-Lussac's high point of his hot-air balloon above Paris in 1804, and his own high point on Chimborazo, but also the elevation of Quito. The image sparks curiosity and imagination, but it also conveys physical exertion and bodily involvement by hinting at Humboldt's mountain ascent.

Eleven columns on the left and nine on the right provide information from characteristic animals to the cultivation of the soil, from barometric pressure to air temperature, and from the chemical composition of the air to the light refraction and blueness of the sky. Significantly, human activity in the form of agriculture, extraction of resources, and exploration, all linked to colonialism, are included in the "Tableau," as such activity would be in an Anthropocene understanding of an earth system, where human beings and their activities are seen as integral components rather than a disconnected force. Stephen T. Jackson called this profile "an entirely new sort of graphic, combining elements of traditional cartography, botanical illustration, landscape profiles (like La Condamine's), and statistical graphics (still in its infancy)."[40]

Despite Chimborazo's prominence in the "Tableau," Humboldt did not publish much about his ascent.[41] Aside from a description in the diary and a brief account in a letter to his brother Wilhelm dated November 25, 1802, only two engravings of the mountain, with accompanying short essays, appear in *Views of the Cordilleras*. The first published description of the climb itself appeared thirty-five years later in the 1837 essay "On Two Attempts to Ascend Chimborazo" ("Über zwei Versuche den Chimborazo zu besteigen"), long after his altitude record had been surpassed and even higher mountains had been measured in the Himalaya. Humboldt later reworked this essay into "On One Attempt to Scale the Top of Chimborazo" ("Über einen Versuch den Gipfel des Chimborazo zu ersteigen") and published it in a volume with the negligible title *Kleinere Schriften* (Smaller texts) in 1853.[42] His written texts about Chimborazo are marked by a peculiar tension between pride in his accomplishment and modesty in the recognition of his failure. Indeed, Humboldt seemed torn about the mountaineering quest in itself. On one hand, he admits his desire to scale the "highest" mountain and boasts of his record achievement, yet on the other he makes sure to dismiss such cravings as scientifically worthless.[43] Overall,

Humboldt's description of his Chimborazo climb does not occupy a special place but rather mirrors the depictions of his earlier ascents in sequence, focus, and tone.

In the diary, Humboldt creates tension and a narrative arc. As Lubrich and Ette have documented, Humboldt dramatically interrupts his entry in the middle of the word "cre-vasse" with six pages of excursus to visually and literally depict the team's realization of failure. "Instead of an art of mastery in his Chimborazo texts, Humboldt develops an art of failure—entirely different than one would generally expect from him. This practice delivers an aesthetics as well as an epistemology of failure."[44] At the same time, Humboldt was acutely aware of the importance of his altitude achievement and duly proud of it. In this vein, he dramatized the climbers' troubles: "The hands were bloody, and our diseased, abscess-covered feet constantly hit sharp rocks. Every step had to be calculated because one could not see the snow-covered path—in such a manner was my rather unpleasant state of affairs. If one is used to stresses and strains, one easily prevails over physical pain."[45]

With shrewd foresight, Humboldt collected rocks from the mountain's slopes, reasoning, "who in Europe would not want to have a rock from Chimborazo, and where is there a cabinet nowadays that already owns one?"[46] As on Pichincha, he imagines a fall from the mountain's slope, yet he manages to couch his worries in humor and irony: "To the left the slope was terrifyingly steep and covered with surface-frozen (crusty) snow. To the right there was not a single atom of snow, but the slope was strewn (covered) with large rocks. One had the choice whether one would rather break his bones when hitting the rocks which greeted us 1,000 feet below, or whether to slide over snow into an even deeper abyss to the left. The latter fall seemed to be the more gruesome to us. . . . Therefore we always leaned our bodies to the right."[47]

This passage and others became famously exaggerated in Daniel Kehlmann's 2005 fictional representation of Humboldt's climb, even though Humboldt adds plenty of drama in his own account.[48] As they did on Pichincha, the climbers "amuse[d] themselves" by throwing rocks down the slope to demonstrate the consequences of a fall.[49] Humboldt observes, "No living creature enlivened the air, no insect, not even the condor, which hovered above our heads on Antisana."[50] The diary entry concludes with ample evidence of self-gratification: "The same day three years ago we ascended Pic de Teide. It was the last excursion we undertook on the *nevados* of Quito, we completed it with the highest mountain and ascended to the greatest height, which we ourselves (and any other human being) had attained."[51]

After his return to Paris, Humboldt repeated these details in countless lectures throughout Europe. Indeed, the various aspects of the climb—physical suffering, difficult climbing, the crevasse, danger encountered, measurements, the height record, but also negation of the overall value of the expedition—resurface in his later depictions of the Chimborazo climb. *Views of the Cordilleras* includes two plates with views of Chimborazo from below in volumes 1 and 2. The first image shows the mountain and its neighboring peak Carguairazo in sharp relief with little snow, while the second image, according to Humboldt sketched "only one day after our excursion to the top," reveals the mountain blanketed in snow and provides more detail on the Tapia plains below.[52] Rather than depicting the climbers or replicating their perspective from above, Humboldt thus only indirectly refers to his ascent by hinting at the snowstorm that hindered the climb. As he elaborates, the images before and after the snowstorm are supposed to give the viewer "an exact idea of the imposing appearance of the Cordilleras at the time of both *maximum* and *minimum* snow levels."[53] Both views of Chimborazo against a cloudless blue sky still stand in marked contrast with the written account, since the travelers' view was reportedly blocked by thick fog.

The two accompanying essays likewise straddle the extremes, as Humboldt simultaneously elevates and downplays both the mountain and his climb. The essay in volume 1 begins with a detailed description of the terrain that diminishes the height of the Cordillera range in general and Chimborazo in particular: the mountain only rises above the Tapia plains as much as Mont Blanc above Chamonix, and Pic de Teide outperforms both peaks in vertical rise. In consequence, the impact on the viewer is, in the case of Chimborazo, not as awe inspiring as it could be. Yet soon enough Humboldt discloses his efforts and achievements on the mountain, which he indicates must surely overshadow Mont Blanc:

> It was on a narrow ridge jutting out from amidst the snows on the southern
> slope that Mr. Bonpland, Mr. Montúfar, and I attempted, not without dan-

ger, to reach the top of Chimborazo. We carried our instruments to a considerable height, although we were surrounded by a thick fog, and the thin air gave us serious trouble. The point where we stopped to observe the incline of the magnetized needle appears to be the highest that any man has reached on this mountain ridge; it is eleven hundred meters higher than the top of Mont Blanc, which that most skilled and fearless of travelers, Mr. de Saussure, had the good fortune to reach, struggling against even greater difficulties than we had to overcome near the top of Chimborazo. These grueling excursions, the results of which generally stir the public's imagination, offer only very few results that are useful to scientific progress.[54]

While Humboldt does not elaborate on this mountaineering feat, great satisfaction emanates from these lines although he manages to ensconce his words in humility. Humboldt mentions the dangers encountered but does not elaborate; he publicizes his altitude record but refers to de Saussure, who allegedly surmounted greater difficulties on Mont Blanc; and he acknowledges the public's curiosity but downplays the scientific utility of his mountain expedition altogether.

The essay in the second volume continues this ambivalence. The scene is filled with the standard vocabulary of sublime awe—"imposing," "calm," "majestic," and "enormous"—yet once again Humboldt disappoints visions of grandiosity.[55] And as if to top the negation, he adds that while the mountain may seem high, ranges in Tibet are said to be much higher, and for the scientist, height is not an important criterion after all: "The absolute elevation of mountains is an unimportant phenomenon to the true geologist, who, being engaged in the study of rock *formations,* is accustomed to viewing nature on a large scale. He will hardly be surprised if at some point in the future and in some other part of the globe, someone discovers a peak that surpasses Chimborazo by as much as the highest mountain in the Alps soars above the highest point in the Pyrenees."[56]

This seemingly detached analysis contrasts with Humboldt's previous boasting, illustrating the irreconcilable clash between achievement and failure, fantasy and reality. Humboldt's aforementioned essay about the ascent, "On Two Attempts to Ascend Chimborazo," published in 1837, continues this dualism. Humboldt professes: "Chimborazo became the tiring object of all questions asked after my first return to Europe," thus acknowledging public lectures in which he recounted the climb, all the while withholding a published account of his ascent.[57] In a similar vein, Humboldt dismisses the public's curiosity about his Chimborazo ascent as scientifically unsound yet yields to it by publishing a belated account long after the oeuvre on the American journey had been completed, admitting: "The story of the ascent itself, which can only offer limited dramatic interest, was reserved for the fourth and last volume of my *Travels to the Equinoctial Regions*."[58] Thus Humboldt ultimately satisfies the public's curiosity yet does so much too late, after his record had been broken and higher mountains had been discovered, and only while negating the importance of his achievement.

The essay begins by mentioning the anniversary of the Teide climb. Following the description of the climb in his diary, Humboldt continues his already established mountain discourse. With regard to altitude sickness, he notes:

> The breathing also was strongly affected, and what was even more unpleasant, we all felt nausea and an urge to vomit. A fellow-countryman (a *chagra* from San Juan) who followed us with much goodwill who was a very robust man, assured us that he never before in his life had felt so much pain in his stomach than in this moment. In addition our gums and lips were bleeding. The white in our eyes was bloodshot. For Montúfar, whose body contained the most blood, these symptoms were the worst. We felt weakness in the head, a constant dizziness which was very dangerous considering our situation.[59]

According to Humboldt, Montúfar fared worst, as he had before on Antisana, giving the scientist an opportunity to evaluate and assess his friend's symptoms. Once again Humboldt doubts whether it is humanly possible to reach the top of the mountain, because of both physical limitations and the inaccessibility of the terrain. What exactly happens at such altitude is still unknown, and Humboldt can only speculate: "Meanwhile it is certainly difficult to gauge the degree in which the afflictions increase and very well one's lung vessels could burst (because of the lack of atmospheric counterpressure), and one could cough blood."[60]

Nevertheless, the unclaimed summit of Chimborazo gives Humboldt ample cause to fantasize about the possibilities of a successful ascent and the obstacles standing in his way, whether cold, altitude, or soft snow making travel nearly impossible. While he affirms that it is of no use to lug his instruments even higher, Humboldt cannot help but dream of a possible ascent, thus continuing the fantasies of scaling Chimborazo that already infused the description of his Antisana climb.

> Of what use would it be if one carried his instruments 200 toises [389 m/ 1,278 ft.] higher, to a terrain where the rocks withdraw from observation, on a mountain unsuitable for magnetic experiments because the bedrock influences the magnetic needle and exhibits poles itself.
>
> But it would be interesting to get to the summit and to see whether there is a crater.[61]

Here scientific, aesthetic, and mountaineering interests intersect, in veritable Humboldtian fashion. With its multifaceted, belated, and conflicting narratives, Chimborazo continues to be a fickle, incongruous jewel in Humboldt's crown. Humboldt's obsessive measurements, however, still have value: in 2015, scientists used his data on Chimborazo from two centuries ago to document a strong upward shift in plant distribution due to warming temperatures.[62] What a sad irony to think that Humboldt's mules could have advanced much farther today, possibly changing the course of his ascent.

Coda: The Descent into the Crater of El Jorullo

Although by 1803 Humboldt had completed his major ascents of Andean volcanoes, El Jorullo (1,330 m/4,364 ft.), a Mexican volcano that had violently erupted less than fifty years earlier and rigorously changed the surrounding landscape, became another significant milestone of his journey, not because of the climb itself but because Humboldt was able to descend into the crater and explore its depths.[63] The interplay of height and depth presents yet another oscillation between extremes that Humboldt cleverly used in his finely honed skill set of creating narrative tension. Although the eruptions of Jorullo had only ceased some twenty-five years before his arrival, Humboldt decided to embark on an ascent of the smoking mountain, completed in a team of five (Bonpland, Ramón Epelde [a local estate owner], and two Indian guides).[64] Pico de Teide again served as a point of reference, both for the ascent and for exploring the crater. Humboldt's narrative of the arduous struggle upward, achieved by clutching rocks and plants that easily ripped out of the ground, employs the by now familiar markers of his climbing depictions. In this way, he imagines the consequences of a fall to either side of the slope and describes in some detail the exhausting haul up the steep and loose slope, involving backward slides, repeated falls, tumbling rocks, and tearing vegetation: "One does not progress other than by thrusting his body forward with momentum, creating steps in the ashes. At any instant one falls on his face, slides backwards two toises while barely advancing one tenth."[65] More than other climbing accounts, the narrative is filled with humor and self-effacing irony, combining both understatements and overstatements. Humboldt characterizes the walk along the crater rim as "unsuitable for vertigo-prone persons" and portrays the successful summiteers as pathetic rather than triumphant: "Finally, after a thousand concerns about the survival of the barometer, and while those who had made headway laughed about the sorry shape of those behind crawling on their stomachs, finally we reached the top."[66] After scaling much higher peaks in the Andes and setting two altitude records, on Jorullo Humboldt provides a refreshingly frank and witty narrative of summiting a mountain.

The true focus of the description, however, lies in the transformative descent into the crater. It involves some daring jumps over gaping cracks and stepping on sulfur deposits and volcanic cinder, which once more trigger Humboldt's rich imagination: "If one had the misfortune to break into the crust and halfway fall through, one's legs would have burned to one's bones before one could retract them."[67] As previously on Pichincha, Humboldt is undeniably mesmerized by this otherworldly, perilous environment. His description is yet again marked by superlatives, fusing aesthetic marvel, scientific measurement, and physical challenge. He proudly proclaims, "We are the first who climbed into the crater of Jorullo, and perhaps no one ever before has been in such an enflamed crater," only to add a later footnote rejecting the claim.[68] Battling the heat, sulfurous stench, and precarious footing, the party descends almost to the very bottom of the crater, measuring temperature, barometric pressure, height, and the composition of the air. Humboldt thrives in this environment, his senses heightened by the unusual and formidable experience: "But the majestic enormity of the objects surrounding us, the satisfying notion of standing in the center of the Cyclops's forge, caused us to forget any thought of danger. One emboldened the other, and only Mr. Epelde, who could not discover anything beautiful in that what made us inebriated, warned us of danger, and incessantly asked when we would terminate our descent."[69]

While Humboldt reverts to the vocabulary of sublime intoxication, he also frames his experience as an adventurous, absorbing, and entertaining narrative. In this way, the diary text concludes with the invention of a handy mountaineering tool, and a proper happy ending:

> We retraced our footsteps and descended along the crater, whereupon we glided down on our behinds and ripped our pants. Epelde acquired an especially ingenious method. He made himself a kind of broom from a few tree twigs, sat on it, and let himself glide down in this fashion. We also descended the hill strewn with cauliflower lava. We had breakfast in the shade of a mimosa, on the field of lava debris at the volcano's foot, very glad that the expedition had been so successful. Mr. Epelde vowed never again to descend into the crater.[70]

In *Views of the Cordilleras*, Humboldt does not focus on his ascent or descent. Rather, his illustration shows the mountain from afar, revealing a bizarre, foreign landscape of numerous basalt cones, which the Tarascan Indians use as dwellings, as the accompanying essay elaborates. In the foreground, a cross section of the volcanic rock reveals various layers and cracks, giving the viewer an impression of what is found underneath the earth. In the background, several volcanoes, Jorullo among them, lord over the scene, with smoke rising from some fumaroles. Humboldt's brief essay outlines the features of the horizontal layers of lava from the various eruptions, emphasizing the land's barrenness and inhospitality after being shattered by earthquakes and plagued by volcanic eruptions. He devotes only one sentence to the ascent: "We went all the way into the interior of the crater by scaling the hill of scoriaceous branched lava that is shown on the left side of the engraving and that rises to a considerable height."[71]

Before his departure to Cuba and the United States, Humboldt climbed the Mexican volcanoes Toluca (4,680 m/15,354 ft., on September 29, 1803) and Cofre de Perote (4,282 m/14,049 ft., on February 6–7, 1804), but in the diaries the description of these climbs remains indistinct and focuses mainly on measurements taken as part of Humboldt's study of Mexico.[72] Likewise, the depiction of Perote in *Views of the Cordilleras* is limited to a short essay conveying measurements and a picturesque illustration of the mountain from below.

Volcan de Jorullo, from *Vues des Cordillères*, 1813, plate 43 (Drawing by Hans Konrad Escher von der Linth, provided by the Zentralbibliothek Zurich)

Emerging Mountaineering Discourses

Over the course of nine major ascents described in detail in the diaries, Humboldt's language and style steadily evolved. While Humboldt initially approached the American volcanoes based on European models, framing Teide in the visual spectacle of the sublime, he soon left behind the European paradigm and instead immersed himself in a different world, experiencing, analyzing, and articulating what he saw, smelled, felt, and physically accomplished. Along the way, Humboldt was formed by the people he met and increasingly made room for other, previously undefined experiences. On his climbs of Teide and Silla, he began to focus keenly on physical sensations and material reality, emphasizing the body's role in aesthetic and scientific models. On Antisana, Cotopaxi, and Pichincha, he honed his storytelling of the mountaineering quest, incorporating fantasy and imagination, embellishing when needed, and filling his narrative with "what if" scenarios. On Chimborazo, he created tension by vacillating between success and failure. On Jorullo, finally, he ventured into the abyss of the mountain, skillfully narrating both ascent and descent in a reflection of height and depth.

Taken as a whole, we come to know a different Humboldt in the mountains. While initially grounded in the language of the Romantic sublime and scientific enlightenment, Humboldt admits to being addicted and intoxicated with unknown heights and even boasts of altitudes and first ascents. He encounters the unknown lands with all his senses, seeing, smelling, listening, tasting, and feeling in his zest for experience. He revels in the companionship of Carlos Montúfar, disclosing a certain amount of intimacy that expands our understanding of Humboldt's masculinity. He dexterously moves between what is said and what remains unsaid. Humboldt also employs a good deal of sarcasm and irony, making his mountain narratives biting, discriminating, and funny. Gradually he comes to fashion a narrative arc of a mountain ascent, incorporating built-up tension, humorous release, a high point, and a conclusion. All the while, he hints at a certain moral freedom that comes with being in the mountains, beginning to make a case and build a rationale for mountaineering in the face of his claims that it is scientifically pointless. At the conclusion of his American journey, Humboldt not only ascended to previously unknown and unrecorded heights but also helped create a narrative of mountain climbing that proved highly influential in the further development of the burgeoning sport. Perhaps more important, Humboldt, by viewing the mountaineering quest as intrinsically connected to important scientific, aesthetic, moral, and political questions of the day, teaches us that mountaineering, rather than being an isolated leisure activity, is always embedded in a cultural and historical context.

PART II
ALPINE ADVENTURES

CHAPTER 3

THE ALPS

A Brief History

Once feared as dreadful and dangerous places, mountains in the Western world became environments of interest and beauty. In the seventeenth
century and the early eighteenth, wealthy young Englishmen on their educational Grand Tour would pass through the Alps as quickly as possible on
their way to reach the cradle of civilization and culture, Italy. This practice
began to change in the late eighteenth century, when—thanks to the burgeoning sciences of geology, meteorology, and geography, the philosophical paradigm of Romanticism, and European industrialization—the Alps
became a destination rather than a passageway.[1] In the same way that their
predecessors were chiefly fascinated by cultural antiquities, young men increasingly turned their attention to the mountains. With the rapid development of infrastructure making mountains more accessible to a rising middle class with leisure and means to travel, the activity of mountaineering
was born at the crossroads of scientific exploration and a philosophical
paradigm of the sublime. By the end of the nineteenth century, mountaineering had emerged as a sport of radical individualism that solidified and
simultaneously challenged new models of masculinity and broadly affected
patterns of tourism, leisure, and consumption.

As visitors can easily discern, the Alps are a mountain range that has been greatly shaped by humans. Prehistoric pastures, medieval cities, railways, tunnels, ski lifts, huts, tramways that whisk tourists to impossibly placed restaurants atop sharp peaks, and, more recently, large sheets of plastic covering glaciers to keep them from melting, all reveal the presence and the impact of man throughout human history. Although a systematic exploration of the Alps did not begin until the late eighteenth century, the mountains had been visited for centuries of trading, warfare, and pleasure. In 1991 German climbers on the remote Similaun glacier came across Ötzi the Iceman, a corpse five and a half feet tall that was remarkably well preserved in the ice. From the arrowhead buried in his shoulder (that presumably caused his death), blood from another human on his clothes, and a rudimentary backpack made from animal skins and a wooden frame, scientists concluded that Ötzi had traveled across the mountains as a trader or shepherd and had encountered other people up high.[2] The body was dated to circa 3500 BC, giving evidence that even in prehistoric times Neolithic humans regularly frequented the mountains. In fact, the receding glaciers ten thousand years ago enabled Alpine communities to flourish even before Ötzi's time, as confirmed by rock carvings and evidence of cave dwellings throughout Switzerland.

Around 1000 BC, Celtic tribes settled in the Alpine regions, founding villages and establishing an economy of salt mining and trading. When the expanding Roman Republic threatened Iberian, Gallic, and Celtic communities, as well as Carthage in today's Tunisia, its ruler, Hannibal, famously crossed the Alps with forty thousand men and many elephants during the Second Punic War. While scholars still debate which pass Hannibal's troops used to traverse the mountains on their way to Italy in 218 BC, his military feat and legendary crossing have inspired the imagination of historians, writers, and painters ever since. Still, over the next centuries, the Romans established themselves in the Alps, building monuments, gates, walls, and bathhouses, but also opening roads, bridges, and mountain passes. Eventually they set into motion efforts to convert the regional citizens to Christianity.

After the end of Roman rule, Frankish, Bavarian, and Saracen tribes struggled to control the regions until the various dukedoms and princedoms were incorporated into the Holy Roman Empire under Charlemagne, re-establishing stability. From then on, the Holy Roman emperor was nominally in charge of most of Europe, while in reality aristocratic families became powerful rulers throughout the Alps. During the time when Rudolf von Habsburg was the Holy Roman emperor, the Gotthard Pass, a major pass crossing the Alps, was opened to the general public via the Teufelsbrücke crossing the Schöllenen Gorge. Since the town of Lucerne was the natural point of departure for this pass, its citizens feared that the passage would be used for tax revenues on goods and people. In the face of the perceived Habsburg threat, the leaders of four Swiss cantons adjacent to Lake Lucerne (Uri, Schwyz, Nidwalden, and Obwalden) formed an *Eidgenossenschaft* on August 1, 1291, at Rütli, assuring themselves of mutual military assistance. The document they signed is heralded as the founding of Switzerland and was famously dramatized by Schiller in his play *Wilhelm Tell* (1802).

In the Middle Ages, the Alps were presumed to be the home of witches, wild beasts, devils, and giants, and more specifically a place where dragons abounded. Multiple legends and sightings added to the vivid mythology visible in sculptures and paintings of the day. Even as late as the eighteenth century, Johann Jakob Scheuchzer (1672–1733), a professor of physics and mathematics at Zurich University who undertook annual pilgrimages to the Alps in the years between 1702 and 1711, in the description of his fifth journey in 1706 endeavored to provide "a history of Helvetic dragons . . . whose existence many still doubt."[3] Though he did not claim to have seen a dragon himself, Scheuchzer compiled accounts of numerous eyewitnesses who described dragon encounters, organized by canton (of which Lucerne boasted the most), distinguishing footed and nonfooted, winged and nonwinged species, and providing detailed information on coloring, habitat (preferably caves), and feeding. Finding an astonishing variety— some snakelike, some with cat faces, some with scales, some aggressive and some friendly—Scheuchzer also provided as many as eleven images of the impressive and terrifying *Ungeheuer* (monsters). In his elaborate and extensive works written in Latin and German, Scheuchzer, an avid hiker, however, went much beyond gory tales. Alongside his account of Alpine myths and legends, he assembled detailed information on the Swiss topography, geology, meteorology, glacier motion, flora, fauna, and Alpine inhabitants, including the first barometric height measurements, intricate maps, and

Johann Jakob Scheuchzer, figure 9, "Dragons," from
Ouresiphoites Helveticus, sive, itinera per Helvetiae alpinas regiones, 1723
(Provided by ETH Zurich; with special thanks to Melanie Lerch)

illustrations of plants, rocks, and human artifacts. His work relied on the efforts of other Swiss naturalists, such as Conrad Gessner (1516–65) and Josias Simler (1530–76), who had already begun to describe flora and fauna, as well as the beauty and human impact of the region. Gessner combined the study of botany and zoology with a humanistic quest and the study of languages and literature; his student and biographer Simler focused on a topographical description of the Alps, outlining high passes and their passages in his *Description of the Valais and the Alps,* published in 1574.

At the beginning of the eighteenth century, poor roads and rough passes, scarcity and inhospitality of accommodations, and the prevailing poverty of Swiss peasants kept most travelers from visiting the Alpine mountains. Although some Swiss cantons were among the first democratic republics, religious strife, cantonal quarrels, corruption and repression, different languages and many more dialects, and uncoordinated coinages and transportation hindered safe and enjoyable travel. Yet many Britons had to cross the mountains on their educational Grand Tour to Italy. As the wealthiest nation in the world, Britain boasted a substantial upper class with abundant money and leisure who believed that seeing the sites of Western civilization, especially classical Geneva, Venice, Florence, Rome, and Naples, exerted a formative influence on the minds of the young men who formed Britain's future elite. The inevitable as well as elaborate crossing of the Alps was accomplished via the Mont Cenis Pass and entailed carriages being disassembled and hauled by pack animals and travelers carried by porters, a process that slowed the trip considerably and led to many complaints of discomfort. Given these conditions, travelers hastened through a landscape they viewed as disharmonious and scarce, eager to reach the monuments of Roman civilization while cursing the mountains thwarting their passage as hostile and ugly.[4]

In the wake of the Enlightenment, Swiss scholars and scientists began to explore the regional mountains. The Bernese physiologist, anatomist, botanist, and poet Albrecht von Haller (1708–77) repeatedly visited the nearby mountains, observing geology and geography and collecting plants and crystals. Upon his return from one of these trips, he wrote the influential hymn of Alpine life "Die Alpen" (1732, The Alps), which turned the harsh and remote mountainous landscape into a biblical mission. Haller not only gave a glorious portrayal of mountain scenery but helped create the myth of Alpine peasants who lead modest and happy lives away from a corrupt courtly society in the lowlands. Translated into French, English, Italian, and Latin, and (re)published in as many as thirty editions, Haller's poem enjoyed a smashing and lasting success. In Haller's footsteps, the philosopher, novelist, and social theorist Jean-Jacques Rousseau (1712–78), who was born in Geneva but spent part of his boyhood in the Savoy Alps, touted the Alpine landscape in ecstatic and Romantic terms. In particular, Rousseau's epistolary novel *Julie, ou la nouvelle Héloïse* (1761) fashioned the mountains as a peaceful refuge for its autobiographical hero, the middle-class teacher Saint-Preux, who hopelessly falls in love with Julie d'Etange, the daughter of an aristocrat. While the illicit affair fails, Saint-Preux finds solace in the mountains for his melancholic, tormented state: "High in the mountains where the air is pure and subtle, one breathes more freely, one feels lighter in the body, more serene of mind; pleasures there are less intense, passions more moderate. Meditations there take on an indescribably grand and sublime character, in proportion with the objects that strike us, an indescribably tranquil delight that has nothing acrid or sensual about it. It seems that by rising above the habitation of men one leaves all base and earthly sentiments behind."[5]

Whereas the conservative Haller upheld the healthy air and moral integrity of the Alpine villagers, Rousseau employed the stupendous landscapes and fresh air precisely for his visions of freeing body and soul from social bonds and religious constraints enforced in the lowlands.[6] Influenced and mentored by both, the young naturalist, botanist, and geologist Horace-Bénédict de Saussure (1740–99) first came to the Alps at age twenty and found himself beguiled. The following chapter explores Saussure's depiction of Alpine travels in his four-volume *Voyages dans les Alpes* (1779–96), a work that laid the foundation for his reputation as the father of Alpinism, and details in particular his obsession with Mont Blanc.

The Alps: A British Romance

The British agricultural revolution increased both food production and population through means of mechanization and crop rotation, giving rise to a new upper middle class eager to display its wealth. And the wealthiest nation became even richer when Britain's gross national product per capita

increased two and a half times from 1750 to 1850 during the ensuing Industrial Revolution.[7] Britain's industrialization had a profound effect on the
development of the Alps, both by introducing new methods of transportation and by creating a class with the means and leisure to temporarily escape urban society. After the conclusion of the Seven Years' War between
Britain and France in 1763, borders once again opened, and travel became
as fashionable as ever. Toward the end of the eighteenth century, Britons
thus began to view the Alps as a destination in itself rather than a passageway. The spirit of Romanticism also fostered such development by making the territory, once feared to contain witches, demons, and dragons, the
subject of spiritual and aesthetic marvel in literature and painting. As western Europe was becoming increasingly urbanized and industrialized, an
unprecedented Romantic appreciation of the natural landscape was beginning to take hold. In the decades after Edmund Burke had proposed that
uncontrollable, potentially dangerous forces such as grand mountains both
please and scare the observer, at once producing feelings of awe, pleasure,
and terror, the prevailing Romantic paradigm gained currency in philosophy, literature, music, and the visual arts, even causing neatly manicured
English gardens to be fashionably transformed into untamed "wilderness."[8]
In search of Romantic solitude, William Wordsworth (1770–1850) and his
friend Robert Jones covered two thousand miles on foot on their first trip to
the Alps in 1790, celebrating the Alpine scenery.[9] While Wordsworth's poem
"Descriptive Sketches Taken During a Pedestrian Tour Among the Alps"
echoes Haller and Rousseau in its praise of peasant life, Wordsworth wrote
for an educated British audience with the money and leisure to travel.

Yet the alluring lands became off-limits once again for Britons after the
French Revolution and France's declaration of war against Britain in 1793.
In the wake of the French Revolution and encouraged by revolutionary
demonstrations in Zurich, French revolutionary armies overtook Switzerland in 1798, declaring it an independent "Helvetic Republic." Just two
years later, Napoleon Bonaparte became another famous military ruler to
cross the Alps, leading an army of forty thousand men and lavish provisions on his way to Italy to retake territory seized by the Austrians. To advance his military interests against Habsburg Austria, Napoleon ordered
the construction of several roads and passes. Most prominently, he improved the carriage road pass at Mont Cenis, which, already used by Char-

lemagne, had become the main route for crossing the Alps and connected the provinces of Savoy and Piedmont, which both belonged to the Kingdom of Sardinia until 1859. After Swiss cantons rebelled against the French rule in 1803, Napoleon allowed for the restitution of cantonal governments, though Switzerland remained under nominal French control until Napoleon was defeated at Waterloo. The Congress of Vienna in 1815 finally established the post-Napoleonic order, guaranteed Switzerland's neutrality, and determined the Swiss borders as they are today.

During this new prolonged period of peace, Britons swarmed to the continent once more, in even greater numbers. As they had done before, travelers visited Paris and Italy, reviving the traditions of the Grand Tour, but increasingly lingered in Switzerland, admiring not only the artifacts of human civilization but also the natural sights. The convenience and ease of traveling steadily improved, as well. In meticulous triangulation work, the region was topographically surveyed from 1809 to 1862, and the exceptionally detailed Dufour topographic maps, on a scale of 1:100,000, covered all of Switzerland by 1864, a testament to both Swiss national identity and the growing attraction of the Alps. The first steamships crossed the English Channel in 1816, and by 1821, a regular cross-steamer service connected the British Isles with France. New or improved roads and more comfortable carriages using spring-based suspension greatly cut travel times and increased comfort. Finally, the availability and hospitality of Swiss inns and hostels expanded. With these improvements, the number and composition of British travelers also changed, including more upper-middle-class men and increasingly women.

In the summer of 1816, George Gordon Byron (1788–1824) and Percy Bysshe Shelley (1792–1822) settled in Geneva with their lovers Claire Clairmont (1798–1879) and Mary Wollstonecraft Godwin (1797–1851), Claire's stepsister. With their scandalous lifestyle and shocking reputation, the poets attracted a great deal of curiosity and gossip and were watched like celebrities as they followed the locations of Rousseau's *La nouvelle Heloise* and visited other tourist sites. Rather than celebrating pure peasant life and viewing the mountains as morally uplifting, Shelley's and Byron's works portrayed the Alps in sensuous and intensely Romantic terms, conveying an immediate and ecstatic experience as well as a deeper and darker Romantic philosophy. Shelley's future wife Mary was inspired by the stormy weather to conceive her Gothic novel *Frankenstein* (1818), and the character-istic sublime mixture of awe and terror spilled into all three writers' poetic texts, radically transforming the Alps' reputation.

Prepared by the texts of Saussure, Wordsworth, and Byron, John Ruskin first visited the Alps on a six-month carriage tour at the age of sixteen. Ruskin found the Alps so compelling that he saw them as a work of art shaped by the Sculptor, created for human delight. In direct contrast to Bur-net's assessment, Ruskin fashioned mountains into a graceful and vibrant expression of God's presence, defining their meaning for post-Romantic generations. Ruskin also proved influential in introducing and explaining the works of modern landscape painters such as J. M. W. Turner, whose works revealed the drama and sublimity of Alpine locations in unprece-dented color and light.

The revolutions of 1848 in Italy, France, and Germany led to the estab-lishment of the Second Republic in France and the First National Assem-bly in Germany. In the same year, Switzerland was founded as a federal state of republican cantons, with a uniform system of measurement and currency, laws guaranteeing equality and freedom of speech, and Bern as the federal capital. As continental Europe was becoming increasingly po-litically and economically stable, England rose to new heights of industri-alization and urbanization—but also became increasingly filthy, making a temporary escape all the more alluring for those who could afford it. By the time England was displaying its industrial prowess at the Great Exhi-bition in London in 1851, the number of English tourists eager to leave for more "natural" heights had also reached new records and included the upper middle classes eager to join the former domains of aristocracy.

Thanks to intense railway building, modern transportation systems ca-tered to the new demands. The first steam locomotives were used between Liverpool and Manchester in 1831, and the railway net grew rapidly in Great Britain, gradually expanding to the mainland and the Alps. After the founding of a Swiss national parliament that expressed the desire to create a national railway system, English financiers, engineers, and contractors helped design and build railway lines along principal valleys and riverbeds that connected the main cities and branched out to various Alpine desti-nations. In addition, thousands of new hotels and health resorts opened, many of them catering specifically to English visitors by offering currency exchange, English mealtimes, and afternoon tea. This, in turn, made Swiss innkeepers wealthy men with power and influence. Travel guidebooks were also widely published. In Britain, John Murray, son of a leading publisher in London, wrote *A Hand-Book for Travellers on the Continent* in 1836, followed by a *Hand-Book* on southern Germany in 1837, and one on Switzerland in 1838. Based on Murray's firsthand experiences, all books followed a similar format, beginning with an introduction to the history and manners of the region, followed by practical travel information, suggested itineraries, and detailed chapters on each subregion, outlining in straightforward style what "*ought to be seen.*"[10] This format, combined with the books' compact size and recognizable bindings, filled an obvious niche in the booming travel market, shaping the travel routes and habits of generations of tourists to come. Soon thereafter, others followed suit by copying the books' style, and the young Karl Baedeker, who owned a small publishing firm in Germany, began issuing his own travel guides to the Rhine region (1839), Germany and Austria (1842), and Switzerland (1844). Baedeker imitated the format, organization, and size of his British predecessor's books but made his own guides cheaper by printing on thinner paper and by adding colorful and more accurate maps, which made his books popular with tourists beyond Germany.[11]

Specific climbing guides, such as John Ball's *The Alpine Guide* (1863–68), a comprehensive and up-to-date route guide, the first of its kind, followed next. After an accident killed three guides who fell into a massive crevasse, in 1821 the Compagnie des Guides de Chamonix, a first mountain guiding organization, was founded.[12] The Compagnie, still in existence to this day, established strict rules on the number, price, and rotation of guides, enforced by fees and fines by the commandant of Savoy. For instance, an ascent of Mont Blanc required four guides to be paid forty livres each, but no climbing could be undertaken on Sundays or holidays before Holy Mass.[13] While some Britons like Alfred Wills circumvented these rules by hiring their guides outside the bounds of Chamonix, most accepted the new safety and salary guidelines for those leading customers up the mountain and carrying their provisions. As discussed in chapter 6, Albert Smith made his famed fortieth ascent of Mont Blanc in August 1851 and cleverly capitalized on the expedition's success by developing the Piccadilly show *The Ascent of Mont Blanc,* accompanied by products such as mountain miniatures, a board game, and book. The success of these products fed into an even greater travel appetite fueling the transportation and lodging business.

Meanwhile, the British cabinetmaker and temperance teacher Thomas Cook developed yet another product that propelled tourism to new heights: the package tour. As a passionate Christian, Cook ingeniously conceived the combined use of both entertainment and travel to distract people from drinking and other forms of debauchery. At first, Cook convinced the Midland Counties Railway to offer a reduced fee in exchange for a guaranteed number of (working-class) passengers herded to regional temperance meetings. The overwhelming popularity of these tours encouraged Cook to move beyond church excursions and offer both food and entertainment as part of affordable trips, first within England (1845), then Scotland (1846), the Continent (1855), and finally Switzerland. Cook's first Alpine excursion received more than five hundred applications and took place from June 26 to July 15, 1863, involving sixty people who reached Geneva by rail and then trekked by mule to the Mont Blanc region. The trip became a resounding success owing to its immaculate organization, ranging from transportation to lodging to meals to provisions. Breaking class barriers, Cook promoted working-class travel and advocated the benefits of recreation and fresh air for all. His trips proved especially attractive to single women barred from traveling by Victorian etiquette, who made up a majority of his passengers. While Cook drew criticism from those wishing to preserve upper-middle-class exclusivity, he profited from the growing tide of visitors, causing a hotel building boom and further railway development. In the 1860s, a new era of railway tunnel building commenced, with increased tributary railway lines to the high mountains. Thanks to rock blasting with dynamite, pneumatic drills, and a ventilation system, the English and French engineers Thomas Brassey and Germain Sommeiller built, with English capital, the Mont Cenis railway tunnel, which opened in 1871, the first in a series of tunnels that included Gotthard (1882), Arlberg (1884), Simplon (1905), and Lötschberg (1913). The deployment of the electric telegraph and the establishment of the Swiss banking system in the nineteenth century further helped the burgeoning travel industry.

As Victorian Britain adopted an increasingly sedentary lifestyle, sports and adventure gained new allure. Organized sports, it was believed, provided a socially and morally formative outlet for excess energy and competitive drives. By midcentury, numerous sporting associations from rugby to football had been founded.[14] During the same period, mountaineering grew into a favorite pastime that, beyond scientific or aesthetic motives, primarily involved testing one's physical and mental abilities. During the so-called Golden Age of Alpinism, in the years between Alfred Wills's 1854 Weisshorn and Edward Whymper's 1865 Matterhorn ascent, nearly all the major Alpine peaks were scaled by British, Swiss, French, Italian, and German climbers and their guides.[15] The central location of the Alps, combined with increased ease of accessibility and improved infrastructure, made this mountain range the premier venue for British gentlemen to temporarily flee the constraints of Victorian culture while engaging in pursuits of both danger and heroism and visions of purity and sublimity.

As the perception, representation, and publicity of mountaineering began to change, in 1857, the first Alpine Club was founded in London, an idea hatched by the Cambridge-educated mountaineers William Matthews and Thomas Stuart Kennedy. Membership was decided by a qualification committee and entailed not only the completion of difficult mountaineering ascents but also scientific or literary Alpine contributions. The exclusive association met at suitable hotels in London and soon counted over 150 members, most of them Cambridge and Oxford graduates—James Forbes, John Ruskin, Alfred Wills, and the publisher John Murray among them.[16] Women were not permitted entry. With such intellectual prowess among its membership, the club's first president, John Ball, soon proposed a publication, and in 1859 the first volume of *Peaks, Passes, and Glaciers* was published, with records and descriptions of climbs accomplished by its members, accompanied by elaborately produced woodcuts, maps, and colored plates. The Austrian (1862), Swiss and Italian (1863), German (1869), and French (1874) Alpine Clubs soon followed, building for their members Alpine huts with bunk beds, stoves, cooking utensils, and blankets; establishing signed trails over the passes; and providing mountaineering training.

In this climate, the Irish physicist John Tyndall and the wood engraver Edward Whymper both had their eyes set on the first ascent of the imposing Matterhorn, one of the last Alpine summits to be "conquered." After seven attempts, Whymper's team of seven climbers and guides succeeded in summiting the Matterhorn on July 14, 1865, yet the climb culminated in tragedy when, on the descent, one member of the group slipped and dragged three others to their deaths before the rope that joined them broke. At home and abroad, Whymper was forced to defend himself against repeated accusations that the rope had been cut or that he had deliberately used a weak rope. As a consequence of these widespread discussions, Queen Victoria considered banning Englishmen from climbing altogether, but it was already too late to stem the tide of peak baggers, onlookers, media coverage, and tourist development. The queen herself made her first trip to the Alps in 1868 and trekked up Mount Pilatus on a mule. In 1871, finally, three key books of the Golden Age were published: Leslie Stephen's *The Playground of Europe,* John Tyndall's *Hours of Exercise in the Alps,* and Edward Whymper's *Scrambles Amongst the Alps,* all of which invent, narrate, and market mountaineering as a fusion of scientific task, sublime experience, competitive masculinity, and escapism.

After the Franco-Prussian War (1870–71), which had kept visitors to Switzerland at bay, western Europe entered a long period of peace, with political stability guaranteed by treaties among nation-states.[17] After a brief economic depression in 1873, a sustained period of prosperity ensued. At the same time, both the number and type of Alpine vacationers greatly increased, based on two new developments: convalescence from tuberculosis in an Alpine climate and skiing. Since Roman times, Alpine natural springs had been hailed as a remedy for arthritis, heart disease, gout, depression, and infertility, and resorts in the Dauphine, Tyrol, and the Grisons began to flourish in the 1760s. In the second half of the nineteenth century, mountain enthusiasts such as John Forbes and John Tyndall touted Alpine vacations as a healthy respite from the filth of England's rapid industrialization. These beliefs were soon bolstered by science through the theories of the German-Swiss physician Alexander Spengler. After his visit to Davos in 1853, Spengler concluded that Alpine villagers were immune to tuberculosis because of the dry and warm climate. Spengler's theory of an "Alpine cure" for lung diseases soon attracted much attention in Britain, where tuberculosis, like many other diseases, was rampant owing to the high concentration of people, damp climate, and abundant coal smoke and soot. The first tuberculosis patients arrived in the Alps in the early 1860s, giving way to a steady stream of middle- and upper-class British, German, Austrian, and Dutch cure seekers. The remarkable growth of Davos as a spa town is an impressive example of the tangible effects of such beliefs. Situated at 1,600 meters, Davos used to be a minor village. In 1870, however, after the first *Kurgäste* (sanatorium guests) arrived, the village counted two thousand inhabitants, the starting point to a growth of astonishing pace: in the next twenty years, Davos doubled in size, and it doubled again in the following ten years.[18]

A second trend involved an extended winter tourist season: in the 1890s, the British travel agent Henry Lunn began to offer religious and educational Alpine winter tours, convincing resort owners to open their facilities exclusively for his guests. The growing appeal of winter sports also helped promote Lunn's endeavor. Soon Alpine resorts created areas for skating, curling, and sledding. Most significantly, Alpine skiing was introduced in the 1880s and 1890s and, promoted by Lunn's first Alpine skiing competitions in 1911, eventually made the winter season as fashionable as the summer.[19]

As it became easier, faster, and cheaper to reach the Alps, the British lost their domination of Alpine tourism to Germany and Italy, new nation-states that had risen to prosperity and were eager to follow the industrialized British model. Americans also made up a substantial part of the new Swiss tourists; in the late 1870s, Mark Twain passed through Switzerland, calling the country "simply a large, humpy, solid rock, with a thin skin of grass stretched over it."[20] The Saint Gotthard tunnel offered an easy principal passage from Germany to Switzerland and Italy, providing a model for numerous other tunnels in the Alps and the Canadian Rockies. In the 1890s, railway building culminated in the ambitious project of blasting a line right through the middle of the Eiger, destroying Alpine meadows and scenery but bringing tourists and money to the Kleine Scheidegg. There were fiercely contested plans for building a railway line to the summit of Mont Blanc and a shaft through the Matterhorn. Soon, however, railway building was surpassed by yet another invention when the first automobiles crossed the Alps in 1894.

From Heidi to Hitler

Even the formerly poorest regions of the Alps now prospered, opening their doors to tourists no matter their nationality, wealth, age, sex, and class, aided by a booming tourist industry that cleverly marketed Swiss products from milk to watches to chocolate. By the beginning of the twentieth century, the Alps had become not only a popular tourist destination but also center stage for projections of purity and chastity, as manifested in Johanna Spyri's influential *Heidi* novels. *Heidi's Lehr- und Wanderjahre* (1880, *Heidi's Years of Learning and Travel*) and *Heidi kann brauchen, was es gelernt hat* (1881, *Heidi Makes Use of What She Has Learned*) tell the story of a devout orphan girl who grows up in the Swiss mountains with her beloved grandfather, her goats, and the goatherd Peter. When she is forced to move to Frankfurt to be a companion to the invalid girl Clara, a homesick Heidi quickly charms Clara with her innocent genuineness and unmannered kindness but offends the heartless housekeeper, Fräulein Rottenmeier, and the restrictive conventions of city life. An overjoyous Heidi finally returns home, turns her faithless grandfather to God, and even teaches her friend Clara to walk with the help of pure mountain air and goat's milk. The trope of peaceful and happy mountain living amid hardworking, pious, and honest peasants unmistakably harkens back to Haller and in simplified form proved incredibly successful and marketable. Heidi was translated into French as early as 1882 and into English in 1884; to date the novels have been translated into more than fifty languages, reaching an audience of over twenty million readers.[21] The books have also inspired numerous film and television adaptations, from a Hollywood motion picture starring Shirley Temple in 1937, a Japanese animated series in 1974, a highly popular twenty-six-episode German-Swiss television series in 1978, to the German-Swiss feature film *Heidi*, directed by Alain Gsponer, in 2015.

Rather than a site of spiritual and physical regeneration, the eastern Alps became the epicenter for a series of battles between Austria-Hungary and Italy during World War I. After the Armistice and the collapse of the Austro-Hungarian Empire, the fighting ceased, but in the interwar period, the Alps continued to be seized for ideological reasons. To the Nazis, the mountains presented a welcome battleground for national domination.[22] While German *Bergfilme* celebrated heroic mountain deeds completed by Aryan supermen, Jewish members were infamously barred from membership in the Austrian and German Alpine Club. Hitler himself, an avid mountain enthusiast, established his retreat, the Berghof, above Berchtesgaden, where he wrote the second volume of *Mein Kampf* in 1925. The Nazis saw mountaineering as an extension of the war experience, which embraced courage, sacrifice, and heroism, encouraging risky, high-profile mountain excursions, from the Eiger North Face to Nanga Parbat, all with the high risk of losing human life.[23]

In the twenty-first century, images of the Alps made headlines for glacial melting and climate change. With sixty to eighty million visitors each year, tourism in Switzerland generates close to fifty billion dollars annually and provides over 10 percent of the country's jobs.[24] Yet revenue at over six hundred ski resorts in the Alps is declining. A recent Europe-wide assessment identified "increasing losses in winter tourism due to reduced snow cover and increased exposure of settlements and infrastructure to natural hazards as the primary vulnerabilities to climate change in the Alps."[25] According to recent research, the most important impacts of climate change on tourism in Switzerland are snowpack reduction, melting glaciers, and water scarcity. At a time when clean air, freshwater, and glaciers have become invaluable yet quickly disappearing resources, it is worthwhile to reflect on how the early mountaineers appreciated and advocated for these resources. Their influential texts promoted touristic exploitation as well as environmental concerns, both of which continue to bear much relevance today.

CHAPTER 4

HORACE-BÉNÉDICT DE SAUSSURE'S
QUEST FOR MONT BLANC

On Top of Mont Blanc

On August 3, 1787, fifteen years before Humboldt attempted Mount Chimborazo, Horace-Bénédict de Saussure stood atop Mont Blanc, the fifth person ever to do so, his wife looking on via telescope from Chamonix. That day, Saussure realized a dream he had harbored for more than two decades, and the financial resources and scientific research he had put into this project finally came to fruition. Yet the experience proved altogether different than imagined. After a dinner "eaten with appetite but digested with disgust" and a "detestable night," the party set off at 6:00 a.m., making slow progress up the col.[1] Dizzy and exhausted, Saussure was forced to take frequent breaks, and his guides did not fare much better. Finally, atop the mountain, Saussure was pleased to observe the flag his eager onlookers had hoisted in his honor down in Chamonix. He lingered for four and a half hours, fumbling with his bulky instruments (some of which he had designed himself) while gasping for air and fighting nausea. He determined the boiling point of water, the temperature of the snow, the moisture and electricity of the air, the color of the sky, and his pulse and that of

91

his guides. They drank some wine and ate some food, finding smell and taste unaffected by the altitude, fired a pistol to verify that its thud sounded the same at altitude, and filled bottles with air and snow from the summit. Still, Saussure felt regret that his party had to leave before all measurements were completed. What had been envisioned as a triumphant march to the top turned into an experience of mixed emotions, with sensations ranging from pride to pain, as Saussure recorded in his diary:

> My work would have been far more complete had I been in any ordinary situation, and I venture to boast that it needed no common effort to accomplish what I did in the condition I was. Despite the delight which this superb spectacle gave me, I felt a painful sense of not being able to draw from it all the profit possible, and that my power of appreciation was limited by my difficulty in breathing. I was like an epicure invited to a splendid festival and prevented from enjoying it by violent nausea.[2]

The metaphor that Saussure reaches for is one of intense physical pleasure, yet the dissatisfaction of the experience is just as tangible in its torturing effects. Owing to material conditions at altitude and the ensuing bodily afflictions, Saussure is precisely not capable of enjoying the "superb spectacle" unfolding in front of his eyes but instead becomes physically involved, reacting to the environment that he is not only seeing but experiencing. If shortness of breath hinders both aesthetic consumption and scientific measurement, Saussure considers this a loss but still provides us, in his diary, with a vivid description of the conflict. Conversely, in his later opus magnum, the four-volume *Voyages dans les Alpes, précédés d'un essai sur l'histoire naturelle des environs de Genève* (1779–96), he changed his tone in hindsight, depicting the summit and its all-encompassing view in more familiar and predictable terms of sublime reverence.

> Still the grand spectacle I had under my eyes gave me a lively pleasure. A light haze suspended in the lower layers of the atmosphere, hid, it is true, the more distant and low-lying objects, such as the plains of France and Lombardy, but I did not greatly regret this loss; that which I came to see, and now recognized with the greatest clearness, was the order of the great ranges of which I had so long desired to ascertain the grouping. I could hardly believe my eyes, it seemed a dream, when I saw under my feet these majestic peaks, these formidable Aiguilles du Midi, d'Argentiére [Aiguille

Verte] du Géant, of which I had found even the bases so difficult and dangerous of approach. I seized their connections, their relation, their structure, and a single glance cleared away doubts which years of work had not sufficed to remove.[3]

In this depiction, the bodily experience that in the diary overshadowed the "grand spectacle" is erased as the visual reward of the climb leads to reflection and understanding, similar to the sublime process that Kant (who admired Saussure and his feats) outlined in *The Critique of Judgment* (1790).[4] The unique perspective gained from the top therefore justifies the hardships of the ascent, but ambiguities remain: if widespread haze hindered an expansive view, how could Saussure arrive at insights of the "greatest clearness"? And if the experience seemed like a dream far removed from reality, how could it afford an intellectual discovery surpassing years of research? Even here, physical needs cannot be pushed aside entirely, as Saussure admits a little later: "I found myself constantly compelled to leave off work to take care of my respiration."[5]

The unevenness of the summit experience resurfaces in a later passage in *Voyages*, when in the chapter "Descriptions des rochers & other détails du Voyage" Saussure further acknowledges the disappointments of the trip:

> Since I had had for the last two hours under my eyes almost all one sees from the summit, the arrival was no *coup de théâtre*—it did not even give me all the pleasure one might have imagined; my most lively and agreeable sensation was to feel myself at the end of my uncertainties; for the length of the struggle, the recollection and the still vivid impression of the exertion it had cost me, caused me a kind of irritation. At the moment that I trod the highest point of the snow that crowned the summit I trampled it with a feeling of anger rather than of pleasure. Besides, my object was not only to reach the highest point, I was bound to make the observations and experiments which alone gave value to my venture, and I was very doubtful of being able to carry out more than a portion of what I had planned.[6]

This wonderfully frank description stands in stark contrast to the sublime spectacle Saussure delighted in previously, detailing once more physical interventions rather than victorious stirrings. The physical demands of the climb cannot be pushed aside in favor of sublime rapture; instead they disturb and even prevent measurements. Complementing his previous pleasure with growing anger, Saussure even begins to question the intrinsic value of his ascent, something that comes to bear even more explicitly in Humboldt's mountaineering descriptions, as we have seen.

Although Saussure had put decades into the preparation for climbing Mont Blanc, which he elevated to a matter of utmost scientific urgency when he declared, "Mont Blanc is one of the mountains of Europe whose comprehension seems to throw the most light on the Theory of the Earth," his famed ascent remained a precarious and uneven undertaking.[7] And his motivations for climbing prove as contradictory as his widely fluctuating experiences on Mont Blanc. In the preface to *Voyages*, Saussure defined the term *geology* as "the Theory of the Earth," claiming that "it is above all through the study of mountains that the progress of a Theory of the Earth can be accelerated."[8] The volumes of *Voyages* accordingly pose at the outset an interest in the geologic study of the Alps but become increasingly multilayered, blending measurements and observations on rock and snow with aesthetic landscape descriptions and advertisement, with narratives of various tours, including mountain ascents. In this way, Saussure resembles Humboldt: if the initial impetus for scaling a mountain is scientific, soon other rationales, desires, sensations, and fears come into play, making the undertaking as rich as it is entangled. As one of the first naturalists to couple scientific and aesthetic interests with an intense desire to actually climb mountains, Saussure exemplifies one of the key dilemmas of tourism: he hailed the Alps for their spectacular scenery, bucolic villages, and friendly folk. Yet his own privileged life was a far cry from these depictions, as he came to the Alps for temporary respite, and was very much familiar with the comforts of city life. In short, Saussure much enjoyed the cultural opportunities and luxuries only cities could offer, yet he upheld the ideal of pure Alpine life from a position of power and wealth. By titling his volumes *Voyages*, Saussure departed from his Swiss predecessors, whose titles of works ranged from *historia* to *descriptio* to *commentario* (Gessner, Simler, Scheuchzer), to align his works to travel in the age of exploration, as exemplified by Georg Forster, Charles Marie de La Condamine, and Pierre Bouguer. Saussure thus helped shape travel accounts by Humboldt and a generation of British travelers who turned the Alps into a tourist destination for a rising middle class.

Influences and Upbringing

While Saussure has long been credited with initiating interest in the Alps and indeed plays a central role in the emergence of mountaineering, his works have not been translated into English, hindering a wide reception and detailed knowledge of his texts. The first two volumes of *Voyages* were translated into German; but since the last two volumes, including the elaborate description of the Mont Blanc excursion in the fourth volume, were never translated into either German or English (except for short excerpts), widespread confusion still exists about many particulars of Saussure's later trips, not unlike the case of Humboldt.[9] The gap of information is all the more regrettable because Saussure was of seminal importance in matters concerning geology and mountains, for Humboldt and beyond. Saussure's biographer Douglas Freshfield emphasized, "Saussure was the true author of our modern passion for Alpine scenery, as well as the first systematic Alpine explorer."[10] Saussure's contemporaries agreed: Humboldt called Saussure a grand master in whose footsteps he was to follow, Johann Wolfgang von Goethe requested to meet Saussure in Geneva for travel advice on his Alpine tour in 1779, John Ruskin abundantly quoted from Saussure's works, and Forbes referred to him as the "great historian of the Alps," modeling his *Travels Through the Alps of Savoy* in format and style on Saussure's *Voyages.*[11]

Saussure was born into a well-to-do patrician family in Conches near Geneva on February 17, 1740. Both grandfathers held high posts in the Genevan government, and his father, Nicolas de Saussure, successfully entered the agriculture business after publishing treatises on the cultivation of crops. Yet Saussure seems to have developed a much stronger bond with his mother. Complementing schoolwork with rambles in the nearby hills and mountains, where he collected flowers and other botanical specimens, Saussure, like Humboldt, preferred solitude over the restrictions of society. In the preface to the first volume of *Voyages,* he recalled: "Such are the pleasures tasted by those who devote themselves to the study of mountains. For myself, I have from childhood felt for them the most positive passion: I still recollect the thrill that I experienced the first time that my hands clasped the rocks of the Salève and my eyes enjoyed its panorama."[12] This quote is remarkable in its revelation of the physical effects of climbing.

While Saussure mentions the views, they are secondary to the sensual experience of touching rock with his hands, the quintessential definition of
rock climbing, as an intrinsic pleasure of climbing. "Thrill," "passion,"
and "pleasures tasted" become the predominant memories of mountains,
forming an early and lasting drive to climb long before scientific rationales.
These material perceptions continue to play a role in his later mountain
explorations.

In 1756 Saussure's aunt married the eminent naturalist and philosopher
Charles Bonnet (1720–93), who encouraged the sixteen-year-old to pursue
a scientific career. Another important influence in Saussure's early intellectual life was Albrecht von Haller, whom Saussure met after his first trip to
Chamonix in August 1760. At the time when the young Saussure and his
mother visited the "Great Haller" at his château in Roche, Haller was at
the peak of his career serving as the director of the Bernese salt works.[13]
Saussure was utterly taken with the famed naturalist and poet of "The
Alps," and Haller in turn invited the aspiring scientist to collect plants,
encouraged subsequent trips to the Chamonix region, and began a lifelong
friendship and avid letter exchange.[14] Saussure's impressions from this first
trip to the Alps, recorded in the first volume of *Voyages,* are very much
shaped by Haller's verses in "The Alps," elevating the mountainous terrain
to a place of worship and veneration. In this vein, Saussure exults: "The
fresh and pure air one breathes, so different from the close atmosphere of
the basins of Sallanches and Servoz, the good cultivation of the soil, the
pretty hamlets met with at every step, when seen on a fine day, give the
impression of a new world, a sort of earthly paradise, enclosed by a kindly
Deity in the circle of the mountains."[15] Saussure's emphasis on fresh air,
fertile soil, honest villagers, and a benevolent God resonates with Haller's
praise of Alpine modesty that concluded "The Alps":

> O happy you who here, with steers of your own rearing,
> Plough your ancestral fields and tend paternal leas,
> Who wear your flocks' warm wool, no wintry weather fearing.
> And live on unspiced food, on milk and country cheese;
> Who, when soft zephyrs blow, upon the yielding turf
> Can soon be lulled to sleep by some cool waterfall;
> Who never wake to hear the raging ocean's surf

Nor yet in troubled times the shrilling trumpet's call;
Who would not seek to change, who live the life you love!
Lo, Fortune has no gifts that could your state improve.[16]

If Haller, in contrast to some earlier assessments that vilified the mountains as a place of evil, made a biblical argument in favor of the Alpine landscape, then Saussure expanded this line of argumentation.[17] While Haller, plagued by ill health and apparently too heavy to make excursions to higher-lying terrain, lauded a pastoral landscape, Saussure reveled in the actual climbing experience and encouraged others to do so as well, posting notes throughout the Chamonix Valley that promised a generous reward to the first person to climb the Old World's highest mountain, Mont Blanc.

Other trips followed in 1761, 1764, 1767, 1771, 1776, and 1778. After an unsuccessful application for the chair of mathematics at the Academy of Geneva, a professorship of philosophy opened at the same institution, and with the support of Haller, Saussure received the post in 1762, at just twenty-two years of age. Later he became the dual chair of physics and metaphysics at the academy, a position he held until he resigned in 1786. On his third trip to Chamonix, in March 1764, Saussure became particularly fascinated with glaciers. He delivered a lecture titled "A Description of the Glaciers of Savoy, and a Theory of Their Formation" (which later formed the basis for his chapter on glaciers in *Voyages*) but withheld publication, fearing it would duplicate Gottlieb Sigmund Gruner's three-volume *Die Eisgebirge des Schweizerlandes* (1760)—which Saussure initially could not read for his lack of German.[18]

After his return from Chamonix, he married the twenty-year-old Albertine Amélie Boissier, the eldest daughter of a family of prosperous bankers, which allowed Saussure to buy a house in Geneva and spend the rest of his life in wealth and comfort. The marriage, however, put a temporary hold on his travels. He did not return to the Alps until after the birth of his daughter, Albertine Andrienne, when he completed a tour of Mont Blanc in 1767 before returning promptly to Geneva for the arrival of his son, Nicolas Théodore. In 1768 the family, along with his sister-in-law, embarked on a yearlong Grand Tour to Paris, Holland, and London. In Paris, they rented an extravagant apartment for four months, frequenting theaters and comedies while Saussure also devoted himself to botanical and geological studies. In London, they visited the theaters and opera, as well as horse racing in York, while Saussure met with members of the Royal Society, including Benjamin Franklin, and explored the surrounding parks and caverns. In addition, Saussure traveled to Germany, Italy, and Sicily, reaching the top of Mount Vesuvius and Mount Etna in 1772 and 1773 to perform barometric measurements. These climbs fueled his enthusiasm for mountains and prepared him for his increased Alpine activities in the coming two decades. Still, Saussure's adulation of the Swiss Alps should be considered in the context of his travels to the European metropolises. If Saussure hailed the mountains as a peasant sanctuary, he himself was more at home in the worldly and bustling lifestyle of the cities, a tension that continued with British climbers in the nineteenth century and beyond.

Voyages

Saussure's *Voyages dans les Alpes,* published originally in four, then in eight, volumes from 1779 to 1796, collects the results of more than thirty years of geologic study and Alpine exploration. Nevertheless, this account omits many trips only narrated in private letters and diaries owned by the family. In the main, *Voyages* focuses on trips to the Mont Blanc region in the 1770s and 1780s. After the French publication of the first volume, Saussure received an offer from a Bernese friend, the pastor Jacob Samuel Wyttenbach (1748–1830), to translate the book into German. Wyttenbach, himself an avid hiker who had already published a small guidebook of his own, oversaw the German translation (most likely completed by a female geologist) of the first two volumes of *Voyages,* publishing them in four volumes as *Reisen durch die Alpen* between 1781 and 1788.[19] Toward the end of the fourth volume, Wyttenbach inserted a short report on the first ascent of Mont Blanc and Saussure's ascent the following year, which had just been accomplished.

While Saussure—like Haller—was initially interested in the flora of the Alpine environment, his view became more comprehensive as he sought to understand geologic phenomena and the topography of the earth, popularizing the term *geology,* rather than *geognosy,* which had been used previously. Going beyond Haller, Saussure's diverse and wide-ranging interests resembled those of Humboldt, who greatly admired the achievements of his predecessor. Saussure also invented several instruments that aided his own research as well as Humboldt's and others: he developed the first electrometer, the cyanometer to measure the color intensity of the sky, and a hair hygrometer to measure the humidity of the air by using human or animal hair under tension. Blending scientific treatises such as the "Description of a Magnetometer," observations on rock and ice layers, and descriptions of his trips, Saussure's format proved highly influential for Humboldt's *Personal Narrative* and nineteenth-century texts of Alpine explorations.[20]

Unlike Humboldt in Latin America, Saussure might not have had the necessary distance from Europe to free his mind from established and preconceived notions. Although Saussure's scientific observations led to many original interpretations to come (James Hutton, for instance, drew on Saussure's findings for his theory of uniformitarianism), Saussure himself did not draw any radical conclusions, perhaps because he was too reluctant to openly refute others and especially religious ideology. Thus his scientific insights were often thwarted by the prevailing beliefs of his time and remained bound to an old-world paradigm. Nevertheless, Saussure's scientific concepts are worth exploring: with his sustained examination of rock strata, glaciers, and meteorology, he helped to give the field of geology much currency, even though he subscribed to the by now outdated theory of Neptunism that was popular at the time. As a Neptunist, Saussure was predisposed to look at all rocks on earth as marine layers and even to regard erratic blocks that had clearly traveled far as evidence of a giant flood. In *Voyages,* he avoids mentioning God in the shaping of the earth's geological features, yet his acceptance of Neptunism implied God's hand in the creation of the earth and ultimately limited independent thinking. In this vein, Saussure believed that a giant ocean had covered the earth, depositing debris underwater and forming mountains that were later lifted up when fires within the earth raised and ruptured the earth's crust. When the waters receded, they transported huge boulders over great distances, leaving in their path residual water in the form of lakes and enabling the growth of plants and animals. Saussure's unquestioned belief in these forces prevented him from recognizing the true origin of geological features such as the fact that the moraines he observed were caused by the movement of glaciers.

In other instances, his explanations came close to an accurate under-standing of geologic processes. His observations on different rock layers, for example, almost anticipate the modern theory of plate tectonics, which did not come into currency until the twentieth century: "These layers lie atop of others that are also chalk-like and vertical, but that form the con-tinuation of almost horizontal tiers. One could say that an unknown force bent the tops of these layers into straight inclinations in order to force them into a vertical position."[21] Puzzled by the discovery of other jagged, straight, or curved bent rock layers, he considered the theory of a subterranean fire but dismissed it as an "almost supernatural explanation," deciding instead that the probable cause for dislocated and distorted rock strata was com-pression rather than internal explosion or another "unknown force."[22] While Saussure wrote off these dynamic theories as too unlikely—in con-trast to Humboldt, who, in the face of the New World, came to embrace the ongoing dynamic forces shaping the earth's surface—he had no diffi-culty believing in scenarios that seem equally far-fetched to a contempo-rary audience. In this vein, Saussure rebutted at length the opinion of local villagers who claimed to have seen a volcanic eruption near Turin by asserting that the rocks he collected nearby were of sedimentary origin. Expounding on this idea, he claimed that many Italian statues ostensibly made from volcanic basalt were in fact made from sandstone, using his own sculpting experiments with sandstone as proof (2.219–20). In another instance, Saussure correctly identified large moraines as remnants of sea-sonal snow and ice but theorized that the rocks and sands were deposited when the spring thaw waters and rains transported debris downhill.[23] Freshfield concludes: "He at once recognized that the character of the boulders showed that they had come from the recesses of the central chain. But as to the mode of their transport, so obvious to our eyes, he remained absolutely blind; he was too firmly imbued with the current belief in the agency of prehistoric floods" (151).

A similarly misguided argument informed his thoughts on glaciers. Saus-sure was captivated by the presence of ice, snow, and glaciers, and the chap-ter "On Glaciers in General" is the longest one in *Voyages*' second volume, referring to Simler, Scheuchzer, and Gruner before offering observations on the thickness, fissures, shape, and substance of the ice.[24] Yet again Saus-sure makes leaps of the imagination when he posits that an inner, subterranean heat of the earth caused glaciers to melt underneath and propelled them downslope. In contrast to his own far-fetched theories, he dismisses the villagers' belief in seven-year-long periods of ice advancement and withdrawal as an erroneous belief in magic numbers. Despite its contradictions and limitations, Saussure's work pushed forward diverse fields of inquiry: he took numerous measurements at different altitudes, studied the electricity of the atmosphere, experimented with hot air balloons, measured the temperature and depth of Swiss lakes, and published botanical works.[25] Rightfully so, Humboldt, Forbes, and Ruskin all referred to Saussure's *Voyages* as a model for their own work.

As Saussure readily admits, stylistic considerations and artistic success remained secondary, since *Voyages* primarily sought to pique readers' scientific interests. Notably, he justified stylistic flaws with the physical demands of climbing: "As to my style, I shall make no apology—I know its faults; but more accustomed to climb rocks than to turn and polish phrases, my only object has been to describe clearly what I have seen and felt. If my descriptions give my readers some part of the pleasure I have had myself in my travels—above all, if they serve to incite in some of them a desire to study and to advance a science in the progress of which I take an eager interest, I shall be well pleased and well rewarded for my exertions."[26] Indeed, Saussure tends to rely on established rather than original terms. If Haller had already praised the picturesque splendor of an Alpine idyll, Saussure for the most part follows this ideal of bucolic beauty. In this vein, he describes charming and quaint villages, situated in fertile valleys, surrounded by lush meadows, and crossed by bubbly streams. Apparently Saussure did not mind numerous repetitions of the adjective "beautiful" to characterize the scenery, readily employing established eighteenth-century tropes to stage a visual experience of joy and beauty. In keeping with this pastoral emphasis, he repeatedly describes the *vues* (view) of a particular scene and also evokes the bucolic idyll when praising the generosity and moral uprightness of the Chamonix villagers when, for instance, recalling a peasant woman who offered him pears from her orchard despite her own lack of means.[27]

In the case of the Chamonix Valley, Saussure praises, on one hand, the clean air and beautiful paths in the style of Haller, but on the other he introduces a new diction, including sublime loudness, suddenness, and enormousness. "But at times one is awakened from his slumber in terror because a loud bang with roars like thunder moves through the long valleys and gives the surprised traveler an indication of the incredible size of the loads of ice whose collapse causes such racket. The immensity of the matter causes the eye's deception in terms of distances."[28] Beyond the contrast between pastoral and sublime landscape, the quote reveals Saussure's fascination with ice and snow and hints at his understanding of the mind's fallacies. Indeed, the passage is paradigmatic for Saussure's going beyond purely visual consumption: he begins by praising the view in keeping with the century's emphasis on the visual but follows with remarks on the air and a description of the path to arrive at sensations of sound. In another instance, he admits that the cold on a glacier rendered his body and mind temporarily useless.[29] These immediate, physical interruptions of touch, sound, and smell surpass a merely visual approach, complementing traditional modes of the pastoral.

True to its title, *Voyages* takes its readers on a journey, inviting them to follow the author on foot and by mule. In this way, the text refers not to readers but to travelers, and "walking" refers to both the author and the presumed reader, as in "thus the stunned traveler does not walk away without some kind of fear."[30] As is the case with a modern travel guide, Saussure favors the pronoun "we" or "one" over "I": "However, we want to continue our way to the Buet and walk straight to the village of Valorsine, which lies at the base of that mountain."[31] He offers his expertise to an imagined hiker: "We will walk by the base of this mountain, and I will describe it in the second part," but instead of merely pointing to vistas and attractions, he takes his reader on a rigorous mountain tour: "After one has ascended the mountain of Chede for almost half an hour, one can rest at a very beautiful water pool that nature seems to have excavated in order to collect the water of a stream rushing down the mountain."[32] At times, traditional hiking evolves into laborious scrambling, an all-encompassing physical activity reminiscent of Saussure's childhood impressions of touching rock in his diary: "One follows a kind of groove carved out by nature and some irregularities of the rock, which one has to grasp almost more with the hands than with the feet while climbing."[33] Sometimes tiring and even dangerous, the path leads over snow-covered rocks, demanding utmost caution. However, such rigorous activity rewards the climber with not only geological insights but also sublime views: "The admirable regularity of this sublime peak's [Mont Breven] layers deserves the attention of geology aficionados, and the view that one enjoys in itself would compensate anyone for the efforts of the ascent."[34]

In another attempt to invite readers to follow in his literal footsteps, Saussure includes much practical travel advice, a practice later imitated by Forbes and Wills. He advertises the names of guides (2.290) and innkeepers (2.239) and delivers detailed information on sheds used for lodging, as well as passes that can be traveled by mule. Regarding altitude and snow travel, Saussure references Bouguer's findings in South America to observe that humans and animals alike become exhausted and sick at altitude. In particular, he reports nausea, fainting, and vomiting and observes that the "vivacity of the light" causes exposed skin to turn red and peel, noting that Alpine citizens seem less affected by these afflictions.[35] Saussure correctly traces the cause of altitude sickness to the lowered pressure at altitude, which in turn reduces the partial pressure of oxygen, a theory that Humboldt adopted and expanded on. Another useful piece of advice concerns glacier travel, when Saussure made improvements on iron-made hooks that can be attached to boots and enable better traction when traveling on snow-covered slopes: "We armed ourselves forthwith with foot-irons that made our steps secure, so that we could continue our journey without hindrance."[36] Those who venture into the Alpine terrain and onto mountaintops, a space Saussure calls "a different world, forgotten by nature, or a comet, far away from the sun," are rewarded with magnificent sights and sublime experiences: "Only those who have entertained similar thoughts on the tops of the high Alps know how deeper, farther, and more enlightened they envision the nature of the soul, rather than if one is enclosed among the walls of his cabinet."[37] In sentences like these—which anticipate late-nineteenth-century mountain discourses from Stephen to Tyndall to Muir—Saussure expands on Haller's plea for pastoral beauty and health in a rural setting with the deep and spiritual experience of the sublime found only on the mountaintops.

Saussure's *Voyages* therefore represent an important historical pivot. While the text remains indebted to its predecessors and does not aspire to go beyond established conventions, not only does it become the paradigmatic manual on Alpine travel for Humboldt and beyond, but Saussure's construction of the mountaineering quest, particularly visible in his obsession with Mont Blanc, introduces tensions that come to bear in nineteenth-century mountaineering narratives and beyond, such as exhaustive descriptions of physical debilitation, loss of control, and general suffering intermingled with pride and pleasure about the achievement of feats previously thought impossible. If Saussure embraces an inclusive "we," taking his readers along on his journeys, the sublime experience he delineates celebrates a radical individualism in the mountains that eschews worldly attachments while relying on long-established privileges.

Mont Buet, Mont Blanc, and the Col du Géant

Before devoting his attention to Mont Blanc, Saussure climbed Mont Buet (3,096 m) in 1776 and 1778, a feat that formed the concluding high point of the first volume of *Voyages* and in many ways prefigured his later ascents. For one, his measurements on the summit allowed Saussure to determine via barometer and triangulation the height of Mont Blanc, confirming its status as the highest mountain of the Alps against previous claims that the Schreckhorn was higher. For another, climbing Mont Buet, especially on the second ascent, foreshadowed some of the disappointments and failures that awaited Saussure on Mont Blanc. When his party finally reached the top of the mountain, they found themselves plagued by nausea and deprived of the "beautiful view" they had hoped for.[38] Despite the disappointing sight, his insights proved valuable: according to Saussure, the exposed positions of mountaintops encourage the mind to ponder about the formation, age, and development of mountains. On the top of Mont Buet, he ruminates: "If one searches for the origin of these elements [mountains], observes the changes that they go through and those that they are still expecting: what an abyss of thoughts!"[39] What Saussure contemplates but ultimately dismisses as an "abyss of thoughts" is actually an important insight into the dynamism and changeability of nature, one that Humboldt would later pursue more open-mindedly and successfully. On the summit of Mont Buet, Saussure also drafted an inventive if unexpected drawing that provides a 360-degree perspective by combining the views from both ascents.

According to Saussure, standing atop Mont Buet made him realize the necessity of illustrations that provide readers with more precise informa-

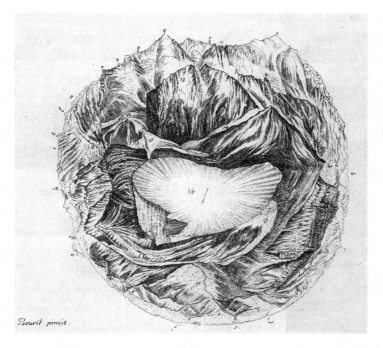

"Circular View of the Mountains from the Summit of the Buet"
(*Vue circulaire des Montagnes qu'on decouvre du sommet du Glacier de Buet*),
from *Voyages dans les Alpes*, vol. 8 (1779) (Wikipedia)

tion. But rather than choosing only one perspective or view, Saussure opted for a panoramic perspective that reveals the totality of the mountains to be seen. He achieved this perspective by rotating the sheet of paper as he drew the various peaks visible from the top, an act of drawing that mirrors the act of viewing, as a spectator slowly turns around to take in all angles and viewpoints. Yet the readers' viewpoint differs from that of the climbers, in that readers assume a bird's-eye perspective, hovering in the air above the mountain, from which they can detect two tiny figures on the summit, at the center of the drawing. With this unusual omnidirectional and circular perspective, Saussure pays tribute to the all-encompassing and engulfing view from a mountaintop. Like Humboldt, Saussure searched for new ways to do justice to the grand experience, and both men invented visual forms of representation that conveyed perspectives and information that the human eye could not obtain. While Humboldt presented a cross section of the mountain with information on vegetation, altitude, and temperature, Saussure adopted a horizontal circular perspective from a sovereign position that revealed comprehensive information on the mountain's environment. As Peter H. Hansen recognizes, such an all-encompassing perspective—previously reserved only for God—now marked the summit position of the sovereign individual.[40]

Mont Blanc, beginning and dominating the second volume of *Voyages*, embodied for Saussure the epitome of his desire, both visually and in terms of climbing. It comes as no surprise that the mountain elicits all sorts of conflicting descriptions, assessments, measurements, sensations, and physical responses. Moving from the pastoral to the sublime, Saussure emphasizes a picturesque view (*vues*), a picture (*tableau*), and a *spectacle*, terms that lend mountains more agency and power. He refers to Mont Blanc repeatedly as a "colossus" and designates its summit as "inaccessible."[41] By underscoring nature's force and man's smallness and insignificance, his sentiments resonate with Burke's and Kant's previously published treatises on the sublime. Saussure introduced his first impressions of the mountain as follows:

> Almost during the entire voyage through the high mountains, the top of this mountain [Mont Blanc] is withdrawn from sight, and it only becomes visible between the waterfall and the village St. Martin. From the bridge in this village, the summit can be seen very well, and even better from Sallenche, where it presents itself in its astonishing height. But the mountain's height produces the most astonishment when the largest part of its body is veiled in clouds, leaving an opening through which one can see nothing but the summit. In that case one thinks it is almost impossible that the object which one distinguishes in this manner is a part of this globe; and those who see it [Mont Blanc] like this for the first time cannot be convinced that they aren't seeing white clouds of the kind that often crowd above the mountaintops. Their mistake only vanishes when the clouds disperse and the large and solid base connecting the ever-reaching summit with the earth becomes visible.[42]

For one, the passage emphasizes astonishment and amazement vis-à-vis the fast-changing mountain scenery, veiled and unveiled by swiftly moving clouds. For another, Saussure's passage must have inspired Humboldt, who depicted his first view of Pico de Teide in a similar fashion. Both Saussure and Humboldt use the sight to make a larger point: framed by a curtain of clouds that only allows momentary glimpses, the mountain grows exceedingly high and impressive, a process that is in fact so dramatic that an onlooker could easily be fooled. Like Humboldt, Saussure personifies the mountain as simultaneously presenting and concealing itself, turning the visual sight into a dynamic and forceful interaction.

Saussure's advances on Mont Blanc proved more toilsome and laborious. Despite having posted "a fairly significant reward" for the mountain's ascent on his first trip to the region in 1760, for some fifteen years the offer went without serious consideration, as Saussure admits in *Voyages*' second volume.[43] In 1775, four guides advanced onto the ice as far as the level of the Grands Mulets, and in 1783, another party proceeded some two thousand feet higher. These early mountaineers turned around not because of the difficulty of the climb or particular obstacles but because they complained of "suffocating heat," "such disgust," "exceeding starvation and exhaustion," "pain," and "an insurmountable desire to sleep," which, by today's standards, is no surprise, given the climbers' tendency to sleep low on the mountain, start late in the morning, and drink wine while climbing, which all contributed to altitude sickness, general misery, and soft snow on the slopes.[44]

In the 1780s, however, the determined and eccentric Marc Théodore Bourrit would not be as easily deterred and resumed the attempts, reporting in 1784 that he and his guides advanced to the base of the summit peak and could see a path to the top. After a long spell of bad weather, Bourrit returned to Mont Blanc in September 1785, accompanied by his son, Isaac, and Saussure. The group spent the night in a simple cabin that Saussure had built to carry out his research. While his measurements on the boiling point of water at altitude proved a failure owing to faulty equipment, Saussure was captivated by witnessing the sunset on the slopes of Mont Blanc, and he recorded the occurrence in the second volume of *Voyages* in strikingly sublime terms: "But the beauty of the evening and the magnificence of the spectacle presented by the sunset from my observatory consoled me for this disappointment. The evening vapours, like a light gauze, tempered the brilliancy of the sun and half hid the vast expanse under our feet, forming a belt of the most beautiful purple which embraced all the western horizon, while to the east the snows of the base of Mont Blanc, illuminated by the rich glow, offered a singularly magnificent spectacle."[45]

Initially, Saussure perceived the experience visually, reveling in the various nuances of the light and repeating the words "spectacle" and "magnificence." When he returned to the same spot after nightfall, however, he experienced something different: "The peace and complete silence which reigned over this vast space, magnified further by the imagination, affected me with a kind of terror. I fancied myself the only survivor of the universe, and that I was gazing on its corpse stretched at my feet. Sad as are ideas of this description, they have a fascination which it is difficult to resist. I turned my eyes more frequently towards these obscure solitudes than towards Mont Blanc, whose brilliant and seemingly phosphorescent snows still retained the sense of life and movement."[46] Here the environment takes on a more immediate character, invoking a physical experience beyond visual consumption. Not only magnificent, brilliant, and visually spectacular, the terrain conveys terror, silence, loneliness, and a sense of death, and in these moments, Saussure reconfigures his environment imaginatively, reaching beyond clichés and allowing for multiple responses and reactions.

A letter to his friend the Prince de Ligne conveyed both gratification and regret after his unsuccessful ascent the following day:

> Not to keep you in suspense, I will begin by telling you that its success was not complete, but nevertheless I reached a higher level than any observer before me had in the Alps, and I satisfied myself that in a more favourable season, starting from a higher point, and with the aid of a good head and stout limbs, the top of the mountain might be gained. . . . I observed the barometer, and the height of 18 inches 1 line ¾ at which it stood proved that we were about 1,900 toises above sea level, and consequently on the level of the Peak of Teneriffe, a height no physical observer had ever obtained on a European mountain. I made several observations of the thermometer, the hygrometer, and the electrometer. I observed the structure and nature of these elevated crags, and we enjoyed a view of immense extent and beauty, since we looked down on our lake over the high ranges which separated us from it. . . . These enjoyments did not, however, give us pure pleasure: our satisfaction was marred by the regret at not getting higher and by some anxiety as to our return. (Freshfield, 206–8)

This passage, reminiscent of Humboldt's letters describing his mountain feats, exudes pride in his accomplishments while acknowledging the failure of not having reached the top; fresh snowfall had forced the party to turn around. As Humboldt did later, Saussure insists on the success of his measurements, naming off his instruments while repeatedly referring to his (brief) altitude record. He also admires the beautiful view and moreover imagines the summits of mountains being scaled with the help of modern technology: if Humboldt on Chimborazo envisioned building huts to enable a siege-like tactical ascent, then Saussure goes a step further, conceiving an ascent via balloons. "While climbing with so much fatigue these steep rocks I envied the lot of aeronauts who rise to such great heights comfortably seated in their gondolas, and I even speculated on the possibility of using these aerial cars for attaining inaccessible peaks like Mont Blanc" (Freshfield, 208).

In the following summer, however, climbers reached the summit of Mont Blanc without such aids. Dr. Michel-Gabriel Paccard, a physician from Chamonix who had scoped out various approaches, and Jacques Balmat, a crystal hunter who had slept on a glacier a few months earlier, came to a hasty agreement to join forces so as not to outdo each other. On August 8, 1786, the two men could be seen approaching the summit of Mont Blanc at six-thirty in the evening, after fourteen hours of climbing and spending the night bivouacked on top of the Montagne de la Côte. A few days later, when Balmat came to Saussure to claim his reward, Saussure immediately made plans for his own ascent. While a long-standing conflict between Balmat and Paccard ensued, writing Paccard out of the ascent, Saussure busied himself with preparations for his summit attempt, hiring Balmat as a guide.[47] Balmat succeeded in taking two other guides (Jean-Michel Cachat and Alexis Tournier) to the top of the mountain on July 5 of the following year, but Saussure's attempts were hampered by bad weather. On August 1, finally, he started another attempt, his expedition outfitted with a bed complete with mattress and sheets, ladders, change of clothes, and scientific equipment. With mules, horses, and some eighteen guides carrying equipment, the party advanced slowly, reaching the Montagne de la Côte after six and a half hours. The next day, they carefully navigated a crevassed glacier on snow bridges, camping on a snow platform on the Grand Plateau—ninety toises (175 m/575 ft.) above Pico de Teide's summit, as Saussure points out. While his guides dug a cave into the snow, Saussure completed barometrical measurements, but all began to feel sick from the altitude. Saussure noted, "These hardy men, to whom seven or eight hours' walking counts as nothing, did not throw out more than five or six shovel-fuls of snow before they found it impossible to continue, and were obliged to relieve each other from one minute to another," admiring Paccard and Balmat's previous courage and perseverance.[48] After a miserable night in a hot, stuffy tent, the party proceeded the next morning, facing considerable difficulties. Fainting and falling, Saussure slowly stumbled the final nine hundred feet up the slope to arrive at the summit at 11 a.m. on August 3, 1787, in the anticlimactic moment described at this chapter's beginning.

If Saussure's own assessment of the summit push remained contradictory and ambivalent, in secondary sources it usually turned into a triumph. Already in 1788, Saussure's translator Wyttenbach rejoiced: "Here our observer could at once have a look at the entirety of all the sublime peaks whose configuration he had long wished to know. He could observe more closely their proportion, relationship, and structure, and a single glance put away any doubts which could not have been cleared through years of work."[49] With words like "observer," "glance," and "to overlook," Wyttenbach perceives the summit experience in solely visual terms, omitting its intense physicality. Most recently, Peter H. Hansen's careful analysis deemed Saussure's ascent "the culmination of the twenty-seven-year odyssey he described in *Voyages in the Alps* and the embodiment of the masculine heroism he celebrated in those volumes."[50] As we have seen, numerous physical interventions made such experience more complicated and multifaceted, preventing the consumption and conquest of nature. Long before he scaled Mont Blanc, Saussure outlined an all-encompassing bodily climbing experience in the preface to *Voyages:*

> But in order to obtain these general ideas it is not enough to follow the high-roads, which, as a rule, wind in the bottom of the valleys and cross the mountain chains in their deepest defiles; one must leave the beaten track and climb the lofty peaks, whence the eyes can embrace at once a multitude of objects. These excursions are, I admit, laborious, one must do without carriages, or even horses, endure great fatigue, and even at times expose oneself to somewhat serious risk. Often the Naturalist on the point of reaching a peak which he eagerly desires to gain is seized with doubt whether his

strength will carry him to the top, or whether he can succeed in conquering the cliffs that bar his way, but the brisk and fresh air he breathes sends through his veins a tonic which restores him, and the hope of the great spectacle he is about to enjoy, and of the new discoveries which he may gain, reanimate his vigour and his courage.[51]

Here, physical exhilaration (the tonic through his veins), sight (the spectacle to be seen), and scientific promise (the discoveries to be made) all come together to form the essence of the climbing experience.

Somewhat ironically, most of Saussure's mountaineering career took place in the years after he resigned from the professorship at the Academy of Geneva in January 1786 for reasons of ill health. After an attack of whooping cough forced him to take a leave of absence, Marc-Auguste Pictet succeeded his post at the academy, leaving Saussure more time to devote to writing and climbing. Although Saussure never again advanced to a height comparable to Mont Blanc, he continued to climb and completed more difficult achievements. In 1788 Saussure, his son, and a small group of guides remained at the Col du Géant at an altitude of eleven thousand feet for seventeen days, completing elaborate measurements such as the daily variations of winds while battling cold, severe storms, and the effects of altitude. This feat garnered no recognition as a mountain ascent but was a more laborious and fruitful accomplishment than the Mont Blanc expedition. In the following summer, Saussure trekked through a remote and unknown region around Monte Rosa, determining that the mountain was the second highest in the Alps. In 1792 he returned with his son to the nearby Matterhorn, the last trip Saussure recorded in *Voyages*.

Images

Two prominent watercolors associated with Saussure's travels emerged from previous drawings made by Henri l'Evêque, who accompanied Saussure to Chamonix in 1788. While the images are often labeled as depicting the ascent and descent of Mont Blanc (as Freshfield speculates, a savvy publisher probably thought the latter titles more profitable), they likely portray Saussure's excursion to the Col du Géant the following year.

The popular images show a line of climbers advancing in tow, amid a surrealistic landscape of jagged blocks of ice positioned in the foreground.

"Dr. Saussure's Ascent of Mont Blanc, 1787" (1828) (*Summits of Modern Man* image gallery at Worcester Polytechnic Institute)

The sheer number of the climbers, their uniform dress, and even spacing evoke a well-organized, skilled, and victorious advance in which an alien, lifeless, and dangerous terrain is conquered by manpower and technical aids, such as rucksacks, alpenstocks, and ladders. But one could also read the images differently: in both pictures, gigantic ice blocks loom as the largest objects in the foreground, and majestic peaks rise to invisible heights in the background, which has the effect of reducing the climbers to ant-sized proportions, making their endeavors appear insignificant and point-less. Looking down rather than up, the climbers seem more defeated than defiant, and it remains unclear whether they were triumphant. As Hansen points out, Saussure had requested that the second image be changed so as not to show him sliding down the slope on a rope but rather standing upright.[52] Open to such interpretations, the images evoke opposing con-cepts: enormous ice versus small climbers; skilled mountaineers and their climbing aids versus an uncontrollable and dangerous terrain; the sharp and spiky blocks of ice, later colored in a cold bluish-white, versus hunched

"Saussure Returning from the Summit of Mont Blanc" (Getty Images)

men in brown and gray coats (the original illustrations were black and white). And what would be the most important image—men standing atop Mont Blanc—remains missing, denying audiences a final victorious reading of the endeavor. By omitting the climbers' destination, the two illustrations of ascent and descent thus attest to the journey itself, emphasizing the capability of the climbers but also the resistance and undiminished dominance of their environment.

In the wake of the French Revolution and the resulting revolution in Geneva in 1792, Saussure worked on committees designed to democratize the government, presided over Geneva's Constituent Assembly, and even proposed a plan for free national education until he withdrew from politics after increasing massacres in 1794. During this time, Saussure's wealth steadily declined as investments failed and taxes were raised, forcing the family to retire to their farm in Conches and sell the home where Saussure had grown up. To supplement their income, Saussure sought employment at academic institutions in France, Germany, Russia, and the United States, all to no avail.

Horace-Bénédict de Saussure, engraving by Charles Simon Pradier
after Jean-Pierre Saint-Ours (Wikimedia)

To make matters worse, his health steadily deteriorated, especially after a seizure in March 1794 left him partially paralyzed. Still, he continued to work, writing and editing the final two volumes of *Voyages* from 1794 to 1796. In 1796 the Society of the Arts requested an oil painting be made of Saussure before it was too late. While his wish to be painted on the slopes of Mont Blanc was not granted, Saussure insisted that the mountain be included in the painting. In the end, the portrait completed by Jean-Pierre Saint-Ours, a well-known Swiss painter of the day, shows Saussure next to a theodolite, with a rock and a geologist's hammer in his hands, and Mont Blanc rising in the right background. If, judging from the dark rings under sunken eyes, the painting hints at Saussure's failing health, it also conveys determination and confidence and may well have inspired the prominent portrait of an aging Humboldt in front of Mount Chimborazo. After a second stroke in late 1796, Saussure became unable to walk and talk, enduring periods of feebleness. On January 22, 1799, not long after Geneva was annexed by the French, he passed away at his home in Conches.

CHAPTER 5

ICECAPADES

James David Forbes and Louis Agassiz

The Ascent of the Jungfrau

At four o'clock in the morning of August 27, 1841, James David Forbes, his assistant Mr. Heath, Louis Agassiz, and his friend Édouard Desor, as well as two students and six guides, left the Grimsel Hospice to ascend to the Oberaarjoch, a high mountain pass in the eastern Bernese Alps. Equipped with thermometer, hygrometer, clinometer, and compass, the party crossed the Fiescher Glacier to arrive at the Marjeelen Chalet that evening, determined to scale the Jungfrau the following day. Unfortunately, their early morning start was delayed because they had to wait for a porter to bring a ladder they needed to cross the mountain's bergschrund. They finally set out at 6 a.m., crossing the Aletsch Glacier to ascend a heavily crevassed slope with the help of gaiters, axes, ropes, and the wooden ladder.[1] After four and a half hours of strenuous walking, Forbes felt his "breathing sensibly affected," and the party rested for some bread and wine, which allegedly invigorated Forbes to make a final push for the summit, still some three thousand feet above them.[2]

Plagued by altitude sickness, Forbes crossed the unstable ladder over the yawning bergschrund, then hauled himself hand over hand up a rope the remaining distance. Reduced to four climbers and four guides when the students and two guides did not want to continue, the party then crossed another bergschrund, frightened by the ice's movement, which they could both hear and feel. After another rest with wine, they slowly moved up a steep ice slope with precariously overhanging precipices, holding on to a rope while their guide, Jacob Leuthold, cut steps in the steep snow. Forbes noted, "I felt my toes benumbed, and had some trouble to restore animation by shaking and striking them. This slow progress, on the other hand, took away any suffering from difficult breathing."[3] They finally reached the summit at 4 p.m. in what turned out to be the fourth ascent of the mountain, standing in succession on the precarious summit ridge and planting a self-made flag while taking measurements and enjoying the view to the east and "a magnificent cumulus-headed cloud . . . in wonderful majesty, reaching apparently from the valley to at least 2,000 feet above us" to the west.[4] After still more wine, they began a slow but uneventful descent, arriving happily back at the Marjeelen Chalet at half past eleven.

Forbes, who had initially voiced skepticism about attempting the peak and never before or after ascended to such heights, described the undertaking in a letter to his sister hesitantly, yet with an unmistakable sense of triumph:

> You thought me wiser than to undertake any such expedition, and I own that but for Agassiz, who had an intense anxiety to ascend the Virgin Alp, so often assailed in vain, the idea would never have occurred to me. Since it succeeded, I am, you may believe, very glad to have made the attempt; not only for the thing itself, but because it gives me a perfect idea of what I have long wished to know, the real amount and kind of difficulty of the most formidable Alpine ascents, for I suppose that there is no doubt that the ascent of Mont Blanc, though longer, is by far less formidable.[5]

Despite these sentiments, Forbes was never to attempt Mont Blanc. Not unlike Humboldt and many other nineteenth-century explorers, Forbes remained torn between the scientific value of climbing and the quest to reach a summit. In a letter to his friend William Whewell, he asserted, "The much-tattled of ascent of the Jungfrau was without any scientific result of importance, but led us through scenes of sublimity never to be forgotten."[6]

Drawing by Louis Agassiz, in a letter to Baron von
Werther, Neuchâtel, April 2, 1842 (Provided by the
Berlin-Brandenburg Academy of Sciences and
Humanities, with special thanks to Carmen Götz.
Acta des Königl. Civil-Kabinets, 1tr. Abthl. betr:
den Professor Agassiz in Neuchatel. Geheimes
Staatsarchiv Preußischer Kulturbesitz, I. HA
Rep. 89 Geheimes Zivilkabinett, Nr. 19499)

Reflective of this ambivalence, Forbes withheld his account of the Jung-frau ascent in his first and most influential book, *Travels Through the Alps of Savoy* (1843). Only a decade later, he devoted a chapter to the climb, "The Ascent of the Jungfrau," in his book *Norway and Its Glaciers* (1853), publicizing his ascent in a "certainly not exaggerated" manner.[7] Thus Forbes's account, much like Humboldt's description of his attempt on Mount Chimborazo, appeared only belatedly and in a highly unlikely place. Like many naturalists of his time, Forbes did not seek to climb mountains but instead focused on passes and glaciers to pursue his research.[8] Nevertheless, while he downplayed the scientific importance of the Jungfrau climb, Forbes cleverly capitalized on his climbing skills and mountain aptitude to validate his glacial theories, as detailed later in the chapter.

Agassiz, for his part, who appeared to be the driving force behind the ascent, never wrote or published anything about it. Perhaps that is the reason some veritable confusion still exists about his accomplishment.[9] Notably it was Humboldt who boasted about Agassiz's Jungfrau ascent in a letter asking King Friedrich Wilhelm IV of Prussia for three thousand francs to fund Agassiz's research, referring to "this scholar who . . . accomplished lastly the perilous ascent of the 12,870-foot sharp-edged summit of the Jungfrau."[10] In his letter of thanks to the king, Agassiz did not mention his climb but enclosed three lithographs depicting (1) the profile of the Jungfrau, (2) three climbers summiting the mountain and erecting a flag, and (3) a horizontal plan of the second image. Like Forbes, Agassiz, too, seems to have greatly savored the experience of summiting. According to his friend Desor, "Agassiz remained upon it [the Jungfrau summit] for nearly five minutes, and when he rejoined us, I saw that he was greatly agitated; in fact, he confessed to me that he never experienced so much emotion."[11] In a letter, Agassiz later declared, "I thought I could not do better than to pass some weeks in the solitude of the high Alps; I lived about a fortnight in the region of the glaciers, ascending some new field of ice every day, and trying to scale the sides of our highest peaks."[12] Indeed, he became engulfed in mountain climbing during his glacier research in the Alps and continued combining these two pursuits.

Agassiz's longtime climbing companion Desor (who had already published a diary of their joint explorations to the Matterhorn and Monte Rosa glaciers) published a description of the climb that mirrored Agassiz's sentiments, confessing to "great emotion at a spectacle of such overpowering grandeur."[13] Desor, however, also referred to another quandary of mountain climbing when depicting his summit experience as a moment of great intimacy with Agassiz, on one hand, but a reminder of society's conventions on the other: "I had need of grasping the hand of a friend, and I venture to say, that I never felt so happy in my life as when I had seated myself by his [Agassiz's] side on the snow. I believe that both of us would have wept had we dared; but a man's tears ought to be modest, and we were not alone; and such is the strength of the habits which society makes us contract, that, at 12,000 feet, there was still a regard to etiquette!"[14] Forbes, Agassiz, and Desor mention some key aspects of mountain climbing and mountaineering narratives in the nineteenth century, which serve as the underpinning for this chapter: (1) the tension between scientific enterprise and the thrill of climbing, (2) the overwhelming emotional and physical experience that defies spoken or written expression, and (3) the intimacy between males and the desire to escape societal conventions.

Upbringing and Education

If Humboldt and Saussure were among the first to lug their instruments up the mountains to conduct research in "nature's laboratory," then Agassiz and Forbes continued this quest, becoming interested specifically in glaciers and glaciology. Their fascination if not obsession with ice—Agassiz with his vast claims of a previous ice age and spellbinding illustrations in his volume; Forbes in adding a literary dimension to such claims and using his athletic feats to prop up his research—introduced audiences to an ethereal yet dynamic world of moving glaciers. Moreover, Forbes's *Travels Through the Alps of Savoy*, combining glacier research, trip report, practical travel advice, and poetic ambition, became the blueprint of nineteenth-century mountaineering companions by Wills, Tyndall, and even nonscientists like Whymper and Stephen.

James David Forbes was born to Sir William Forbes and Williamina Belches in Edinburgh, Scotland, on April 20, 1809. As the delicate youngest child in a wealthy aristocratic family with four sons and two daughters, young James received much love and pampering from his mother before her untimely death in December 1810. While the youngster was left with no memories but an adoring reverence of his mother, his father took over the responsibility of raising the children, entertaining them with scientific apparatuses at home, which instilled in Forbes a lifelong passion for the sciences even though he was destined for a career in law. Forbes was entirely home schooled until age sixteen, which reinforced the introversion and secluded life that resulted from losing his mother at such a young age. In 1825 he entered the University of Edinburgh and quickly distinguished himself as a student. In addition, he began an initially anonymous professional correspondence with the renowned scientist and editor of the *Edinburgh Journal of Science,* Sir David Brewster, who began to publish Forbes's scientific papers under a pseudonym.

Forbes missed his entire second year of university schooling owing to an extensive one-year trip with his family from Scotland to Paris, Strasburg, Innsbruck, Venice, Bologna, Florence, and Rome and then back home, crossing the Alps twice. On this Grand Tour, facilitated by modern rail service, the seventeen-year-old had ample opportunities to complement his bookish education with actual experience. In southern Italy, he visited the pillars of antiquity but also explored natural wonders such as Mount Vesuvius, into whose crater Forbes descended, observing what he termed in his journal "the bowels of the earth, where her internal riches were displayed in their wildest form."[15] On the return trip, the family stayed in Chamonix, for Forbes the first of many visits to follow. He and his brother, along with three guides, mules, and spiked poles, ascended to the Mer de Glace, a prominent glacier on the northern slopes of the Mont Blanc massif that had already become a popular destination for British travelers and would later play a critical role in Forbes's glacier research. Being well familiar with Humboldt's and Saussure's texts—he had already published a review of Humboldt's *Cosmos* and frequently referenced his measurements—afforded Forbes a greater, comparative perspective.

While Forbes was duly impressed by the glacier, he became infinitely more curious about one of the guides, Michel Cachat, who had spent seventeen days performing scientific experiments with Saussure on the Col du Géant and had also accompanied him on Mont Blanc. Forbes meticulously recorded their conversation, inquiring "what he thought of the practicability of the ascent of Mont Blanc, and whether a man of ordinary strength might achieve it" (32), and concluding, "I felt that it was with more regret that I left this interesting spot [Chamonix] than any town or scene that we had visited in our travels" (33). After their return to Scotland, Forbes was indeed inspired to complete a research journey similar to Humboldt's, as Forbes admitted in his journal:

> My present thoughts are as follows: to devote a moderate but steady attention to law, which, as far as I understand, may never occupy nearly all my time, and at first will leave me very great leisure. It is my idea not to pass my Scotch law trials till spring 1831. Then, if things go well, go abroad for a considerable time. I confess my private views in this tour to be to examine with a much more scientific view than last time the south of Europe, to form scientific connections in France and Italy, and—I have never before had courage to record it either by word of mouth or on paper—to write a personal narrative like Humboldt, and Travels in Italy. (48)

As the quotation shows, Humboldt's journey evidently stirred in many young men similar desires of escaping a predetermined career in favor of scientific exploration. Research in the mountains provided opportunity to do so by offering a space outside the conventions of Victorian life and family expectations.

Forbes reentered the college in 1827, taking classes in moral philosophy and natural history. His professor Robert Jameson had trained at the Freiberg Mountain Academy under Abraham Gottlob Werner, the staunch proponent of catastrophist theories, and defended them against new ideas of uniformitarianism pioneered by fellow Scot James Hutton. Nevertheless Jameson offered lectures on glaciology (later he even accepted the controversial idea that the British Isles had been glaciated) and established a first-rate collection of geological specimens, fossils, birds, and insects at the university museum. He also taught fellow student Charles Darwin, who reportedly became rather bored with Jameson's lectures.[16] In the meantime, Brewster continued mentoring Forbes and even published some of their correspondence, revealing Forbes's identity in the *Edinburgh Journal of Science*. Brewster proposed Forbes for admission to the Royal Society of Edinburgh, an unusual honor for someone younger than twenty. This marked the beginning of a swiftly rising scientific career. After serious doubts about a career in law, for which "my distaste increased instead of diminishing," and much deliberation with friends and family, Forbes finally decided in

March 1830—against the resistance of Brewster, of all people—"to cast law behind me, and, content with a small competence, to follow science at leisure" (61).[17] Still, Forbes passed his exams and qualified as an advocate the following summer before parting with the field to devote himself fully to natural science.

In accordance with the earlier plans outlined in his journal, Forbes prepared himself for a multiyear journey to western Europe, the Balkans, and perhaps Egypt, setting out in July 1832 together with his friend Louis Necker, a mineralogist and grandson of Saussure, to explore first the Mont Blanc region, the Bernese Oberland, and the Italian lake country. Yet Forbes limited himself to well-established tourist attractions, such as Le Brévent, a 2,525 m/8,284 ft. mountain near Chamonix affording a popular view of Mont Blanc; the Lauterbrunnen Valley with its famous Staubbach Falls, which already enthralled Albrecht von Haller; and the much-visited Saint Gotthard Pass, where Forbes remained unimpressed with the sheer walls of the Schöllenen Gorge and its legendary Devil's Bridge, which inspired many sublime paintings. Covering great distances on foot and by mule, he performed measurements of barometric pressure, magnetic dip, and solar radiation at altitude but remained uninterested in glacial action and missed important evidence of glaciation such as U-shaped valleys and moraine debris, concluding instead—in line with established thinking—that the valleys had been formed by water. Forbes's trip was cut short when he received news that the professor of natural philosophy at Edinburgh University, Sir John Leslie, had passed away, and Forbes quickly returned to Edinburgh in hopes of contesting the vacant chair. At the young age of twenty-three, Forbes was elected to the prestigious position over four competitors, his friend and mentor Brewster among them. He quickly rose to success, building a close-knit circle of students and colleagues and eventually being elected secretary of the Royal Society of Edinburgh.

Meanwhile, around the same time, Jean Louis Rodolphe Agassiz commenced his glacier research in the Alps. Two years older than Forbes, Agassiz was born to the Protestant minister Louis Rodolphe Benjamin Agassiz and Rose Mayor, the wealthy daughter of a physician, on May 28, 1807, in the small village of Môtier near Lake Neuchâtel in Switzerland. Since all her four previous children had died in infancy, Rose cared greatly for her son Louis, the eldest of one more boy and two girls to follow. Like Humboldt and Saussure, Agassiz developed an early interest in natural history, roaming the neighboring woods and meadows to collect plants, insects, fish, and birds. When Agassiz was to leave school at age fifteen and enter the business of his uncle in Neuchâtel, he begged his parents to continue his studies and was able to do so for two more years at the Academy of Lausanne, where he studied the works of the naturalists Georges Cuvier and Jean-Baptiste Lamarck. After his mother's brother, a physician, advised that his nephew be allowed to study medicine, Agassiz entered the medical school at Zurich University at age seventeen. His younger brother soon joined him, and the two embarked on some first excursions to the higher Alps.

In the spring of 1826, Agassiz transferred to Heidelberg University to take courses in paleontology and zoology and, more importantly, remove himself from parental supervision. As president of the local fraternity, he met two fellow students who were to become close friends, Alexander Braun and Karl Friedrich Schimper, both botanists. With Braun, Agassiz developed a special bond, marveling in an intimate letter, "In you I see my own intellectual development reflected as in a mirror, for to you, and to my intercourse with you, I owe my entrance upon this path of the noblest and most lasting enjoyment."[18] When Braun decided to transfer to the newly opened University of Munich in 1827 and invited his friends to come along on account of the excellent instruction in the natural sciences, the rich opportunities in entertainment, and, last but not least, the "beer plenty and good," Agassiz accepted, eager to "drink new draughts of knowledge."[19] Rooming with Braun and soon joined by Schimper, the three took full advantage of newfound opportunities both academically (the university boasted Friedrich Wilhelm von Schelling as professor of philosophy and other eminences in zoology, physiology, botany, and mineralogy) and socially. Known by their nicknames as Molluscus (Braun for his fascination with shells), Rhubarb (Schimper for his botany), and Cyprinus (Agassiz for his interest in fish), they had nightly conversations on botany and embarked on joint trips to the Alps during the semester breaks.[20]

These exhilarating endeavors, however, diverted Agassiz from the study of medicine. A letter exchange in 1828 with both parents reveals just how fiercely he had to fight for a career in the natural sciences. His mother cautioned against the ramifications of such a career, cleverly using metaphors of nature to advise her son to settle down: "Have you reflected seriously before setting aside this profession [medicine]? Indeed, we cannot consent to such a step. You would lose ground in our opinion, in that of your family, and in that of the public. . . . The sooner you have finished your studies, the sooner you can put up your tent, catch your blue butterfly, and metamorphose her into a loving housewife" (January 8, 1828). His father conversely applied pressure more directly: "Begin by reaching your first aim, a physician's and surgeon's diploma. I will not for the present hear of anything else, and that is more than enough" (February 21, 1828), and "Indeed, the natural sciences, however sublime and attractive, offer nothing certain in the future" (March 25, 1828).[21] Agassiz resisted, insisting that wedding plans were not part of his near future: "But the man of letters should seek repose only when he has deserved it by his toil, for if once he anchor himself, farewell to energy and liberty, by which alone great minds are fostered. Therefore I have said to myself, that I would remain unmarried till my work should assure me a peaceful and happy future. A young man has too much vigor to bear confinement so soon."[22] Instead he hinted at extensive future travels, claiming that his career "requires, for instance, but two or three years to go around the world at government expense."[23]

Unbeknownst to his parents, Agassiz had expanded his studies in ichthyology by accepting an invitation to write a description of Brazilian fishes brought home in 1821 by the biologist and ethnographer Carl Friedrich Philipp von Martius and the botanist Johann Baptist Ritter von Spix, who had been sent to Brazil by the King of Bavaria.[24] After Spix had died in 1826, Martius asked Agassiz, his favorite student, to describe about ninety species of fish collected from the Amazon River to complete the work. Written in Latin and dedicated to Cuvier (who had previously scanned the material and deemed it of great importance), *Selecta genera et species piscium* was published in two parts with ninety-seven plates in 1829 and 1831, to great success. Garnering a letter of thanks by Cuvier himself, the publication impressed Agassiz's parents to such a degree that it paved the way for a career in the natural sciences. Meanwhile, Agassiz and Braun had been plotting some grand plans: along with Schimper, they hoped to join Humboldt's expedition to the Caucasus and Caspian Sea, convincing their professor Lorenz Oken to contact Humboldt on their behalf. According to a letter by Braun to his father, "[Agassiz] rolled himself in the snow for joy, and we agreed that however little hope there might be of our joining the expedition, still the fact that Humboldt would hear of us in this way was worth something, even if it were only that we might be able to say to him one of these days, 'We are the fellows whose company you rejected.' "[25] The latter sentiment turned out to be true when Humboldt swiftly replied that he had already chosen his assistants.

In April of the following year, Agassiz completed his doctor of medicine at Munich and wrote to his parents that their goal had been accomplished. For the time being, however, he remained in Munich along with Braun and Schimper, reading and discussing books on natural history, medical encyclopedias, as well as the complete works of Schiller and Goethe. In December 1830, Agassiz, still without permanent employment prospects, returned home to spend nearly a year engaged in ichthyologic studies while seeing patients in a nearby village. In September 1831, he left for Paris to further his studies in medicine and natural history, duly warned by his mother: "Now, all this would seem to me delightful if you had an income of fifty thousand francs; but, in your position, you must absolutely have an occupation which will enable you to live, and free you from the insupportable weight of dependence on others."[26] Yet in Paris Agassiz was able to establish contact with Cuvier and Humboldt, who both greatly aided his budding career: Cuvier granted Agassiz access to the laboratories at the Jardin des Plantes, and Humboldt afforded him a major credit of one thousand francs that ensured the completion of this work, reasoning that "a man so laborious, so gifted, and so deserving of affection as you are should not be left in a position where lack of serenity disturbs his power of work."[27]

This gift from the great Humboldt himself sealed the deal in making Agassiz's parents more amenable to a career in science. Soon thereafter, the president at Neuchâtel preparatory college promised to create a professorship of natural history for Agassiz. Agassiz was eager to accept and assumed his position with an inaugural lecture on November 12, 1832. He also began building the school's museum of natural history. In October 1833, Agassiz married the sister of his best friend Alexander, Cecilie Braun, who as a trained artist in drawing botanical specimens, helped with the newly established lithographic printing of ichthyologic research at Neuchâtel. Cecilie bore Agassiz three children: Alexander (born 1835), Ida (born 1837), and Pauline (born 1841). Despite offers from Heidelberg, Geneva, and Lausanne, Agassiz remained at Neuchâtel, where he completed *Re-cherches sur les poissons fossiles,* dedicated to Humboldt and comprising five volumes of text and an elaborate folio atlas of nearly four hundred plates, which laid the foundation for the new science of paleoichthyology (the study of fossil fish).

Glaciers and Glaciology

While still conducting research on fossil fish, Agassiz became interested in glaciers when in 1834 he heard a paper by the German-Swiss geologist Jean de (Johann von) Charpentier (1786–1855), a former classmate of Humboldt at the Freiberg Mountain Academy and the current director of the salt mines at Bex, who suggested, against the prevailing opinion of Neptunists, that erratic boulders in Switzerland had been transported by ice rather than water. Charpentier based his theories on his own observations in the field, as well as on drawings by Goethe, who had already pointed to a "period of fierce cold" when ice sheets transported erratic boulders. Indeed, Charpentier prefaced his work *Essai sur les glaciers* (1841) with a paragraph from Goethe's *Wilhelm Meisters Wanderjahre, oder Die Entsagenden* (1829, *Wilhelm Meister's Journeyman Years, or The Renunciants*)—the same quote that would later appear in Forbes's work—speculating about glaciers and radical climate change: "Finally two or three quiet guests invoked a period of fierce cold, when glaciers descended from the highest mountain ranges far into the land, forming in effect slides for ponderous masses of primeval rock, which were propelled farther and farther over the glassy track. In the subsequent period of thaw, these rocks had sunk deep into the ground, to remain forever locked in alien territory."[28]

Although Goethe, as has been pointed out, was certainly among the first to suggest such theories, Charpentier credited other predecessors, such as the Valais chamois-hunter Jean-Pierre Perraudin (1767–1858), who put forth the idea of Switzerland's glaciation as early as 1815, and his fellow Valais engineer Ignaz Venetz (1788–1859), who suggested a more widespread European glaciation as early as 1821 and published his work in 1833.[29] However, there was no sustained theory yet about how glaciers formed, moved, or disappeared. Agassiz, for his part, remained skeptical until he was invited by Charpentier in 1836 to spend the summer in Bex, where, to his own surprise, he revised his earlier thinking. Witnessing firsthand the evidence of glacial movement that Charpentier presented at several local excursions, Agassiz became convinced of former glaciation and in fact quickly capitalized on the idea: he would spend every summer between 1837 and 1841 in the Alps and even conducted the first winter examination of an Alpine glacier in 1841.

He also wasted no time in making his new convictions known. At the 1837 Meeting of the Société Helvétique des Sciences Naturelles in Neuchâtel, Agassiz at the last minute switched his planned presidential address on fossil fish to glaciology and for the first time laid out the fundamentals of his glacial theory. In his infamous "Discours de Neuchâtel," Agassiz proposed that after each geological period, a massive drop in temperature wiped out existing life-forms, and new life would reappear during warm-ups in the following period, rendering Hutton's (and Lyell's) theory of uniformitarianism impossible. During a recent ice age, a term he had borrowed from his German friend Schimper, who in a poem from 1837 coined the term *Eiszeit,* Agassiz proposed that a giant sheet of ice had covered an area from the North Pole to the Mediterranean and the Caspian Sea in Iran if not farther, causing rocks to crack, dislocate, and uplift to eventually form the Alps.[30] During the following warm-up, the glaciers, according to Agassiz, retreated to higher elevations in the Alps, leaving boulders and other remnants across Switzerland that had slid downward on the ice.[31] Agassiz's startling presentation, written the previous night, and his far-fetched theories were not received well, by earlier proponents of an ice age or by its skeptics. In fact, both Humboldt and Leopold von Buch urged Agassiz to stick to his research in fossil fish.[32] Humboldt later revised his advice, though he continued to remain skeptical of glacial theories, calling himself "a grumbling rebellious subject in your kingdom."[33]

Nevertheless, Agassiz set out on his first glaciological expedition to the Unteraar glacier in 1838, determined to prove empirically what he had postulated a priori. At the meeting of the Geological Society in France, he was able to draw from his field research evidence of polished and striated rock surfaces, erratics, and moraines, yet he somehow failed to see, as had Forbes and other early glaciologists, one of the largest signs of glaciation: U-shaped valleys. Agassiz was able to convince participants of glacial action, even though the majority of scientists continued to doubt his vast claims about a universal ice sheet and catastrophic climate change. The next summer, Agassiz returned to the Valais and the Unteraar glacier and devoted the winter to writing *Études sur les glaciers / Untersuchungen über die Gletscher*, which, after its simultaneous publication in French and German in September 1840, along with an accompanying atlas of thirty-two plates, established him as a leading glaciologist. The first chapter summarized the history of glacier research, vastly crediting Saussure—"Nobody has studied glaciers on a larger scale than the famous De Saussure"—and, to a lesser degree, Johann Jakob Scheuchzer, Gottlieb Sigmund Gruner, Joseph Hugi, Venetz, and Charpentier while also indicating the inadequacy of their research.[34] Based on the previous "Discours de Neuchâtel," *Études* then closely examined the characteristics of glaciers, including crevasses and moraines, as well as glacier formation, movement, and temperature in chapters 2 through 17; and the final chapter repeated his faulty albeit imaginative ideas about a universal ice age preceding the uplift of the Alps:

> The ground of Europe, previously covered with tropical vegetation and inhabited by herds of great elephants, enormous hippopotami, and gigantic carnivora, became suddenly buried under a vast expanse of ice covering plains, lakes, seas and plateaus alike. The silence of death succeeded to the movement of a powerful creation. Springs dried up, streams ceased to flow, and only by the whistling of northern winds and the rumbling of the crevasses as they opened across the surface of that huge ocean of ice.[35]

Significantly, Agassiz assured his readers that his theories were backed by five years of research and sanctioned through many conversations with friends who reined in all "flights of fancy."[36]

The narrative was matched by the volume's exquisite illustrations, transporting readers to a faraway yet accessible world of ice, snow, and rock. In the plates depicting the Glacier de Zermatt, lone subjects are juxtaposed with huge boulders, expansive stretches of snow, and countless peaks looming above. Yet the depicted landscape always remains aestheticized, artistically rendered in stark black-and-white geometrical forms, with a sense of compositional balance. Rather than chaotic, the mountain masses seem neatly assembled, the ice skillfully crunched, the rocks beautifully stacked. In this way, the illustrations at once rely on established discourses of the sublime but also exhibit an environment that can be measured and assessed

Glacier de Zermatt, upper part, from Agassiz, *Atlas études sur les glaciers,*
plate 3 (Provided by ETH Zurich; with special thanks to Melanie Lerch)

by the scientist. The enormous scale of this awe-inspiring white world conveniently corresponds with Agassiz's vast scientific claims.

Fourteen of the lithographs are accompanied by elaborate "linear plates,"
that is, an overlay that added text to the illustration, providing topographical names, the glacier's features, geological markers, evidence of glaciation,
type of rock, and other information.

With these visually overwhelming and beckoning images, Agassiz cleverly swayed readers in his favor. His accompanying tales of ice masses advancing during ice ages liberally used Romantic metaphors, as in "these
mountain colossus with their white garments and ice trains" and "the frozen cradles of the eternal rivers that from here bring life and movement to
the cheerful lowlands."[37] No wonder that Agassiz's work became instantly
famous, though it also infuriated Schimper (who went unmentioned and
later berated Agassiz as a "thieving magpie") and estranged Venetz and
Charpentier (to whom, incidentally, *Études sur les glaciers* was dedicated),
who had voiced many of these concepts beforehand and felt not properly
credited for their work.[38] The historian of science Frank F. Cunningham
concludes, "Up to the summer of 1840 it would not be unjust to say that

Glacier de Zermatt, middle part, from Agassiz, *Atlas études sur les glaciers,*
plate 4 (Provided by ETH Zurich; with special thanks to Melanie Lerch)

Glacier de Zermatt, last curve of the lower part, from Agassiz, *Atlas études sur les glaciers*, plate 5 (Provided by ETH Zurich; with special thanks to Melanie Lerch)

Glacier de Zermatt, lower end, from Agassiz, *Atlas études sur les glaciers*, plate 6 (Provided by ETH Zurich; with special thanks to Melanie Lerch)

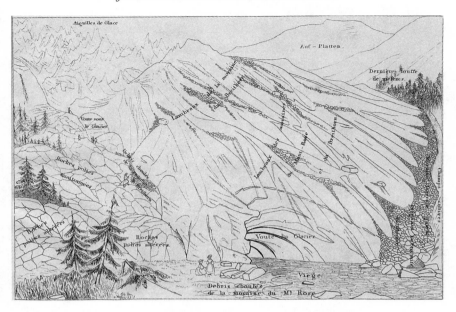

Glacier de Zermatt, lower end with overlay, from Agassiz, *Atlas études sur les glaciers*, plate 6 (Provided by ETH Zurich; with special thanks to Melanie Lerch)

Agassiz had not produced a single major observation or proposal about the Glacier Theory which was both original and correct."[39] Even so, to this date it is Agassiz who remains best known as a pioneering glaciologist.[40]

Teamwork and Strife

At the meeting of the British Association for the Advancement of Science in Glasgow in September 1840, Agassiz once again laid out his theories and for the first time met Forbes, who quickly became mesmerized by theories of glaciers and glaciation. Looking for professional support, Agassiz invited Forbes to join him in research at the Unteraar glacier the following summer. Forbes gladly accepted, and the two agreed to meet on August 8 at the Grimsel Hospice, conveniently located just an hour's walk from the Unteraar glacier, whose low gradient afforded easy travel. On the glacier itself, at 8,100 feet, Agassiz had constructed—somewhat unwisely—a cabin at the top of a moraine, below a previous structure built by Hugi, who had already measured glacial movement. Far from a solitary affair, this so-called

Unteraar glacier with Hugi's Hut, from Agassiz, *Atlas études sur les glaciers,*
plate 14 (Provided by ETH Zurich; with special thanks to Melanie Lerch)

Hôtel des Neuchâtelois housed as many as seven friends and admirers,
along with additional visitors in daytime, who passed the time during spells
of bad weather with books, magazines, food, and wine. In this "Agassian
Club" (266), Forbes passed many social hours, making new friends including the Swiss geologist Bernard Studer, enjoying the latest copies of the
Literary Gazette and *Athenaeum,* sampling Agassiz's routine of daily baths in
ice water, and even smoking his very first cigar, "with no disagreeable consequences, but the reverse" (261). The encampment still boasts a monu-
ment for Agassiz, although it was permanently destroyed in 1846 when the
rock at its base predictably split. The Grimsel Hospice appears to have
been an even more sociable affair, entertaining as many as sixty visitors for
supper and tea during Agassiz's and Forbes's lectures. The worldly, ambitious, and extroverted Agassiz and the devout, skeptical, and solitary
Forbes—characterized by Agassiz's contemporary biographer Jules Marcou as "austere to an extent seldom seen even among Englishmen"—must
have made an unlikely pair.[41] Yet Forbes became undeniably captivated by
Agassiz and his cheerful social entourage, while the rising young Agassiz

was fascinated if not intimidated by Forbes's logical conclusions, quick understanding, and keen observations.

Beyond social exposure, the trip also marked the beginning of Forbes's own glacier study and was to profoundly shape the direction of his research ever after. Seeing the landscape before him anew, as shaped by ice rather than water, Forbes writes in his journal of glacial moraines, roches moutonnées (sheepbacks, or hump-like rocks shaped by glaciers), erratic boulders, and striated and polished rocks, and he scoffs at his own previous assumptions: "To talk of such striae having been produced by water is ridiculous" (270). In hindsight he concludes in *Travels Through the Alps of Savoy:*

> I cannot now recall, without some degree of shame, the almost blindfold way in which, until lately, I was in the habit of visiting the glaciers. During three different previous summers, I had visited the Mer de Glace, and during two of them, 1832 and 1839, I had traversed many miles of its surface; yet I failed to remark a thousand peculiarities of the most obvious kind, or to speculate upon their cause, or else the clearer apprehension which I now have of these things, has wholly driven from my mind the previous faint impression.[42]

Such novel and revolutionary thinking in interpreting the land before him while imagining the agentic forces of ice sweeping the country invigorated Forbes to an unprecedented degree. While Agassiz spent the remainder of the summer boring holes in the ice to measure temperature and thickness, Forbes set out to explore the Rhône Valley and Jura, now finding evidence for glaciation on his own.

Already on their first day, Forbes observed and alerted Agassiz to what he called the "ribboned structure" of the ice, that is, bluish-white vertical bands traversing the ice parallel to its length, a somewhat obvious feature that Agassiz had dismissed.[43] Forbes described narrow bands of hard, clear ice a few centimeters thick, alternating with bands of bubbly ice, and he suggested that the bands stemmed from cycles of thawing and refreezing, allowing sand to enter between the layers of ice. This veined structure became a key factor in Forbes's theories on glacier motion because it attested to glacier flow and could be used to map it. Its discovery was also a major bone of contention in the upcoming dispute between the two men. Back in Scotland, Forbes studied Agassiz's *Études*, as well as Charpentier's later published but earlier researched *Essai sur les glaciers,* to concur with Charpentier rather than Agassiz on the proposed extent of glaciation.

The dispute between Forbes and Agassiz, carried out in hostile letters between the two and their respective camps, broke out when Forbes came across a published letter from Agassiz to Humboldt describing the 1841 tour, in which Forbes not only went unmentioned but Agassiz claimed the discovery of the ribboned ice structure for himself. Forbes reacted mildly, writing to Agassiz in November 1841 to clarify the issue ("I perceive by your letter to Humboldt that you consider that observation of the vertical schistose structure of the ice to be the most interesting part of our summer work") and expressing hope for continued joint studies the following summer.[44] Moreover, Forbes presented papers on the "ice structure" at the Royal Society of Edinburgh in December 1841, as well as the University of Edinburgh, and also inquired about a publication with the renowned publisher John Murray but was rebuffed—unbeknownst to him, Agassiz had already secured a publication deal with Murray. While Forbes wasted no time in approaching Murray's competitor, the *Edinburgh Review,* for reasons of space he had to delay publication of the "Glacier Theory" until April 1842. In the meantime, his lecture at the Royal Society was published in the *Edinburgh New Philosophical Journal* (January 1842), where Forbes laid out details of the ice structure, noting, "I was surprised, on remarking it to Mr. Agassiz as a thing which must be familiar to him, to find that he had not distinctly noticed it before, at least if he had, that he had considered it as a superficial phenomenon wholly unconnected with the general structure of the ice."[45]

Taken aback, Agassiz sent enraged and deprecating letters to professional acquaintances such as Murray and friends like his protégé Desor, who in turn sent an accusatory letter directly to Forbes. Forbes replied sharply to Desor while writing once more to Agassiz in a more conciliatory tone: "I was certainly vexed that in your letter to Humboldt you should have omitted to state my share in the observations, but I should have been sorry to disturb the harmony which so long and happily prevailed between us, by any extreme jealousy upon a point of priority."[46] Whereupon Agassiz wrote a frosty reply to Forbes confirming his position and moreover turned to Murray, denouncing Forbes in a letter that he explicitly asked to be circulated: "I showed him [Forbes] everything interesting about the glacier, all the research was pursued under his eyes. From the first day I myself told him that one of the aspects I had especially decided to study was the internal structure of the glacier and in particular the ribboned appearance of the glacier which I only briefly described in my work."[47] Murray complied, though he would later regret circulating the letter, convinced by support for Forbes by his friends Heath and Studer.

Agassiz's and Forbes's friendship and collaboration had ended. When his review article "The Glacier Theory" was finally published in the *Edinburgh Review,* Forbes expertly outlined his theories, crediting Venetz, Hugi, Charpentier, Rendu, Necker, and Agassiz for their contributions and rising above the details of the quarrel by not even mentioning the ice structure.[48] In its wake, support in Britain tended to sway toward Forbes, underscored by testimony of more impartial witnesses to the summer proceedings, who confirmed Forbes's version of the events. When Forbes attempted reconciliation before his 1842 summer trip to Neuchâtel and sent a note to Agassiz affirming his goodwill and seeing no reason "why we should not take the present opportunity of meeting on friendly terms," Agassiz answered promptly, "I cannot conceive what kind of personal relations you desire to entertain with me."[49] Openly annoyed by the reply, Forbes responded by asking for the return of his alpenstock, and the two men never corresponded with each other again. Still, in the aforementioned account of the Jungfrau ascent published in 1853, Forbes credits Agassiz as follows: "The arrangements, so far as this part of the excursion was concerned, were undertaken and carried out entirely by M. Agassiz, and with him rests the credit of our success."[50]

Travels Through the Alps of Savoy

Forbes's principal inquiry shifted to glacial motion, but rather than continuing to follow in the footsteps of Agassiz by studying the well-researched Unteraar glacier, he decided to pursue his investigations elsewhere. He began to conduct trigonometrical surveys at the Mer de Glace, acquiring the services of Auguste Balmat, the much-experienced great-nephew of Jacques Balmat, who soon became Forbes's most trusted guide, and spent the entire summer in the Mont Blanc region, crossing the Col du Géant pass, where he discovered Saussure's former camp and recalculated some of his measurements. Thereafter Forbes was able to refute both prevailing theories of glacier motion, the gravitational theory supported by Saussure, which claimed that rigid ice blocks slid downward on a slope, facilitated by the presence of a layer of water between the bedrock and the ice, and the dilation theory supported by Scheuchzer, Charpentier, and Agassiz, which stated that the majority of motion occurred overnight after the superficial meltwater on the surface and in the cracks of a glacier refreezes and ex-pands the glacier's volume, releasing the ice downward. Instead Forbes argued that (a) glaciers moved steadily and consistently, day and night, summer and winter (Agassiz had initially claimed that because there was no meltwater, no movement occurred in winter, before his own measure-ments in March 1841 failed to produce evidence); and (b) analogous to a river, the center of a glacier moved faster than its sides (which turned out to be correct and was later confirmed by Tyndall's measurements), con-trary to what Agassiz had proclaimed in *Études* (because there were more crevasses along the sides and more meltwater, Agassiz concluded that the sides moved faster).[51] As we now know, they were all partly correct: glaciers move as solids when the underlying ice flows out from the pressure of the overlying ice. As Forbes recognized, ice continually deforms under stress, though some glacial movement also occurs when blocks of ice slide across a downward surface, as Saussure had claimed. Accordingly, a glacier's veined structure forms when layers of high pressure alternate with layers subject to a high rate of strain.[52]

In the following winter, Forbes busied himself with a roughly chronolog-ical account of his Alpine tour in the summer of 1842. *Travels Through the Alps of Savoy* (the northwestern part of the French Alps), the first text in English to deal with glacier exploration, was published by the small Scot-tish publisher Adam and Charles Black the following year. Forbes followed Saussure's (and to some degree Humboldt's) model in combining natural history, geologic measurements, and travel advice in the form of a personal travel narrative, but he took even greater care to advertise and market his book to the general public. Touting the Alps as the "grandest theatre of natural operations in Europe" (*TS*, 6), Forbes cleverly connected the pre-vailing arts of theater and modern technology to advertise mountains to a nineteenth-century audience and bemoaned the absence of a travel guide-book to the Alps, especially for regions that had not yet been sufficiently explored. *Travels* is more reader friendly, with a clear structure and scientific observations delegated to specific chapters; in fact, Forbes even advises the general reader to omit certain chapters that may provide too much detail (99). Promoting the conveniences of traveling in Switzerland, Forbes outlines specific routes, such as the "Tour of Mont Blanc" in chapter 9 that circles the mountain at its base and provides practical advice on the desired wardrobe and technical equipment (102), endorsing or deploring particular villages, chalets, and local curés (a pastor often providing accommodation, meals, and travel advice).

Forbes acknowledges the Alpine historians Josias Simler, Scheuchzer, Gruner, Hugi, Venetz, and Charpentier besides profusely thanking and crediting Saussure, and he also gives credit to Agassiz while voicing some doubts about the timing and the extent of the latter's proposed glaciation. Decrying the "unfavourable impression" (*TS*, 7) of Saussure's plates and maps, Forbes conversely convinced his publisher to hire a first-rate illustrator and even took drawing lessons himself to draft sketches for the volume's four plates. Their lasting influence was recognized by the president of the Royal Society, George Biddell Airy, who not only admired Forbes's mapping of the Mer de Glace but opined, "I suppose it may be asserted that the present popularity of Zermatt, a place which was before scarcely known, is almost entirely due to Professor Forbes's picture of the Matterhorn."[53] This lithograph must also have inspired Tyndall's similarly dramatic drawing of the mountain.

Forbes has no qualms about claiming the Alps as British terrain. In reference to Saussure, Forbes asserts that "nature is *our* laboratory" (*TS*, 14, emphasis mine) and furthermore picks up on the pastoral tradition, accelerated industrialization, and medical discourses of the day when advertising pure Alpine living to weary British travelers:

> The sense of perfect health—the rapid and refreshing sleep which attends most persons escaped from the hot-bed languor of towns to the freshness of the Alps, stimulate the powers of thought; . . . Mornings of active exercise, from sunrise till afternoon, and evenings of quiet thought and speculation, with here and there a day interposed of easy society with intelligent travelers, or employed in reducing and digesting the knowledge previously acquired by observation, give the sense of living twice over. The body and the mind are alike invigorated and refreshed; weariness from fatigue, and weariness

"Mont Cervin from the Riffelberg," from Forbes, *Travels Through the Alps of Savoy*, plate 7, 313 (Provided by ETH Zurich; with special thanks to Melanie Lerch)

from inactivity, are forgotten, together with the other evils of our more artificial existence. (*TS*, 13–14)

Pitting an "artificial" existence in the cities against a more "natural" existence in the mountains, Forbes shrewdly employs the pastoral tradition to
advertise an Alpine respite to educated middle-class and wealthy Britons.

But the true focus and passion of Forbes's book lie in the glaciers. Forbes
moves from a general account of glaciers, their structure, the veined bands,
and his thesis of liquid movement, to a description of the Mer de Glace
specifically, followed by depictions of his surveying activity in the vicinity.
Fittingly, on its title page, *Travels* sports a German quote by Goethe proclaiming an unrelenting love for ice and rock: "Sage mir was du an diesen
kalten und starren Liebhabereyen gefunden hast" (Tell me what you have
found in these cold and lifeless pursuits/obsessions).[54] By quoting from the
third chapter of the first volume of *Wilhelm Meisters Wanderjahre, oder Die
Entsagenden* (*Wilhelm Meister's Journeyman Years, or The Renunciants*), which had
appeared a couple decades earlier, in 1829, the same text that had graced
Charpentier's volume, Forbes at once credits Goethe with his contributions to glaciology, connects his own research to that of Charpentier, and
positions himself in opposition to Agassiz. But the quote carries further
significance when in Goethe's text, Jarno patiently explains the value of
geology. Far from being "lifeless cliffs," rocks are letters forming words and
sentences in an unknown language: "But suppose I treated these very fissures and crevasses as letters, attempted to decipher them, shaped them
into words, and learned to read them, would you have any objection to
that?"[55] Mountains, in other words, reveal stories of a dynamic earth that
we can only come to know by learning a different scientific language, and
only to a layman do glaciers appear fixed. By putting Goethe's words up
front, Forbes cements the importance of glacier study by linking it to classical *Bildung*. In his introduction, Forbes underscores this interpretation by
calling a glacier "an endless scroll, a stream of time, upon whose stainless
ground is engraven the succession of events, whose dates far transcend the
memory of living man" (*TS*, 22).

Forbes's infatuation with glaciers acknowledges a highly dynamic, volatile,
and agentic environment: in the chapter aptly titled "On the Geological
Agency of Glaciers," he vividly describes the immense powers of glaciers,

"Glacier-Table on the Mer de Glace," from Forbes,
Travels Through the Alps of Savoy, plate 1, frontispiece (Provided
by ETH Zurich; with special thanks to Melanie Lerch)

which chafe and polish the rocks, depositing moraines in their paths. Likewise, the book's impressive frontispiece displays a striking glacial table on the Mer de Glace, which formed when the large erratic rock blocked the sun from melting the snow underneath it. Forbes placed himself beneath the boulder for scale and also included a theodolite on a tripod in the illustration. The image hints at the enormous force of glaciers, particularly when compared to the minuscule humans in the landscape, but also reveals humans' scientific quest to understand the earth's history and, in Goethe's words, to read the foreign language of geology. Indeed, Forbes frequently reaches for literary sources; his chapter on glacial movement is prefaced by an often-quoted verse from Lord Byron's *Manfred* (1816–17): "The glacier's cold and restless mass / Moves onward day by day." Such Romantic and scientific understanding of glaciers revises previous ideas of mountains as immovable barriers in favor of a model that assigns agency to manifold environmental forces. Furthermore, the quote makes another stab against Agassiz, who had claimed that glaciers only move at night.

Glaciology, Masculinity, Bigotry

Both Agassiz's stunning imagery and Forbes's literary references draw attention to glaciers' mesmerizing impact. While the aesthetics of an infinite, overwhelming, and potentially threatening environment connect to discourses of the sublime, there are some aspects particular to glaciers, since coming into contact with a glacier becomes an all-encompassing experience. As part of their great force, glaciers exert loud noises, producing cracking, thunder, and explosive sounds; they also, of course, involve a physical sensation of the temperature. Most importantly, glaciers embody seemingly opposite qualities and remain an enigma: glaciers suggest both permanence and flow; they emit cold and heat, in extreme form. As powerful forces both active and passive, they become a medium that can be conquered and that conquers but remains unpredictable. Surging glaciers, for instance, remain dormant for decades but can suddenly advance extremely quickly (50 to 100 meters per day). As the quarrel between Forbes and Agassiz and others exemplifies, one can think of glaciers as both solid and liquid: in fact, they are a solid that flows when glaciers move, becoming liquid under pressure of its weight. This kind of shape-shifting greatly contributes to their enigmatic power. *Travels* concludes with a poetic metaphor cementing Forbes's theory of viscous flow while imbuing glaciers with life: "Poets and philosophers have delighted to compare the course of human life to that of a river; perhaps a still apter simile might be found in the history of a glacier" (386). Agassiz also emphasized a glacier's agency in *Études:* "Although the massive aspect of glaciers seems to suggest the idea of a certain stability, nothing is actually more mobile and changing than their surface. When we visit a glacier that we have not seen for a certain number of years, we are always surprised to notice so many changes."[56] By introducing audiences to otherworldly fields of ice and snow, Forbes and Agassiz sparked the public imagination with tales of a massive previous ice age and fueled further travel.

After his break with Agassiz, Forbes heralded his theories as hard-won, authentic field science superior to theoretical insights made in faraway laboratories. In this way, he embedded scientific discoveries in his travel narratives, an aspect missing from Agassiz's work. Later, Forbes used his mountain accomplishments to defend his theories against the mathematician

William Hopkins, who claimed in "On the Motion of Glaciers" (1845) that glaciers moved as solids, as demonstrated by his laboratory experiments. Here the third theme of masculinity comes into play. As Bruce Hevly recognized, "Heroism, with its elements of direct action, lonely commitment, and manly risk, helped to shape arguments over glacier physics. It served as a rhetorical resource for those who had ventured into the alpine landscape and who could thus portray those who had not as armchair theorists."[57] In *Travels*, Forbes related in detail a traverse of the Col du Géant via a new route, claiming in a letter to his sister: "I made an excursion over the Mer de Glace in the midst of a snow-storm, which gave me a good idea of an Alpine winter; but these difficulties added something to the value of the results."[58] This statement also subtly dismantled Agassiz's claim of winter research in the Alps. In the same letter, Forbes continues not so subtly:

> I am not sorry that the world should have an opportunity of comparing the results of Agassiz' mode of working with those of mine. His force consisted of a paid surveyor, a paid draughtsman, a chemist, a geologist, a trumpeter—I know not whom besides—in all nine masters, and nine guides who all lived on the glacier. I avoided society, and the disturbances attendant on notoriety, and with one assistant only, except on rare occasion, have performed all my summer's work—my ordinary expenses being eleven francs a day![59]

Silencing the fact that in the previous summer he had enjoyed social life and material indulgencies on the glacier, Forbes uses his solitary, manly modus operandi and even financial thriftiness to bolster his arguments. As Bruce Hevly elucidated, Forbes in essence claimed that his science was superior "on the basis of authentic, rigorous, manly experience" and advocated such "muscular science" for other males to follow.[60] Yet we can see limits to this line of argumentation, hinting at more complex models of masculinities. Hevly's evidence of Forbes's "muscular science" rests mainly on letters and unpublished texts, while both of his main works, *Travels* and *Norway and Its Glaciers*, go unmentioned. Forbes completed *Travels* at a major turning point in his life, right around the time when he proposed to Alicia Wauchope, and he would undertake most of his future journeys accompanied by her. In a rare depiction of actual research, *Travels* included an illustration of Forbes and an assistant measuring the thickness of the Mer de Glace, but the two hunched figures, shown lowering a rope into a berg-

"Contact of Ice and Rock at the Angle, Mer de Glace,"
from Forbes, *Travels Through the Alps of Savoy*, plate 3, 76
(Provided by ETH Zurich; with special thanks to Melanie Lerch)

schrund dwarfed by a yawning crevasse below and a steep cliff above, do not radiate any particular heroism or manliness.

Forbes and Wauchope were married on July 4, 1843, and the couple set off for a journey to the Continent, but prolonged health problems forced him to ask for a leave of absence and allowed for only sporadic research in Switzerland. In the summer of 1851, Forbes attempted to observe the total eclipse of the sun in Bergen, Norway, though thick clouds hindered a full view. Still, he was able to examine some of the Norwegian glaciers, elaborating on his findings in *Norway and Its Glaciers* (1853). After his return to Edinburgh, Forbes became aware of Alfred Wills's publication *Wanderings Among the High Alps* (1856) and struck up a conversation that turned into lifelong friendship. Though giving up on research in the mountains himself, Forbes stayed in touch about mountain matters, following with great interest the foundation of the Alpine Club in 1858, of which he became an honorary member. In this capacity, Forbes passed the baton to a new generation of climbers—"Robust I can never again expect to be. The mountains are for you and your contemporaries"—but continued to give advice.[61] To Wills, for instance, he kindly bemoaned the club's missing recognition of guides: "I regret to see Balmat's name never alluded to in these volumes [the publication series of the Alpine Club, *Peaks, Passes, and Glaciers*]."[62] In 1865 Forbes met Edward Whymper, greatly impressed by his Matterhorn feat and moved by his account of the ensuing disaster in the *Times*. In the fall of 1859, Forbes assumed the presidency of Saint Andrews College, giving university-wide lectures on climate and glaciers without daily presence in the classroom. Forbes's declining health forced him to spend the winter of 1867–68 in a more hospitable climate, and the family chose Cannes and Hyeres in France, where Forbes became bedridden. In spring, the family returned to Clifton, England; in October Forbes turned in his resignation from Saint Andrews and denied requests for postponement. He passed away on December 31, 1868.

Agassiz's life was to take a different turn. Increasingly estranged from his wife, who began to show signs of encroaching tuberculosis, he made preparations for an extended trip to the United States, thanks to Humboldt, who secured a generous grant of sixteen thousand francs from King Friedrich Wilhelm IV of Prussia.[63] Agassiz left Europe in September 1846 and was never to return, leaving Cecilie to die two years later, in July 1848. He made a new home as an appointed professor of zoology and geology at the newly established Lawrence Scientific School at Harvard University, and married Elizabeth Cabot Cary in April 1850, who connected him to the wealthy intellectual elite in Boston. His research turned to jellyfish, and he soon gathered a new circle of students and assistants around him, some of whom became deeply disillusioned with Agassiz's narcissistic and sometimes exploitative mentoring.[64]

In the United States, Agassiz became increasingly known for his rejection of Darwin's theories of evolution and for his scientific racism.[65] Although Agassiz opposed slavery, he did so on the grounds of his deep-seated bigotry, arguing that whites and blacks were created to live in different geographical areas that would prevent any kind of interracial mixing. Firmly anchored in white supremacist beliefs, he claimed that the human races were zoologically distinct, touring Southern slave plantations in 1850 in an attempt to prove his points. His first trip to Brazil in 1865 and 1866, funded by a friend, produced a vast collection of photographs of Brazilian male and female "half-breeds" that were supposed to corroborate Agassiz's belief that racial intermixing produced physical and moral degeneration that was to be avoided in North America. In her incisive analysis, Nancy Leys Stepan interprets these disturbing images as a new form of racialism reflecting, "in extreme form, the shift in attitude towards race that took place in science and politics in the middle of the century."[66]

In 1869 Agassiz suffered a first stroke but, accompanied by his wife, boarded the steamer *Hassler* for another extended expedition to South America in 1871 and 1872. Once again funded by wealthy friends in Boston, the expedition was to produce scientific proof for Agassiz's creationist theories. Agassiz's evidence, however, remained shaky at best, especially in light of his findings on the Galápagos Islands, which failed to outshine Darwin's previous assertions. After her husband's passing in December 1873, Elizabeth assumed Agassiz's legacy by publishing *Louis Agassiz: His Life and Correspondence* eight years later with Houghton Mifflin. Cognizant of the by now highly controversial nature of Agassiz's theories, Elizabeth attempted to document Agassiz's life via documents, letters, and other voices rather than her own, withholding some of his most outrageous writings.[67] Thanks to his wife's selective censorship, scholarship on Agassiz continued to whitewash his abhorrent theories and beliefs well into the 1970s.[68]

In an age of climate change, dwindling glaciers, and massive species extinction, Agassiz's far-fetched theories of catastrophic climate change, even though they originated in a different context, are gaining currency and new meaning. Glaciers not only have become an icon for climate change but, as historian Mark Carey points out, are also depicted in terms of an endangered species.[69] Such emotional attachment leads us back to the passionate research of early glaciologists, who offer insights into the dynamic and even agentic forces of nature and point to a deeper history and sense of time. While Forbes's and Agassiz's depictions of glaciers divulge fantasies of a blank slate, a white world beckoning scientific discovery, recognition, and conquest, they are also marked by an awareness of human limits. Silenced and stunned, humbled and limited, Forbes and Agassiz demonstrate a physical enmeshment with snow and ice, modeling how scientific discoveries can be represented in both narrative and visual form. Their passionate and all-encompassing approaches to science and to mountaineering provide us with fresh perspectives at a time when the pursuit of science or mountaineering without an ecocritical awareness seems ignorant and inadequate.

CHAPTER 6

THE SELLING OF THE ALPS AND THE
BEGINNING OF THE "GOLDEN AGE"

Albert Smith and Alfred Wills

Albert Smith's Ascent of Mont Blanc

Albert Smith had dreamed about an ascent of Mont Blanc since boyhood.[1] On August 1, 1851, Smith, at the age of thirty-five, and his friend William Beverly finally boarded a train in London, determined to at least make an attempt at the climb. Precisely his resolve to aim for the summit stands in marked contrast to previous mountaineering and makes Smith's endeavor a modern one, resembling recreational peak baggers in the twentieth century and the twenty-first. Smith had been planning his trip for a year and had already hired a guide, Jéan Tairraz, in advance, but by his own admission he had not in the least trained for the undertaking; on the contrary, "I came from my desk to the railway, from the railway to the diligence, and from that to the *char-à-banc;* and on the night of my arrival at Chamouni I sent for Tairraz."[2] At the Hôtel de Londres, Smith made the acquaintance of three Oxford undergraduates also in pursuit of Mont Blanc and promptly invited them along. He proceeded to hire four guides and waited for better weather. After long periods of constant rain, the group finally convened on the morning of August 12 to commence the ascent, though not before a lavish breakfast.

Leaving Chamonix, Smith declared, "I believe we formed the largest caravan that had ever gone off together" (159), and the size of his party was impressive indeed: each of the five climbers had hired four personal guides plus twenty porters, with friends and family accompanying the partakers. For the two-day expedition, Smith's elaborate list of provisions included no less than ninety-one bottles of wine, forty-six fowl, and four legs of lamb, among other supplies. At the Glacier des Bossons, the group encountered crevices and crevasses, navigating them by jumping or by using ladders. They laboriously climbed the towers of rock forming the Grands Mulets in the broiling heat, to a salute of firing guns from locals in Chamonix, who eagerly watched their progress through telescopes. The party's "high festival on the Grands Mulets," that is, the overnight camp on a platform among the rocks, was a wild one. Entertainment consisted of singing, stories, and laughter, no doubt facilitated by the vast quantities of alcohol that had been schlepped to the camp. This provided another unexpected amusement when "a fine diversion was afforded by racing the empty bottles down the glacier" (178). By sunset Smith had become so elated that he compared his intoxication to the effects of other drugs: "A scene of such wild and wondrous beauty—of such inconceivable and unearthly splendour— burst upon me, that, spell-bound, and almost trembling with the emotion its magnificence called forth—with every sense, and feeling, and thought absorbed by its brilliancy, I saw far more than the realization of the most gorgeous visions that opium or *hasheesh* could evoke, accomplished" (182).

Tairraz woke everyone shortly before midnight, and armed with a few bottles of wine and a couple of cold fowl, the party began trudging up the snow slope to the Grand Plateau in moonlight. According to Smith, the hangover, exhaustion, sleep deprivation, and cold made this the low point of the journey: "I felt very chilled and dispirited. I had now passed two nights without sleep; and I had really eaten nothing since the yesterday's morning but part of an egg, a piece of fowl, and a little bit of bread—for my illness had taken away all my appetite; and on this small diet I had been undergoing the greatest work" (194).

Overcome by fatigue and sickness, Smith began to hallucinate, meticulously recording the phantoms of his waking dreams, in which he encountered real and literary friends "in such a strange state of mingled unconsciousness and acute observation—of combined sleeping and waking—that

Albert Smith, "The Bivouac on the Grands Mulets,"
from *The Story of Mont Blanc,* 178 (Provided by ETH
Zurich; with special thanks to Melanie Lerch)

the old-fashioned word 'bewitched' is the only one that I can apply to the complete confusion and upsetting of sense in which I found myself plunged" (196). Finally, he collapsed in the snow, unable to keep his eyes open, and was dragged upward by Tairraz, arriving at the summit at an infamously anticlimactic moment: "Gradually our speed increased, until I was scrambling almost on my hands and knees; and then, as I found myself on a level, it suddenly stopped. I looked round, and saw there was nothing higher. The batons were stuck in the snow, and the guides were grouped about, some lying down, and others standing in little parties. I was on the top of Mont Blanc!" (201). In ironic contrast to the chapter's title, "Victory," Smith's first response was to fall asleep for some seven minutes until, awoken by Tairraz, he could bask in the accomplishment. The group proceeded to celebrate their achievement in style: enjoying the view, shaking hands, eating fowl, bread, cheese, prunes, and chocolate, drinking wine, and toasting with champagne.

By his own admission, Smith was wholly uninterested in attaining scientific results. He instead climbed the mountain for its vistas, the thrill of adventure, and the pride in triumphant conquest. Accordingly, he directly contrasted his endeavor with that of Saussure:

> We made no "scientific observations,"—the acute and honest De Saussure had done everything that was wanted by the world of that kind; and those who have since worried themselves during the ascent about "elevations" and temperatures, have added nothing to what he told us sixty years ago. But we had beheld all the wonders and horrors of the glacier world in their wildest features; we had gazed on scenery of such fantastic yet magnificent nature as we might not hope to see again; we had labored with all the nerve and energy we could command to achieve a work of downright unceasing danger and difficulty, which not more than one-half of those who try are able to accomplish, and the triumph of which is, even now, shared but by a comparative handful of travelers—and we had succeeded! (206–7)

Smith here provides an apt explanation of the shifting mountaineering discourse over the past half century: considering the science exhausted, his reasoning for climbing consists in elusive scenery, dangers mastered, and most importantly, the exclusivity of a small club of men who succeed in daring adventures.

Whereas Humboldt, Saussure, and Forbes had lingered on the summit for hours, trying to complete their measurements, Smith contented himself with a mere half hour on top, despite the drawn-out description in his book. At half past nine, the party promptly began their descent, skating, gliding, and glissading down the soft snow. An illustration in *The Story of Mont Blanc* depicts them helplessly tumbling down the mountain slope, a far cry from skilled climbing or mountain triumph and yet reminiscent of many images found in Tyndall and Whymper.

After a brief rest at the Grands Mulets, they descended all the way back to the greenery of the valley. Supplied with milk and mules at the chalet, they made a triumphant entry into Chamonix, parading through the streets in front of cheering men, handkerchief-waving women, and bouquet-throwing girls, accompanied by artillery fire, a violin, and a harp player. The next morning, Smith found himself presented with a bill for 103 lost bottles, among a host of other expenses, but reasoned that "it was better to throw them [the bottles] away than to fatigue the men with the thankless task of carrying them down again" (218). John Ruskin, who was staying in

Albert Smith, "Coming Down," from *The Story
of Mont Blanc*, 210 (Provided by ETH Zurich;
with special thanks to Melanie Lerch)

Chamonix at the time, was less amused, grumbling in a letter to his father,
"There has been a cockney ascent of Mont Blanc, of which I believe you
are soon to hear in London."[3] Indeed, Smith wasted no time, publicizing
his ascent as soon as eight days after his return, and continued to draw
from its entertainment value in his later career.[4]

Alfred Wills's Ascent of the Wetterhorn

Three years later, on September 17, 1854, Sir Alfred Wills, along with his
Chamonix guides Auguste Balmat and Auguste Simond and the local
Grindelwald guides Ulrich Lauener and Peter Bohren, reached the perilous summit of the Wetterhorn after Lauener chopped away an ice block
from the overhanging cornice that had likely turned around a previous
party. Seated atop a narrow ridge, Wills at length described the magnificent panorama, spotting the Ortler, Monte Rosa, the Schreckhorn, and
the Eiger, among many other peaks. Harking back to the age-old transfor-

mative vision of being closer to God on a mountaintop—"We felt as in the more immediate presence of Him who had reared this tremendous pinnacle, and beneath the 'majestical roof' of whose deep blue Heaven we stood, poised, as it seemed, half way between the earth and sky" (295)—he also delighted in conceiving the depths below, with an appropriately sublime shudder: "The imagination shrank from contemplating the abyss, and picturing to itself the fearful precipices which must be beneath" (300). Wills's party spent twenty minutes on the summit, savoring the spectacle that "made our hearts beat quicker with a solemn and strange emotion" (300), while Lauener, more concerned with immediate matters, drove the "Flagge," a three-by-two-foot metal sheet that he had carried on his back, via an iron bar into the ice.

Wills had originally wanted to follow in Forbes's footsteps and scale the Jungfrau to crown his 1854 honeymoon trip with an achievement that would both prove himself and impress his new wife. But Lauener—in part guided by his own motives—convinced him that it was too late in the season for the longer Jungfrau trip, recommending a first ascent of the Wetterhorn instead. In the end, the prospect of a first ascent trumped previous plans and motivated the Wetterhorn climb, even though this "first ascent" was a malleable concept. While Wills was aware that the highest of the three Wetterhorn peaks had possibly already been ascended almost ten years earlier, Lauener withheld the fact that three previous ascents of the lower peak had been made from another side, some of them involving himself and Bohren, who had planted a flag just ten feet below the summit.[5] Leaving Wills in the dark, the two guides hoped for two things: to settle unfinished business by planting the iron slab at the very top, and to procure a large bonus for this "first" ascent. However, not only did Wills reap the acclaim of being the first to scale the Wetterhorn, but his ascent was crowned with the special honor of ringing in the Golden Age of Mountaineering—surprising even to himself.

Dating the 1854 Wetterhorn ascent as the arrival of the Alpine "Golden Age"—an era that established competition, sportsmanship, and climbing skill as foundational principles of modern mountaineering—seems arbitrary at best, and plain wrong when considering the confusions surrounding this so-called first ascent, but points to the many inconsistencies and controversies in the emergence of mountaineering.[6] In hindsight, Smith's "cockney ascent" was surely more influential, but no matter the precise starting date, the heyday of mountaineering emerged in the 1850s as an activity that proved worthwhile in itself, ushering in an industry of consumption and commercialization. Considering both Smith's and Wills's accomplishments in juxtaposition reveals much about the direction, scope, and development of mountain climbing in the latter half of the nineteenth century. Likewise, the reception of their diverse texts sheds light on both the growing group of armchair mountaineers who consumed climbing narratives and staged performances and the rising number of mountaineers raising the stakes of the sport by claiming ever-more-difficult first ascents of Alpine peaks.

Smith and Wills Come to the Mountains

The *Oxford Dictionary of National Biography* lists Albert Richard Smith as an "author, public lecturer, and mountaineer," even though his mountaineering achievements remained rather unimpressive and short-lived: after climbing Mont Blanc once, he never set foot on another Alpine mountain.[7] Born in London on May 24, 1816, Smith trained for a career as a surgeon and apothecary, like his father, but his interest in the Alps was piqued when, on his tenth birthday, he received *The Peasants of Chamouni* (1823), a volume that detailed Dr. Hamel's fatal attempt to climb Mont Blanc in 1820.[8] Smith then attempted to translate Saussure, devoured Captain Sherwill and Dr. Clarke's account of their ascent of Mont Blanc in 1825, and also secured an account of Mr. Auldjo's ascent in 1827, fashioning a moving panorama of the adventure for his sister.[9]

Smith soon switched careers, making his living as a popular and humorous journalist and writer. After an initial trip to Chamonix in September 1838 that led to public lectures on the Alps, he toured Europe, Constantinople, and Egypt in 1849 and afterward developed "The Overland Mail," a successful show combining lecture and visuals at Willis's Rooms in London. Seven months after his Mont Blanc climb, "Mr. Albert Smith's Ascent of Mont Blanc" opened at the Piccadilly in London on March 15, 1852, including a Swiss chalet, Saint Bernard dogs, Alpine milkmaids, chamois

"Mr. Albert Smith's Ascent of Mont Blanc," at the Egyptian
Hall, Piccadilly, *Illustrated London News,* December 25, 1852
(With special thanks to Melanie Kowalski)

sheep, and modern stage technology such as metallic lilies emitting gas and
light.[10] The show ran for more than six years with two thousand performances, earning Smith and his brother, a theater manager at the Piccadilly, an estimated thirty thousand pounds. With slight variations each year
and references to contemporary events, the show included characters such
as two old ladies closing the curtains of their carriage every time they
neared a mountain, an ignorant American tourist confusing Lord Byron
with the Prisoner of Chillon (a figure in his poem), and patter songs such
as "The Young English Traveller." In May 1854, Smith performed before
Queen Victoria and Prince Albert at their summer retreat, and in the
following year he developed popular merchandise such as a board game,
coloring books, and replicas from the show.[11] He also published *The Story
of Mont Blanc* (1853), which depicted earlier attempts and tragedies on the
mountain—including the first ascent and that of Saussure—to culminate
in Smith's own successful climb.

After the Mont Blanc show concluded, Smith traveled to China in 1858, publishing once more an account of his travels, *To China and Back* (1859), as well as producing another Piccadilly show. He married the actress Mary Lucy Keely in August 1959, but their life together was short-lived: Smith died of bronchitis on May 23, 1860, in London.

Compared with Smith, Alfred Wills (twelve years Smith's junior) followed the more traditional mold of a nineteenth-century British mountaineer. Born on December 11, 1828, to the solicitor of Edgbaston, Birmingham, William Wills, and his wife Sarah, he was destined to a career in law. After graduating with highest honors from the University College of London with a bachelor of arts in 1849 and a bachelor of law in 1851, Wills was called to the bar by the Honourable Society of the Middle Temple in London. In the following decades, he married twice, first to Lucy Martineau in 1854, who often accompanied him on his travels and bore him two children, and, after her premature death of a heart condition in 1860, Bertha Taylor in 1861, with whom he fathered three sons and two daughters. As an amateur botanist inspired by Forbes's book, Wills first came to the Alps in 1846 and returned almost every year during his summer vacation, partly to combat his insomnia. In the 1850s and 1860s, he completed numerous ascents, mostly with the Chamonix guide Auguste Balmat, Jacques Balmat's great-nephew, who had helped Forbes conduct his glacier research and also assisted Tyndall during his first Alpine forays in 1857 and 1858.

During these years, Wills developed a keen interest in botany and glaciology, defending Forbes's theories against Tyndall. Wills completed the ascent of the Wetterhorn and also ascended Mont Blanc in 1858 (with Balmat and Tyndall), 1866, and 1873 (with his daughter). After publishing *Wanderings Among the High Alps* (1856), Wills became an inaugural member of the London Alpine Club founded in 1857—as was Smith—and served as its third president from 1864 to 1866. In 1858, after extensive negotiations and against the strong resistance of some local councilmen who feared a Protestant invasion, Wills purchased property in Savoy in the French Alps, where he built a chalet called the Eagle's Nest, to which he returned each summer. His second book, *The Eagle's Nest in the Valley of Sixt: A Summer Home Among the Alps, Together with some Excursions Among the Great Glaciers* (1860), illustrated by his late wife, nostalgically recalls the purchase of the property and his later climbs.

Wills's legal career flourished in the following decades: he was appointed to the Queen's Counsel in 1872, became the first recorder of Sheffield in 1881, and in 1884 was knighted and appointed judge of the High Court, a position he held until his retirement in 1905. Most famously, Wills presided over the trial of Oscar Wilde in 1895, sentencing him to two years' imprisonment with hard labor for committing acts of gross indecency with other males. After his retirement, Wills became a member of the Privy Council and served for two years as president of Hartley University College, Southampton. Sir Alfred Wills passed away on August 9, 1912; a mountain refuge near Chamonix still bears his name.

Texts at the Threshold

Despite their radically different backgrounds, careers, and perspectives, both Smith and Wills helped popularize Alpine climbing to new degrees. Smith showed that even for a common man who had no previous climbing experience, it might be possible to scale a major peak or at least enjoy such scaling vicariously. Wills promoted particular destinations, routes, and peaks, some specifically suited for women. Through their engagement in the Alpine Club, both men staged themselves and their work as constitutive to the beginning of the Golden Age. Through their ties to British corporations—Smith as director of his Piccadilly show and Wills as president of the Railway and Canal Commission—both also made Alpinism a profitable business. Their texts likewise show some unexpected similarities and continuities. Focusing on death and drama, Smith's *Story of Mont Blanc* begins with Dr. Hamel's fatal attempt on the mountain in 1820, sumptuously recounting frostbite, broken limbs, and fractured skulls of previous attempts before turning to "the terrible accident that threw such a frightful interest round the ascents of Mont Blanc" (107). Smith includes eyewitnesses' accounts of the tragic accident when the ascending party was swept away by an avalanche and three guides lost their lives after being carried into a crevasse. With his riveting narration, Smith proves his keen eye for the taste of his time, recognizing the public fascination with, and marketing potential of, mountaineering disasters.

Smith was also among the first to provide a counternarrative to the established discourse of mountaineering, successfully undermining a British upper-crust claim to exclusivity. In contrast to Forbes's and Wills's reverence for Saussure, Smith professed at the outset that he struggled to translate Saussure's four-volume opus from French, assuring readers that "a cheap and excellently-abridged edition of De Saussure can be bought at most of the libraries at Geneva" (vi). In another departure from British tradition, Smith recalls his disappointment at the Mer de Glace on his first travels to the Alps in the late 1830s: "The story that the Mer de Glace resembles the sea suddenly frozen in a storm, is all nonsense. From Montanvert it looks rather like a magnified white ploughed field" (14). When Smith recommends Chamonix as "the nicest place in Europe" (15), he does so on account of its international tourists rather than its natural wonders. Yet despite this populist appeal, Smith anchors his text firmly within the established mountaineering discourse of his time, drawing significantly on previous narratives. The book's second chapter traces the history of Chamonix, referring to Scheuchzer's *Itinera par Helvetiae Alpnas Regiones,* among other works. In chapter 3, Smith provides a brief sketch of Saussure's life and work, complemented by translated excerpts from *Voyages,* and the following chapters dramatically recount the early ascents of Mont Blanc. In chapter 8, Smith compiles a list of Mont Blanc ascents to date, including Henriette d'Angeville's second female ascent (more significant because she was not carried) of the mountain in 1838. Crowning the list with his own ascent in 1851, the account makes a perfect segue into Smith's own ascent and descent, drawn out in a gripping tale spanning the book's five remaining chapters.

In Wills's *Wanderings Among the High Alps,* the narration of the Wetterhorn climb similarly forms the crowning culmination in the final chapters after an extensive buildup. Wills relates in detail a dreadful night on the glacier spent in a stifling cave, an inedible breakfast of meat spiced with garlic (a recurrent theme in Wills's text to which I return later), and skillful technical climbing over slick limestone rock and ice, achieved with the help of crampons, hobnailed boots, and alpenstocks. There is even some last-minute competition when two chamois hunters who had followed Wills's tracks armed with a tree and intending to pass were instead convinced to join the party and, on the summit, planted the tree next to the "Flagge," content with a "second" ascent.

Merging existing discourses in the tradition of Humboldt and Saussure,

Wills's description includes a narrative arc climaxing in the dramatic position of the climbers, the breathtaking views, and the all-consuming sublime sensation on the summit. Beyond that, however, Wills's account abounds with admiration for his guide Lauener, revealing a modern cult of the mountaineer as masculine hero:

> I could not help admiring Lauener's figure, as he stood there, straight as an arrow, more than six feet high, spare, muscular and active, health and vigour glowing in his open and manly countenance, his clear blue eye sparkling with vivacity and good temper, a slight dash of rough and careless swagger in his attitude and manner, which suited well with the wild scenery around, and made him look like the genius of the place.[12]

This quotation introduces a new language that has come a long way since Humboldt's accounts. If Humboldt had described his guides as frightful and weak companions, and Saussure regarded Jacques Balmat as an equal if not superior climbing partner, and Forbes admired the strength and vigor of the local guides, then Wills's depiction furthers Forbes's muscular science in its voyeuristic acclaim. But rather than advancing scientific claims, Wills elevates the rough-hewn mountain man—with chauvinistic undertones—to the epitome of masculinity and virility. This image of the hardy mountain hero as master of his environment will surface in many other narratives, John Tyndall's, Edward Whymper's, and Clarence King's among them. In addition, the emphasis on manliness begins to assume tinges of military poise: Lauener is tall, "straight like an arrow," with striking features resembling a perfect warrior, underscored by the fact that he plants the "Flagge" on the Wetterhorn summit. Wills also mixes some military language into the description of his ascent—"This was the peak we determined to assail" (274)—indicating a subtle shift in the mind-set and narration of mountain climbing.

Despite the conjecture on Lauener, the overriding tone of Wills's depiction remains one of Romantic ecstasy and sublime inspiration rather than virile manliness. When Wills gazes toward the summit at sunset, he feels "stimulated by a pleasing excitement, and filled with all the mingled wonder, delight, and awe, which takes possession of the soul" (280), and at night, the Swiss guides burst into a hymn in German that radiates an "inexpressibly solemn" (283) ambiance. In this way, Wills's account of the Wetterhorn climb reveals the convergence of several shifting mountaineering discourses, from Romantic sublime and scientific measuring to masculine posturing and even military engagement.

Compared with Smith's smashing success, it is easy to overlook Wills's narrative achievements, but after the first publication of *Wanderings Among the High Alps* in 1856, a second edition followed as early as 1858, testifying to the popularity of this travel report and guide. In the preface, Wills professed his aim as twofold: "on the one hand, to convey some idea of the glories of the higher and less accessible regions of the Alps, and if possible to stimulate others to seek those magnificent scenes amongst which I have myself passed some of my happiest days; on the other, to point out some few of the more interesting excursions which lie almost at the traveller's door, at such places as Chamouni and Interlaken; but which, from the routinism or apathy of the inhabitants, are hardly known to themselves— much less to strangers" (vi).

Similar to Smith, Wills sought to promote tourism and traveling but appealed entirely to the touristic interests of a highly educated and well-read upper-middle-class British readership. In the tradition of Swiss writers such as Haller, Rousseau, and Saussure, Wills pictured much of the Swiss scenery along his hikes with awe and delight, logging an established register of the pastoral, such as in his description of the Saas Valley: "Embosomed in this imposing scene of desolation and solitude is the sweetest pastoral valley that ever God created or man enjoyed. The pasture grounds are rich and well-watered; the grass is of the freshest green; trees grow freely and stoutly in the more sheltered spots; corn and flax are safely reared; rough, sunburnt chalets are dotted here and there about the fertile meadows" (122–23). In this pastoral idyll, Alpine peasants conform to the cliché of a morally upright, simple people already evoked in Haller's poem "Die Alpen." This myth is again confirmed when Wills heartily recommends the curé (priest) of the Hotel du Mont Rose, advising that "the pastor of one of these secluded valley is unavoidably a man of narrow means, and it would be absurd to expect in one who belongs essentially to the peasant-class, the kind or degree of refinement which usually marks an educated gentleman" (119–20).

Despite their differences, both Wills and Smith reach for the same literary metaphor by quoting from Byron's *Manfred*, a play written after the author's visit to Chamonix:

> Mont Blanc is the Monarch of Mountains,
> They crowned him long ago;
> On a throne of rocks, in a robe of clouds,
> With a diadem of snow.[13]

In Smith's Mont Blanc show, however, a tourist misquotes Byron, replacing the last two lines with "But who they got to put it on, / We don't exactly know."[14] This parody of the play tellingly diminishes its solemn and foreboding aspects.

In both Smith and Wills, the depictions of virtuous peasants stand in stark contrast to hostile remarks deriding local culture. While Smith describes locals as "people of the humblest grade, who evidently lived upon garlick" (*SMB*, 22), Wills sharpens these remarks: "The natives are so much in the habit of eating garlic, on every possible occasion, that they are quite unable to understand that it can be disagreeable to a traveller" (113). On another occasion, Wills finds himself unable to stomach meat because, to his taste, it has been overseasoned with garlic. Indeed, the (over)use of garlic becomes a recurring theme in the book, culminating in the penultimate chapter when Wills grumbles about eggs "fried in a garlicky pan," bread cut with a knife "that has just been used for chopping garlic," and meat with garlic "scraped over it as it roasted" (340). As a small consolation, he assures his readers that "the rude health enjoyed among the mountains enables you to digest, without inconvenience, food that you would shudder at in England" (340).

At the heels of such contempt for the local cuisine, Wills's descriptions of Swiss villagers range from condescending benevolence to open bigotry, reflecting a modern discourse of British superiority and racial distinction. In the case of the Val d'Anniviers, a place that he never visited, Wills recaps Auguste Balmat's supposed observations about "the natives living in a state of nudity and filth, almost too gross and disgusting to relate" (200), in primitive houses with grimy wooden tables having holes corresponding to the number of household members into which meals are filled. Drawing his own harrowingly prejudiced conclusions, Wills conjectures that this "is too often the case with the fairest spots on earth, inhabited by a race unworthy of such a home" (123). The depictions of the Italian Aosta Valley in both Smith and Wills mirror such discrimination. Smith denounces the place: "Aosta is a miserable place, and the Hôtel de la Couronne dear and dirty. There are some Roman remains, a great deal of frightful *goître,* some poor shops, and all the church clocks strike the hours twice over" (*SMB,* 21). Wills deepens the racist bias when he describes the Val d'Aosta as "one of the loveliest and most fertile valleys in the north of Italy; but it is inhabited by a stunted race, afflicted with goiter and cretinism, to an extent which contrasts painfully with the charms of the scenery" (220). Contrasting the citizens of the Italian Alps with those living in the French- and German-speaking portions, Wills opines about Samoëns in the French Alps: "No squalid buildings meet the eye, no stunted forms whose cowering aspect speaks of want and misery. The men are a fine, broad-shouldered race; the women strong and healthy."[15] And he elevates the inhabitants of the Saas Valley as having "short faces, small noses, white teeth, determined through good humoured mouths, full cheeks, blue eyes and light hair" (123), finding the men "manlier, the women finer and more shapely and good-looking," and the houses "more comfortable and better kept" (123). In these discriminatory comparisons, appearance and character traits are determined based on the colonial bias of a north-south divide, a direction later continued in Edward Whymper's *Scrambles Amongst the Alps* (1871).

At a time when Alpine communities were changing greatly owing to booming tourism, Wills outlined several tours and provided tips and guidance on the quality and cleanliness of inns. His later *The Eagle's Nest* continued this practice, naming particular hotels, landlords, and even rooms, as well as dishes (not) to order. Wills demands nothing short of British standards for tea, coffee, and game, and he eagerly names the accommodations that have adjusted to British tastes. He remains confident that even in lesser-known valleys, businesses would soon adapt to the new economic opportunities: "These valleys [the Saas Valley], however, are becoming so much more visited than they were a few years ago, that I have little doubt that, before long, all these little discomforts [i.e., the garlicky cuisine] will have been remedied" (113). In the case of the southern regions, such as the dreaded Aosta Valley, he retains his biases while leaving modest room for improvement: "Among such a population, it is vain to hope for decency or cleanliness; and, as far my experiences goes, I have found the innkeepers as dishonest as they are dirty. It is very likely, however, that even here, great improvements may be made, in a few years, if they be not already taking place" (221). For laymen mountaineers, Wills readily advertises particular destinations: "I cannot understand why the ascent of the Torrenthorn is not more constantly made. If it were in the neighbourhood of Interlaken or Chamouni, an inn would be built at the top, and numerous parties would sleep here, to witness the sunset and sunrise" (230). In the same vein, he outlines possible future pathways that could accommodate easier travel to sites of interest, such as a trail leading from the base of the Aiguille de Charmoz to the Mer de Glace (85).

Despite his general promotion of tourism, Wills at times bemoans the presence of travelers from nations other than Britain. Specifically, he quips about the presence of six rude and noisy German students during a stop-over below the Saint Bernard Pass, and he is quick to generalize: "As far as my experience goes, it is very unfavourable to the class of German students one meets travelling in Switzerland, in parties of six or eight together" (63). However, the encounter is soon outdone by the arrival of Italians. Wills continues in familiar stereotypes: "There is hardly a more agreeable person to be found than the well-bred and well-educated Italian gentleman . . . but the inferior order of Italians, such as you not unfrequently meet on passes like the St. Bernard, which are much used for business purposes, or on the great diligence roads of the Simplon or the St. Gothard—persons of the class of small tradespeople and commercial travelers—are, almost without exception, a very disagreeable set. These people were noisy, dirty, spitting, and generally ill-conditioned. One of them beat all men I have ever seen, in the nastiness of his way of smoking" (63–64). Aside from their smoking, Wills decries the Germans' and Italians' alcohol consumption, once more drawing a class-based distinction.

Conversely, Wills found himself to be the victim of national prejudice and stereotyping when attempting to purchase property in the Valley of Sixt. Specifically, he faced the opposition of the local curé, who, in the spirit of clerical dominance in his parish and backed by the Sardinian adminis-tration, had convinced the majority of councilmen to oppose the purchase. In his second book, Wills carefully noted the perceived objections: "There would be a protestant crusade in the valley; domestic purity would suffer even more severely than religious orthodoxy; one intruder would give rise to another, and their 'montagnes' . . . would be cut up into building patches to satisfy the vagaries of English taste; then the cattle and goats would stray over the land of this English aristocrat, who could impound them and refuse to release them except upon payment of exorbitant compensation."[16] Despite the overblown fantasies, Wills successfully purchased the property the following year with the help of the local secretary and found locals to hold no ill will toward him. Nonetheless, the claims about religious conversion, moral decay, Anglicizing, a building boom, and food insecurity identify some of the tensions rising from increasing British tourism and its effects.

Despite the book's overall purpose as travel guide, scientific interests continue to play an important role in Wills's text: giving evidence to the recently accepted glacier theories, as well as the extent to which its vocabulary entered the educated class, he mentions roches moutonnées, erratic blocks, and terminal moraines, and the book's final chapter, "Glacier Action and Glacier Theories," provides a succinct summary of glaciology from Saussure to Forbes. Wills credits Saussure, the "great philosopher and naturalist" (351), mentions various vegetation zones on Chimborazo and Cotopaxi in reference to Humboldt, and delineates Agassiz's 1839 and 1840 research at the "Hôtel des Neuchâtelois" and Forbes's results from his 1842 studies at the Mer de Glace. As the sequencing indicates, Wills gives preference to Forbes's notion of a glacier behaving like a fluid, moving faster at its center than its sides, a theory with which Wills concurs owing to Forbes's "mathematically accurate experiments" (361) after disproving Saussure's gravitation theory and Agassiz's dilatation theory. Wills also remarks on the local flora and goes to great lengths to include in each chapter botanical notes on collected specimens, information complemented by an extensive register of plants found at various locations, listed by botanical nomenclature, in the appendix. This information, which by Wills's own admission came from his friend the botanist James Atkins, who accompanied him on an Alpine tour in 1852, anchors Wills's text further in the scientific tradition. Without scientific contributions of his own, Wills's volume therefore gives a nod to the botanists, geologists, and glaciologists who frequented the Alps in the past decades and pays tribute to their findings.

Wills equally recognizes the aesthetic tradition of sublime rapture. As becomes evident in the obligatory accolades, however, the concept of the sublime has moved past its heyday. Wills cannot help but reiterate by now established clichés, a tendency that especially comes to the fore in his descriptions of sights and views. If early on in his text he admittedly borrowed from Saussure to admire the "uncommon brilliancy" of the stars that "hang out of a sky of ebony" (8), he later resorts to a number of repetitions, such as the "sublime" prospect of particular scenes (repeated six times), the "sublimest" view (repeated three times), and the "sublimity" of nature (repeated four times). Furthermore, he marvels at the "glorious" day or view (repeated eleven times), standing in "awe" (repeated eight times) before "grand" scenery (repeated five times) on the "grandest" (repeated nine times) expeditions. All these characterizations are topped by the term "magnificent," which appears no less than twenty-four times in the text. These reiterations indicate that by the mid-1800s, the terminology of describing Alpine scenes was already somewhat exhausted, recycling Romantic terminology and drifting into the commonplace.

Wills solves this dilemma by systematically including literary quotes of mountain glory. If Humboldt, Forbes, and Agassiz included the occasional literary reference or citation, Wills in *Wanderings,* as well as in his later *Eagle's Nest,* prefaces each chapter with one or two epigraphs, ranging from Sophocles, Euripides, Homer, Lucretius, Horace, and Virgil to a heavy emphasis on British Romantic poets such as James Thomson, Ebenezer Elliott, Samuel Roberts, William Wordsworth, Samuel Taylor Coleridge, Percy Bysshe Shelley, Lord Byron, and Thomas Moore, as well as Johann Wolfgang von Goethe. These quotes affirm Wills's firm grasp of classical European eighteenth- and nineteenth-century *Bildung,* as well as his projected educated readership. A quote from Ebenezer Elliott's poem "Vernal Walk" (1798), "Look all around! behold one boundless scene / Of beauty, wildness and sublimity!" (188), provides a poetic grounding to Wills's own exaltations in nature, as it prefaces a chapter on various excursions around Zermatt. At the same time, quotes by Wordsworth and Shelley lend the sometimes cursory and factual descriptions of Wills's mountain adventures a deeper layer of Romantic mystery, terror, and awe. In this way, Wills's description of the Col du Géant passage gives matter-of-fact advice on guides, travel routes, and costs involved, but the preceding quote from Shelley's "Mont Blanc" (1817) creates a tantalizing tension: "Frost and the Sun, in scorn of mortal power / Have piled: dome, pyramid and pinnacle." In other instances, the quotes underscore a literal meaning, as in chapter 6, where Wills prefaces his description of a challenging and time-consuming descent from the Col Imseng back to Zermatt with a quote from Wordsworth's "The Excursion" (1814): "So, to a steep and difficult descent / Trusting ourselves, we wound from crag to crag / Where passage could be won" (155). In a similar vein, the famous words by Horace, "Noctes cœnæque Deûm!" (nights and suppers of the gods), precede chapter 2, which details an overnight encampment with his wife (33).

Fittingly, one of the final chapters, "Hints for Pedestrians," is prefaced by a quote from Goethe's *Faust* in both German and English translation, when Faust, on their hike to the Walpurgis Night, rejects Mephistopheles's request for a broomstick, wanting to continue by foot: "While I'm still fresh upon my legs and gay, / I find this knotted stick enough. / What good is shortening one's way? / To trudge along the winding valley's shoulder, / Then to climb up this rugged boulder, / Whence ever plunging torrent hurls its spray, / This is what lends such paths their zest and charm!"[17] Goethe's words highlight Wills's plea to travel by foot rather than by carriage once in Switzerland, thereby underscoring the book's title and emphasis on "wandering." According to Wills, physical exertion and immersion lead to a deeper and more encompassing travel experience. Notably, such an argument also begins to make a case for climbing as an activity in itself, a sport that does not have to be justified by reasons of science, aesthetics, or even conquest. While not departing from its literary and scientific roots, Wills thus expands a mountaineering discourse created by Humboldt, Saussure, and Forbes and points ahead to Leslie Stephen's philosophy of embracing the difficulties encountered as well as the skills involved.

Accordingly, Wills keeps readers in suspense by mentioning the dangers of yawning chasms and hidden crevasses, slippery ice, loose rocky slopes, and unpredictable weather, but he also draws attention to successful strategies to combat these adversities. For instance, the alpenstock assists travelers by enabling them to examine hidden crevasses—such a valuable tool that Wills readily employs a military metaphor, "a mountaineer leaving his alpenstock among the mountains feels like a soldier leaving his musket on the field" (178–79)—and Balmat screws four iron claws into his boots to facilitate the ascent and descent of snow and ice slopes. Finally, Wills remarks on the quick and skillful art of descending by glissading, referencing a more detailed description of the maneuver in Smith's *The Story of Mont Blanc*. In the final chapter, Wills also provides advice on what to bring, where to dine and lodge, and even how to press flowers. Here we find some startling similarities between Wills's and Smith's texts: while Smith likewise promoted pedestrianism but cautioned that "pedestrians must not expect to find everything *couleur de rose*. Trivial annoyances of every description will be constantly starting up" (28), advising flexibility and laughter to combat disturbances, Wills approaches the topic more systematically, compiling a list of necessities that include a thermometer, telescope, compass, journal, books, screws to be nailed into one's boots, and the alpenstock. Going further, he provides specific information about where to purchase the best knapsacks in London, complete with shoes, socks, and hats to combat the dangers of sunburn. Smith, on the other hand, had decried the knapsacks sold in London as "utterly useless," advocating instead a "soldier's old knapsack" (27) purchased in Paris, with the essential items of a knife, string, and sticking plaster.

A Climb for the Ladies

In addition to these practical considerations, Smith and especially Wills begin to outline new directions in mountaineering texts: they emphasize the benefits of health, acknowledge and advocate the presence of female climbers, and explicitly discuss the politics of guides and guiding. Already Haller and Saussure had mentioned the Alps' healthy air, and Forbes had backed these arguments with references to his increased physical strength in the mountains. Wills specifically advertises a six-week tour in the Alps as a guarantee for improved health, both physically and mentally. In particular, he promotes "pedestrianism" in the Alps as "healthful and manly exercise" in the mountain air, "the finest tonic in all the pharmacopoeia of nature," which brings "strength to the weak, fresh energy to the jaded," and "calm, unbroken slumbers, which no dreams disturb and no restlessness interrupts" (317). In *The Eagle's Nest*, Wills reaffirms, "The restoring effect of the glacier air is wonderful," presenting his own refreshed health as an example.[18] In *The Story of Mont Blanc*, Smith had likewise endorsed the benefits of health when comparing "our bustling, smoky, dusty London to my beloved Chamouni" (36).

Despite his promotion of traveling and hiking, Wills claims exclusivity for skilled mountaineering such as the Wetterhorn ascent, deeming it not suitable for anyone "not tolerably familiar with Alpine climbing, or who had not had practice and experience enough to know whether he could safely trust his head and his nerves" (313). While reserving such attempts for experienced men only, Wills was among the first to provide guidance on how "ladies might see much more of the grander scenery of the High Alps than they usually do" (vii). In *The Story of Mont Blanc*, Smith had recommended as "the most interesting excursion" (138) from Chamonix an overnight stay at the so-called Jardin de Talèfre (2,787 m/9,144 ft.), a vegetated spot in a cirque of the Glacier de Talèfre that could be reached by crossing the lower part of the Mer de Glace. Smith reports: "We were told that, now and then, young ladies were found bold enough to make the attempt . . . although the expedition is certainly one not particularly calculated for females to undertake," pronouncing, "We were rather pleased than annoyed at hearing that the majority of the fair adventurers were English girls" (148–49). Indeed, wealthy women had begun venturing to the Mer de Glace: Sophie La Roche, the first German woman who, like others of similar social status, was mostly carried to the glacier on an armchair, attested in her published diary description from 1787 that tours of this sort were gaining popularity, especially among British women.[19] The Chamonix local Marie Paradis was the first woman to summit Mont Blanc in 1808, though she was also partially carried by guides. Thirty years later, Henriette d'Angeville became the second woman to summit the mountain, making the climb entirely by her own strength.

In *Wanderings*, Wills chose the same route Smith mentioned for an overnight trip to the Mer de Glace in the company of his wife Lucy, using the experience to offer ample advice for women to participate in—albeit modest—mountain travel. Professing his "growing desire to introduce my wife to some of the wilder and grander features of glacier scenery, and to give her a little insight into what exploring the recesses of the High Alps really involved" (34), Wills pushed for female companionship. His chapter describing the endeavor is fittingly preceded by a poem written by a woman: "The Rock of Cader Idris" (1822), by the English poet Felicia Hemans (1793–1835), describing in Romantic fashion the intense experience of nature during a night in the open. In the chapter itself, Wills prides himself

"Overnight Trip to the Mer de Glace," drawing based on a sketch by
Lucy Wills, from *Wanderings Among the High Alps*, 40 (Internet Archive)

in his skillful preparation for the trip, beginning with securing an excellent
guide "who is something of a gentleman, as well as familiar with the ice,
and whose tact and refinement will make him an acceptable companion
where ladies are of the party" (58), bringing along a tempting spread of
food, arranging mattresses, sheets, and blankets for a comfortable night,
and even letting his wife use the coffeepot for her morning ablutions.

On the glacier itself, Lucy drew sketches that eventually provided the
pencil drawings used for the four illustrations in Wills's book. One of these
shows her sitting at the edge of a glacier while Wills and two other companions busy themselves gathering firewood and preparing the night quarters. Though Wills seems somewhat surprised that "my wife proved herself
a capital mountaineer" (38), he takes full credit for the successful undertaking, concluding: "Thirty or forty years ago, two ladies, and a year or two
back, a gentleman and his daughter, crossed the Col du Géant . . . but,
with these exceptions, I believe no lady, before or since, had ever spent a
night on the bare mountain side. We have shown that the thing is practi-
cable, and I hope our example will not long want followers"(56). A later
chapter details another excursion to the Torrenthorn and Gemmi Pass

that Wills undertook together with his wife. Here he provides advice on when the lady should dismount her mule, lauding the view with the only caveat that "not a single lake is to be seen in any direction" (229). Once again, Wills also provides ample time for his wife to sketch, even improvising a paintbrush from his own hair after the proper brush was dropped.

Guides and Friends

In another novel turn, Wills dedicates *Wanderings* to his guide Auguste Balmat, "my tried and faithful companion, in many difficulties and some danger," who, twenty years Wills's senior, had already guided Forbes in the Alps. Two years later, in *The Eagle's Nest*, Wills does not even call Balmat his guide anymore: "I was accompanied by my friend August Balmat."[20] In 1858 Wills even gave Balmat the power of attorney when purchasing his home in the Alps and cared for Balmat during his last months in 1862 before his passing in October of the same year.

These examples not only depict the intimate relationship between clients and guides but also show that the role of Swiss mountain guides was undergoing significant changes. Thanks to trade unions, the guide-client relationship became tightly regulated, especially in Chamonix, at the time part of the Kingdom of Sardinia. The Compagnie des Guides de Chamonix imposed a strict rotation that prevented British travelers from choosing their own guides in advance. Already Smith had mentioned, "The guides at Chamouni are now re-organized, and are obliged to go out with travelers in their turn" (vi). Wills also bemoaned this rule, as well as that the number of guides to be taken and their charge was dictated by the Compagnie.

Although these rules relaxed somewhat in the following years, they hint at the burgeoning popularity of hiking and mountaineering, and growing opportunities to profit from this boom, as well as a newfound self-confidence among guides, who recognized their crucial importance in the business. If Smith named the guides he deemed most capable but offered no advice for circumventing the regulations, Wills, as a judge, recognizes that "the guides of Chamouni are a kind of corporation, governed by their own bye-laws, which are capable of being enforced by legal process," choosing to circumvent what he calls "absurd" rules (2). Indeed, it is Balmat who helps Wills to bypass some of the regulations when the two agree to travel over the Col de Voza pass, outside the jurisdiction of Chamonix, to hire Balmat and avoid the assignment of an unknown guide. Wills offers advice on how many guides are needed under what circumstances, what they are to be paid, and how they are to be treated, also pointing out that a good guide can save his client money by securing better deals at inns and carriages. He also opines on the issue of food for the guides, assuring the reader that "they are content with very simple fare," but at the same time recommends serving guides the same fare as everyone, "to promote that kindly feeling and good fellowship amongst the party, on which so much of the pleasure of the expedition must depend" (31). Time and again, Wills emphasizes the utmost importance of a guide who ideally is "a very intelligent man . . . with manners more like those of a gentleman than are to be found amongst men of any other class" while at the same time "a sort of personal servant, almost a valet," who "will risk his life to save yours" (330). This ideal guide, accordingly, was expected to conform to British middle-class standards and uphold a refined conversation; at the same time, however, he was not to overstep his role as a servant whose life was always worth less than a client's. Thus in Wills's time, the guide-client relationship, fraught with tension, reflected both the expectations of England's upper middle class and the Swiss guides' savvy efforts to adapt to new economic opportunities.

Wills's text stands at a threshold. While he sticks to customary and by now commonplace if not clichéd tropes of sublimity, mystery, and ecstasy, he acknowledges if not celebrates the fact that tourism has already profoundly shaped the Alpine landscape. Some of his quotes, from Wordsworth's poem on the Jungfrau, "The virgin mountain, wearing, like a queen, / A crown of everlasting snow" (240), or from Thomson's "The Seasons," "These lonely regions, where, retired, / From little scenes of art, great nature dwells / In awful solitude, and nought is seen" (254), thus pose an odd contrast to the chapters they preface. Although the Romantic quotations celebrate a spiritual experience in solitude, Wills actually designed his book as a hands-on travel guide with the express goal of stimulating British tourism: each chapter concludes with a summary of the advantages of the specific tour, the costs involved, the required level of fitness, advice on guides, and more. Adding further discrepancies, Wills revels in hegemonic masculinity while promoting women's climbing; embraces both sportsmanship and the militarization used in mountaineering language; and furthers stereotypes of Alpine villagers while also setting a notable example by treating his guide Balmat as a valued friend.

Along with Smith's *The Ascent of Mont Blanc,* Wills's book thus testifies to the manifold and evolving mountaineering discourses and aptly foreshadows developments to come. In this vein, it is no coincidence that Wills mentions, as many as eight times, the view of "the tremendous, indescribable peak of the Matterhorn" (193), "an object which never failed to fill me with astonishment and awe" (171). Proving that the Matterhorn was already imagined as the pinnacle of an alluring yet still improbably difficult ascent, *Wanderings* anticipates the highly charged and contested race for the peak's first ascent that was to take place in the 1860s.

CHAPTER 7

POETIC SCIENCE AND

COMPETITIVE VIGOR

John Tyndall and Edward Whymper

Race to the Matterhorn

On his second attempt of the Matterhorn's Italian Ridge from Breuil in July 1862, John Tyndall and his guides Johann Joseph Bennen and Anton Walter, with the cousins Jean-Antoine and Cesar Carrel as porters, advanced to some 230 meters below the mountain's summit. All had gone well thus far, and after exchanging some cordial words with Edward Whymper, who was descending from his own, unsuccessful attempt, the party had even been able to use Whymper's tent, still pitched on the mountain. However, on top of the mountain's southwest ridge, now called Pic Tyndall (4,241 m/13,914 ft.), a deep cleft separated the climbers from the final cliffs, halting their progress. Tyndall's initial confidence quickly shattered, and bitterly disappointed, he opted to turn around amid a "tempest of hail . . . as if the Matterhorn, not content with shutting its door in our faces, meant to add an equivalent to the process of kicking us downstairs."[1]

Three years later, on July 14, 1865, shortly before 2 p.m., Whymper and his spur-of-the-moment team of four climbers and three guides raced to the mountain's prized summit via its Swiss side after eight unsuccessful attempts on the Italian side from Breuil. To mark their success, they planted a makeshift flag made from one of Whymper's tent poles and his guide Michel Croz's shirt. After this moment of triumph, however, tragedy befell the team. On their descent, Douglas Hadow, a young and particularly inexperienced member of the group, slipped and knocked Croz off his feet, dragging two more climbers downslope before the rope broke between four people, who tumbled to their deaths, and the three remaining men, Whymper and two guides, Peter Taugwalder and his son of the same name.[2] While this accident has received plenty of attention in both popular and academic culture, the stakes of competitive masculinities at play in the various Matterhorn climbs, as well Tyndall's and Whymper's differing backgrounds, perspectives, and rationales for climbing, deserve to be fleshed out further. This chapter delves deeper into their respective texts to uncover the mixture of science, aesthetics, competition, and contest, and to elucidate contrasting yet sometimes similar attitudes. Both Tyndall and Whymper harken back to previous scientific and aesthetic discourses on mountains but also engage in the summit-driven quest for first ascents that came to characterize twentieth-century mountaineering, acting as important hinges in a transitional moment.

Notwithstanding their superficially convivial relationship, the competition between Tyndall and Whymper ran deep: already in 1861 Whymper professed to be excited by only two peaks "which had remained virgin," the Weisshorn (4,506 m/14,783 ft.) and the Matterhorn (4,478 m/14,692 ft.).[3] Upon learning that Tyndall had climbed the higher Weisshorn, Whymper admitted, "My interest in the Weisshorn abated" (37), and he intensified his efforts on the Matterhorn. And when offering his tent to Tyndall in the episode described earlier, Whymper, by his own admission "tormented with envy and all uncharitableness," remained nearby, fearing that "they carried off the prize for which I had been so long struggling" (113). In *Scrambles Amongst the Alps* (1871), Whymper later offered a detailed analysis of Tyndall's failure, reasoning that Tyndall's guide Bennen was too timid to push on (in the previous year, Bennen had declared the Matterhorn an impossible peak); that his second guide Walter yielded to Bennen; and that the Carrels, though they were the group's most accomplished climbers and capable of circumventing the cleft, declined to help because they were only hired as porters, not guides, and wanted to claim the summit for themselves.

Tyndall, for his part, refuted this analysis in an "Additional Note" published in the second edition of *Hours of Exercise in the Alps* (1871), bemoaning Whymper's "inaccuracies" and "general tone towards myself."[4] Here Tyndall also revealed that he had invited Whymper to take part in the 1862 attempt, but Whymper behaved in a manner "the reverse of reasonable" by demanding to lead the expedition.[5]

On his successful summit bid, Whymper made a number of consequential mistakes as well: blinded by his zeal, he rushed onto the mountain as soon as getting word that the Carrels, together with Quintino Sella, the Italian minister of finance and founder of the Italian Alpine Club, had set out on July 10 to claim the mountain for Italy.[6] Whymper, by his own words "a general without an army," hastily put together a large party of available climbers and guides in an attempt "to outmanœuvre the Italians" (354). After running into Lord Francis Douglas and convincing him to join the team—if only because Douglas had hired the guide Peter Taugwalder and was unwilling to dispense with him—Whymper hired Taugwalder, along with his father (called Old Peter), as well as his longtime friend Michel Croz as the most experienced guide. Whymper also came across two other Brits, Charles Hudson and Douglas Hadow, whom he likewise invited to join. Competitive nationalism with the Carrels clouded Whymper's judgment in putting together such a large party of unknown climbers and guides. Luckily, the climb on the Matterhorn's Swiss side proved much easier than expected, and the party made relatively quick and easy progress, despite some of the climbers' inexperience. Still fearing that the Italians arriving from the other side had beaten him to the top, only on the summit was Whymper reassured that his was indeed the first ascent. Spotting the Italians a thousand feet below, he promptly responded by hurling down "a torrent of stones" (365) toward the Italians to announce his victory.

Later, however, Whymper was terribly shaken and devastated by the ensuing accident, which resulted in the loss of his favorite guide Croz as well as three Englishmen. He blamed the accident on Old Peter Taugwalder's unintentional use of an old rope that "should not have been employed, for the purpose for which it was used" (372). In addition to the weak rope, the roping arrangement proved most unfortunate, since Croz, the most experienced climber, descended first rather than last, where he would have had a better chance of catching a fall. In his book, Whymper cast the disaster in military terms: "So the traditional inaccessibility of the Matterhorn was vanquished, and was replaced by legends of a more real character. . . . It proved to be a stubborn foe; it resisted long, and gave many a hard blow; it was defeated at last with an ease that none could have anticipated, but, like a relentless enemy—conquered but not crushed—it took terrible vengeance" (378).

Upon his return to London nine days later, Whymper was publicly vilified and blamed, both for the accident and for the follies of climbing in general. Whymper defended himself in a letter published in the *Times,* offering a minute description and analysis of what had happened. In an overall defeatist tone, Whymper speculated that had the rope not broken, the entire party would have fallen to their deaths, and emphasized that he had suggested leaving a rope tied to rocks for the down climb.[7] There is no triumph in summiting the Matterhorn, not even a description of the descent. In his later *Scrambles Amongst the Alps* (1871), a book continually revised, polished, and amended, with a large number of wood engravings making it the finest of its kind, Whymper offered a thorough reworking of his description of the climb, focusing much on his rivalry with "Professor Tyndall."

Upon hearing of the tragic accident, Tyndall rushed to Zermatt to propose an ambitious if not harebrained plan to recover the still missing body of Lord Douglas, which would have involved Tyndall climbing the mountain, then being lowered thousands of feet to the site of the accident; on account of the weather and protest by the guides, this plan never materialized. In 1867, finally, Tyndall, with the Maquignaz brothers as guides, completed the seventh ascent of the Matterhorn and its first traverse by ascending the Italian Ridge from Breuil in Italy and descending the Hörnli Ridge into Zermatt. In his *Hours of Exercise in the Alps* (1871), published in the same year as Whymper's *Scrambles* and Leslie Stephen's *The Playground of Europe,* the actual summit experience occupies less than half a page, with no description of triumphant feelings or an expansive view. Tyndall only notes the footprints of some climbers (the party of Julius Elliot) who had made the ascent a couple days earlier. After the party "stood for a moment silently and earnestly looking down towards Zermatt" (286), they had an obligatory bite to eat and gulp of wine before they descended, spending no more than fifteen minutes on the summit.

On their way down, they passed the scene of the 1865 disaster. Tyndall ponders about future accidents and soon turns to philosophizing when considering the ongoing geologic changes at hand. For Tyndall, witnessing the Matterhorn's jagged cliffs, rocks, and debris stirs feelings not of fear or awe but rather of sadness: "Hacked and hurt by time, the aspect of the mountain from its higher crags saddened me. Hitherto the impression that is made was that of savage strength, but here we had inexorable decay" (291). The overall melancholic tone of the ascent contrasts starkly with Whymper's and Tyndall's previous vigor, though Tyndall subtly continues the competition by stressing that for his 1862 attempt he had "a rope specially manufactured in London, and guaranteed by its maker to bear a far greater strain than was ever likely to be thrown upon it" (154). Drawing another contrast to Whymper's crude and virile language and attitude, Tyndall marvels reverently, "The Matterhorn, in fact, was our temple, and we approached it with feelings not unworthy of so great a shrine" (156). In turn, Whymper deftly passed over Tyndall's Matterhorn traverse in the fifth edition of *Scrambles*, published in 1900. While giving due credit to the Carrels' successful ascent of the Italian Ridge three days after his first ascent, and elaborating on other ascents in his final chapter, "Subsequent History of the Matterhorn," Whymper relegates Tyndall's achievement to merely two short sentences, greatly diminishing the importance of his contribution.

Two Untraditional Climbers

Although Tyndall and Whymper have come to define Alpine mountaineering in the latter half of the nineteenth century and beyond, neither of them fit the conventional mold of British climbers. Coming from a lower- and lower-middle-class background, respectively, both were acutely aware of the not-so-fine distinctions between themselves and their often privileged climbing fellows. Tyndall was born on August 2, 1822, in Leighlinbridge, Ireland, into a poor Protestant family of five children (of whom only two survived).[8] His mother, Sarah McAssey, was the daughter of a farmer; his father, John Tyndall, was an impoverished shoemaker and part-time policeman who raised their son in the Protestant faith, with a great emphasis on education.

With no access to a university education, Tyndall began working at age nineteen, first as a surveyor in Ireland and later as a railway engineer in England, where he met his longtime friend, the considerably younger Thomas Archer Hirst (1830–91), who also worked on railway surveying. In 1847 Tyndall accepted a teaching post in mathematics at the Queenwood College boarding school in Hampshire, where he met fellow teacher and chemist Edward Frankland (1825–99), who knew the German chemist Robert Bunsen and often spoke of the excellent education in Germany. After one year of teaching, both men decided to depart for Marburg, Germany, to continue their education under Bunsen—although Tyndall barely knew any German. Hirst followed Tyndall's example the following year by studying mathematics, physics, and chemistry in Marburg. After completing his doctorate, Tyndall remained in Germany, pursuing research at the University of Marburg and later Gustav Magnus's laboratory in Berlin. Here he was granted an audience with Alexander von Humboldt, who was apparently quite taken by Tyndall and handed him an inscribed copy of one of his books—Tyndall, on the other hand, later complained that he could barely get a word in.[9] Tyndall returned to England in 1851, determined to establish himself in the scientific community. While resuming his post at Queenwood—soon followed once more by Hirst—he published papers and attended meetings of the British Association, getting to know fellow scientists such as Michael Faraday (1791–1867) and Thomas Huxley (1825–95). As a newly elected fellow of the Royal Society, Tyndall gave a rousing first lecture in London at the Royal Institution in February 1853 and was promptly offered the position of professor of natural philosophy at the same institution.

Founded in 1799, the Royal Institution from 1852 to 1867 was headed by Faraday, one of the most important scientists of his time, who also came from a working-class background. The institution employed a number of scientists who, in exchange for use of the library and basement laboratories, gave afternoon lectures to amateurs and students, as well as "Friday Evening Discourses" for paying members, an audience of up to a thousand people of London's social elite who could afford membership. The job suited Tyndall well: by all accounts, he was a riveting lecturer who delivered as many as fifty-five discourses and even more afternoon lectures to which fellow scientists, the high society, and laymen alike flocked in great numbers. Owing to his anxiety, Tyndall meticulously prepared his lectures and left nothing to chance, performing experiments with precision and paying as much attention to his lecturing style as to the content. Working first as Faraday's assistant, Tyndall eventually became his successor in leading the Royal Institution after Faraday's death. In later years, he received honorary degrees from Cambridge, Edinburgh, Oxford, and Trinity College and was elected into almost forty scientific societies in Europe and beyond.

As a member of the X-Club, a group of nine scholars (including his friends Hirst and Frankland) who met regularly in London over dinner and, following Darwin, lobbied for the support of science education, Tyndall advocated an education for everyone, regardless of social status and class; he also gave evening lectures at the Royal School of Mines in London, to an audience of mostly working-class men. Heralding the education he received at Marburg as an exemplary model, he not only supported the establishment of a doctorate degree in physics at the University of London but also suggested that science education for the working class would help advance society as a whole: "Besides this, our factories and our foundries present an extensive field of observation, and were those who work in them rendered capable, by previous culture, of *observing* what they *see*, the results might be incalculable. . . . Grant these Samsons sight, and you multiply the chances of discovery, and with them the prospects of national advancement."[10] In this vein, a grounding in basic physics, such as electricity, magnetism, optics, and heat, would prepare students for the advancements of a modern world that included the electric telegraph, telescopes, microscopes, photography, and the steam engine, which today has become a symbol of the Anthropocene.

Twenty years Tyndall's junior, Edward Whymper was born on April 27, 1840, to the wood engraver Josiah Wood Whymper and the orphan Elizabeth Claridge, mother of eleven children, who died shortly after giving birth to her last child, when Edward, the second born, was nineteen. Like Tyndall, Whymper grew up accustomed to financial hardship, with a keen awareness of class divisions. The family had arrived from Holland in the seventeenth century as part of a group known as Dissenters—that is, devout Baptists who insisted on strict moral codes, biblical rules, and patriarchal authority. Whymper's father, Josiah, opened his own wood-engraving business in London, changing his name from Whimper to Whymper to appear more British. Combining aspects of woodcuts and metal engraving by using the harder end grain of boxwood, which allowed for finer lines and more detail, wood engraving proliferated throughout the nineteenth century, as engraved wood blocks could fit into letter presses (metal plates could not), allowing for the printing of image and text on the same page. Thanks to the ever increasing demand for printed books, Whymper's business slowly rose to success, though it continued to be vulnerable to periodic upswings and downswings. For tradesmen, upward mobility into the middle class was challenging, but Josiah eventually worked for reputable publishers such as John Murray and William Longman and later also became known as a watercolor painter. When his son Edward turned fourteen, it was decided that he should enter the family's engraving business rather than continue school. As an apprentice of his father, Whymper was unenthusiastic, passing his free time by watching cricket and horse racing and devouring sensational news, as detailed in his diaries from 1855 to 1859. But as he became more financially independent, self-reliant, and gained physical strength, Whymper indulged in dreams of fame and glory. In 1858 he twice attended Albert Smith's Mont Blanc show, which fully satisfied his high expectations and might have fueled his quest for mountain adventures.[11]

Alpine Beginnings

In July 1860, the publisher William Longman, a member of the Alpine Club and editor of its journal, commissioned young Whymper to fashion some sketches of the Dauphiné Alps for a forthcoming publication. With no mountain experience whatsoever, Whymper first visited well-known tourist sites such as the baths of Leuk, the Visp Valley, and Zermatt before passing through Breuil and Chamonix. Though he appears to have been unmoved by the Matterhorn ("grand it is, but beautiful I think it is not"), he met Leslie Stephen in Zermatt, following him and his brother across the Grimsel Pass.[12] Whymper also ventured beyond well-known sites, crossing glaciers and climbing passes and minor peaks with veritable challenges along his way. While the trip yielded no major achievement, to Whymper's own admission it sparked his "passion for mountain-climbing" (19). To complete his assignment, he then hurried to Mont Pelvoux, sketching the peak and witnessing Professor Bonney's unsuccessful attempt at the summit. Longman was sufficiently happy with the drawings that he commissioned Whymper again next summer.

Tyndall's first visit to the Alps had happened a good decade earlier, when he embarked with his friend Hirst on a first Alpine holiday in August 1849 while still studying in Germany. To save money, the two men traveled by foot via Heidelberg to Basel, Zurich, and Bern, though at the time Tyndall was not interested in mountaineering and would not return for another seven years.[13] After he read Forbes's *Travels Through the Alps of Savoy* in 1856 at Huxley's suggestion, Tyndall's interest in glaciology was piqued when he suspected that his research on the cleavage of slate might be related to the structure of ice described by Forbes: "In order to appreciate Forbes's theory I must see what *he* has seen."[14] He decided to travel to the Alps en route to the meeting of the Deutsche Naturforscher Versammlung in Vienna that same year, accompanied by Frankland, Huxley, and the botanist Joseph Dalton Hooker. Following in the footsteps of Agassiz and Forbes, Tyndall visited the Jungfrau glaciers, the by then ruined Hôtel des Neuchâtelois, the Mer de Glace, and saw the Matterhorn, becoming passionately involved in both mountain climbing and glaciers. "Next day we engaged a guide and ascended the slope which bounds the glacier. It was most beautiful, and most instructive. . . . But there was a scientific pleasure superadded."[15] In the following year, he returned to the Mer de Glace to continue his research studies and built on the works of Charpentier, Agassiz, and Forbes. Quickly becoming known both for his devoted work and for his athletic and daring feats, Tyndall was elected into the Alpine Club soon after its founding in 1857.

With his gregarious personality, Tyndall entered the scientific debates on the nature of glacial movement and soon found himself in a major conflict with Forbes, that, according to Frank F. Cunningham, lastingly tarnishing Forbes's reputation.[16] Both Forbes and his student Peter Guthrie Tait argued that ice was viscous, whereas Tyndall, based on field and laboratory experiments partly conducted with Huxley, asserted that ice melted and refroze continually, thereby only resembling viscosity. To Tyndall, ice was of crystalline composition and melted under pressure, that is, its own weight, causing the veined structure that Forbes had detected to form under compression. The amateur scientist Ruskin also entered the debate, arguing against Tyndall out of respect for Forbes, which only added to the publicity and open hostility of the attacks. Not one to shy away from a fight, Tyndall also had a falling out with Stephen when the latter dismissed scientific motives in mountaineering.

In other areas, too, Tyndall was at the center of controversy. He advocated for science to replace the classical canon of school curricula and challenged the efficacy of prayer by publicly questioning whether prayer could have a measurable effect, such as changing the weather or curing a disease. According to Tyndall, only advances in the sciences could divert minor disasters, and thus science must have authority in investigations of the natural world.

When, duly warned by his friend Huxley, Tyndall used the occasion of the 1874 opening address of the British Association for the Advancement of Science at Belfast, one of the most renowned and publicized events of the year, to accuse theology of obstructing scientific discovery, he faced mounting criticism from not only the clergy but also the general public, who saw his speech as subversive. Tyndall's "Apology for the Belfast Address," later published alongside the address, only made matters worse, as it confirmed and actually intensified his claims. While even former supporters could not help but disapprove of the address, some scholars see the speech as a watershed, after which Tyndall's public image became lastingly tarnished, preventing the widespread reception of his ideas to this date.[17]

In 1876, at age fifty-six, Tyndall married Louisa Hamilton, daughter of Lord Claud Hamilton and twenty-five years his junior, who not only provided material and emotional support but prompted a rise in social standing and remained devoted to Tyndall after his death. That same summer, after a successful vote in the community council (he did not face the same difficulties as Wills had), Tyndall purchased a property in Belalp, where he had spent the previous twenty-five summers in the hotel's very own "Tyndall-room." After completion of their second home in November 1877, the Tyndalls spent fifteen more summers in Belalp, relishing the healthy environment, relaxed pace, and village community.[18] Tyndall retired from the Royal Institution in 1887 for reasons of health but became dismayed at how quickly the scientific world would forget his research. That same year he was elected honorary citizen of Naters/Belalp. He died on December 4, 1893, after his wife had accidentally administered an overdose of chloral, a sleeping medication. Allegedly, after realizing that she had given him chloral instead of magnesia, Louisa said to Tyndall, "John, I have given you chloral," to which he replied, "Yes, my poor darling, you have killed your beloved John."[19] Louisa was devastated by the error and spent her remaining forty-seven years collecting and arranging the vast material for a definitive biography of Tyndall, which finally appeared five years after her death in 1940.

Like Humboldt, Tyndall was an unceasing scientist, publishing more than 150 articles that laid the groundwork in many research fields, but he could not claim a single most important scientific discovery, perhaps another reason why he was largely forgotten after his death. Tyndall reportedly found writing to be challenging and revealed in a letter after publication of his first book, *The Glaciers of the Alps* (1860), "My book is getting on but it is horrible work and I hate it. I think I shall never undertake to write a *book* again."[20] Nevertheless he continued publishing books to great success, particularly because he tried to make his research relevant for laymen. In this vein, he claimed in the preface to *Heat: A Mode of Motion* (1868), "My aim has been to rise to the level of these questions from a basis so elementary, that a person possessing any imaginative faculty and power of concentration, might accompany me," providing ample examples from his mountain climbs in the text itself.[21] In contrast to Forbes, however, who capitalized on his achievements in the mountains to prop up his science, Tyndall was sometimes criticized for embellishing his scientific theories with climbing narratives. A review of his book *Forms of Water* wailed: "His narratives of last year's climbings and observations read very much like those of older ones with which he has already made us familiar."[22] Although Tyndall's publications initially slipped into obscurity, his research was rediscovered in the twenty-first century, especially his work on the greenhouse effect, showing that gases in the atmosphere absorb heat to different degrees.[23]

While Tyndall rejected the strict rules and traditions of established religions, he cherished spirituality in nature, becoming greatly impressed by Ralph Waldo Emerson. Tyndall met Emerson in Boston on his trip of 1872 and 1873 to the United States, along with Henry Wadsworth Longfellow and Louis Agassiz, and later hosted Emerson at his home in London, as the respect between the two men seems to have been mutual. Tyndall was also well familiar with German philosophy and literature in general and Johann Wolfgang von Goethe's scientific and poetic texts in particular, the latter of which proved highly inspirational.[24] This exposure to natural philosophy and literature gave Tyndall a framework with which he began his forays to the Alps: terming himself "a student of nature" (*Glaciers of the Alps,* 38), Tyndall approached mountains with devotion and imbued climbing with an intrinsically spiritual dimension. Tyndall's meditative experience replaced religion practiced in churches or other predetermined contexts and even took precedence over science, such as on top of the Weisshorn when Tyndall revealed, "I opened my note-book to make a few observations, but I soon relinquished the attempt. There was something incongruous, if not profane, in allowing the scientific faculty to interfere when silent worship was the reasonable service" (106). Tyndall acknowledged that nature (which he, like John Muir, always spelled with a capital $\mathcal{N}$) actually surpasses the human imagination: "In the application of her own principles, Nature often transcends the human imagination; her acts are bolder than our predictions" (180), greatly influencing the writings of Muir. In a similar vein, Tyndall called for a different, more respectful approach to nonhuman matter, with his theory of materialism anticipating contemporary theories of new materiality. In his essay "Vitality," Tyndall suggested that all matter holds the potential for life, reasoning that since organic matter can be reduced to inorganic matter, the reverse must also be true. Not surprisingly, Tyndall's statements questioning both the divine origin and permanence of life enraged many clergymen, who saw his words as openly inflammatory.[25]

As was the case with Humboldt, Tyndall's language in how he approached, experienced, and described the mountains steadily evolved. The depictions of his second Alpine trip in 1856 included somewhat timid advances in climbing, respect if not fear of the formidable environment, and predictable sublime exaltations: "A glorious expanse was before me, stretching itself in vast undulations and heaping itself here and there in to mountainous cones, white and pure, with the deep blue heaven behind them."[26] Soon, however, Tyndall relinquished the aesthetic distance to immerse himself in his environment. On his 1857 trip to the Mer de Glace, he mused, "Wandering slowly upwards, successive points of attraction drawing me almost unconsciously on, I found myself as the day was declining deep in the entanglements of the ice" (*Glaciers of the Alps*, 53). The wording "entanglements of the ice" picked up and intensified the discourse on snow and ice initiated by Agassiz and Forbes (harking back to British Romanticism and Goethe), but rather than speaking in general terms of the dynamic force of ice, Tyndall added an explicitly material dimension of physical enmeshment, connecting his bodily movements to the ice's advance. That same summer, Tyndall embarked on his first major climb, summiting Mont Blanc for the first time on August 13, along with his friend Hirst while guided by Edouard Simond. Multiple letters give evidence of the deep impression left by the ascent of the "Monarch of Mountains," as Tyndall, like Smith and Wills before him, called Mont Blanc in reference to Byron's *Manfred*.[27]

Tyndall's 1858 journey was marked by more rigorous climbing—the ascent of the Eggishorn and Finsteraarhorn, along with two ascents of Monte Rosa, including a first solo ascent on August 17, and again Mont Blanc—to advance several scientific projects, such as placing thermometers on the top of the Finsteraarhorn and Mont Blanc to record low winter temperatures, and measuring the boiling point of water on Monte Rosa. Tyndall's depiction of the latter climb recalls Humboldt's earlier description of climbing Chimborazo's ridge: "The precipice to my left was a continual preacher of caution, and the slope to my right was hardly less impressive" (*Glaciers of the Alps*, 140). Like Humboldt, Tyndall also inserted humor into his climbing descriptions while letting his imagination run wild with the consequences of a potential fall. Tyndall returned to Mont Blanc in August 1859 with Frankland, spending a rather miserable twenty-two hours as the first people to camp overnight on the summit, during which they lit candles to measure the rate of burning and fired pistols to assess the nature of sound. In December, Tyndall returned to the Mer de Glace for a first winter excursion, marveling: "The glacier excited the admiration of us all: not as in summer, shrunk and sullied like a spent reptile, steaming under the influence of the sun, its frozen muscles were compact; strength and beauty were associated in its aspect" (*Glaciers of the Alps*, 181).

Being in the mountains, as part of a dynamic and volatile nature, takes on a physical dimension that visibly enriched Tyndall's previous approach of sublime adulation. In *Mountaineering in 1861*, he characterized this all-encompassing experience: "The mutations of the atmosphere, the blue zenith and the glowing horizon; rocks, snow, and ice; the wondrous mountain world into which he looks, and which refuses to be encompassed by a narrow brain: these are objects at once poetic and scientific, and of such plasticity that every human soul can fashion them according to its own needs" (67). Tyndall's emphasis on what he calls "plasticity," that is, the material demands of being in the mountains, harkens back to Humboldt, Saussure, and Forbes. But whereas for his predecessors, such bodily experience arose in the text as an interruption of scientific measurement or poetic waxing, Tyndall seeks to specifically delineate it, boldly imbuing the very categories of science and aesthetics with an inherent material dimension. Somewhat comically, the essay "A Letter from Bâle" exemplifies—on the occasion of a train ride to Basel—the effect of physical sensations on both poetic reflection and scientific observation:

> The morning of the 1st of August found me on my way from Paris to Bâle [Basel]. The sun was strong, and, in addition to this source of temperature, eight human beings, each burning the slow fire which we call life, were cooped within the limits of our compartment. We slept, first singly, then by groups, and finally as a whole. Vainly we endeavored to ward off the coming lethargy. Thought gradually skips away from its object, or the object glides out of the nerveless grasp of thought, and we are conquered by the heat. But what is heat, that it should work such changes in moral and intellectual nature? Why are we unable to read "Mill's Logic" or study the "Kritik der reinen Vernunft" [Kant's *Critique of Pure Reason*] with any profit in a Turkish bath? Heat, defined without reference to our sensations, is a kind of motion, as strictly mechanical as the waves of the sea, or as the aërial vibrations which produce sound. (61)

Tyndall takes the physical sensation of lethargy as an opportunity to reflect on both the philosophical and the scientific ramifications of heat, reaching for Kant (along with John Stuart Mill) as an epitome of German idealism to question the power of human control and will in the face of physical parameters. Linking scientific and philosophical inquiry with bodily function, Tyndall provocatively continues, "Human action is only possible within a narrow zone of temperature. . . . The intellect is in some sense a function of temperature. . . . Physically considered, however, the intellect of noon is different from that of 8 P.M. simply in the amount of motion possessed by the molecules of the brain" (61–62). Tyndall continues by reflecting on the connection between poor food and health, also pointing to the larger material factors at play.[28] His statements have far-reaching consequences for political and economic sciences especially in the face of climate change, and also gain renewed relevance in the context of new materialisms that view the human body as an open system in continual intercorporeal exchange with its environment.

Textual Encounters

Hours of Exercise in the Alps, Tyndall's second mountaineering book, published in 1871, includes nine out of twelve essays published previously in *Mountaineering in 1861,* but as Tyndall freely admits, he aimed to republish them, since the earlier book was out of print. Once again, Tyndall hails mountaineering as an experience invigorating both body and mind. Already in the preface, he calls his book "for the most part a record of bodily action" (v), finding himself "infected" (2) by the desire to climb. In Switzerland, previous symptoms of weariness subside: "After this day's journey, which was a very hard one, the tide of health set steadily in. . . . Each day's subsequent exercise made both brain and muscles firmer" (16). This emphasis on physical well-being continues Wills's endorsement of vacations in the mountains for reasons of increased health and echoes in Muir's later campaign of restoring workers' senses and bodies with time spent in the North American wilderness. Yet Tyndall tends to restrict himself to his own experience, and his claims of vigor and strength remain juxtaposed with tales of weakness and helplessness, as discussed later in the chapter.

In a mixture of genres not unlike Humboldt's texts, *Hours of Exercise* combines outings undertaken for pleasure, philosophical musings, descriptions of research projects, measurements of the velocity of ice, and scientific excursuses such as the "Note on Clouds." Tyndall seamlessly moves from a depiction of his experiences to scientific explanations that remain easily understandable to laymen, in the process inventing a language that furthers Humboldtian writing as it imbues scientific observation with a poetic dimension. In sentences like "Stormy cumuli swept round the mountains, between which, however, the illuminated ridges seemed to swim in the opalescent air" (63) or "Through the shadowed water needles of ice were darting: all day long the molecules had been kept asunder by the antagonistic heat; their enemy is now withdrawn, and they lock themselves together in a crystalline embrace" (74), scientific terms are joined with poetic metaphors in a vernacular of both analytic specificity and literary depth. Tyndall employs this language when describing the effects of glaciation and imagining previous geologic ages, such as at the Urbach Valley, where he becomes mesmerized both by the view itself and by its imaginative possibilities:

> Looking at these charactered cliffs, one's thoughts involuntarily revert to the ancient days, and we restore in idea a state of things which had disappeared from the world before the development of man. Whence this wondrous power of reconstruction? Was it locked like latent heat in ancient inorganic nature, and developed as the ages rolled? Are other and grander powers still latent in nature, destined to blossom in another age? Let us question fearlessly, but, having done so, let us avow frankly that at bottom we know nothing; that we are imbedded in a mystery, towards the solution of which no whisper has been yet conceded to the listening intellect of man. (69)

If Humboldt had emphasized the importance of the imagination in scientific approaches, and Agassiz and Forbes delineated theories of glaciation and glacial movement, Tyndall connects imagination with theory, past with future, and knowledge with lack of knowledge. In this way, he takes the ice age theory as an opportunity to ponder about future geologic change and as proof that we do not (yet) possess enough knowledge about these workings. Conversely, science informs Tyndall's aesthetic vision. Using the geologic force of erosion as an opportunity to refute catastrophism and instead argue for Darwin's emerging concept of evolution and gradual change, Tyndall professes, "There is a grandeur in the secular integration of small effects implied by the theory of erosion almost superior to that involved in the idea of a cataclysm. Think of the ages which must have been consumed in the execution of this colossal sculpture" (251). This is a significant move in that Tyndall expands the traditional concept of the sublime—suddenness, grandness, loudness—to include gradual, small, and constant change that ultimately proves even grander than sudden upheaval. Science therefore encourages a revision of the sublime paradigm.

For Tyndall, as for Humboldt before him, these observations do not remain isolated insights but connect to a larger philosophy. Whereas Forbes and Agassiz had contented themselves with analyzing the structure, movement, and extent of glaciers, Tyndall takes glacial action as an opportunity to reflect on more general tendencies of mankind. In the Grimsel region, he observes evidence of glaciation and once more enlists the imagination when envisioning the "scene of unspeakable desolation" when "all Europe was thus encased in frozen armour" (78). Tyndall uses this imagery to envision a dynamic earth notably shaped by forces of nature rather than God: "She [nature] buildeth up and taketh down. She lifts the mountains by her subterranean energies, and then blasts them by her lightnings and her frost. Thus grandly she rushes along the 'grooves of change' to her unattainable repose" (79). Going further, he uses the example to formulate a philosophy pertaining to life in general, positing that all living things must remain in motion to avoid death: "Matter longs for rest; when is this longing to be fully satisfied? If satisfied, what then? Rest is not perfection; it is death. Life is not only compatible with mutation; when equilibrium sets in life ceases, and the world thence forward is locked in everlasting sleep" (79). This powerful analogy connects the activity of mountaineering to the very essence of life and a universe in constant motion.

In utter contrast to Tyndall's musings, Whymper establishes from the get-go that his motivations decidedly differ from those of his peers. Departing in structure and style from previous mountaineering narratives, Whymper terms his endeavors a "sport, and nothing more" (2), and—in a stab against scientific and aesthetic traditions—assures readers that his volume comprises a much condensed version of his travels, with only "salient points" elaborated to "spare the reader from much useless repetition" (2). He professes his interest in ascending Mont Pelvoux solely because it was thought to be the highest mountain in France and still unclimbed. After putting together a makeshift group of climbers and guides, on August 4, 1861, Whymper embarked on an ascent of what turned out to be the wrong summit. The next day, the party regrouped and ascended to the top of Mont Pelvoux, only to discover an even higher unclimbed summit in the vicinity, subsequently named Barre des Écrins. Still, on account of Whymper's first ascent of Mont Pelvoux, which he described in the 1862 second issue of *Peaks, Passes, and Glaciers,* William Longman proposed to elect Whymper into the Alpine Club, even though his background in trade was unusual among the club's 158 members at the time.

Rather than dwelling on geology and botany or waxing lyrical, Whymper

"The Mont Cenis Road and the Fell Railway,"
from *Scrambles Amongst the Alps*, 30 (Internet Archive)

inserts a chapter on the history of railway construction in the Mont Cenis Pass. Fascinated by railway engineering and the "railway mania" of his day, Whymper actually interrupted both his first and second trips to the Alps to inspect the tunnel construction at the pass and, in September 1871, was able to experience the first rail passage of the Cenis tunnel as an invited guest. In the spirit of modernity, Whymper's chapter celebrates the transformation of the rough path built by Napoleon into "one of the finest highways in Europe" (49), minutely describing the horse-drawn diligences of the early 1860s, the opening of the first mountain railway, the Mont Cenis Pass Fell railway running in serpentines along a steep incline in 1868, and finally the construction of the Fréjus Rail Tunnel west of the pass, a task involving decades of intense work, human toll, and vast expense. With its focus on technology, the chapter supersedes both sublime awe and scientific exploration. On one hand, Whymper supplies table after table of measurements on the progress of the work, costs involved, rock encountered, men employed, accidents, heights and gradients, and even temperatures inside and outside the tunnel. On the other, he transfers the vocabulary of the sublime to technology itself. In ambivalent language typical of literary modernism, he terms the railway over the pass both "a marvel" (51) and "a monstrous serpent" (53) that can barely be stopped with Fell's patented center-rail system, using a third rail for additional drive wheels— the pads needed replacement after each trip. Rich illustrations depict both the Cenis road and railway as an impressive example of human prowess. Whymper also basks in some national pride, since the railway was built with the help of British investors, contractors, and engineers, among them most notably John Barraclough Fell (1815–1902), though the project turned into a financial disaster after its late completion, coupled with the early open- ing of the tunnel thanks to pneumatic drilling and dynamite. To Whymper, the newly built tunnel allows for an even more impressive "monster train" (71) epitomizing speed and power.

Placed right after the railway chapter, the ensuing description of Whymper's Matterhorn attempts reads like a logical sequence from the conquest of nature via railway and tunnel to Whymper's eventual triumph on the Matterhorn. To underscore this victory, Whymper employs a mili- tary language of mountaineering that later became staple fare in twentieth- century texts. Already the preface speaks of "conquer[ing]" (1), "assault" (1), and "attacks" (2), and the descriptions of his eight failed summit attempts repeat and intensify this language: faced with "defeat" (83), Whymper re- sumed the "attack" and "assailed again in 1861" (88), vowing "to lay siege to the mountain until one or the other was vanquished" (88). Others rush in, too, to "do battle with the mountain" (89). In between attempts on "my old enemy—the Matterhorn" (255), Whymper decided to ascend the Dent Blanche, which, "as the saying is, still remained virgin" (252). This largely new terminology, coupled with the nationalistic tinge of Whymper's writ- ing, hints at the increasing national pride and tensions at a time when other nations also established themselves as industrialized epicenters, and foreshadows the national appropriation of mountaineering in the wake of World War I.

Because of these overtones and his insistence on mountaineering as mere "sport," it is less known that Whymper also anchors his text firmly in the tradition of his predecessors, both by engaging in the scientific discourses of the day and by imbuing his book with a poetic dimension. Though Humboldt goes unmentioned in *Scrambles*, Whymper was intimately famil- iar with Humboldt's texts, as we know from frequent references in his later book, *Travels Amongst the Great Andes of the Equator* (1891). He widely credits other naturalists, mentioning Saussure no fewer than fourteen times in the text, and carefully comparing his own observations on glacial features but also Alpine customs with those of Saussure. He meticulously records altitudes and temperatures, inserting tables of comparative heights of Alpine peaks, offering meteorological explanations of the atmosphere, collecting and classifying Alpine flora, and devoting a significant part of the book to the discussion of glacial features and competing theories. Whymper quotes Agassiz, Forbes, and Tyndall to follow with his own (false) claims that, rather than predominant glacial action, "sun, frost, and water have played an important part in modelling the Alps" (249). Mostly, Whymper emerges as an exceedingly knowledgeable and careful reader of previous texts. He corrects mistakes in Forbes's *Travels* and revises Ruskin's assessment of the Matterhorn: "'There is no aspect of destruction about the Matterhorn cliffs,' says Professor Ruskin. Granted, when they are seen from afar" (138). He credits Saussure and Forbes with the crucial discovery that a mountain consists of "a series of stratified beds" (266) rather than continuous cliffs, which importantly leads to Whymper's decision to attempt Matterhorn's Swiss side. He calls Stephen "the fleetest of foot of the Alpine brotherhood" (251) and offers an astute interpretation of Tyndall's published Matterhorn descriptions in *Mountaineering*. Like Wills, Whymper prefaces most of his chapters with literary quotes (Homer, Aeschylus, Euripides, Virgil, Pliny, Cesar, Cicero, and Shakespeare, among others), at once situating his book in a larger classical tradition and elevating his mountaineering plea to the realm of aesthetics, politics, and philosophy.

Scrambles therefore is a text replete with inconsistencies and unexpected turns. A solo Matterhorn attempt stirs feelings of grandeur and solitude: "The earth seemed to become less earthy and almost sublime; the world seemed dead, and I, its sole inhabitant" (101). Surprisingly, Whymper here comes to question—in the tradition of Humboldt and Forbes—the value of the mountaineering quest altogether: "Those who would, but cannot, stand upon the highest Alps, may console themselves with the knowledge that they do not usually yield the views that make the strongest and most permanent impressions. . . . And when those happy moments are over, which always fly with too great rapidity, the summit is left with an impression that is seldom durable, because it is usually vague" (145–46). In another turn, he characterizes mountains as remainders of destruction and collapse, harking back to Burnet's apocalyptic *Sacred Theory of the Earth*. During the ascent of Mont Pelvoux, Whymper opines, "A more cheerless and desolate valley it is scarcely possible to imagine" (28), though his depictions of the Matterhorn exceed the devastation: "But here, all was decay and ruin," and "In the whole range of my Alpine experience I have seen nothing more striking than this desolate, ruined, and shattered ridge at the back of the Great Tower" (104). The north side fares still worse: "Nothing can seem or be more inaccessible than the Matterhorn upon this side, and even in cold blood one holds the breath when looking at its stupendous cliffs. . . . This side of the mountain has always seemed somber-sad-terrible. It is painfully suggestive of decay, ruin, and death; and it is now, alas! more than terrible by its associations" (137–38). These haunting images and futile thoughts seem to render impossible the notion of conquest, questioning masculine prowess altogether.

Gendered Approaches

On other occasions, Whymper describes mountains in highly gendered terms that suggest they must be conquered and defeated. His view of the Aiguille de Trélatête recalls Humboldt's description of Teide becoming veiled and unveiled, yet Whymper connotes the mountain as distinctly female: "Our mountain, like a beautiful coquette, sometimes unveiled herself for a moment, and looked charming above, though very mysterious below. It was not until eventide she allowed us to approach her; then, as darkness came on, the curtains were withdrawn, the light drapery was lifted" (220). Adding to the overt eroticism, Whymper terms himself a "foolish lover" (114) in the face of the Matterhorn, adding a tinge of self-mockery to the sexually charged discourse.

Tyndall's gendered approach to mountaineering also reveals inconsistencies. In a gesture of male triumph, Whymper, Tyndall, and Stephen (discussed in more detail in the next chapter) marked their first ascents with makeshift flags, celebrating their achievements. Ann C. Colley reads such moments as heroic masculinity replacing sublime awe.[29] The Matterhorn engravings found in Tyndall's, but also Whymper's and Stephen's, texts illustrating impossibly steep cliffs that rise sharply to boundless heights visually underscore such a transformation: rather than an individual becoming disoriented and humbled by the overwhelming sublimity of the mountainous landscape, they instead depict one distinctly phallic object, begging to be surmounted. Tyndall, a staunch opponent of women's suffrage and emancipation, also terms his climbing attempts on the Matterhorn "assaults" and admonishes a fellow climber who fell into a crevasse, "If you behave like a man, we shall save him; if like a woman, he is lost" (147).[30] In this vein, he celebrates a masculine vigor that thrives at altitude:

> There is assuredly more morality in the oxygen of the mountains, as there is immorality in the miasma of a marsh, and a higher power than mere brute force lies latent in Alpine mutton. We are recognizing more and more the influence of physical elements in the conduct of life, for when the blood flows in a purer current the heart is capable of a higher glow. Spirit and matter are interfused; the Alps improve us *totally*, and we return from their precipices wiser as well as stronger men. (156)

The quote merges Rousseau's and Haller's ideals of a pure Alpine space, a focus on the body and health, an early social Darwinist dimension, and masculine ideals of strength and power.[31] In an incisive analysis, the historian Michael S. Reidy contends that Whymper, Tyndall, and Stephen moved an exclusive male terrain ever higher, distinguishing such a space from more accessible peaks. Arguing that "definitions of masculinity were at the bottom of the Matterhorn tragedy," Reidy proposes that male mountaineers, influenced both by studies of human physiology and by Darwin's contribution to the idea of natural selection, were obsessed with the body and its limits, expunging all that was considered effeminate in an exclusively male space marked by altitude.[32] Yet Tyndall deliberately confuses the binary of female beauty in the lowlands versus male sublimity up high when he writes: "Grandeur is conceded while beauty is sometimes denied to the Alps. But the higher-snow-fields of the great glaciers are altogether beautiful—not throned in repellent grandeur, but endowed with a grace so tender as to suggest the loveliness of woman" (143). Using the traditionally gendered vocabulary of the sublime, Tyndall seems conscious of its loaded connotations but in response merges the distinct categories.

Tyndall was also interested in, if not supportive of, the fact that female climbers increasingly encroached on vertical spaces, and mentions female

"View of the Matterhorn," from a sketch by E. E. Cooke,
from *Mountaineering in 1861*, 82 (Internet Archive)

climbers throughout his travels. On the Matterhorn, for instance, Tyndall
admires a female climber, crediting her with scaling the mountain long
before he himself ascended it: "At Val Tournanche I saw a maiden niece
of the Chanoine who had gone high up the Matterhorn, and who, had
the wind not assailed her petticoats too roughly, might, it was said, have
reached the top. I can believe it. Her wrist was like a weaver's beam, and

her frame seemed a mass of potential energy" (273–74). While the description unwittingly posits femininity and muscular vigor as opposites, the skirts
that Tyndall cites as reason for her failure indeed posed a major challenge
and hindrance to women's climbing, as Colley has revealed. In her carefully researched chapter "Ladies on High," Colley effectively refutes the
prevailing opinion that (a) women generally did not climb in large numbers or at high altitude, and (b) there was widespread discouragement if
not discrimination against the women who tried to do so. Instead, Colley
states, "A closer look at British Victorian women mountaineers suggests that,
even though these climbers sometimes faced disapproval and their achievements occasionally elicited snide remarks, these individuals also frequently
benefited from an admiration for their mountaineering ambitions."[33]

Unheroic Performances and Prejudice

Contrary to a heroic performance, Tyndall's own body and those of
others often become limp, distorted, and uncontrollable when falling, dodg-
ing rockfall, or being hauled up by ropes. Tyndall showcases such vulnerable and weak rather than virile bodies in the illustration "Recovery of Our
Porter" (148), with its accompanying description detailing an elaborate rescue when both Tyndall and Bennen lowered into a crevasse to revive a
porter with brandy, excavate him from the ice, and finally lift him back up.
Fear and failure come to the fore in Tyndall's various Matterhorn attempts.
Already during the first "Inspection of the Matterhorn," Tyndall and Bennen encounter some veritable challenges. On what turns out to be a wrong
path, they cautiously move up a cliff "by aid of the feldspar crystals pro-
tuberant from its face" (*Mountaineering*, 259). Tyndall elaborates on what
sounds like a precursor to modern rock climbing in a description mixing
terror, bravado, and humor that surely inspired Clarence King's later tale
of scaling Mount Tyndall.

> Here is the grand difficulty of the Matterhorn; the rocks are sound, smooth,
> and steep, and hardly offer any grip to either hands or feet. Midway up the
> cliff referred to, Bennen asked me to hold on, as he did not feel sure that it
> formed the best route. I accordingly ceased moving, and lay against the rock
> with legs and arms outstretched *like a huge and helpless frog.* Bennen climbed
> to the top of the cliff, but returned immediately with a flush of confidence

in his eye. "I will lead you to the top," he said excitedly. Had I been free I would have cried "Bravo!" but in my position I did not care to risk the muscular motion which a hearty bravo would demand. (*Mountaineering*, 259, emphasis mine)

Notably, Tyndall omitted the words "like a huge and helpless frog" in the reprint of the essay in *Hours of Exercise*, thus excluding an image of utter vulnerability. Still, the discrepancy between Tyndall's precarious position and Bennen's premature confidence exudes some undeniable humor. The "second assault" of the Matterhorn likewise remained unsuccessful, forc-

"Recovery of Our Porter," from *Hours of Exercise in the Alps*, 148 (Internet Archive)

ing Tyndall to his knees instead of a triumphant summit pose: "So savage a spot I had never seen, and I sat down upon it with the sickness of disappointed hope" (163–64). Rather than conquering their environment, Tyndall and his companions repeatedly find themselves victims of circumstance, at the mercy of natural forces.

In Whymper as well, competitive drive and nationalistic overtones are kept in check by humorous and often self-deflating anecdotes. After his 1864 ascent of the Barre des Écrins, his first major new ascent, Whymper warns future peak baggers that anyone hoping to scale the mountain after a snowstorm "is likely to experience misery far deeper than anything with which he has hitherto been acquainted" (199). Describing in witty language reminiscent of Mark Twain a position equivalent to Tyndall's helpless frog pose, Whymper uses himself as an object of humor when depicting a jump across a crevasse:

> The second which followed was what is called a supreme moment. That is to say, I felt supremely ridiculous. The world seemed to revolve at a frightful pace, and my stomach to fly away. The next moment I found myself sprawling in the snow, and then, of course, vowed that it was nothing, and prepared to encourage my friend Reynaud. (207)

Like Tyndall, Whymper dwells on falls, mistakes, and failures despite the text's overall emphasis on conquest. After he boasts that a snow slope of 45 to 50 degrees can easily be mounted by skilled climbers equipped with axes, such mastery is called into question when Whymper discloses a fall on precisely such a slope, without apparent reason: during his solo attempt on the Matterhorn, Whymper slipped and fell nearly two hundred feet, leaving him temporarily unconscious, badly cut, and bruised, with wounds on his hands and head. The elaborate description of the accident in *Scrambles* is complemented by an illustration depicting a passive and powerless body, not unlike Tyndall's rescued porter.

If some scholars have pointed to British mountaineers' increasing proclivity for risk and danger in an evolving culture of imperialism and individuality, Tyndall happily entrusts himself to guides and climbing equipment such as axes and ropes.[34] R. D. Eaton considers vulnerability as a major theme in Tyndall's *The Glaciers of the Alps and Mountaineering in 1861*, concluding that "his work reveals the dynamic, unstable, and highly prob-

"In Attempting to Pass the Corner I Slipped and Fell,"
from *Scrambles*, 54 (Internet Archive)

lematic nature of mid-Victorian attitudes toward danger."[35] *Hours of Exercise* continues to acknowledge the sometimes deadly dangers of mountaineering and contrasts tales of successful ascents with descriptions of harrowing accidents. During the Weisshorn ascent, Tyndall and Bennen are plagued by constant rockfall, leading Tyndall to recommend only the mountain's arêtes to future climbers, since "at any moment the mountainside may be raked by a fire as deadly as that of cannon" (110). Although Tyndall compares the act of climbing to a military battle, the ascent remains a far cry from victorious conquest: "I thought of Englishmen in battle, of the qualities which had made them famous: it was mainly the quality of not knowing when to yield—of fighting for duty even after they had ceased to be animated by hope. Such thoughts helped to lift me over the rocks" (104). The imagery evoked is one of plowing onward, without enthusiasm or energy, defenselessly exposed to the elements of weather, rockfall, and avalanches.

Bennen's tragic death—he perished tied to another climber when an avalanche wiped six people off an unstable snow slope in March 1864—hovers over the volume as a catastrophic loss. Tyndall heralds the Swiss Johann Joseph Bennen [Benet] (1824–62) as a first-rate guide, assuring readers he needed no other guide besides "my faithful Bennen" (144), whose skills Tyndall recalls with great admiration. The chapter "Death of Bennen," placed in the center of the volume and graced with a portrait of the late guide, is narrated not by Tyndall himself but by an eyewitness to the disaster. This depiction is mirrored by another accident involving Tyndall and four other climbers who likewise uncontrollably swirled down a steep slope on the back of an avalanche but luckily came to a stop just before a deep chasm. Tyndall relates, "I thought of Bennen on the Haut de Cry, and muttered, 'it is now my turn'" (214). Throughout the text, these accidents serve as reminders that, far from being in control, climbers are constantly at the mercy of rockfall, avalanches, and weather.

Whymper likewise recognizes the crucial role that guides played in climbing successes while also pointing to their weaknesses. In particular, he distinguishes the Italian Jean-Antoine Carrel, Bennen, and the French Michel Croz, harboring the greatest respect for Carrel, a former Bergsaglieri (defending Italy against Austria), whom he calls "the cock of Val Tournanche" (110) and describes as "the finest rock-climber I have ever seen" (82–83). Yet during the Matterhorn competition, Whymper remained distrustful of the "well-made, resolute-looking fellow, with a certain defiant air" (74). Croz, whose "magnificent strength" rises above "the range of ordinary mortals," became Whymper's most preferred guide, "the man who was most after my own heart" (162), though he too died in the mountains while guiding, leaving Whymper shocked and grieving.

In the face of unstable and harsh environments that even guides are unable to master, male camaraderie and friendship take on renewed importance. According to R. D. Eaton, "There is very little in these narratives to support the idea, advanced by Peter Hensen [Hansen], that the English alpinists put on display the virtues of heroic, individualistic English masculinity. Mountaineering in Tyndall's accounts is richly social, both in the business of climbing and the eagerness to share the experience with the audiences back home."[36] Indeed, plenty of evidence suggests that Tyndall, though he accepted or at least acknowledged female presence, viewed mountains primarily as a space for forging male friendship. *Hours of Exercise* is dedicated to Tyndall's close friend Hirst, introduced in the preface as "a friend whom I taught in his boyhood to handle a theodolite and lay a chain" (viii). Eight years his junior, Hirst was a lifelong friend and climbing partner who offered Tyndall part of his inheritance to enable Tyndall's continued study in Europe, calling him affectionately "my angel of mercy, my guiding star."[37] Frankland was another friend with whom Tyndall spent time in the mountains, with his devotion also including guides:

> We [Tyndall, Hirst, and their guide Simond] gathered round the pine fire, and I can hardly think it possible for three men to be more happy than we then were. It was not the goodness of the conversation, nor any high intellectual element, which gave the charm to our gatherings; the gladness grew naturally out of our own perfect health, and out of the circumstances of our positions. Every fibre seemed a repository of latent joy, which the slightest stimulus sufficed to bring into conscious action. (*Glaciers of the Alps*, 77)

Notably, heroic deeds, intellectual prowess, and scientific findings are absent from this description, which focuses on the joy of joint outings in the Alps. Following his general philosophy of linking physical and mental faculties, Tyndall suggests that male camaraderie emerges from shared physical struggles in the awe-inspiring environment of the mountains. To Francis O'Gorman, "homosociality slips almost into the homoerotic here," a dimension that underscores but also begins to question our understanding of heroic masculinity in the mountains.[38]

Similarly, Whymper affectionately recounts a night camping out in the open with his guide Croz, having adjourned to "a most eligible rock" after being unable to sleep: "How well I remember the night at that rock, and the jolly way in which Croz came out! We were both very wet about the legs, and both uncommonly hungry, but the time passed pleasantly enough round our fire of juniper, and until long past midnight we sat up recounting, over our pipes, wonderful stories of the most incredible description, in which, I must admit, my companion beat me hollow" (198).[39] Whymper's depiction, playfully veiling and unveiling an intimate night in public form, echoes that of Tyndall, and both in turn influenced Clarence King's description of a night camped with his friend Cotter. That Tyndall did not marry until age fifty-six and Whymper remained single until age sixty-four strengthens the idea of such intimate male bonding. During their youthful years, both Tyndall and Whymper focused on their professional careers and times spent with other males in the mountains, excluding women from both of these areas.

In general, Whymper preferred to keep the lines of distinction between clients and guides, British and what he called "natives." Continuing and sharpening the bigoted overtones of Wills's text, Whymper frequently portrayed local citizens as a superstitious and unreasonable people. In particular, he drew a sharp distinction between the Swiss and Italian sides of the Alps that Wills, and to a lesser degree Forbes, had already dwelled on. According to Whymper, the Italian "inhabitants of the Val Tournanche are behind the times. Their paths are as bad as, perhaps worse than, they were in the time of De Saussure, and their inns are much inferior to those of the Swiss side" (148). He goes on to speculate that wealth would increase if the local citizens were to improve roads and paths and serve meals more suited to an English taste, with more meat. Whymper's prejudices become most apparent in his chapter on the Italian Aosta Valley, where he charges the villagers with cretinism (a congenital deficiency of the thyroid hormone resulting in stunted physical and mental growth) and goiters: "The extreme form of idiocy which is called Crétinism is so highly developed in the Valley of Aosta, and the natives are so familiarised with it, that they are almost indignant when the surprised traveler remarks its frequency" (277).

Like Wills, Whymper contrasts the beautiful scenery with the deplorable state of its inhabitants but, expanding on his predecessor's views, offers a pseudomedical explanation for the phenomenon: establishing a connection between cretinism and goiters, which is indeed medically correct, Whymper linked goiters to "the use of chemically impure water, and especially hard water" (279). Going further, he claims that the frequency of cretinism in the Aosta region proved that the disease is caused by inbreeding, especially in the lower classes, expressing hope that the opening of a new railway could produce "the happiest effects" "in a natural way" (284). As we now know, cretinism is caused by iodine deficiency and, because most iodine stems from the oceans and enters the atmosphere as rain, was most prevalent in inland and mountainous areas, especially those without outside food sources. Decades later, Whymper's type of reasoning resurfaced when he complained about the dirty, impoverished, and flea-ridden conditions in Ecuador, not investigating the political causes of such living environments, as Humboldt had done in his time.

Chimborazo Again

After sojourns to Greenland to pursue glacier research in 1867 and 1872, Whymper returned to the Matterhorn in 1874, summiting the mountain one more time together with his old rival Jean-Antoine Carrel, but his main objective was to take photographs he could use on his lecture tours. By this time, the Survey of India had confirmed the Himalaya as the highest mountain range in the world, and the brothers Adolph, Robert, and Hermann Schlagintweit had published six volumes on their trip to Tibet and northern India of 1855, claiming to have reached twenty-two thousand feet. Whymper set his sights on an extended trip to India, but the increasing amount of wood-engraving work prevented concrete planning, and in 1879 he opted for a trip to South America instead. Together with Carrel, he embarked on a trip to Ecuador, with the aim of bagging the first ascent of Mount Chimborazo.

In contrast to Humboldt, Whymper and Carrel climbed the mountain slowly, deliberately, and in siege style: they started on December 26 as a large party with fourteen mules, but already after their first cold night at 14,300 feet, most of the porters abandoned the endeavor. Over the next six days, Whymper and Carrel established two more camps above 16,500 feet on the rocky southwest ridge, suffering greatly from altitude sickness. Whymper detailed his afflictions as well as his numerous barometric measurements in *Travels Amongst the Great Andes*. On their first summit attempt on January 3, they reached the top of the ridge, but a violent wind forced them to retreat. The next day, they were able to advance to the saddle between Chimborazo's summits and proceeded to climb the nearer eastern one (which they had presumed to be higher), reaching the top after ten hours of strenuous climbing at 4 p.m., only to discover a higher summit to the west. After another hour of "flogging, wading, and floundering," they finally arrived at the top, planting a pole and struggling to set up the barometer in the fierce wind.[40] Like his predecessors, Whymper focused on his measurements, determining the mountain's height at 20,608 feet, a full 817 feet lower than Humboldt's estimate (and a very accurate measurement by today's standards, which measure the mountain at 20,549 ft.). After sixteen hours of strenuous climbing, they finally returned to their tents, utterly exhausted.

Still, Whymper undertook a second ascent during that same trip half a year later, on July 3, 1880, this time via the northwest ridge, taking a photograph on the summit. Notably Whymper included in his account an appendix titled "Humboldt's Attempt to Ascend Mount Chimborazo," previously published in Karl Bruhn's *The Life of Humboldt,* providing translated excerpts of Humboldt's essay on the ascent. While Whymper complained, "I am unable to tell from his own writings where he actually went" (16), he carefully reevaluated Humboldt's words, quoting from his essay and comparing it to that of Baussingault (also included in an appendix) to question both altitude claims based on their fast rate of descent.[41] Although Cotopaxi had been climbed by a number of German scholars in the meantime, Whymper became similarly taken with this "ideal volcano" (70), and he and Carrel even spent a night in a tent pitched on the summit's crater to ascertain the effects of altitude during a longer stay. Like Humboldt previously, Whymper stares, spellbound, into the abyss with its "fiery fissures," "flames traveling to and fro," and "scintillations scattering as from a woodfire," interpreting the volcanic pipe as a "channel of communication with lower regions" (90), as Humboldt had.

After his return from Ecuador, Whymper gave a triumphant illustrated lecture in front of nearly a thousand people at the Royal Institution in London. In the years following, however, he largely gave up climbing and instead turned to researching altitude sickness—both he and Carrel had been severely stricken—and writing *Travels Amongst the Great Andes.* He also continued with his wildly successful lectures, spanning the history of Alpinism by beginning with slides of Scheuchzer's dragons and Saussure to cul-

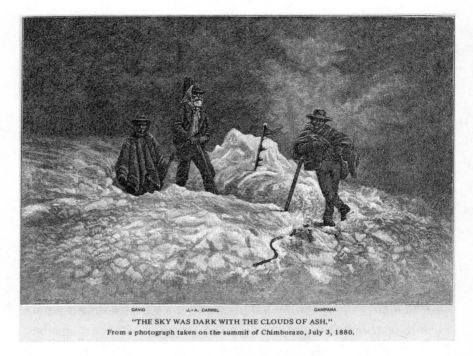

"The Sky Was Dark with the Clouds of Ash," from
Travels Amongst the Great Andes, 326 (Internet Archive)

minate with his own ascent of Chimborazo. His *Guide to Chamonix and Mont Blanc,* containing a richly illustrated climbing history of Chamonix, was published in 1896. After public lectures in Boston and New York, Whymper was employed by the Canadian Pacific Railway and offered a free ride to Vancouver to advertise the company's facilities, especially around Lake Louise and the Banff area. In 1900 he oversaw publication of the fifth and final edition of *Scrambles,* which had already turned into a mountaineering classic, ensuring the text's continued popularity in the new century.

Throughout his life, Whymper harbored friendships with older, independent women, but two days before his sixty-fifth birthday, he rashly married a butcher's daughter, Edith Mary Lewin, forty-three years his junior. The arrangement failed miserably and was broken off after four years; Whymper was drinking heavily, and Edith eventually became engaged to another man, leaving Whymper bitter and disappointed. Their daughter, Ethel Rosa (1908–69), however, became an accomplished climber. Whymper's health steadily declined, aggravated by insomnia and rheumatism. In 1911 he embarked on a final trip to the Swiss Alps, visiting Geneva, Grindelwald, and Zermatt before arriving at Chamonix on September 9. He locked himself into his room, not feeling well but refusing medical help. A week later, on September 16, he died in his room.

Both Whymper and Tyndall had a profound influence on North American mountaineering, especially Clarence King and John Muir. While King honored Tyndall by naming his first Sierra Nevada peak after him, Muir called Tyndall his model in the same vein as Charles Darwin, Asa Gray, and Thomas Huxley. Muir also owned a copy of Whymper's *Scrambles* and *Travels,* and a scrapbook from Muir's South American journey contained an article titled "Mr. Whymper in the Andes."[42] Whymper conversely knew about, and was fascinated by, California's mountains: in an extensive footnote on meteorology, he mentioned the Sierra Nevada as a "happy place" (100) for its scarcity of severe summer storms, quoting from the chapter "The High Sierra" in *The Yosemite Book* (1869), by Josiah Whitney. With his daredevil attitude, reckless climbing (even if exaggerated), and witty style, Whymper anticipated King's depictions of climbing in the Sierra Nevada. King's writing especially bears the mark of Whymper when jumping crevasses, inching up chimneys, and lowering down ropes. Both Whymper and King also proved to be meticulous editors, continuously revising, altering, and expanding their books in revised editions after original publication.

Aside from their respective literary influences, Tyndall and Whymper offer a more practical transition to the twentieth century. Both not only benefited from the increasing railway network but actively worked to support its expansion: Tyndall began his career as a railway engineer, and Whymper propagated the new rail lines, such as the Mont Cenis Pass, in writings and wood engravings. One of the first mountaineers to make a career out of climbing, Whymper supported his expeditions by fashioning wood engravings, illustrations, and popular travel descriptions: his *Scrambles Amongst the Alps* featured twenty-one full-page and as many as ninety smaller illustrations that underscored the narrative and became narrative vehicles in themselves. No wonder many reviews first and foremost dwelled on the quality of illustrations. Whymper also provided the illustrations and engravings for Stephen's *The Playground of Europe* and Tyndall's *Hours of*

Exercise, and both authors were both sufficiently pleased with the results. Around the same time, Whymper began to experiment with glass plates spread with collodion to produce a negative. In this important shift, Whymper welcomed and supported the use of photography (like King) while still involved in the trade of wood engraving, which would become obsolete in the twentieth century. Indeed, Whymper straddles both centuries most visibly when summiting Mount Chimborazo in 1880 for the first time and completing the mountain quest that Humboldt had begun at the beginning of the nineteenth century, transforming mountaineering into the high-altitude pursuit of the twentieth century.

CHAPTER 8

THE MAKING OF MODERN CLIMBING

Leslie Stephen

The Playground of Europe

Although published in the same year as Whymper's and Tyndall's books, Sir Leslie Stephen's *The Playground of Europe* (1871) in many ways takes off where Whymper's closes. Whymper concluded *Scrambles Amongst the Alps* with a self-serving assessment of the Matterhorn disaster, later adding a short history of ensuing ascents and accidents. Stephen, too, grapples with the aftermath of this tragedy, pleading for more safety, guided travel, and rope usage. More significantly, Stephen foresees a new era of mountaineering, in which all Alpine peaks have been claimed and their summits can be attained by anyone with reasonable fitness, favorable conditions, and good guides. This profound change affects the language of climbing as well: "Since the first summer I spent in the Alps, more than one excellent mountain of my acquaintance has passed through the successive stages denoted by the terms 'inaccessible,' 'the most difficult point in the Alps,' 'a good hard climb, but nothing out of the way,' 'a perfectly straightforward bit of work'; and, finally, 'an easy day for a lady.'"[1] Stephen's chauvinistic language aside (for now), the grappling with this dilemma, familiar in an age when even the highest Himalayan peaks have become attainable by any-one with fitness and funding, permeates Stephen's mountaineering writing, thus outlining many challenges and opportunities of modern climbing.

Not coincidentally, Stephen frames his mountaineering classic—once again in reference to Byron—with the "Monarch of the Alps," Mont Blanc, a mountain that by the 1870s had most strikingly made the transition from inaccessible to doable. Accordingly, the ascent of Mont Blanc, so eminently important for Saussure and Smith but now "a most commonplace exploit" (178), does not prominently figure into *The Playground of Europe*.[2] Instead, the mountain aptly encases the volume without being its high point: in the second edition's affectionate dedication to his friend and climbing partner, the painter Gabriel Loppé (1825–1913), Stephen recalls their joint Mont Blanc ascent "to watch the sunset from the summit" twenty-one years be-fore, in August 1873.[3] The chapter "Sunset on Mont Blanc," included in the latter part of the text, expounds on this evening on top of Mont Blanc. Since climbers usually travel in the early morning hours, Stephen aims to capture a view rarely perceived with Loppé "in a desperate attempt to fix upon canvas some of the magic beauties of the scene" (186), while climb-ing the mountain in itself is not a topic of great length. In addition, Ste-phen completed winter trips together with Loppé in the 1870s and 1880s to describe, paint, and photograph Alpine scenes.

Referring to various viewpoints and experiences rather than to his most renowned climbing achievements, Stephen hints at a decisive future direc-tion of climbing at a time when being the first on top of a major Alpine peak is no longer relevant, and scientific inquiry and Romantic searching have likewise faded into the background. While some mountaineers began to venture to higher ranges, Stephen does not abandon the Alps but in-stead locates the driving impetus for climbing in the novelty of experience. By focusing on individual interaction and fulfillment rather than ultimate achievement, this move carries the seeds of a radical democratization and revolution of the sport in relinquishing the summit position. With the em-phasis on one's own original and unclaimed experience, Stephen begins to outline a philosophy of mountaineering for an age where untrodden peaks and blank spots no longer exist on the map. To a large degree, this philos-ophy consists in attention to the physical quality of mountain climbing, its ever present bodily involvement, which Stephen outlines in all its gymnastic detail. Stephen locates this corporeal dimension within an agentic mountainous environment, claiming that new faculties of knowledge emerge in interaction with the mountain. Mountaineering, then, becomes a learning process, not about one's skills and techniques but about awareness and understanding of the self and nature. In a departure from many of his contemporaries, Stephen highlights physical and mental pleasure accessible to anyone as a guiding stimulus for climbing. Tracing this significant development, however, one stumbles across inconsistencies and controversies in Stephen's exclusive and elitist framework that ultimately grants experience up high only to a privileged few.

A Distinguished Family, a Prosperous Career

Stephen's prosperous life is exceptionally well documented in extensive biographies: *Life and Letters* (1906), by his official biographer, Frederic W. Maitland; and a later, more critical study, *Leslie Stephen* (1951), by Noel G. Annan. Stephen was born in Kensington Gore, London, on November 28, 1832, into a distinguished family of the intellectual elite with a tradition in law and evangelical reform. His grandfather was a master in chancery; his father a lawyer, colonial administrator, and member of the Privy Council; and his mother the daughter of the rector of the Clapham Sect of Anglican evangelicals. His older brother, Sir James Fitzjames, eventually became a judge at the High Court, and his younger sister Caroline Emilia was a Quaker. While the robust and outspoken Fitzjames appealed to his father's austere asceticism, Leslie was a delicate and asthmatic child, favored by his mother, who taught him reading and shorthand. Both boys began their education at the public boarding school Eton College, which they abhorred, but later received a first-rate education at King's College and Trinity Hall at Cambridge University. At Trinity Leslie became interested in athletics, especially long-distance running and rowing, and eagerly participated in the academic and social life of the college. After completing his B.A. in 1854 and his M.A. in 1857, he worked at Cambridge as a clergyman and coach. Famed for his athletic feats, such as running a mile in just over five minutes and walking fifty miles to London in twelve hours, Stephen also became interested in philosophy and American history, reading Auguste Comte, Charles Darwin, and Herbert Spencer, which by his own admission caused his faith to waver.[4] Faced with modern thought and the discoveries of science such as Hutton's, Lyell's, and Darwin's groundbreaking work, Stephen felt increasingly unable to reconcile these findings with the church's teachings and renounced the holy orders in 1862, which also meant giving up his teaching post. Still, he remained at Cambridge for some years as a college tutor while he began to write and publish.

A firm abolitionist, Stephen visited North America from July to October 1863, meeting with President Lincoln and General Meade, as well as Henry Longfellow, Charles Eliot Norton, and Ralph Waldo Emerson (who disappointed Stephen's expectations). He published his opinions in the *Times* upon his return. In 1866 he moved to London to pursue his career as a writer, making contributions to the *Pall Mall Gazette,* the *Nation,* and *Cornhill Magazine,* and eventually became editor of the *Cornhill Magazine* from 1871 to 1882. After more than a decade of religious doubts, Stephen officially renounced the Anglican order in 1875. He married Harriet Marian Thackeray on June 19, 1867, promptly departing for a honeymoon in the Alps. Stephen fathered one daughter, Laura (born 1870), but in 1875, his wife, pregnant again, unexpectedly died from eclampsia. Laura, slow to develop and hence a source of indignation for her father, was eventually placed in a home for the "imbecile." Stephen later married his London neighbor Julia Prinsep Jackson (1846–95), a widowed mother of three, in March 1878. Together they had two more sons and two daughters: Vanessa Bell and Virginia Woolf. In her novel *To the Lighthouse* (1927), Woolf offered an unflattering fictional portrait of her authoritarian yet insecure father as Mr. Ramsey, who, unable to listen to or accommodate the needs of his wife and children, remains caught in the patriarchal patterns of his culture. In her later essay "Leslie Stephen" (1932), published almost three decades after his death, Woolf described her father more softly as a solitary, deaf, and outdated yet kind man living in memories of his mountaineering and writing career while being plagued by self-doubt. Woolf here also credited her father with encouraging her to read and write.[5]

Beginning in the late nineteenth century, Stephen wrote several popular biographies, such as *Samuel Johnson* (1878), *Alexander Pope* (1880), *Jonathan Swift* (1882), *George Eliot* (1902), and *Hobbes* (1904), for the English Men of Letters series published by Macmillan. He also published three volumes of critical studies and two important volumes in philosophical theory, all culminating in his appointment as the first editor of the *Dictionary of National Biography* from 1882 to 1891, where he contributed as many as 378 articles for sixty-three volumes. After his second wife's death in 1895, Stephen threw himself into his work and completed the family photograph memoir *Mausoleum Book*, published posthumously in 1977. In addition, he was able to complete the long-awaited three-volume *The English Utilitarians* (1900). While Stephen had been recognized throughout his life, receiving honorary degrees from Edinburgh, Cambridge, Oxford, and Harvard, in 1902 he was elected as one of the founding fellows of the British Academy and that same year received the crowning award of Knight Commander (KCB) during the coronation of Edward VII. But Stephen's later years were also marred by family strife, illness, decreasing social life, and developing deafness. Two years after being diagnosed with cancer, Stephen died in his sleep at his home in London on February 22, 1904. His book on key intellectual concepts, *English Literature and Society*, appeared in the year of his death.

Alpine Sojourns

Already during his first trip to Bavaria and Austria in 1855, when he climbed the minor Schafberg (1,783 m/5,850 ft.) and visited the Grossglockner glacier, Stephen became enthralled with mountains to the point of religious rapture. Fellow mountaineer and president of the Alpine Club Douglas Freshfield remarked, "The Alps were for Stephen a playground but they were also alternately a cathedral in which to worship and a row of idols to fall down before."[6] Influenced by John Ruskin's praise of the Alps but also Alfred Wills's *Wanderings Among the High Alps*, both published in 1856, Stephen made his first visit to Courmayeur in 1857 and ascended to the Col du Géant. This formed the first of all told twenty-five summer and eight winter holidays in the Alps, during which Stephen completed numerous first ascents, such as the Bietschhorn in 1859, the Schreckhorn in 1861, and the Zinal Rothorn in 1864.[7] He joined the London Alpine Club in 1858, a year after its founding, and served as its president from 1865 to 1872.

The Alps gave Stephen an outlet for his athletic impulses and proved a fertile ground for his initial writings. His first book was a translation of Baron Hermann von Berlepsch's *Die Alpen* (1861), and his first essays on ascents of the Schreckhorn and the Eigerjoch appeared in 1862 in the second volume of *Peaks, Passes, and Glaciers.* In the years following, Stephen contributed a number of essays to the *Alpine Journal,* which he edited from 1868 to 1872. In the aftermath of the Whymper tragedy, Stephen advocated first and foremost for safety in the mountains, insisting on the importance of skilled guides and writing some articles on proper rope usage. Later he compiled many of his Alpine essays, which had appeared in periodicals, in his book *The Playground of Europe* (1871). Blending climbing descriptions and philosophical though often humorous reflections that signaled his sarcasm about the emerging Alpine tourism, the volume was revised and updated in a second edition (1894) and quickly became a mountaineering classic.

Both the first and second editions of *The Playground of Europe* move from depictions of successful ascents of peaks and passages of passes to descriptions of places and conclude with general reflections on mountaineering, a part much expanded in the second edition. While the first edition began with two essays contrasting the old and new schools of mountaineering and concluded with an essay titled "The Dangers of Mountaineering," the second edition added more contemplative essays, such as "A Bye-Day in the Alps," "Sunset on Mont Blanc," and "The Alps in Winter." Both editions mirror Stephen's path from exploratory and competitive mountaineering to a reflective and critical approach: quite consciously, Stephen took mountaineering in a new direction after the 1865 Matterhorn disaster. Whereas the earlier essays celebrate achievements and first ascents, the later ruminations add critical reevaluation to the enterprise as a whole.

Readily admitting to his own summit fever, Stephen rejoices atop the Rothorn: "I can, at any rate, say that I have seldom known a happier half-hour than that in which I basked on the mossy turf in the shadow of the conquered Rothorn—all my internal sensations of present comfort, of hard-won victory, and of lovely scenery, delicately harmonized by the hallowing influence of tobacco" (41). While using a language of conquest, Stephen still infuses an ironic twinkle by linking triumph with gratification, serenity, and the pleasure of nicotine. In this way, his climbing descriptions are mingled with mockery, his summit experiences tinged with playfulness. This is also the case when Stephen details one of his most impressive achievements in "The Ascent of the Schreckhorn," a chapter that already

formed the opening essay of *Peaks, Passes, and Glaciers.* Comparing the gran-
deur and impressiveness of various Swiss mountains, Stephen begins with
Mont Blanc and the Matterhorn but then voices his preference for the
Bernese Oberland, specifically mentioning the Jungfrau, Mönch, Eiger,
Wetterhorn, and finally the Schreckhorn. He details the Schreckhorn's
climbing history, including Joseph Hugi's attempt in 1828, and Édouard
Desor's (Agassiz's friend and assistant) in 1842, who claimed the first ascent
until it turned out his party had climbed a secondary peak of the Lauter-
aarhorn by mistake. Stephen describes this history in a language mirroring
the mind-set of assault: "The others [peaks] had fallen before the zeal of
Swiss, German, and English travelers; but in 1861 the Schreckhorn, the
most savage and forbidding of all in its aspect, still frowned defiance upon
all comers" (10). Stephen's description of his own climb continues in this
vein but foregrounds an intimate and intense physical experience: "We
were frequently flattened out against the rocks, like beasts of ill-repute
nailed to a barn, with fingers and toes inserted into four different cracks
which tested the elasticity of our frames to the uttermost" (15–16). While
boasting about his most renowned Alpine successes, Stephen acknowledges
with ambivalence the fame that comes with the "victory" (17) over a peak:

> In 1861, however, the prestige of the mountains was rapidly declining. Many
> a noble peak, which a few years before had written itself inaccessible in all
> guide-books, hotel registers, and poetical descriptions of the Alps, had fallen
> an easy victim to the skill and courage of Swiss guides, and the ambition of
> their employers. In spite, therefore, of the supposed difficulties, I was strongly
> attracted by the charms of this last unconquered stronghold of the Ober-
> land. Was there not some infinitesimal niche in history to be occupied by its
> successful assailant? The Schreckhorn will probably outlast even the British
> Constitution and the Thirty-nine Articles: so long as it lasts, and so long as
> Murray and Baedeker describe its wonders for the benefit of successive gen-
> erations of tourists, its first conqueror may be carried down to posterity by
> clinging to its skirts. (12)

In his essay on his ascent to the Jungfraujoch, Stephen uses the fact that
he climbed a pass rather than a summit to distance himself from overeager,
single-minded mountaineers, celebrating instead a gentler moment of reflection. Using British references for British travelers, he mocks his fellow

summit-crazed mountaineers: "The top of the Jungfraujoch comes like the bathos in poetry. It rises so gently above the steep ice-wall, and it is so difficult to determine the precise culminating point, that our enthusiasm oozed out gradually instead of producing a sudden explosion; and that instead of giving three cheers, singing 'God Save the Queen,' or observing any of the traditional ceremonial of a simpler generation of travelers, we calmly walked forwards as though we had been crossing Westminster Bridge" (73). While admitting that mountains hold more value as long as they are still unclimbed, Stephen imbues such anthropocentric perspective with irony. This denunciation of conquest rings familiar: Already Humboldt, Saussure, and Forbes had emphasized the nonimportance of their mountain quests, though Stephen more generally reframes the very idea of humans' claims on mountains in that he acknowledges multiple forces at play, lending his texts a modern and timely bent. Rejecting a fixed moral message that emanates from nature, Stephen urges us to approach our environment unencumbered and open-minded.

Summit Positions and Modern Climbing

Stephen's humorous and sometimes cynical tone extends to depictions of his summit experiences. On the Bietschhorn ascent, Stephen remarks that the view, according to Ball's *Alpine Guide*, should be one of the most beautiful in the entire Alps, but masses of clouds prevented a confirmation. On the Rothorn, he jests, "No doubt some enthusiast will ask me about the view" (39), and on the Weisshorn, he admits to not remembering anything outstanding at all. In a similar vein, Stephen downplays his mountaineering achievements, especially when compared to his guides. Owing to Chamonix's strict regulations, Stephen ended up with three guides on the Schreckhorn—in his opinion "one, if not two, too many" (13). Yet here as well as elsewhere he emphasizes the indispensability of guides: "I utterly repudiate the doctrine that Alpine travellers are or ought to be the heroes of Alpine adventures" (13), crediting Swiss guides for their skill, strength, and courage, even though on the whole, his relationship to guides appears to have been more formal.

Like Humboldt and Saussure before him, Stephen pays acute attention to physical sensations interfering with his climbing experience. In "The

Eigerjoch," he grumbles about early morning starts and finds it difficult to enjoy fully the rewards of his efforts: "I looked at it [the loveliest of Alpine views] with utter indifference, and thought what I should order for breakfast. Bodily fatigue and appreciation of natural scenery are simply incompatible" (62). "The Rothorn" similarly blends Stephen's appreciation of beautifully colored clouds at sunrise with the fact that he feels grumpy at such an early hour and the clouds thwart his chances of climbing success: "At this moment [the clouds] were tinged with every shade of colour that an Alpine sunrise can supply. I have heard such clouds described as 'mashed rainbow'; and whatever the nature of the culinary process, their glorious beauty is undeniable. But for the time the ambition of climbing the Rothorn had quenched all aesthetic influences, and a sulky growl was the only homage I could pay them" (31). "Rising," "streaming," and "raging," the clouds arguably possess more agency than Stephen himself, who grudgingly retreats.

As Humboldt, Forbes, Wills, and Tyndall had done, Stephen depicts climbing as an activity that involves every part of the body, "sometimes using our hands, knees, and eyelids" (5). About this all-encompassing activity, he specifies: "In a few places I found myself fumbling vaguely with my fingers at imaginary excrescences, my feet resting upon rotten projections of crumbling stone, whilst a large pointed slab of rock pressed against my stomach, and threatened to force my centre of gravity backwards beyond the point of support" (37). Delineating rock climbing as the athletic, precarious, and gymnastic moving over stone, Stephen puts more emphasis on the actual process of climbing than on the summit experience. Once again the direction of agency is not one-dimensional: instead, the self and the rock take turns in a delicate sequence of movements. Stephen's fingers fumble, the stone crumbles, the rock presses, and the subject struggles to maintain a sense of balance. While Saussure remembered the moment his hands first touched rock, Stephen here goes much further, portraying climbing as an intricate and sensual movement, a reciprocal interplay of body and environment. In *The Playground of Europe,* an illustration of his climb on the Rothorn's knife-edge ridge, a climb that is now rated as D+ (difficulty plus), captures this moment as if an early version of present-day photographs displaying outstretched climbers in extreme positions perched on steep if not overhanging rock. Departing from his predecessors, Stephen

"Ascent of the Rothorn," frontispiece in
The Playground of Europe (Internet Archive)

does not view these physical challenges of mountain climbing as wearisome impediments but embraces, indeed welcomes, the taxing activity as a sport that, requiring both physical and mental stamina, brings one in touch with one's environment and ultimately affords much passion and pleasure, regardless of whether one reaches a summit or not.

The essay "Dangers of Mountaineering" that originally concluded *The Playground of Europe* compares Alpinists to gymnasts, beginning to outline modern forms of rock and ice climbing. While Stephen makes an argument for guides, he emphasizes movement, balance, agility, and power, all ingredients of contemporary climbing. Refuting the opinion that in an era when "the mountains are exhausted, the only remaining excitement will depend upon future travelers learning to dispense with the guides," Stephen instead advocates the training of one's gymnastic faculties while benefiting from the guidance of leaders to prevent further accidents.[8]

To Stephen, the modern era of Alpine climbing, when "there is no more glory to be won by making new ascents," has also ended the time of scientific discovery.[9] Science cannot provide a rationale for climbing anymore, and accordingly, Stephen only pokes fun at scientific motives for climbing, anticipating by a decade the satirical depictions of Alpine climbing in Mark Twain's *A Tramp Abroad* (1880).

> "And what philosophical observations did you make?" will be the inquiry of one of those fanatics who, by a reasoning process to me utterly inscrutable, have somehow irrevocably associated alpine travelling with science. To them I answer that the temperature was approximately (I had no thermometer) 212° (Fahrenheit) below freezing-point. As for ozone, if any existed in the atmosphere, it was a greater fool than I take it for. As we had, unluckily, no barometer, I am unable to give the usual information as to the extent of our deviation from the correct altitude; but the Federal map fixes the height at 13,855 feet. (39–40)

Yet despite Stephen calling scientists fanatics—which, unsurprisingly, deeply offended Tyndall and other contemporaries—multiple references to Saussure, Forbes, Tyndall, and Wills appear in his text. Paying due respect to his scientific predecessors, and still undeniably fascinated by the imagination of a glacial epoch, Stephen's ridicule emphasizes that one has no need to lug around instruments in an age when peaks have been mapped, temperatures recorded, and other measurements taken. In the spirit of his reflective approach to climbing, Stephen deliberately uncouples climbing from science.

If science no longer provides fitting motivations for modern climbers, then Romantic rapture has run its course, too. Stephen admits that the act of climbing actually pulled him away from Ruskinian mountain ecstasy:

> When long ago the Alps cast their spell upon me, it was woven in a great degree by the eloquence of *Modern Painters*. I hoped to share Ruskin's ecstasies in a reverent worship of Mont Blanc and the Matterhorn. The influence of any cult, however, depends upon the character of the worshipper, and I fear that in this case the charm operated rather perversely. It stimulated a passion for climbing which absorbed my energies and distracted me from the prophet's loftier teaching.[10]

Though admiring the Victorian writer, artist, architect, art critic, social critic, and amateur geologist John Ruskin (1819–1900) and even borrowing some phrases of his, Stephen deliberately sets himself apart from Ruskin's transcendental visions.[11] By way of contrast, Stephen inserts a good deal of irony and sarcasm into the mountaineering discourse, claiming that "a sense of humour is not incompatible with imaginative sensibility" (219). With a nod to Ruskin and Romantic clichés, Stephen pokes fun at writers who "burst out in sentences which swell to paragraphs, and in paragraphs which spread over pages; to plunge into ecstasies about infinite abysses and overpowering splendours, to compare mountains to archangels lying down in eternal winding sheets of snow, and to convert them into allegories about man's highest destinies and aspirations" (218). Ruskin, conversely, charged British mountaineers in general and Stephen in particular with being vain, boastful, and competitive, complaining that their sport paid little attention to the realities of mountain life and Alpine dwellers.[12]

Musings on Materialism

If first ascents were no longer to be had, and neither science nor the sublime could promise a fitting reward for climbing, then what motivation remains? Following the philosophy of materialism, which held that mental deliberation was rooted in material interaction, Stephen embraced climbing's physical dimension: "It follows, however, that my passion for the mountains had something earthly in its composition. It is associated with memories of eating and drinking. It meant delightful comradeship with some of the best of friends; but our end, I admit, was not always of the most exalted or aesthetic strain."[13] Delineating climbing as a fusion of physical and mental faculties, Stephen lends poetic power to the experience. The essay "The Dangers of Mountaineering" outlines this process most explicitly: addressing his readers as persons with "genuine love of the mountains," Stephen advocates first "quiet walks" then "second-rate mountain[s]" so as "to practise not only your muscles but your eyes and your understanding."[14] Making a case for modern mountaineering, Stephen finally advises: "You will find, especially, that you are developing new faculties. You learn how best to economise your strength, and how most effectually to tackle any little difficulty that occurs. You learn still more to interpret the real meaning of the sights before you. The mountains, for example, will grow daily in apparent size. The little white or purple patches which said nothing to you at first will become full of poetical meaning."[15] Mountaineering here becomes a physical and psychological educative path, as it encourages the climber to adapt and develop. In the interaction of subject and environment, both continually change, to the point that the mountaineer simultaneously develops skill and wisdom, namely, "a new faculty of enjoyment."[16]

The essay "A Bye-Day in the Alps" (only included in the second edition of *The Playground of Europe*) puts such ideas into practice by transitioning from trip report to a multifaceted contemplation of the dynamic entanglements between man and nature. Stephen details an excursion to the top of the Dent d'Oche, a minor peak near Evian. Although the excursion does not promise a renowned ascent, Stephen sees other qualities in this "perfectly easy" (120) undertaking: "No elaborate preparations were necessary to carry out so modest a scheme; and next morning, instead of summoning guides, ordering provisions, and testing ropes and axes, I surreptitiously conveyed a roll from the breakfast-table in my pocket, and started with a domestic walking-stick upon an exploring expedition" (113). This contemplation ends up being one of the most interesting chapters in Stephen's book and includes a minute description of the climb, peppered with intertextual references from Ruskin, Milton, Goethe, Shakespeare, Wordsworth,

Byron, Shelley, Rousseau, and Voltaire; a glimpse into Stephen's mountain philosophy; and a revelation of his thoughts on agency.

In marked contrast to the frenzied activity of mountain conquest, "A Bye-Day in the Alps" begins with a reflection on sleep. Prefacing the chapter with lines from Wordsworth, "The silence that is in the starry sky, / The sleep that is among the lonely hills," Stephen ponders the relationship between exertion and rest and, by extension, the interplay between body and mind.[17] Harking back to Haller's celebration of Alpine peasants' robust health and sound sleep, Stephen contrasts the refreshing and soothing Alpine sleep with London's "depressing dreams" (108). However, Stephen much extends this discourse by turning to the restorative aspects of hiking. Hiking, according to Stephen, quenches "conscious intellectual effort" to the point that "thought, that is, becomes indistinguishable from emotion . . . and therefore, I find that nothing is more conducive to the proper state of delicious drowsiness than the regular monotonous rise and fall of a pair of feet in hobnailed boots forcing me upwards through a perpendicular height of about 1,500 feet in an hour" (108–9).[18]

Outlining the rewards of a restless mind put at ease by constant and demanding activity of the body, Stephen devises an original yet powerful and enduring rationale for climbing. While hiking in itself offers some meditative reward—in his essay "In Praise of Walking," Stephen celebrated "the delightful sensation of independence and detachment enjoyed during a walking tour"[19]—the benefits are exponentially expanded with mountaineering: "When climbing upwards, you first feel that the bundle of earthly cares rolls off your shoulders, and that you have finally cleared the 'slough of despond'" (118). Using the inclusive "you," Stephen advertises climbing as an activity that recompenses itself, no matter the summit attained, since the act of climbing provides an intense contact and communication with one's environment, what Stephen terms "absorbing or being absorbed into the mountain-spirit" (122).

On the summit, Stephen succumbs to this experience: rather than enjoying the view, he closes his eyes and throws himself on the ground, elucidating: "I lazily fingered a little clump of gentians and tried to sink into a temporary Nirvana" (123). Significantly, Stephen's bliss is grounded in material reality and is soon disrupted by more mundane preoccupations of the mind: "Had I been a bona fide anchorite, I might possibly have remained on the summit of the Dent d'Oche till my nails grew into my flesh. . . . But the Western mind refuses to lend itself long to such uncongenial efforts. In a few minutes the most sublunary considerations began to force themselves upon my mind. Thoughts of dinner and speculations about a certain short cut became irresistible, and before long I descended from my peak and my poetizing" (124). After the bliss found in nature, Stephen happily returns to modern life. He does not pit one against the other but seeks to open such experiences to the average Alpine traveler.

If in "A Bye-Day in the Alps" Stephen depicts the mountain as a voice beckoning him to its summit, where, in a pantheistic moment, "I endeavored to be simply an animated top of the mountain" (124), the essay "Sunset on Mont Blanc" goes even further in delineating nonhuman agency. Once again, Stephen ties together literary quotes, a trip report, and philosophical ponderings on man and nature. As the title hints, the essay begins with Romantic reverence but soon casts doubt on any single meaning found in nature: "Natural Scenery, like a great work of art, scorns to be tied down to any cut-and-dried moral. To each spectator it suggests a different train of thought and emotion, varying as widely as the idiosyncrasy of the mind affected" (180). While Stephen here still assumes the role of a "spectator," who, in the tradition of the sublime, is moved to inner contemplation, he rejects a fixed moral message and ceases to decode and define nature. Going further, Stephen surrenders visual distance to describe the deep and physical enmeshment with his environment:

> Does not science teach us more and more emphatically that nothing which is natural can be alien to us who are part of nature?
>
> Where does Mont Blanc end and where do I begin? That is the question which no metaphysician has hitherto succeeded in answering. But at least the connection is close and intimate. He is a part of the great machinery in which my physical frame is inextricably involved, and not the less interesting because a part which I am unable to subdue to my purposes. The whole universe, from the stars and the planets to the mountains and the insects which creep about their roots, is but a network of forces eternally acting and reacting upon each other. (180–81)

In her insightful reading of the passage, Catherine Hollis interprets Stephen's words as a testament to materialism, suggesting that Stephen's later turn to philosophic empiricism emerged in this context. To Hollis, Stephen achieves unity with the mountain not through conquest or Romantic rapture but through the act of climbing, which entails the mountain's resistance and the human's insight that the mountain cannot be subdued for his purpose. As she elucidates, "The kinship Stephen sees is not that mountains resemble humans, but that in the action of climbing, a climber becomes more like a mountain, more material, more [a] thinking body than an embodied mind. You might say that Stephen advocates that we allow the mountain to 'geomorphize' us, rather than the other way around" (40–41). Indeed, Stephen posits the mountain as a sentence subject, situating himself in a reversal of agency as a "loyal adherent" (178). Challenging the division between humans and nature, emphasizing the role of the physical body, and outlining a network of interacting forces, Stephen's thoughts resonate in recent findings in the field of biosemiotics, which investigates processes of communication among all forms of life, including touch, sound, smell, electric fields, and waves.

In "The Regrets of a Mountaineer," Stephen returns to notions of human intentionality versus mountain agency. This time, he bases his ruminations on a simple fact with far-reaching consequences: "That a mountain is very big, and is faced by perpendicular walls of rock, is the first thing which strikes everybody, and is the whole essence and outcome of a vast quantity of poetical description" (223). Faced with the sheer size of a mountain, mountaineering "brings one into contact with the sublimest aspects of nature" and "helps one indirectly to absorb and be penetrated by their influence" (218). Stephen engages the common premises of the sublime, but instead of rational detachment, he stresses the physical immediacy of the experience: "Any one standing at the foot of the Wetterhorn may admire its stupendous massiveness and steepness; but, to feel its influence enter in the very marrow of one's bones, it is necessary to stand at the summit" (238). In this immersion, visual consumption gives way to an immediate connection down to the level of cellular interaction. More recently, scholars have pursued this line of inquiry further in the context of material ecocriticism. In *Becoming Animal,* the philosopher and cultural ecologist David Abram delineates a mountain's field of energy with the example of its shadow: "To step into the shadow of this mountain is to step directly under the mountain's influence, letting it untangle your senses as the rhythm of your breath adjusts to its breathing, to the style of its weather. To step into its shadow is to become a part, if only for this moment, of the mountain's life."[20] Challenging the notion of the interaction of separate natural and social realms altogether, the theoretical physicist and feminist Karen Barad instead proposes the concept of "intra-action" to recognize the dynamism and entanglements that structure relations of space, time, and matter.[21]

Sublime Stereotyping

Alongside its proto-ecocritical significance and contemporary resonance, however, Stephen's work contains troubling and backward aspects, particularly when it comes to elitism and supremacy. As Wills had done, Stephen acquired the services of the Swiss guide Ulrich Lauener in the summer of 1859 for his push to the Eigerjoch, becoming similarly enthralled with Lauener's figure and physique. If Wills, in 1854, admired Lauener's tall, muscular frame, piercing blue eyes, and manly vigor, Stephen correspondingly marvels at "the gigantic Ulrich Lauener, the most picturesque of guides. Tall, spare, blue-eyed, long-limbed, and square-shouldered, with a jovial laugh and a not ungraceful swagger, he is the very model of a true mountaineer" (46). Stephen's admiration for the Aryan ideal becomes only slightly tainted by less-flattering insights when he acknowledges Lauener's "autocratic" rule, which back in 1854 self-servingly triggered the Wetterhorn ascent. If Wills observed an ensuing conflict between the Chamonix and the local Grindelwald guides, Stephen affirms Lauener's "views as to the superiority of the Teutonic over the Latin races, which rather interfered with the harmony of the party at a later period" (46). Statements like these reveal the origins of patriarchal disposition, class snobbery, and xenophobic trains of thought that still pervade a mostly wealthy and white mountaineering culture to this day.

Stephen also takes up Forbes's, Wills's, and Whymper's disparaging views of Alpine peasants. Like Wills, Stephen recounts tales of natives using "holes in their tables as a substitute for plates" (24), based not on his own but on Balmat's observations. And while Wills had complained about noisy German students, Stephen similarly objects to "the clatter of sundry German tourists, who had flooded the little coffee-room and occupied my beloved sofa, and who kept up a ceaseless conversation" (43). As in Whymper,

Stephen's observations lead to some national stereotyping, though he does so with a characteristic chuckle: in the Mont Blanc chapter, he laments that watching the Alpine glow on the mountain has become "a little too popular," explaining: "The very sunset seems to smell of *Baedeker's Guide.* The flesh is weak and the most sympathetic of human beings is apt to feel a slight sense of revulsion when the French guests at a *table d'tôte* are exclaiming in chorus, '*Magnifique, superbe!*' and the Germans chiming in with '*Wunderschön!*' and the British tourist patting the old mountain on the back, and the American protesting that he has shinier sunsets at home" (182). Mocking the growing commercialization and nationalization of Alpine travel, Stephen lays bare both the narrow-mindedness of tourists and the prejudices of seasoned mountain travelers. Ruskin had condemned the popularity of Alpine travel in somber tones; Stephen, on the other hand, seems to include himself in the "crowd of upstart rivals" (178) attempting Mont Blanc and likewise realizes that his very text helps advertise Alpine travel. Assuming the position of both the mountaineering crowd and the readers who consume these feats back in England, Stephen elucidates in the preface to the first edition of *The Playground of Europe:* "Somehow, in reading, London fogs have rolled away, and I have caught glimpses of the ever-glorious Alps; above the chimney-pots over the way I have seen the solemn cliffs of the Schreckhorn and the Jungfrau" (xxi).

In returning to the familiar contrast between a foggy and smoky London home and glorious Alpine heights, Stephen echoes similar thoughts voiced by Smith and Whymper, but goes further by drafting an infamous height profile of the Alps, in which he distributes Alpine travelers according to plant zones:

> Travellers, like plants, may be divided according to the zones which they reach. In the highest region, the English climber—an animal whose instincts and peculiarities are pretty well known—is by far the most abundant genus. Lower down comes a region where he is mixed with a crowd of industrious Germans and a few sporadic examples of adventurous ladies and determined sightseers. Below this is the luxuriant growth of the domestic tourist in all his amazing and intricate varieties. (211)

The passage recalls the well-known illustrations of Humboldt's plant geography, which grouped plants according to their native habitat and high-

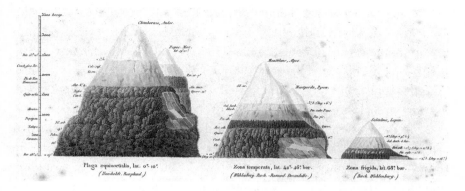

Alexander von Humboldt, *Geographiae plantarum lineamenta*, 1817
(Provided by the Zentralbibliothek Zurich)

lighted their relationship to climate and geography. But instead of plant
zones, Stephen situates mountaineers, tourists, and women on a vertical
scale, as if to follow a natural distribution according to gender, nationality,
and physical fitness. Stephen thereby profoundly misreads Humboldt, who
had provocatively proposed that vertical vegetation zones correspond to
horizontal climatic zones. Whereas Humboldt proposed a carefully cali-
brated ecosystem rather than following Linnaeus in regarding life-forms as
classified and isolated species, Stephen precisely reintroduces such categories in entirely unnatural divisions.[22] Stephen's taxonomy drew considerable criticism, both positive and negative. In the introduction to the 1937
edition of Stephen's book, the British Alpinist and writer Geoffrey Win-
throp Young (1876–1958), in the spirit of his time, did not hesitate to
sharpen Stephen's views by declaring that "mountaineering as a sport was
the invention of these few cultured and imaginative Englishmen" (vii). In
Germany and Austria, fervent nationalists bluntly enlisted such divisions in
the service of their chauvinistic and racist ideology when separating Aryan
über-climbers from the masses of hikers below. The German and Austrian
Alpine Association's functionary Eduard Pichl, for instance, successfully
agitated for the exclusion of Jewish members from the association, delineating the Alps as a politicized pan-German space of racial purity.[23]

In his gendered critique of early mountaineering, Michael S. Reidy
points out that Stephen and others "attempted to codify the high Alps, the
third and uppermost Switzerland, as an all-male preserve."[24] Indeed, in his

model of traveler zones, Stephen departs from his predecessor Wills, who had advocated female mountain travel, to reinsert gender stereotypes into the mountaineering discourse. Yet as Hollis reveals, despite his words, Stephen took his fiancée Thackeray and her sister up to the Gorner Glacier and the Riffelhorn and was impressed with her adaptability to the Alpine terrain on their honeymoon.[25]

A similar wavering is mirrored in his later biographical writings, when Stephen strictly distinguished between so-called masculine and feminine traits—and moreover in his own life, when Stephen, after his wedding to Harriet Marian Thackeray in 1867, declared his renunciation of mountaineering in "The Regrets of a Mountaineer," the concluding essay to both editions of *Playground* and originally published anonymously in the *Cornhill Magazine* a few months after his nuptials. As a married man, Stephen described to a friend the "pangs at staying at the bottom, instead of bounding from peak to peak" during his honeymoon and voiced his unhappiness about having given up mountaineering before he was physically incapable of climbing.[26] Yet the essay somewhat melodramatically and prematurely dramatized Stephen's self-imposed postmarriage departure from Alpine climbing. He continued to make yearly Alpine excursions and completed "The Alps in Winter" and "Sunset on Mont Blanc" after "The Regrets of a Mountaineer." His "drama of renunciation set up the mountains and marriage in opposition, as a romantic rivalry between competing loves," as Catherine Hollis has perceptively noted, "an ultimately false choice generated by a temperament attracted equally to the stoicism of climbing and the sentimental attractions of domesticity."[27] Yet what Hollis does not mention is that Stephen was well aware of this pitfall and in a later essay (which he mused could be called "Relapses of a Mountaineer") mocked his previous words: "Following the precedent of dramatic performances, I bade a solemn farewell to the mountains, and—still according to that precedent—I have to confess that the farewell was perhaps a little premature."[28]

A similar slipperiness informs Stephen's xenophobia: on one hand, he injects nationalism into the mountaineering discourse; on the other, he reserves some harsh words for the increasing numbers of tourists from his own country: "I studied with a philosophic eye the nature of that offensive variety of the genus of *primates,* the common tourist. His main specialties, as it seems to me from many observations, are, first and chiefly, a rooted aversion to mountain scenery; secondly, a total incapacity to live without *The Times;* and thirdly, a deeply-seated conviction that foreigners generally are members of a secret society intended to extort money on false pretences" (74–75). While descending into common prejudice and bigotry, Stephen keeps a tinge of sophisticated sarcasm: when he, like many of his predecessors, takes notice of unsanitary conditions in the Italian village of Santa Catarina, he adds, "But Italian dirt, though unpleasant, is not of that uncompromising character," calling the dirt, in reference to Heinrich Heine, "grossartiger Schmutz" ("magnificent dirt," 134).[29] Returning to the problematic elevation profile, Stephen contrasts the Italian, who "appears to pass his day in elaborate indolence" (135), with the Briton, who spends his days searching Alpine heights, and his nights consuming a modest meal before retiring early for a short period of sleep. In his preference for the latter, despite continued jabs at "muscular Christianity" (135) and the "scrambling Briton" (136), Stephen once more uses physical fitness as a key distinguishing factor, drawing attention to physicality and the body when it comes to Alpine space. His disdain of tourism and even of the locals seems to stem from the presumption that those who do not physically interact with the mountain are unable to achieve a greater understanding of, or deeper connection with, the land.

Stephen expands this calculus in "The Alps in Winter" when evaluating the Alpine inhabitants according to their level of activity:

> As one penetrates further into the valleys, and the bagman element—the only representative of the superincumbent summer population—disappears, one finds the genuine peasant, neither the parasite which sucks the blood of summer tourists nor the melodramatic humbug of operas and picture-books. He is the rough athletic labourer, wrestling with nature for his immediate wants, reducing industrial life to its simplest forms, and with a certain capacity—not to be quite overlooked—for the absorption of *schnapps.* (204)

Once again, Stephen imbues what he calls the "genuine" Alpine peasant with characteristics that relate to a physical interaction with the environment—strength, vigor, and athleticism. His opinions on both Alpine citizens and travelers thus follow along a trajectory that places a physical engagement with the landscape at its center. This emphasis on material contact with the land has both deeply troubling and refreshingly progressive ramifications. While Stephen's mountain profile relating to the kinetic experience of its visitors introduces problematic classifications and stereotyping into the mountaineering discourse, the emphasis on one's own sensual experience irrespective of a summit position carries the potential to open up and democratize the mountaineering experience. Stephen's framework at once highlights the elitist and restrictive dimensions of nineteenth-century mountaineering and outlines a modern climbing experience that emphasizes physical entanglement and bodily pleasure.

In this vein, Stephen characterizes mountaineering as a sport that "calls into play a great variety of physical and intellectual energies, and gives the pleasure which always accompanies an energetic use of our faculties" (218). From the physical effort arrives a connection to one's environment that affords happiness: "I say that I enjoy being on the top of a mountain, or, indeed, half-way up a mountain; that climbing is a pleasure to me" (217). Openly acknowledging the pleasure gained from mountaineering—which Stephen here compares to the equally physical act of dining on culinary delicacies—not only captures his passion and motivation for climbing but also outlines the key motivation of modern climbing, with its focus on movement, form, and gratification. Equally, the resulting questions about privilege, exclusivity, and bias continue to bear relevance in John Muir, Clarence King, and beyond.

PART III
EXPLORING THE AMERICAN WEST

CHAPTER 9

TRANSCONTINENTAL SHIFTS

Clarence King's Representation of the American West

To the Highest Summit

Nearly seventy years after Alexander von Humboldt lugged his heavy brass instruments up to a considerable height on Mount Chimborazo in 1802, the presumed highest summit in the world, Clarence King in 1871 carried similar instruments to what he believed to be the highest peak in North America. On top, King and his partner Paul Pinson found a cairn with an Indian arrow, but this historical record detracted little from their triumph. Taking pride in being the first *white* men to have climbed the highest mountain in the United States, they left a note to this effect, proclaiming its height at fifteen thousand feet (even though their measurements on top indicated a lower elevation). As was the case for Humboldt and many others, the cloud-enshrouded summit did not afford a gratifying bird's-eye view; instead, a thick fog obscured King's vision to such a degree that he claimed he could not see that an even higher peak lay five miles to the north.

This brief sketch reveals some of the continuities and differences in the transnational evolution of climbing in North America. Profoundly influ-

enced by his European predecessors, King emulated their aesthetic sen-
sibilities, competitive drive, and scientific claims. As Patrick Kupper and
others point out, traditions of European Romanticism informed notions
of nature and wilderness on both sides of the Atlantic, also establishing the
idea that modern civilization and wild places were mutually exclusive.[1]
While, as we have seen, British climbers had idealized some Alpine peasants and used others as a foil for racial stereotyping, the environment King
encountered during the westward expansion was in the process of being
expunged from its indigenous inhabitation and appropriated in the service
of national identity. When King stylized himself into a western hero in an
imagined wilderness, he helped develop a sense of place and pride in North
American identity predicated on driving indigenous populations from
their homes and erasing their histories. By opening the western landscape
to its beckoning exploration and possession, he pegged an American sublime that leaves behind the aesthetic categories of European Romanticism.
King's adventures, therefore, were bound up in the political, racial, and
ethical ramifications of the frontier experience. King's later work as geologist in charge of the United States Geological Exploration of the Fortieth
Parallel aggressively continued such exploitation when mountain slopes
were stripped of forest to supply timber for the burgeoning mining operations and railroad construction along the survey.[2] At the same time, King's
narratives betray a certain ambivalence (which John O'Grady termed
"psychological repression") about the larger ideological thrust of such conquest.[3] Couched in humorous and satirical tales are moments of fear, of
homoerotic desires, and of encounters with Indians that all unsettle a one-
dimensional narrative of heroic expansion of the West.

For two years, King basked in the glory of having climbed the highest
mountain in the United States, until his achievement turned into a public
disgrace when, in 1873, the geologist Watson Goodyear and a companion
"climbed" (by riding a mule) the same mountain, only to detect a higher
peak from its summit. Goodyear rushed back to announce the news to the
California Academy of Science in San Francisco. It was discovered that
both parties had mistakenly climbed Mount Langley, then called Sheep
Mountain. Based on two erroneous magnetic bearings from 1864 (one by
King himself), King's former expedition companion, the German cartog-

rapher Charles F. Hoffmann, had misidentified Langley as Whitney, and the mistake had been reproduced in an incorrect map of the entire Sierra Nevada by Hoffmann and Wheeler in 1873, which turned out to be the map Goodyear and King had used. When King raced to rectify his mistake by climbing the true Mount Whitney in September of that same year, he discovered to his dismay that he had been beaten by a few weeks by three locals from Lone Pine (Charles D. Begole, Albert H. Johnson, and John Lucas), who had summited the mountain on August 18, unsuspectingly naming it Fisherman's Peak. King's response to the disappointment, published in a revised chapter of the 1874 edition of *Mountaineering in the Sierra Nevada*, projects eloquence, wit, and mockery:

> My little granite island was incessantly beaten by breakers of vague impenetrable clouds, and never once did the true Mount Whitney unveil its crest to my eager eyes. Only one glimpse and I should have bent my steps northward, restless till the peak was climbed. But then that would have left nothing for Goodyear, whose paper shows such evident relish in my mistake, that I accept my '71 ill-luck as providential. One has in this dark world so few chances of conferring innocent, pure delight.[4]

Mountaineering in the Sierra Nevada (mostly compiled from essays previously serialized in the *Atlantic Monthly* from May to December 1871) appeared with the Boston publisher J. R. Osgood in 1872, the same year as Mark Twain's *Roughing It;* a London edition followed soon thereafter, and a new 1874 edition in both the United States and England contained some additional pages on the Whitney calamity. The book not only made the range known and palatable to the nation but reflected a highly original American-European convergence. King harked back to his European predecessors while advancing the tall tales of the Wild West and embracing an American masculinity that, according to Mark Allister, a professor of environmental studies, "is notable for its emphasis on a certain conservative outward demeanor, on physical prowess, personal restraint, doing rather than thinking."[5] In this way, it established an imaginative and captivating mountaineering discourse with a distinctly North American bent: catering to an East Coast readership feasting on popular dime novels about frontiersmen, King cast himself as a western hero with pluck, reserve, and perseverance.

An Eastern Education, a Western Quest

Clarence Rivers King was born on January 6, 1842, to the sixteen-year-old Florence and the somewhat older James Rivers King, a merchant in trade business in Canton, China. King's father saw his son only between the ages of three and five before returning to China, where he perished in 1848, most likely from a fever. Growing up as an only child (two sisters had died as infants), under the tutelage of his doting young mother in Newport, Rhode Island, and Hartford, Connecticut, King formed a strong maternal connection and simultaneously developed an early urge to escape the parental home and wander about. Thanks to the continued profits from the China trade, Florence was able to afford her son an excellent education at several New England institutions that supported and fostered his early interests in the natural world. Though King was dismayed when Florence decided to remarry a good decade after her husband's death, his new stepfather soon stepped in with financial support, funding King's attendance at the Sheffield Scientific School at Yale, to which he was admitted in September 1860.

Along with his best friend from high school, James Terry Gardner, King took classes in chemistry, physics, and German with William Whitney, brother of Josiah Whitney.[6] King and Gardner became particularly engrossed in geology classes with the school's newest luminary, James Dwight Dana, and George Jarvis Brush, who had visited Humboldt while in Berlin. After completing the three-year program in two years, graduating in July 1862 in the midst of the Civil War, King considered joining the Union Army—he was a longtime abolitionist like his grandmother and his mother, but he had also adopted his family's biblical faith, which rejected any killing. Allegedly, King found an altogether different answer to the dilemma at a reading by his professor Brush, who had just received a letter from his friend and former classmate William H. Brewer, in which he described a harrowing ascent of Mount Shasta, at the time thought to be North America's highest mountain. King reportedly responded to the reading with the words "that settles it" and committed himself to further vigorous training as a geologist.[7] He read Dana's new book, *Manual of Geology* (1863), studied Humboldt's *Kosmos,* and familiarized himself with glacial theories by reading the works of John Tyndall and traveling to Harvard to hear Louis

Agassiz's lectures on glaciology. These European models exerted a great influence, shaping King's approach to mountains not only in scientific but also in aesthetic terms. In honor of John Ruskin's contemplation of nature in *Modern Painters* (1843–60), King, Gardner, and five other friends even formed a Pre-Raphaelite brotherhood called "the Society for the Advancement of Truth in Art" in New York, where King and Gardner now shared an apartment.

King's life bears some striking resemblance to that of Alexander von Humboldt: both grew up largely fatherless, in affluent, sheltered environments that they escaped as boys by exploring the outdoors, and both developed an early interest in the natural sciences. Humboldt and King received a first-rate education that kindled their quest for scientific exploration. By all accounts, both were strikingly handsome, charismatic men and especially gifted speakers who could, with their ravenous charm and larger-than-life tales, capture the imaginations of crowds, whether in Paris, Berlin, or New York. Yet both also felt deeply dissatisfied with many of the traditions and conventions of elite nineteenth-century culture: Humboldt and King battled melancholy, isolation, and depression with an incessant need to travel. Only by escaping the restrictions of their societies were they able to explore not only the world around them but also inward drives and sexuality, forming intimate friendships and ties with other men and women of different ethnicities. The two men, finally, were outspoken abolitionists and liberal thinkers but ultimately avoided involvement in open political struggles such as the French Revolution and the Civil War, respectively. Like Humboldt, King also became more settled in the second half of his life, after he had achieved considerable success by writing about his adventures. In this way, both explorers reentered the societies they had fled as young men, with the adventures of the first part of their lives defining them.

That King lived in the latter rather than the first half of the nineteenth century, however, made his life profoundly different from Humboldt's. In King's time, the field of geology was thriving after Sir Charles Lyell's renowned book *Principles of Geology* was published in 1830, promoting the influential theory of uniformitarianism. Lyell viewed catastrophism as a polar opposite to uniformitarianism and advocated empirical fieldwork that to his mind would only win the argument for the latter. His theories in turn influenced Charles Darwin, who applied them to biology in *On the Origin of*

Species (1859), and the wealth of fossils found by King's Fortieth Parallel Survey supplied ample evidence for Darwin's theories. Yet as uniformitarianism became widely accepted, King discovered abundant evidence of glacial activity in the mountains of California, which supported the existence of ice ages, suggesting climatic catastrophes rather than gradual changes. This discovery caused ongoing friction with his former boss, Josiah Whitney, as King found himself defending catastrophism against uniformitarianism. In his commencement address at the Yale Sheffield School in 1877, he pleaded for a model in which both theories could coexist.

The progressions in the sciences paralleled other deep-seated changes taking place in King's time. The California gold rush of 1849 spurred not only the quick development of transportation and settlements but also state funding of paleontological research on strata where gold could most likely be found, and extensive mapping of the state. In the decades to come, a growing tide of immigrants came to California, first by wagons, coaches, and sailing ships, later by steamers, and finally on the newly constructed transcontinental railroad (completed in 1869). Even after the gold flow slowed, investors were searching for the next great discovery, be it silver, diamonds, or coal, and early maps of the Sierra Nevada indicated not only mountains, rivers, and routes but also mineral deposits. The aftermath of the gold rush helped finance King's explorations but also tied him to the interests of politicians and businessmen. Whereas Humboldt was financially independent, King's surveys were contingent on state and federal budgets, which greatly influenced the surveys' path, outcome, and representation.

In 1863, King and Gardner took the opportunity to head to the western frontier, armed with a letter of recommendation from Professor Brush. After an adventuresome, multimonth crossing of the continent by train to Missouri, by horseback to Sacramento, and by steamboat to San Francisco (some chapters in King's later book embellish this journey), they chanced on the same Brewer whose account of climbing Mount Shasta had inspired King to come to California in the first place. Brewer, in turn, introduced them to the head of the California Geological Survey, Josiah Whitney, coincidentally the older brother of their former German professor. With his youthful energy and enthusiasm, King charmed Brewer and Whitney alike, persuading Whitney to hire King, without pay, for an upcoming outing with Brewer.[8] Not as financially independent as King, Gardner stayed behind.

The California Geological Survey

As the son of a wealthy New England banker, Josiah Whitney studied chemistry, mineralogy, and astronomy at Yale and continued his education after graduating in 1839 on a five-year trip to Europe, studying chemistry with Justus Liebig in Germany and geology with Elie de Beaumont in France and attending lectures by Alexander von Humboldt in Berlin. After working at state geological surveys in New Hampshire, Iowa, and Wisconsin and securing the support of Agassiz, Dana, and Brush, among others, Whitney convinced legislators to appoint him as director of the California Geological Survey to map the state and provide descriptions of rocks, fossils, and mineral deposits. The survey's first goal was to create accurate topographical maps of the state, beginning with the coastline and stretching to the western side of the Sierra (where most gold mines had been found), the Sierra Crest, and finally, the Sierra Eastside. Whitney hired as his principal assistant Brewer, another graduate from Yale, who had also studied chemistry with Liebig in Munich, with Bunsen in Heidelberg, and with Chevreul in Paris; and as an additional assistant William Ashburner, a former student of Agassiz at Harvard. In 1861, Hoffmann, who had immigrated to the United States at age nineteen, joined the team as first geological assistant for triangulation surveys and the production of maps. The team's strategy was to climb a high peak of known position and measure the angular relations to unknown peaks, fixing their position by establishing the intersection of lines before repeating the process from another known point.

Whitney's survey, however, depended on the California legislature and remained vulnerable to the state's unreliable funding. In response, Whitney pursued both scientific and commercial interests, keeping his team engaged in the question of where the gold was most likely to be found, but also with an eye toward mapping and exploring California's unrivaled landscape. When in the fall of 1861 the state ran out of money, the team continued its work without pay while Whitney took a loan to buy supplies, fresh mounts, and logistical support for his men. During the 1862 season, the survey made great strides when Brewer and Whitney each lugged a barometer all the way to the top of Mount Shasta, measuring its height at 14,500 ft. (now assessed 14,180 ft.). In September 1863, King and Brewer made some fossil finds in the gold-bearing strata of the western Sierra Nevada before turning northwest to the volcanoes of the Cascade Range and successfully climbing Mount Lassen. Influenced by Humboldt's explorations of volcanoes, the men approached the Cascade Range with knowledge and interest in volcanism but concluded wrongly that Lassen was extinct—it erupted violently later, in 1915. Other European artists and scientists also supplied the means of how to approach, understand, and climb mountains. Once on the summit, King reportedly shouted, "What would Ruskin, the most famous living critic of art, have said if he had seen *this!*" before glissading down the treacherous slope, as he had read in the accounts of Tyndall in the Alps.[9] On a second ascent three days later, King filled his journal with pages and pages of glorious musings, using his erudition of Ruskin to frame the summit experience in exalted, Romantic terms. If the Puritans had initially emulated the European bias against mountains as hostile and infertile grounds, with the import of Romantic ideals, the image of an idealized North American wilderness began to emerge, leading to distinctly American landscape aesthetics such as the Hudson River school.

While King preferred to roam in the mountains rather than to excavate fossils, upon his return, he was assigned to several paleontological excursions designed to locate fossils in the auriferous slate on the western slopes of the Sierra Nevada. During one of these missions, while climbing Mount Bullion near the town of Mariposa, King spotted "a vast pile of white peaks" to the south, of whose "great height I was fully persuaded" (45). To explore these heights, five months later he had convinced Whitney to assemble a team consisting of Brewer as director, Hoffmann as principal cartographical assistant, King as volunteer assistant geologist, and Gardner as volunteer assistant surveyor (both were paid only for their travel expenses), and a friend from the cross-country trip, Richard D. Cotter, as packer. The party reached the western Sierra Nevada slope in June 1864, in the area today known as Sequoia and Kings Canyon National Parks. In

Mountaineering, King heavily emphasized the ensuing expeditions in summer and fall of 1864, which make up over half of the book's chapters.

If King initially perceived the American West aesthetically and scientifically as a continuation and expansion of existing European discourses, *Mountaineering*'s first chapter follows in this vein by framing the evolution of the Sierra range in the context of Mozart's *Magic Flute:* "As the characters of the *Zauberflöte* passed safely through the trial of fire and the desperate ordeal of water, so, through the terror of volcanic fires and the chilling empire of ice, has the great Sierra come into the present age of tranquil grandeur" (25). By referring to an opera that—in the spirit of colonialism— illustrated the effects of the Enlightenment on the "Dark Continent," King compares Africa to the American West, justifying its exploration and exploitation. He then heralds the Sierra Nevada, with its "tranquil grandeur," as a sublime paradise and supreme destination for North American travelers, linking the mountain range to familiar depictions of the Alpine sublime from Rousseau to Wordsworth to Byron. The connection is made explicit when King christens the Whitney range the "new Alps" (45), marveling that "the view was so grand, the mountain colors so brilliant, immense snow-fields and blue alpine lakes so charming, that we almost forgot we were ever to move" (85). By measuring the two mountain ranges and enlisting the Sierra as a source of national pride, King capitalized on a newly forming sense of American identity, cleverly exploited by a growing travel industry that touted the natural wonders of the American West as equal or superior to European ruins, castles, and cathedrals.

Yet the actual climbing experience caused King to leave behind familiar European discourses and instead borrow from western-style adventure fiction popular in dime-store novels. This soon becomes evident in his depiction of the Mount Tyndall climb. After the survey arrived in the western part of the Sierra, Brewer and Hoffmann climbed what they named Mount Brewer on July 2, 1864, thinking it was the highest peak of the range, only to discover they had ascended a lower ridge (the Great Western Divide), with the actual Sierra Crest and many higher peaks still eight miles to the east. While the discovery confirmed King's earlier theory, the peaks to the east were separated from those of the west by a deep, seemingly impassable gorge. Nevertheless, Brewer reluctantly agreed to have

King and Cotter attempt "a campaign for the top of California" (71). On July 4, the entire team set off with six days of provisions, climbing for four hours to the crest of the Great Western Divide. There the party separated: Brewer, Hoffmann, and Gardner proceeded to climb Mount Brewer once more to complete their observations, while King and Cotter carefully descended the treacherous, rocky slope into the deep gorge. By nightfall they arrived in an amphitheater covered with snow and endured a cold night on a granite shelf above a frozen lake. The next day, they ascended the ridge separating the two mountain ranges, first on snow, then on rock, cutting steps into the ice with Cotter's knife and hoisting their packs and instruments up with a rope. With a sheer cliff above and the option of turning around impossible, King saw only one course of action: "It was to lasso one of these blocks, and to climb, sailor-fashion, hand over hand, up the rope" (82).

Daniel Arnold, who retraced King's steps with the same gear (or lack thereof), later described King's words as sheer exaggeration: "In reality, the cliffs on this side of the pass are steep—but not that steep; the climbing is tricky, but not impossible, even by nineteenth-century standards. If they lassoed a spike with their rope, then ascending it would have been more like tugging on a rope to walk up a roof of an average house rather than the dangling, free-hanging affair that King described."[10] Undoubtedly, King's adventuresome tales freely mix unadulterated descriptions of mountain scenery with harrowing dangers real or imagined, while brimming with wit and sarcasm. "The smooth-precipice-face against which my body swung offered no foothold, and the whole climb had therefore to be done by the arms, an effort requiring all one's determination. When about half-way up I was obliged to rest, and, curling the feet in the rope, managed to relieve my arms for a moment. In this position I could not resist the fascinating temptation of a survey downward" (82–83).

From the crest, King and Cotter could see the headwaters and the divide between the Kings and the Kern Rivers, as well as the "sublime white giant" (85) they had set out to climb. They decided to lower themselves down the cliff into the Kern valley by tightening a rope around their waists and looping it around protruding rocks. This crossing of the mountain range from west to east involved some technical climbing and descents of cliffs that— even with the precise difficulties debated—mark a notable achievement in

North American mountaineering history. Once on the valley floor, they looked for a bivouac site beneath the mountain that seemed to be the highest peak of the crest. King and Cotter awoke on July 6 at 3:30 a.m. and began ascending a snowfield by cutting steps until they encountered a large bergschrund separating the ice from the wall. In *Mountaineering*, King described his precarious position comically: "In the friendly seat which this wedge gave me, I stopped to take wet and dry observations with the thermometer,—this being an absolute preventive of a scare,—and to enjoy the view" (93). In a witty comment on scientists before him, King turns the objective act of measuring into a mere response to human fear. Continuing to climb by embracing a column of ice and inching upward, King and Cotter finally reached the summit. In *Mountaineering*, King celebrates the moment properly: "I rang my hammer upon the topmost rock; we grasped hands, and I reverently named the grand peak MOUNT TYNDALL" (94), establishing a direct link not only to European science but also to the Alpine mountaineering tradition, in honor of his predecessor Tyndall.

To King's surprise, they glimpsed still higher peaks to the south, the highest of which, a mountain "looking glorious but inaccessible" (95), they decided should bear the name of the survey's director, Whitney.[11] Standing on Tyndall's summit, King, overwhelmed, put aside Romantic marvel: "Looking from this summit with all desire to see everything, the one overmastering feeling is desolation, desolation!" (98). As he contemplated the descent and sensed the exposure and precariousness of his position, the magnificent mountains turned fearsome: "Vacant cañons lie open to the sun, bare, treeless, half shrouded with snow, cumbered with loads of broken débris, still as graves, except when flights of rocks rush down some chasm's throat, startling the mountains with harsh, dry rattle, their fainter echoes from below followed too quickly by dense silence. The serene sky is grave with nocturnal darkness. The earth blinds you with its light" (97). Here, deep canyons become barren, the brilliant light blinding, the sublime landscape a graveyard.

Turning away from references to European culture, King outlines a North American landscape characterized by canyons rather than Alpine valleys, by harsh western light and loose talus rather than a thick snow cover. King's remarks on the stark light anticipate John Muir's conception of the Sierra as the "Range of Light" and formulate a uniquely North American mountain quality: "The light, although surprisingly lively, was of a purity and refinement quite different from the strong glare of the plains" (68). More generally, this change in tone and style indicates a departure from prevailing Alpine discourses. King's team descended from Mount Tyndall with both elation and disappointment. Later that month, King attempted to climb Mount Whitney, but to no avail. He claimed that he reached an altitude of 14,740 feet, which is impossible, as Whitney today is measured at 14,505 feet.

Mountaineering and American Heroism

King's contemporaries as well as later critics disparaged his writing for embellishing the dangers encountered. Muir commented dryly, "He must have given himself a lot of trouble. When I climbed Tyndall, I ran up and back before breakfast."[12] Although more empathetic, Arnold's assessment goes in a similar direction: "But it's as if King worried that his travels wouldn't seem adventurous enough, so he squeezed his thrilling moments for every last splash of drama, trying to give his reader the tales he thought they expected, in which men dangled over precipices clinging to bits of shrubbery and lives were saved by the lucky snatch of a shirt-sleeve. In King's version of the Sierra, it is hard to tell where the projecting shadows of story end and the real stone begins."[13] But rather than rooted in worry, King's exaggerations seem based on clever calculation. Relying on the success of his publications, he framed his experiences in terms established and familiar to an educated East Coast audience while appealing to the emerging myth of the American West. With respect to the West, the popular dime novels of his day commonly and indiscriminately mixed fact and fantasy in sensationalizing their subjects. King undoubtedly took his cues from these novels when inflating his own actions but also infused his writing with a humorous and sarcastic dimension. Rather than trying to separate fact from fiction, it thus becomes more valuable to focus on the themes and effects of his self-aggrandizing and mocking ruminations.

Though based on European discourses on the Alps, *Mountaineering* pokes fun at this discourse to complement and replace it with a distinctly American perspective. In this way, King uses his knowledge of the Alps' popularity, guided climbing, and booming tourism to satirize the European-style peak bagging that would soon infiltrate the Whitney region:

> I realized we had felt none of the conventional sensations of nausea, head-ache, and I don't know what all, that people are supposed to suffer at ex-treme altitudes; but these things go with guides and porters, I believe, and with coming down to one's hotel at evening there to scold one's picturesque *aubergiste* in a French which strikes upon his ear as a foreign tongue; possibly all that will come to us with advancing time, and what is known as "doing America." They are already shooting our buffaloes; it cannot be long before they will cause themselves to be honorably dragged up and down our Sier-ras, with perennial yellow gaiter, and ostentation of bath-tub. (99–100)

Here the Alps, while still a reference point, serve as a negative example in that they illustrate what happens when Alpine exploration becomes a soar-ing industry of amateur climbing, focused on a range's highest peaks. By insinuating that the Europeans might soon be "doing America," King jus-tifies the necessity of a distinctly American exploration. In fact, his fears of an impending European invasion serve to define an American identity in the West that deftly takes possession of "our buffaloes" and "our Sierras" and grossly disregards indigenous populations. These parameters at the very foundation of the American myth are never questioned.

King's brazen exploits furthermore serve to outline a conceited gender identity even though, at the same time, he seems to scoff at conventional models of masculinity. During the first half of his life and in particular while in the field, King had much closer ties with men than women, first and foremost with his best friend and partner on both western explora-tions, James Gardner. Already as a student at Yale, King wrote intensively romantic letters to his friend: "My heart is taken up with you. Although I don't write much and even when I do write—I don't say much but my love for you grows always and is a most absorbing passion. The deeper I feel the more it becomes an effort to express myself, and at times I almost reason myself into resolving to be silent henceforth."[14] In turn, Gardner described in a letter to his mother on December 26, 1867, his first night in a comfort-able hotel after weeks of cold camping during the Fortieth Parallel Survey: "That night I slept in Clare's arms on luxurious mattresses and between snowy sheets; instead of rolling myself in a blanket on the ground."[15] When

Gardner decided to join another western survey in 1873, possibly so that he could finally emerge from King's shadow, King was angry and hurt, and the seventeen-year intimate friendship between the two men abated, though it never ceased.

In *Mountaineering*'s first chapter, King finds a characteristically humorous setup to introduce the relationship with Gardner on their approach to the Sierra Nevada:

> My mount was a tough, magnanimous sort of mule, who at all times did his very best; that of my friend, an animal still hardier, but altogether wanting in moral attributes. He developed a singular antipathy for my mule, and utterly refused to march within a quarter of a mile of me; so that over a wearying route of three hundred miles we were obliged to travel just beyond the reach of a shout. Hour after hour, plodding along at a dog-trot, we pursued our solitary way without the spice of companionship, and altogether deprived of the melodramatic satisfaction of loneliness. (33)

Juxtaposing "the spice of companionship" with "melodramatic loneliness," King is explaining the workings of his relationship with other men while also lampooning male bonding *and* the lone western hero. He even more explicitly taunts gender expectations and homoerotic notions alike in *Mountaineering*'s description of the cold bivouac that he endured with Cotter during their attempt on Mount Tyndall:

> A single thickness of blanket is a better mattress than none, but the larger crystals or orthoclase, protruding plentifully, punched my back and caused me to revolve on a horizontal axis with precision and frequency. How I loved Cotter! how I hugged him and got warm, while our backs gradually petrified, till we whirled over and thawed them out together! . . . In this pleasant position we got dozing again, and there stole over me a most comfortable ease. The granite softened perceptibly. I was delightfully warm and sank into an industrious slumber which lasted with great soundness till four, when we rose and ate our breakfast of frozen venison. (79–80)

By merging stereotypical gender expectations and provocative images of homoeroticism with semi-scientific details and numerous exclamation marks, King deliberately manipulates the imagination of his readers. His account of sharing heat with Cotter surely raises eyebrows, with words such as "warm," "pleasant," "softened," and "sank" unsettling the image of hard-edged masculine explorers. At the same time, King makes us laugh about male affection and seems to mock his own comfort. In a similarly ostentatious yet teasing tone, he dramatizes a sensual encounter with an Amazonian woman of enormous size, a run-in with a violent buffalo, his capture by Indians who want to torture him with burning coals, and his outwitting a couple of Mexican bandits following him with murderous intent. In all these tales, King only barely escapes his relentless suitors but manages to hold on to his flamboyant humor.

Mountaineering ingeniously complements European narrative traditions of scientific adventures with the colorful and unbound imagination of "blood and thunder" pulp novels. This genre, predating the popular Buffalo Bill shows and the American western, flourished after the invention of the steam-powered printing press in the 1840s and included hundreds of popular tales that fictionalized and aggrandized the lives of Daniel Boone, Kit Carson, Jim Bowie, and other frontiersmen in gripping (if hopelessly inflated) stories and thrilling terms.[16] Many dime novels also featured larger-than-life female characters, which might have inspired King's depiction of the aforementioned Amazonian woman. King merged the stock violence of these lowbrow best sellers with his East Coast literary sensibility. Entertaining his largely nonscientific audience, he embellished his adventures with larger-than-life imagination, skilled eloquence, and sharp wit. *Mountaineering*'s tall tales, then, reflect Romantic grandeur and frontier-style heroism, marking a departure from European models and creating a distinctly American image of the explorer.

Photographs

In a similar vein, King recognized the power of a new medium of representation—photography—that had not yet established a European tradition but quickly became an instrumental tool in depicting and popularizing the American West. King pioneered the use of photography in field studies, attempting to wed modern technology and ancient myth, and compared his impressions of nature to a photographic plate. "I was delighted to ride thus alone, and expose myself, as one uncovers a sensitized photographic plate, to be influenced; . . . and let Nature impress you in the dear old way with all her mystery and glory, with those vague, indescribable emotions which tremble between wonder and sympathy" (142). John Muir, King's famous contemporary and rival mountaineer, arrived at similar conclusions in his (unpublished) journal: "One day's exposure to mountains is better than cartloads of books. See how willingly Nature poses herself upon photographers' plates. No earthly chemicals are so sensitive as those of the human soul. All that is required is exposure, and purity of material."[17] Despite their differences, both men proclaim to be entirely open to new and unexpected sensations, like a blank slate, denying their own bias, as well as the influential roles they played in creating the lens through which the American West was perceived. King for his part hired the Civil War photographer Timothy H. O'Sullivan, who possessed not only the substantial technical skills needed to work with the cumbersome early equipment of wet-plate photography, but also a keen eye and photojournalistic sense to document the fieldwork of the Fortieth Parallel Survey from 1867 to 1872.[18] As his teammate Brewer noted, "King was the first to carry out these ideas on a grand scale."[19]

Already in 1863 and 1864, King's team was using the medium to promote and popularize their work, shaping a photographic image of the western explorer and adventurer. One particular pair of photographs testifies to the rapidly developing sense of showmanship. In the first photograph of the California Geological Survey with King, assistant Chester Averill, paleontologist William M. Gabb, Ashburner, Whitney, Hoffmann, King, and Brewer (from left to right) stand and sit in respectable suits and solemn looks, as if to convey the seriousness and respectability of the undertaking. Clearly these men represent the intellectual elite, coming from the most prestigious institutions on the East Coast, ready to apply their knowledge to the western landscape. Placed in the background, King seems to be the youngest and least conventional, as he is the only person not wearing a suit.

In a photograph taken just a year later, at the same popular studio of Silas Selleck in San Francisco, the serious expressions are replaced with a rugged and playful attitude that at the same time advances and mocks a new image of the surveyor. Gardner, Cotter, Brewer, and King (from left to right) pose for the camera in ragged clothes and dirty boots, as if just returned from the field. Instead of formal suits, the men are dressed in boots, slacks, shirts, and hats, and, in King's case, a white scarf reminiscent of Alexander von Humboldt. They proudly show off their instruments and

The California Geological Survey of 1863, photograph by Silas Selleck
(Courtesy of University of California Museum of Paleontology)

weapons: a sextant, two mercury barometers, a geologist's hammer, two
daggers, a musket, and a pistol. Yet the exaggerated poses and expressions
leave some doubt as to whether the men are solely concerned with tediously
measuring the world: they project an image of the rugged adventurer exud-
ing pride, stamina, and toughness. Clearly these are men of action who
pursue a scientific quest with a great deal of excitement and moxie.

The progression of these photographs also vividly illustrates the transition from New England's Victorian-influenced culture to the western frontier in all its allure. With the exposure of just one year of fieldwork in the
American West, the sons of the exquisite intellectual elite were transformed
into virile heroes embodying a new model of masculinity and frontier
spirit. To David Mazel, this revision of masculinity was closely connected
to America's economic crisis in the late nineteenth century, which threatened to end the traditional sources of power and wealth while creating
new venues for economic enterprises.[20] Yet King's multifaceted personality
both embodies and transcends competitive masculinity: On one hand, his
writings reveal his desire to "penetrate the Terra Incognita" (71), celebrat-

Clarence King and the Field Party of 1864, photograph by Silas Selleck;
albumen silver print, 1864, National Portrait Gallery, Smithsonian Institution
(Courtesy of National Portrait Gallery, Smithsonian Institution)

ing a primal masculine heroism. On the other, King—like Humboldt—climbed mountains precisely to escape defined gender expectations (such as a family), sharing his most intimate thoughts in intensively romantic letters marked PRIVATE to Gardner.

The lasting allure of symbolism in the 1864 photograph also emanates from the seal created for the California Geological Survey. It depicts three men in clothing and with instruments derived from the 1864 photograph, most easily recognizable in a man with a neck scarf. The Latin motto of the seal, "Altiora Petimus" (we seek higher things), not only appears on the title page of King's *Mountaineering* but was also adopted as "Altiora Peto" (I seek higher things) by John Muir as the Sierra Club's motto on its seal.

By the end of the 1864 field season, the survey had identified, measured, mapped, and named the highest mountains of the Sierra, outlined the course of the Kings and Kern Rivers, and defined the positions of the Great Western Divide and the Sierra Crest. In the following years, its former members continued with careers that demanded much greater involvement in public life. Brewer accepted an appointment at the Sheffield School at Yale, focusing on writing his account *Up and Down in California, 1860–1864*. Whitney and Hoffmann remained with the survey through 1874 but confronted increasing budget constraints and pressure to produce more information on gold findings. Both also became affiliated with Harvard University: Whitney as professor of geology and Hoffmann as professor of topographical engineering.

King, Gardner, and Cotter were commissioned to a survey of the newly established Yosemite Park to collect data for a map, fix boundary lines, and study the geology of the area to open it for development. There, among the sheer polished-granite cliffs, King found abundant evidence of glacial activity, which refuted the theories of his boss Whitney, who claimed that the valley floor must have dropped out at some point along fault lines. Avoiding conflict with Whitney's theories, King struck a delicate (and incorrect) balance: "Although much is due to this cause [glacial erosion], the most impressive passages of the Sierra valleys are actual ruptures of the rock; either the engulfment of masses of great size, as Professor Whitney supposes in explanation of the peculiar form of Yosemite, or a splitting asunder in yawning cracks" (27). King concluded that the glaciers advanced only after the valley was already formed by block subsidence, and glaciation was not extensive.

Indeed, King's tendency to accommodate rather than question authority helped establish his brilliant career after the California Geological Survey. After briefly returning to the East Coast in 1865, he and Gardner were hired by the U.S. Army for survey work in California and Arizona, traveling both east and west via the Isthmus of Panama. This route, which involved taking a steamer from New York to Panama, crossing the isthmus, and taking another steamer to San Francisco, was the quickest way of traveling from coast to coast before the days of the transcontinental railroad. They returned to Yosemite in 1866 and climbed Mount Clark and Mount Conness, naming the latter in honor of the congressman who had pushed the Yosemite bill. Surely it was not a coincidence that on top of this mountain, King and Gardner would outline their plans for exploring the land along the fortieth parallel, counting on John Conness's support in Congress.

King resigned from the California Geological Survey in 1866, returning to the East Coast once more via the isthmus to rally the support of heavyweight scientists such as Agassiz, Dana, Brewer, and Whitney, and influential people such as Colonel Robert Williamson, who all wrote letters on King's behalf (and, as it turns out, all had Sierra peaks named after them). With their endorsement, King relentlessly lobbied for his ambitious plan, convincing the secretary of war Edwin Stanton and Brigadier General A. A. Humphreys of the need for a survey that would yield valuable information along railroad routes that were already under construction. With the support of Conness, the proposal was attached to a pending appropriations bill and passed both houses in March 1867, the first time Congress funded a geological survey. At twenty-five, King was appointed geologist in charge of the United States Geological Exploration of the Fortieth Parallel, with full control over staffing. The politicians' broad support of the project was rooted in the prospect of moving troops around, as well as the promise of finding coal deposits, tying King to military and expansionist goals. By producing information on the geology and geography of the terrain, the survey eventually provided the basis for settlement and mineral exploitation, especially after the completion of the transcontinental railroad in 1869.

For the fieldwork of the survey (1867–72), King recruited a team of civilian scientists, among them his old friends Jim Gardner (as first topographic assistant) and Dick Cotter, the photographer Timothy H. O'Sullivan, three topographers, and a team of geologists. Per orders by Humphreys, the survey began in Northern California and Nevada, stretching to Utah and Colorado while also exploring southern Idaho and Wyoming. As King became increasingly enmeshed in the political life, his role gradually shifted from rugged explorer to a public representative responsible to General Humphreys and Congress at large. King directly depended on finding mineral resources in the West, and although most sites of assumed coal deposits turned out to be volcanic rock, the first publication of the Fortieth Parallel Survey was a 650-page illustrated report called *Mining Industry* (1870).

Some of the survey's most enduring representations include O'Sullivan's haunting photographs of western landscapes. O'Sullivan often included humans in his landscape shots and was also the first person to take photographic equipment into mining shafts, vividly depicting the harrowing working conditions of miners at the Comstock Lode.[21] Still, his images continued the allure and mythmaking of the American West. This is also the case with two other survey photographs likely taken by the former landscape painter Andrew Russell in the Uinta Mountains in Utah in 1868 (until recently the uncredited images were thought to be O'Sullivan's).[22] In what the historian Maurice Isserman calls "the first photographic image in the United States of a rock climb in progress," King is seen in mid-action, though actually not climbing up but lowering hand over hand down a rope, with his feet stretched out onto footholds.[23] Outfitted in buckskin field attire with a barometer slung over his shoulder, King seems fully in his element, skillfully descending what appears to be a large and impossibly steep rock wall. Yet on closer inspection, it becomes obvious that the barometer case must be empty, as it bends against the rock. The further staging and manipulation of the photograph become evident if we compare the image to a second photograph taken at the same place and time, which shows nine members of the Fortieth Parallel Survey, including King, scrambling up the same rock without too much difficulty or the assistance of a rope. As the second image reveals, King was descending not a cliff but merely a small boulder, and not executing risky climbing moves in solitude, as the first image suggested.

Clarence King descending a rope, Uinta Mountains, 1868
(Provided by the George Eastman Museum)

King's Elusive Final Years

The years of the Fortieth Parallel Survey marked King's transition to a businessman and dandy who appreciated fine foods, joined exclusive men's clubs, mingled with the rich and famous, and hired Jim Marryat, a young Jamaican, as his cook and personal valet. At the survey's first winter quar-

Fortieth Parallel Survey in the Uinta Mountains, 1868
(Provided by the Union Pacific Railroad Museum)

ters in Virginia City, Nevada, King and Gardner took full advantage of the
bustling social life, outfitting themselves with elegant clothes, taking danc-
ing lessons, and becoming involved with two young schoolteachers. Both
romances were short-lived: King swiftly ended his engagement with Miss
Ellen Dean after a trip to Rhode Island when his mother apparently was

not happy with her son's choice. Gardner did marry his love interest Josephine Rogers in September 1868, but in 1872 she died of tuberculosis. Seven years after listening to Brewer's account of the first ascent, King and a small team climbed Mount Shasta in the summer of 1870. Here King made a significant scientific discovery in finding a large glacier that had hitherto been ignored on the mountain's north flank, even though Whitney, Brewer, and Dana had all visited the region. While Dana, Agassiz, and Whitney doubted the existence of active glaciers in North America, King shrewdly named his discovery the Whitney Glacier. When he wanted to expand his study of glaciers on the Cascade volcanoes, however, Humphreys briskly rejected the plan, warning that it could "hardly be authorized under any existing act or appropriation."[24]

At the zenith of his career in 1872, after King had discovered the nation's first glacier and allegedly climbed its highest mountain, he exposed a large-scale diamond hoax. During the survey's last field season, King's team picked up rumors of a large diamond field in northwestern Colorado, familiar territory from the Fortieth Parallel Survey. Suspecting the field's probable location, they took off and soon discovered the gems, celebrating their find that night. The next morning, however, they realized that they had found a wild mix of stones highly unlikely in nature, and only in places where the ground had been tampered with, and no findings below the surface. Suspecting a swindle of great magnitude, King rushed back to San Francisco to publicly expose the fraud. As it turned out, Philip Arnold and his partner John Slack had bought uncut diamonds mixed with garnets, rubies, emeralds, and sapphires and planted them in an area now known as Diamond Peak. They deposited the diamonds at a San Francisco bank, cleverly indicating their find to the financial institution's director, William Ralston, who in turn showed the diamonds to a San Francisco businessman, George D. Roberts. By spreading the news to powerful investors, Roberts created a frenzy fed by expert evaluations and mining engineers, with stock being sold all over the world. Only after Arnold and Slack had sold their shares and disappeared did King's survey discover the rigged diamond field.

As King rose to become a national hero who had saved the nation from greater damage, his life as an explorer in the field came to an end. Although he remained head of the Fortieth Parallel Survey until its termination in

1879, the survey's remaining work was completed on the East Coast and was limited to writing and publishing its findings and maps.[25] After serving for two years as director of the newly established United States Geological Survey, King resigned from his post in March 1881 to become a mining geologist who accepted consulting and promotion work in exchange for stock options. He visited promising mining properties across the western part of the nation and tried to convince affluent friends to invest in them, but the wealth he had hoped for never materialized. When a bank that he had founded in Texas failed, King was forced to borrow large sums of money from friends. In addition, he battled several medical problems, including bouts of malaria and rheumatic pain, as well as an inflammation of the spine that led to acute depression.

As his health and his assets declined, King, at age forty-five, married a twenty-six-year-old African American nursemaid named Ada Copeland under the name of James Todd in September 1888 and kept his marriage secret from family and friends. He fathered five children with Ada but spent much of his life traveling on business—he had told her that he was a railroad porter. After learning in spring 1901 that he had contracted tuberculosis, King went to a clinic in Arizona and wrote to Ada, revealing his true identity. He died in Phoenix on December 24, 1901, deep in debt, having failed to provide for his wife and children. Ada Todd King received sixty-five dollars per month from Gardner (who died in 1912) until she began legal proceedings against his heirs to recover money from a trust fund that Gardner claimed had been established for her. In 1933, however, it was found that no such fund was ever established.

The posthumous revelation of King's affiliation with a black woman marred his reputation after his death, and his obvious negligence in providing for his wife and children continues to stain his image. Yet his secret marriage sheds light on King's difficulties adhering to expected gender and racial roles. Like Humboldt, King both embodied and escaped dominant models of white masculinity and engaged in complex, ambiguous relationships with other cultures and races. Apparently King found the Victorian-era women of his own class unattractive, artificial, and too formal, and he had no intimate involvements with them. His life in the field allowed him to free himself from traditional gender expectations, but even when King reentered upper-middle-class East Coast society, he became involved with dark-skinned women of different ethnicities and social classes. He raved about the "naturalness" of Hawaiian women on his trip to Hawaii in February 1872, engaged in an affair with an Indian called Luciana while staying at a Southern California hacienda in 1885, and three years later married Copeland.

Even if meant to be complimentary, recent scholarship has continued to cast King's involvement with women of other races in stereotypical terms. "Although he reveled in the popularity," James Gregory Moore maintains, King "was not attracted to what he considered the tradition-bound, seemingly affected and artificial, Victorian women of his own class. Instead, he was drawn to, and felt comfort with, natural, unaffected, dark-skinned women. He was interested in the arts and cultures of other peoples, and enjoyed making modest conversation with older Mexican or Indian women in their villages or camps, and was clearly attracted to younger women from simpler cultures" (4). Moore justifies King's choices with the artificiality of Victorian culture, staging King as a rebel who rallied against established notions of class and beauty. This assessment problematically pits so-called simpler, more natural cultures against the perceived artificiality of society. King himself, however, was extremely aware of such stereotyping, approaching it with his characteristic wit. Describing a first encounter with Indians in *Mountaineering*, he first relies on common categorizations: "You come upon them [Indians] as you travel the trails, proud-stepping 'braves' leading the way, unhampered and free, followed by troops of submissive squaws loaded down with immense packages and baskets" (56). Yet he goes on to question his own judgment, after a "mountaineer acquaintance" urges him not to "judge too hastily" (56–57) when they meet an Indian chief who seemingly does not mourn the death of his wife. King admits, "So I refrained from expressing my convictions concerning Indians, which, I won, were formerly tinged with the most sanguinary Caucasian prejudice" (57), to find the chief in tears at the ceremonial burning of the corpse. Concluding that the Indian chief was "not a stoical savage, but a despairing husband" (59), King's narrative takes even another twist when he discovers that the chief took a new wife on the same night, and King returns to camp as "an enlightened but disillusioned man" (60). By inserting familiar clichés (the noble savage, the despairing husband, the enlightened man) that quite obviously do not suffice to describe the situation, King cleverly questions his own observations, the terms of the discourse, and generally unfitting expectations.

Mountaineering in the Sierra Nevada continues to be read as a chronological account of events that happened, although scholars have pointed to the author's generous liberties and aberrations.[26] The book's photographic detail, scientific measurement, and aesthetic renderings on the sublime are mixed in with provocations and clichés of the western explorer and mountaineer, making King's work rightfully a literary text. Like Humboldt, King engenders a multitude of discourses that tend to be read in formulaic terms, be they mythical exploration, detached science, colonialist exploitation, racist supremacy, or white masculinity. In the main, his tales helped promote a gendered American heroism featuring ruggedness and prowess in the face of obstacles and adversity. Yet when we look closer at King's playful and humorous narratives, rigid categories begin to dissolve into complex matters and interactions. With prose reminiscent of Ruskin's exalted musings and heroic Kit Carson tales, of Humboldt's large-minded observations and Twain's biting satires, King continues to elude attempts at classification and explanation.

CHAPTER 10

THE SOLITARY MOUNTAINEER

John Muir

Mounts Ritter, Whitney, and Shasta

Camping alone amid barren piles of rocks below Mount Ritter at eleven thousand feet, in the dark and under threat of an approaching storm, John Muir admitted, "In tone and aspect the scene was one of the most desolate I ever beheld."[1] By 1872, Muir had spent three years in his glorious Sierra Nevada, and for him to arrive at such a bleak outlook must have taken some seriously forbidding prospects, though he immediately attempted to turn the scene into one of spiritual revelation. "But the darkest scriptures of the mountains are illumined with bright passages of love that never fail to make themselves felt when one is alone" (*Mountains*, 350). Muir had started out with two artists who stayed behind and camped lower in a grove while he, tempted by the "untouched summit of Ritter" (347), decided to embark on a climbing attempt. Outfitted with shoes capped with iron, he crossed an ice field and proceeded to climb a smooth cliff of ice and snow until multiple slips forced him to retreat. Looking for an alternate route, he began climbing another icy cliff just as steep. Muir soon found himself dangerously exposed and, with retreat impossible, continued to carefully inch up the rock and ice, contemplating the consequences of a slip as Humboldt had done seventy years before, until he reached a point when the danger of a fall became imminent. "The tried dangers beneath seemed even greater than that of the cliff in front; therefore, after scanning its face again and again, I began to scale it, picking my holds with intense caution. After gaining a point about half-way to the top, I was suddenly brought to a dead stop, with arms outspread, climbing close to the face of the rock, unable to move hand or foot either up or down. My doom appeared fixed. I must fall. There would be a moment of bewilderment, and then a lifeless rumble down the one general precipice to the glacier below" (355).

In this moment of utter danger, however, Muir felt a sudden calm ease his panic and propel him forward. Surprised at himself, he noted, "Then my trembling muscles became firm again, every rift and flaw in the rock was seen as through a microscope, and my limbs moved with a positiveness and precision with which I seemed to have nothing at all to do" (355). With ease, Muir scaled the remaining climb, confessing, "The strange influx of strength I had received seemed inexhaustible" (355). He arrived at Ritter's summit (now pegged at 13,149 ft.) in the early evening, describing the expansive view before carefully picking an easier yet much longer descent route and returning to his camp well into the night. Muir had not only summited Mount Ritter for the first time but also outlined the discovery of adrenaline-induced concentration and calm in conditions of extreme danger that much contribute to the appeal of modern-day (solo) climbing. In short, on Ritter, Muir had turned into a climber.

In the following year, Muir resolved to climb California's highest peak, Mount Whitney (14,949 ft.), asserting: "Men ascend mountains as instinctively as squirrels ascend trees, and, of course, the climbing of Mount Whitney was a capital indulgence, apart from the enjoyment drawn from landscapes and scientific pursuits."[2] A few weeks earlier, Clarence King had scaled the mountain from its western side, rectifying his previous mistake even though he had missed the first ascent. Guided by the same erroneous map, Muir also climbed Langley but was apparently oblivious to the uproar that had unfolded in the meantime. When he saw the true Whitney to the north, he quietly turned around and promptly climbed the higher peak—by a much harder eastern route. Muir found this climb to be easier than Ritter, though he reluctantly admitted to steep and potentially dangerous snow and ice slopes. To this day, Muir's route remains a challenge, as it follows a narrow couloir to the right of the east face, ascending a steep section to the summit. In a letter published in the *San Francisco Daily Evening Bulletin,* Muir debased King by claiming that Langley (which King had taken for Whitney) "may easily be ascended to the very summit on horse-back" and that the western, more gradual ascent that King had chosen for Whitney was suited for "those travelers who dislike climbing."[3]

On a third mountain expedition, on November 2, 1874, Muir climbed Mount Shasta, the volcano rising from the Cascade Range in Northern California. A passerby had declared the ascent impossible during "the wrong time of the year," duly warning Muir of violent winter storms. Un-deterred, Muir replied "that clean snow was beautiful, and that storms were not so bad as they were called."[4] He still faced some considerable challenges, however. On the approach, the deep snow prevented the horses from reaching camp, so that Muir and his guide Jerome Fay, who accom-panied him to the timberline, had to camp some 800 to 1,000 feet lower than planned. The next day, Muir rose shortly after midnight and pushed through deep snow, rocks of lava, thin air, intense cold, and fierce wind all the way to the summit, even though it was evident a storm was ap-proaching. In characteristic fashion, he subsumed his difficulties in a grander framework of sublimity when describing the climb in the *Daily Evening Bul-letin:* "The steepness of the slope—thirty-five degrees in many places—made any species of progress very fatiguing, but the sublime beauty of the snowy expanse and of the landscapes that began to rise around, and the intense purity of the icy azure overhead thrilled every fibre with wild en-joyment and rendered absolute exhaustion impossible."[5]

The next day, the storm began to bear down in full force, and Muir—happily—became tent bound, burning a constant fire until after three days his worried companion Justin Sisson sent Fay with two horses to the rescue (which Muir claimed he didn't need). This peak turned out to be Muir's favorite, and he returned three times to climb Shasta, becoming caught in a violent storm once more in April 1875, when he and Fay were forced to spend a miserable and freezing unplanned bivouac just below the sum-mit. Seeking warmth in the mud next to some hot springs, they emerged bruised and frostnipped the next morning.[6] The lonesome volcano Shasta appealed to the mostly solitary climber Muir because of "the extent of its individuality," and he professed: "I seem to be more than married to icy Shasta."[7]

During this decisive time, Muir found his calling. "I expected to have been among the foothill drift long ago, but the mountains fairly seized me," he wrote to his good friend, mentor, and adored muse Jeanne Carr a month before attempting Shasta. "I was alone, and during the whole excursion, or period rather, was in a kind of calm, uncurable ecstasy. I am hopelessly and forever a mountaineer" (*Letters*, 252). Muir first and foremost identified himself through his mountaineering pursuits in California. This newfound self-stylization united and expanded previous motives: like many before him, Muir arrived at the mountains seeking escape and solitude and became enraptured by the land and the challenges it presented. Muir celebrated this solitary immersion in nature in letters and essays, consciously setting an example for others to follow. His motivations include a host of contradictions. Muir did not arrive in a pristine wilderness untouched by humans, but wandered in the long-held home of indigenous tribes, such as the Yosemite Miwok, during a time of their extermination. Not only did Muir refuse to acknowledge this rich cultural history, but he actively participated in the white settlement of Indian lands, working first as a sheepherder and then in the logging business and construction in Yosemite, until later in life, when he drew profits from his publications while managing a large farm in Martinez. In other words, Muir embraced the dualism of touting respites in nature separate from a social life in the cities. While "Muir's inconvenient entanglement with other people and lowland life mostly stayed well off the page," as Jedediah Purdy recently put it, mountain life became the root of Muir's identity.[8] Thereby Muir introduced a paradox that remains immensely influential in North America to this day when nature lovers proclaim their true home to be the "wilderness" they encounter on hiking or camping trips.

Muir both epitomized and complicated this dualistic mind-set. He actively promoted and aided tourism, arguing that city dwellers needed vacation time in the mountains. While becoming instrumental in making wilderness accessible to white men, however, he also grew politically engaged and became one of the most effectual advocates for the national parks. The mountain respite therefore did not foster a retreat from politics but on the contrary turned into a political battleground where Muir toured lawmakers and politicians in pursuit of his cause. Although Muir operated within a fixed framework of what constituted nature worthy of preservation, he modeled a physical immersion in the landscape that transcended the strict boundary between human and nature, suggesting that all humans inherently possess a fondness for nature. In yet another inconsistency, Muir found Romantic rapture in nature but hardly practiced a "leave no trace" ethic: when sleeping in the open, for instance, he regularly built stone shelters, cooked by the fire, made a bed from pine and willow branches, and picked large bunches of (now endangered and rare) wildflowers for his pillow.[9] In the wake of his outings, he also became engaged in scientific research, identified the state's glaciers, and developed a philosophy of nature that sought to connect a dynamic environment, his physical body, sublime exaltation, and lingering faith. Decades later, Muir sold the carefully crafted narratives of his achievements, calibrating his adventures and promoting tourism in Yosemite Valley and beyond to both a West and an East Coast readership.

From Scotland to Wisconsin

John Muir's life is exceptionally well documented, especially in Donald Worster's extensive biography *A Passion for Nature* (2008). This chapter foregrounds specifically Muir's climbing exploits and their textual representation to explore Muir's wandering life through the relationship to his own (as well as others') bodies. Against the backdrop of Humboldt and British mountaineer-scientists, a more fully embodied Muir complicates all-too-idealistic concepts of wilderness and foregrounds tensions between emotions, desire, prejudice, gendered expectations, and aesthetic vision. Muir was born on April 21, 1838, in the Scottish seaport of Dunbar. At the time, Scotland, especially Glasgow, was growing rapidly thanks to a booming textile and engineering industry, standing at the forefront of the Industrial Revolution. In 1769, James Watt, a self-taught instrument maker at the University of Glasgow, first patented the steam engine, which eventually created a new mode of production throughout the world. Although Dunbar by all accounts was a gray, urban place with a modern harbor for business and enterprise, Muir later romanticized his hometown. His memoir *The Story of My Boyhood and Youth* begins, "When I was a boy in Scotland, I was fond of everything that was wild, and all my life I've been growing fonder and fonder of wild places and wild creatures." Already here Muir fashioned the "gardens of California" into an Eden where he was eventually to arrive, and he claimed to have acquired "fine mountaineering exercise" on the roof of his family's house.[10] In hindsight, he even turned the ruins of Dunbar Castle into a testing ground for his later wilderness experience, where "we tried to see who could climb highest on the crumbling peaks and crags, and took chances no cautious mountaineer would try" (*Boyhood*, 14).

Muir's father, Daniel, was a stern and strictly religious shopkeeper who managed to become a merchant for grain and livestock by marrying a butcher's daughter, Ann Gilrye, who lived next door. John was the third of eight children. Under Daniel's old-fashioned and harsh rule, the children were brought up in rigorous adherence to his belief system. The only activity both father and son enjoyed was gardening—in the backyard, filled with fruits and vegetables, every child had his or her own plot. Young Muir escaped whenever he could, professing: "After I was five or six years old I ran away to the seashore or the fields almost every Saturday, and every day in the school vacations except Sundays. . . . In spite of the sure sore punishments that followed like shadows, the natural inherited wildness in our blood ran true on its glorious course and invincible and unstoppable as stars" (*Boyhood*, 7). By arguing that all humans have an inherent, bodily ingrained passion for nature, Muir, influenced by growing genetic debates at the beginning of the twentieth century, significantly expanded the discourse on nature of his Alpine predecessors, to make a biological as well as social argument for time spent in the mountains.

Already at the young age of three, Muir was sent to an infant school and drilled in academic subjects; at the age of seven, he transferred to Woodbush School and for the next four years received instruction in grammar, mathematics, and other fundamentals in addition to his father's insistence on memorizing the Old and New Testaments.[11] His education was cut short, however, when in January 1849 Daniel Muir somewhat unexpectedly determined to leave for North America. This decision was mainly motivated by religious beliefs, as he had begun to follow a Secession Church and had grown particularly fond of a minister who had emigrated to Pennsylvania. Making a patriarchal choice for the entire family, Daniel decided to likewise begin a new life in Pennsylvania and on March 3 took three of his children aboard the sailing vessel *Warren,* with the rest of the family following shortly. After their arrival at Staten Island on April 10, the family first stayed with a fellow Dunbar grocer in Buffalo and then decided to resettle in Wisconsin, where they would grow wheat. Daniel purchased 160 acres, and another 160 acres the following year, and also became a citizen of the United States. To the young Muir, the long voyage presented a welcome change from the strict everyday routine, and once in Wisconsin, he had no formal schooling of any kind. Under his father's watchful eye, Muir acquired a small library, with works by the explorers Mungo Park and Alexander von Humboldt among his favorites.[12] Park, a fellow Scot, had written about his travels to the African interior, but Humboldt was to leave an even more lasting impression. In 1858, a small school opened that Muir attended for a little over two years before he left home in summer 1860 for Madison with plans to find work at a factory and dreams of traveling to South America or Africa.

A Humboldtian Quest

With meager financial help from his father, Muir was able to enroll at the University of Wisconsin, taking classes in history, Latin, algebra, trigonometry, and navigation while developing a passion for botany. In his second term, he attended a course on natural science taught by Ezra Carr and subsequently met Carr's wife Jeanne; both would have a profound impact on the direction of Muir's future life. After only six terms, however, Muir, a pacifist, left for Ontario, Canada, for fear of being drafted into the Civil War. In hindsight, Muir concluded his written memoir *My Boyhood and Youth* with an emotional and teary farewell from Wisconsin after four (instead of three) years, proclaiming to trade "the Wisconsin University for the University of the Wilderness" (*Boyhood*, 142). In reality, Muir began to work at a mill in Canada while reviving a passion for inventions that already infused his boyhood, when he invented a self-setting sawmill, a morning fire starter, and an alarm clock bed. None of his inventions bore fruit, and a fire destroyed his machines; and in 1866, after the Civil War ended, Muir recrossed the border into the United States. He found work at a factory in Indianapolis but—styled after Humboldt's fondness for tropical nature—kept dreaming about a botanical exploration of South America, the West Indies, or the American South. From Canada, where he carried a volume of Humboldt's writings with him, the twenty-two-year-old declared, "How intensely I desire to be a Humboldt!"[13]

An accident put a sudden end to both his work and his dreams. On March 6, 1867, while setting up a new circular saw, Muir noticed that a looped belt connecting the main shaft had stretched and needed shortening. When he tried to unlace it by prying at the stitches with a sharp file, the file slipped out of his hands and flew upward, piercing his right eye near the cornea. Muir felt the liquid from his injured eye dripping into his hand as he went blind. Within hours, the other eye turned temporarily sightless as well, leaving him in fear of having become permanently blind. An oculist assured Muir that his sight would be restored within a few months, and indeed, eventually he fully recovered. But the incident motivated Muir to never return to factory life again. Instead he would leave behind the city to venture to South America on an open-ended journey with no fixed agenda or end points, just as Humboldt had done. If Muir had revealed his desire to "be a Humboldt" in his first letter from September 13, 1865, to Jeanne Carr, then thirty-five, who had proposed "an exchange of thoughts" (*Letters*, 29, 31), he now wrote: "I wish I knew where I was going. Doomed to be 'carried of the spirit into the wilderness,' I suppose. I wish I could be more moderate in my desires, but I cannot, and so there is no rest. Is not your experience the same as this?" (*Letters*, 57).[14] Inspired not only by Humboldt but also by Frederic Edwin Church and Charles Darwin and aided by encouraging words from his mentors, Muir bade farewell to his family and the Carrs and boarded a train to Louisville, Kentucky, embarking on a journey on foot through the Appalachian Mountains in Tennessee and Georgia to eventually arrive at Florida's Gulf Coast.

The journey, however, proved tough from beginning to end and culminated in Muir's insight that he was not cut out for tropical climes. In the first three weeks of September 1867, Muir crossed through Kentucky and Tennessee, mostly walking along roads and sleeping in farmhouses, barns, or out in the open. In the area of today's Great Smoky Mountains National Park, he collected an abundance of flowers in magnificent fall weather, exalting: "Oh, these forest gardens of our Father! What perfection, what divinity, in their architecture!"[15] These landscapes contrasted starkly with what Muir considered backward, dreary, and filthy human settlements, breeding an uncivilized, uneducated, and violent demeanor. He announced, "This is the most primitive country I have seen, primitive in everything," but he did not fare much better in Georgia.[16] In Savannah, Muir found himself completely broke, lonely, and afraid of crime and starvation. For lack of a better abode, he camped in a cemetery outside town for almost a week, dwelling on thoughts of death in longing letters to Carr while waiting for a package with money from his brother. Finally, seventy-five dollars drafted from his account in Wisconsin arrived, and on October 14, Muir boarded a coastal steamer bound for Florida. Muir harbored high hopes for the trip, as Florida was the subtropical gateway to his actual destination, the Humboldtian tropics. Though duly impressed by the huge, large-leaved palm trees, Muir was too fearful of snakes and alligators to find his way through the wild, traveling on foot via railroad tracks instead. As a homeless recluse, he carried a tightly written journal inscribed with the words "John Muir, Earth-planet, Universe," which after his death was published as *A Thousand-Mile Walk to the Gulf.*

Having at last arrived at the Gulf Coast, Muir found a job repairing a mill at Cedar Key, but his ill fate continued: on October 23, he unexpectedly collapsed owing to a bout of malaria. Nursed back to life by the mill owner's wife, Sarah Hodgson, he eventually recovered, but once again he used the bodily injury to change the course of his life. Deciding that the disaster must have struck from God himself with intention and purpose, Muir reasoned that his body was simply not suited for the tropics. Having these limits in mind, Muir still hoped to follow in Humboldt's footsteps and see the snowcapped Andes of South America and boarded a timber schooner on its way to Cuba. Spending parts of January and February 1868 in Cuba, Muir was soon exhausted once again from the heat and humidity. For fear of returning malaria, he abandoned his South American plans altogether when he saw an advertisement for cheap fares to California. With a new destination in mind, Muir boarded a boat filled with oranges as an illegal passenger and arrived in late February in a cold New York City. On another vessel ten days later, he traveled to San Francisco via the Isthmus of Panama, arriving at his destination on March 29, 1868.

On the ship, he met a fellow immigrant called Chilwell, with whom he left for the Sierra Nevada at once. In his later recollections, Muir embellished his arrival to mythical proportions: "Arriving by the Panama steamer, I stopped one day in San Francisco and then inquired for the nearest way out of town. 'But where do you want to go?' asked the man to whom I had applied for this important information. 'To any place that is wild,' I said."[17]

Paradise Found: California

Compared to the misfortunes of his previous travels, California from the beginning felt like, and would prove to be, paradise for Muir. Admitted as a state in 1850, California at that time counted a half million residents, mostly in the San Francisco Bay, with a dwindling Indian and Hispanic population.[18] Muir and Chilwell crossed the California Coast Range into the Central Valley, and from there traveled up the Merced River to Yosemite Valley, looking for work. Muir found some odd jobs in the foothills before becoming a sheepherder, first for John Connel and then for Pat Delany, driving sheep to the headwaters of the Merced and Tuolumne Rivers during the summer of 1869. While Muir detested sheep as "outrageously foreign and out of place in these nature gardens" (267), he experienced that summer as a spiritual and sensual awakening, an intense and intimate contact with his surroundings, which he considered, in Humboldtian fashion, interconnected: "When we try to pick out anything by itself, we find it hitched to everything else in the universe."[19] During this time, Muir kept a journal that he revised and in 1911 published as *My First Summer in the Sierra*, one of his most successful books.

The Carrs soon joined him in California, where Ezra Carr accepted a teaching post at the state university in Oakland. Although they would not see each other for several years, the letters between Muir and Jeanne Carr multiplied and intensified, with her being at once a mentor, sounding board, guide, and friend, as well as an idealized lover and mother. Carr had an immense practical influence on Muir's life, too: not only did she introduce him to influential friends, writers, and politicians, but she picked his future wife, revised and edited his essays, and sent them to publishers. After the summer, Muir briefly resumed his South American plans but soon decided to move to Yosemite Valley for the winter. He found work for the next two years with James Hutchings, a hotel proprietor, who in 1864 (the year Abraham Lincoln had signed a bill designating Yosemite Valley as a state park) had bought a two-story wooden structure not far from Yosemite Falls and needed Muir to cut logs for construction. Muir built himself a cabin, sleeping in a hammock above a stream running through his room. While Muir apparently favored Hutchings's monopoly to keep other construction away from the valley, in 1872 the U.S. Supreme Court turned down Hutchings's land claim after Josiah Whitney protested against privatization in a newly established "national public park."

At the time, Muir chose to not become involved. He also seemed indifferent to the expulsion of the Miwok from the valley, depicting the land instead—as Albert Bierstadt had before him—as being devoid of humans or signs of civilization. Muir preferred communing with nature: "But I'm in the woods, woods, woods, and they are in *me-ee-ee*. The King tree and I have sworn eternal love," he wrote to Jeanne Carr in 1870.[20] At the same time, he became quite adept as a guide and naturalist by taking a growing number of tourists on wildflower walks in the valley. In 1871, he hosted the sixty-eight-year-old Ralph Waldo Emerson. The two of them spent a few days touring the Mariposa redwood trees, though Emerson refused to sleep on the ground or return for a longer trip, which disappointed Muir.[21] Meanwhile he became a wild but charismatic main protagonist in the novel *Zanita: a Tale of the Yo-semite* (1872), by Theresa Yelverton, an Englishwoman who had spent three months at the Hutchings hotel. Muir's relationship with his employer soured, however, when Muir struck up a friendship with the young Mrs. Hutchings, who consequently fell in love with him, left her husband, and eventually married another man. Muir was fired and then reemployed but soon quit his job for good. In the coming years, he would spend winters in Yosemite, boarding at a different hotel, but during the summer he stayed away from the increasingly bustling valley.

Muir's time in the mountains sparked his renewed interest in science, and he even inquired at the University of Wisconsin about returning for further study, but his dismal financial situation and the prospect of moving back east quickly put an end to such plans. Emerson invited him to come to New England and live closer to Asa Gray and Louis Agassiz, though Muir declined, explaining, "I have been too long wild."[22] Instead, he furthered his scientific education in California when guiding Joseph Le Conte, a former student of Agassiz and geology professor at the University of California, to Tuolumne Meadows and Mono Lake, learning much about glacial theories along the way. Like Forbes, Agassiz, and many others before him, Muir's fascination with glaciers had been piqued, and in October 1871 he made the startling discovery of active glaciers in California on Mount Lyell, Mount Maclure, and later Mount Shasta. Previous geologists had generally believed that glaciation in the United States had not reached California and was, moreover, a past event. Muir began to measure glacial movement as proof for his theories, eventually convincing Agassiz and Le Conte of his findings, the latter appropriating, if not stealing, Muir's theories.[23] Yet much of the scientific elite, including Whitney and King, continued to doubt Yosemite's glacial origins and belittled Muir's findings as those of a geological amateur.

Rejecting a literal reading of the Bible, Muir embraced uniformitarianism as laid out by James Hutton and expanded by Charles Lyell. Believing in steady, ongoing, and uniform changes rather than sudden outbursts fit well with Muir's view of a benevolent if dynamic environment. In contrast to Agassiz's creationism, Muir enthusiastically embraced Darwin's emerging theories of evolution (*On the Origin of Species* had appeared in 1859 and *The Descent of Man* in 1871) and formed a lasting friendship with Darwin's North American botanist follower, Asa Gray. Together with Gray and the English botanist Joseph Dalton Hooker (a friend of Darwin's), Muir reclimbed Mount Shasta in 1877, the three men merrily camping and discussing plants. Adding Darwin and Gray to his models, Muir defended a liberal, science-based worldview against staunch Christianity.[24] He read Emerson, and fellow Scots Forbes and Ruskin, as well as Stephen and Tyndall, educating himself in science, philosophy, and literature. In this way, Muir was able to considerably complement his brief education and broaden his interests.

Around the same time, Muir purchased an ice ax and hobnailed shoes and methodically trained himself in climbing techniques, quickly gaining confidence. Armed with knowledge and skill, he set out to climb some major peaks, beginning with Mount Ritter, as described previously. In the wake of these mountain climbs, Muir began to formulate his wilderness philosophy. His ideas were rooted in Burke's theories of the sublime and Ruskin's mountain glory, but he revised both positions. To Muir, nature was neither threatening nor fearful but rather engendered what William Cronon, a historian of the American West, has called "the domestic sublime," a concept that proved more palpable and effective for Muir's North American audience.[25] This becomes obvious when we compare King's shudder on the top of Mount Tyndall in the face of the barren, desolate lands with Muir's remarks on his first climb of Mount Hoffman in July 1869: "The broad gray summit is barren and desolate-looking in general views, wasted by ages of gnawing storms; but looking at the surface in detail, one finds it covered by thousands and millions of charming plants with leaves and flowers so small they form no mass or color visible at a distance of a few hundred yards" (*Summer*, 241). By shifting his perspective from grand vistas to what is right under his feet, Muir's discovery of charming nature effectively disrupts notions of sublime awe and terror.

Unlike Ruskin, Muir did not ever view nature as hostile or dirty: "How cordially I disbelieve him [Ruskin] tonight, and were he to dwell a while amongst the powers of these mountains he would forget all dictionary difference betwixt the clean and the unclean, and he would lose all memory and meaning of the diabolical sin-begotten term *foulness*."[26] In Muir's philosophy, "winter storms in Yosemite must be glorious" (*Summer*, 223), and even violent upheavals such as earthquakes, destructive winds, or sudden storms had their place and purpose in God's great nature. Unlike his predecessors, Muir often downplayed danger and risks encountered in the mountains. While inching his way on precarious cliffs toward Yosemite Falls, barefoot and carefully selecting hand and footholds, he rejoiced: "While perched on that narrow niche I was not distinctly conscious of danger. The tremendous grandeur of the fall in form and sound and motion, acting at close range, smothered the sense of fear, and in such places one's body takes keen care for safety on its own account" (*Summer*, 221–22). Once again, sublime fear and awe are replaced with a climber's calm awareness and a focus on one's body. Looking at the larger context of play in the nineteenth century, the professor of English Matthew Kaiser termed such a perspective "the boyish sublime," pointing to the playful, perhaps foolish, nature of Muir's adventures.[27]

Muir remained oblivious to the Native American genocide around him, preferring to believe in a preserved and depopulated "wilderness" he declared sublime.[28] This was a nature of complete harmony and no ill wills.

Such idealism arguably ignored nature's inherent vigor and ferocity, cleansing and domesticating it instead. In his journal, he made an apt comparison: "The cleanness of the ground suggests nature taking pains like a housewife, the rock pavements seem as if carefully swept and dusted and polished every day."[29] Meanwhile his gaze toward "wilderness" turned a blind eye toward social injustice, especially when it came to those not privileged to enjoy nature's remedies, such as minorities and most women. Later he became a vocal spokesperson in making these landscapes publicly available, suggesting that Americans from the West and East would enjoy mental and physical invigoration by spending time in the mountains. While Muir conceptualized nature as pure and clean, its inhabitants (besides himself and other temporary dwellers) were dirty and destructive, as he noted in *My First Summer in the Sierra:* "The worst thing about them [Indians] is their uncleanliness. Nothing truly wild is unclean" (285). As a self-pronounced savior, he attempted to rescue his beloved Yosemite from foreign intrusion by sheep, cattle, and developers, as well as—paradoxically—its inhabitants.[30]

Quite possibly Muir's dislike of the Yosemite Miwok—"A strangely dirty and irregular life these dark-eyed, dark-haired, half-happy savages lead in this clean wilderness" (274)—had to do with Native Americans' use of fire. As recent studies suggest, different tribes used fire strategically and deliberately to control undergrowth, promote biodiversity, and prevent large-scale forest fires.[31] Ironically, these strategies helped create the Yosemite meadowlands Muir so admired. In his zeal for conservation, however, Muir came to view fire as a destructive enemy that had to be avoided at all costs. In his essay "God's First Temples," published in 1876, he faulted tribes for their use of fire: "Indians burn off underbrush to facilitate deer-hunting," he wrote, wrongly concluding that "fire, then, is the arch destroyer of our forests, and sequoia forests suffer most of all."[32] Muir set into motion federal forest protection measures whose destructive impact is still visible today in the form of a decline in tree diameters and reduced biodiversity.

Rather than pondering social differences and complexities, Muir tended to operate within a fixed framework that pitted holy nature against the perils of modern society without much middle ground. However, his own life course questioned such strict boundaries, as Muir slowly but surely established a second home in the city. He came to San Francisco in November 1873, tired of the snowbound valley and determined to enjoy friendship and culture. Through the Carrs, Muir met much of the Bay Area intelligentsia, including the superintendent of schools in Oakland J. B. McChesney, the poet Ina Coolbrith, the painter William Keith, and the educator John Swett. Along with his wife, Swett became Muir's landlord at their three-story house the following winter. Aside from socializing, it was here that Muir began writing in earnest. First he attempted a comprehensive, groundbreaking book on the Ice Age but had trouble finding a publisher in the competitive publishing market in the East. Instead Muir found magazine writing, though still challenging and time-consuming, much easier, and he quickly created an eager readership for his pieces. From 1871 to 1875, the *Overland Monthly*, a West Coast equivalent to the *Atlantic Monthly*, published eighteen articles of his, making Muir increasingly known for his inspiring if flowery prose on the natural wonders of the Sierra Nevada. After the *Overland Monthly* went bankrupt, Muir found another venue in the *San Francisco Daily Evening Bulletin*, publishing almost eighty essays on his adventures. Along with King, Muir helped create an armchair audience for adventurers in the post-frontier age.

An Apostle of Sustainability

Muir added the new theme of conservation and sustainability to representations of the West. After visiting a fish hatchery in Northern California, he concluded that the salmon population was declining because hydraulic mining in the foothills was clogging rivers with sediments and gravel. His concerns soon included California's forests, threatened by grazing operations, lumbermen, and sawmills alike. While openly disdainful of the Native American practice of regularly setting fires to encourage the growth of shade-intolerant species, Muir called for more governmental control to protect "God's first temples," using as a model European forest management. "In European countries, especially in France, Germany, Italy, and Austria, the economies of forestry have been carefully studied under the auspices of Government, with the most beneficial results. Whether our loose-jointed Government is really able or willing to do anything in the matter remains to be seen."[33] Rather than turning to local knowledge, Muir thus relied on top-down models of administration and control that had emerged in monarchies in Europe. With Muir's support, these arguments became influential narratives of the early environmental movement, though today their logic, function, and effect have been questioned.

During a visit to Nephi, Utah, in May 1877, on assignment to cover the growing tensions between Latter-day Saints and the U.S. government, Muir was struck by the Mormons' prosperity but disturbed by their notions of superiority. In particular, he disapproved of polygamy and efforts to increase the Mormon population by having as many children as possible; he argued instead that the environment demands a curbing of human fertility. His warnings about overpopulation acquire contemporary urgency, especially when he relates population growth to freshwater scarcity: "There is a limit to this crop [of human babies] as to every other. It is control[l]ed by the quantity of water available for irrigation."[34] Muir soon expanded his experiences in Utah to general calls for human restraint in the face of lands whose riches and resources were not limitless but finite. His calls for sustainability soon became a central pillar of his environmentalist agenda and shaped the conservation movement in the United States to this day.

While Muir and others assigned a higher spiritual value to nature, they were not opposed to economic profit from fish hatcheries and forest management. Over the years, Muir often learned how to compromise, arguably a recipe for his success and possibly a reason for his failure in Hetch Hetchy. Although he believed that wealth mattered little and all creatures on earth had the right to a peaceful existence—which led him to arrive at holistic and nonanthropocentric views—his public position did not put human development and natural conservation at odds. Instead Muir mixed religion, science, and aesthetics into his environmental vision, appealing to conservatives and liberals alike. Similarly, he did not distinguish between conservation (a responsible use of resources) and preservation (no extraction of resources), as the later environmental movement often did. With his friendly, outgoing nature, Muir also relied on cooperation, which might have been another reason for his widespread popularity.

During these years, Muir's career as a journalist began to flourish. In 1875 he placed his first article, "Living Glaciers of California," in *Harper's New Monthly Magazine,* with three more to follow, in addition to ten essays published in *Scribner's Magazine* in the years between 1878 and 1881. In fact,

Muir helped *Scribner's* to great success, raising circulation to over 100,000 by 1880, with its editor gushing, "We desire to see everything you write."[35] In the summer of 1876, Muir accompanied the U.S. Coast and Geodetic Survey as an invited guest along the thirty-ninth parallel, crossing the Great Basin with a group of scientists. In personal matters, too, Muir's life advanced: determined to end Muir's bachelor life, matchmaker Jeanne Carr cherry-picked for him Louie (Louisa) Wanda Strentzel, the daughter of John Theophile Strentzel, a physician who had immigrated from Poland and owned a farm of orchards and vineyards near Martinez in Contra Costa County, California. Louie, the Strentzels' only daughter (their son John had died prematurely), not only was well educated and well read but also played the piano, helped at the farm, and supported women's suffrage as a liberal Christian, appealing to Carr and Muir alike. "I wish I could give him [Muir] to some noble woman 'for keeps' and so take him out of the wilderness into the society of his peers" (*Letters*, 236–37), Jeanne had written to Louie as early as 1872, but the two did not meet until 1874. In June 1879, John and Louisa became engaged, to the delight of the Carrs and the Strentzels, who warmly welcomed Muir into the family. Instead of fully switching to family life, however, Muir would embark on several trips to Alaska in the coming years.

Leaving behind an anxious fiancée, Muir left for his first Alaskan journey that same June. Though he claimed, "I am going home. going to the mountains, to the ice & forests & flowers," in contrast to California, Alaska was not the home he had imagined.[36] No government was in place yet, and tensions with the local Indian tribes ran high. After spending more than six months in Alaska and one month in Portland, Oregon, Muir returned to California in February 1880. The following April, he and Louisa were married, but already in July, Muir left for Alaska once more, this time leaving behind a pregnant wife. Once again he became overwhelmed by the scale of the wilderness in Alaska, which completely overshadowed the mountains of California. In his best-selling memoir *Stickeen: An Adventure with a Dog and a Glacier* (1897), Muir famously described crossing large crevasses together with his companion, a mutt called Stickeen, culminating in a particularly precarious traverse, which involved balancing on cut steps over a tenuous snow bridge. Stickeen not only bravely surmounted all dangers but more importantly turned into a gleeful, daring, and proud mountaineer over the course of the outing, lending proof to Muir's philosophy of an inherent drive toward wild nature in all beings.

In late September, he returned to California, ready to care for his pregnant wife and be present at the birth of their daughter, Annie Wanda, on March 25, 1881. A little more than a month later, Muir left for a third time to Alaska, this time to accompany as a naturalist the anthropologist Irving Rosse and the ornithologist E. W. Nelson on the U.S.S. *Corwin*. For six months, they traveled farther north, exploring the Aleutian Islands, the Bering Strait, and the Arctic Ocean. Enamored by the stark landscape of mountains, tundra, lakes, and ice, Muir collected evidence of glaciation. With his keen eye, he also observed a state in change, and he criticized the loss of balance between native societies, animals, and the land in part owing to alcohol and guns.

Back home, Muir decided to devote his time to tending to his farm and family and began managing the Strentzel estate. Thinking that grain would deplete his valuable soil, Strentzel had instead planted peaches, figs, plums, grapes, apples, pears, almonds, and olives, exporting them fresh, dried, or in the form of wine to the East Coast, which turned into a profitable market. Muir took over the domestic and farming responsibilities, aside from a trip to see his ailing parents in summer 1885. A stopover in Yellowstone did not leave a lasting impression before he arrived in Kansas City, Missouri, where his parental family had settled. Muir witnessed his father's death in October, sorting family affairs and supporting the family, but returned to California in time for the birth of a second daughter, Helen, resuming his farm duties and eventually becoming sole manager after John Strentzel's death in the fall of 1890. In 1887, Muir assumed responsibility for editing *Picturesque California*, writing a substantial number of essays himself.

Muir traveled to the Cascades in the summer of 1888, climbing Mount Rainier for the first time, which remains a substantial feat even for contemporary climbers, who still ascend the same line, passing Camp Muir, named in his honor, at ten thousand feet, with state-of-the-art clothing and equipment. The next summer, Muir met Robert Underwood Johnson, associate editor of the influential New York magazine the *Century*. During a joint camping trip to Tuolumne Meadows, Muir pointed to the damage in the valley and high country caused by tourism, cattle, and sheep. Johnson quickly realized and promoted Muir's talents, urging him to found a new organization to preserve California's wilderness and in particular suggesting Yosemite as a second national park. Though Muir rejected such a leadership role, he did write two essays, "The Treasures of the Yosemite" and "Features of the Proposed Yosemite National Park," published in summer 1890, arguing passionately yet pragmatically, in his typical rapturous prose, for the land's conservation. Specifically, he maintained that humans would benefit most from a wide boundary that included the watersheds of the Merced and Tuolumne Rivers. These essays had a profound impact in alerting the public to what was at stake, though Muir was not there to witness their impact, as he had boarded another steamer for a fourth trip to Alaska in June 1890.

Upon his return, Muir found wide support for the proposed national park. Eventually Congress would establish three more national parks, going beyond what Muir had proposed and setting a precedent for an unmatched conservation policy that soon included national forests as well. The new Yosemite National Park, signed into law on October 1, 1890, consisted of almost two million acres, a considerably enlarged area. Moreover, a few days earlier, on September 27, Sequoia National Park had been approved, protecting the southern Sierra and forest groves. Muir and Johnson did not cease their efforts, however, but urged Congress to create a third park protecting Kings Canyon along the Kings River, which constituted the deepest canyon in North America but had been left out of Sequoia Park. In 1893 this area was included in a Sierra forest reserve comprising some four million acres.

After a lecturer at the University of California wrote to him about the formation of a Sierra Club, Muir agreed to the proposal and accepted the position of president for the rest of his life. By all accounts, he was a highly gifted speaker, arguably even more effective than as a writer, and thus an obvious choice for the club's leadership, though he initially preferred not to be too involved.[37] Instead Muir sought to use his talents and fame by meeting prominent businessmen and politicians, swaying them to his cause. In 1893 he attended the World's Columbian Exposition in Chicago and was so impressed by his fellow European immigrant Nikola Tesla (1856–1943) and his ingenious design of an alternating current (AC) power supply that he visited Tesla's laboratory in New York.[38] There Muir also visited the *Century* offices and met with the naturalist and author John Burroughs, who became a lifelong friend. On a short trip to Concord, Massachusetts, Muir also had the opportunity to see Emerson's house and graveyard and Thoreau's Walden Pond. From there, Muir embarked on a European trip, his first since leaving Scotland, visiting Edinburgh, Dunbar, London, Zurich, Geneva, and Paris, as well as glaciers in Norway and Switzerland.

Back home, Muir (under some pressure from Johnson) compiled his first book, *The Mountains of California* (1894), with two essays newly written and the remaining fourteen drawn from journal articles, a work that famously coined the term "Range of Light" for the Sierra Nevada.[39] Muir also took on more public responsibilities, joining the Forestry Commission along with William Brewer and Louis Agassiz's son, Alexander Agassiz, to recommend federal policies for forests in the West. As part of his work for the commission, Muir toured public lands in Wyoming, Idaho, Oregon, and Washington and also saw the Grand Canyon. After annual voyages to Alaska in 1896 and 1897, he joined Burroughs on his seventh and final Alaska trip at the invitation of the railroad capitalist Edward Harriman. In 1903, Muir found himself in even more famous company when none other than President Theodore Roosevelt personally asked Muir to accompany him on a camping trip to Yosemite. In May, both men embarked on the now famous two-night trip on horseback, fondly recalling their conversations for years to come. Although Roosevelt, a passionate hunter, and Muir, a gentle animal lover, had some differences in opinion about leisure and manhood, they agreed that humans should have unrestricted access to federal wilderness lands, not the least to return to the cities as happier and more productive workers.

Nature Worship and Its Discontents

In this vein, Muir's second book, *Our National Parks,* published by Houghton Mifflin in 1901, also consisting of mostly revised pieces, addressed an increasingly urban audience to hail the benefits of western parks. Muir exulted:

> The tendency nowadays to wander in wilderness is delightful to see. Thousands of tired, nerve-shaken, overcivilized people are beginning to find out that going to the mountains is going home; that wildness is a necessity; and that mountain parks and reservations are useful not only as fountains of

timber and irrigating rivers, but as fountains of life. Awakening from the stupefying effects of the vice of over-industry and the deadly apathy of luxury, they are trying as they can to mix and enrich their own little ongoings with those of Nature, and to get rid of rust and disease.[40]

The tenor of Muir's praise of "mountain parks" ties into long-standing arguments in favor of healthy and simple Alpine life, free of luxury and vice. In keeping with the times and rapid industrialization, however, Muir directly addressed an audience in the cities: "Few in these hot, dim, strenuous times are quite sane or free; chocked with care like clocks full of dust, laboriously doing so much good and making so much money,—or so little,— they are no longer good for themselves."[41] Muir made an astonishingly thrifty argument: rather than arguing for wilderness to exist in its own right, he suggested that wilderness should exist because city workers would be more efficient when rewarded with temporary outdoor respites. This anthropocentric, capitalist, and exploitative thrust already characterized Muir's early argumentation in his time-motion studies showing increased productivity in factory workers who worked fewer hours. Moreover, such a strategy for conservation proved more effective and successful than pleas to leave nature undisturbed for its own sake, especially during a time when the United States exceeded Britain and Germany in industrial production, and the oil, wheat, and automobile businesses were especially booming.[42]

Muir's willingness to be co-opted by economic and financial considerations was not without problems: for one, by emphasizing his "wilderness cure," he downplayed the importance of labor regulations, unions, and reform, thus arguably forestalling improvements in workers' daily lives. For another, Muir was able to forge important alliances with developers and businessmen, including the railroad imperialist Harriman, but these relationships compromised his ability to remain at a critical distance. For instance, Muir defended his friend Harriman as a founder of prosperity, remaining silent when Harriman supported a large-scale agricultural development in the Klamath Basin, a bird sanctuary, to build dams, canals, and rails. Both of these points confirm Muir's tendency to operate within a dualistic framework of extraordinary and ordinary nature.[43] On one hand, he hailed precious if temporary sanctuaries for city dwellers as extraordinary, promoting their protection as promised lands. On the other, he consented to open for development and exploitation what he considered ordinary lands. As Cronon recognized, this set up a binary of worthy versus unworthy nature that ultimately prevented people from looking at nearby sites for recreation and finding wilderness in their own backyards.

Immediately after the camping trip with Roosevelt, Muir left for New York to embark on his most extensive journey: a twelve-month trip around the world with the Forest Commission head, Charles Sargent, and his son, a landscape architect, partly to tour forests and collect Asian plants. Despite its promise, the trip proved not as rewarding or successful as planned, as Muir faced some differences in opinion with his travel companions, battled illness, and was altogether unsuited for the pace and scale of the journey. They started with cities in Europe, visiting museums and botanical gardens in London, Paris, Amsterdam, Berlin, and Saint Petersburg before embarking on an arduous trip on the uncompleted Trans-Siberian Railway. Over the course of six thousand miles, Muir became increasingly sick and generally annoyed; he fared better only when, once at the Pacific coast, they boarded a ship to Shanghai and parted company, with the Sargents heading to China's interior and Muir leaving the country to spend three weeks in India. Feeling better, Muir became especially elevated when seeing the Himalaya and Mount Everest, the high point of his trip. Next, he traveled to Australia and New Zealand, enthralled by the rich vegetation but dismayed at the damage done by sheep. After visiting the Philippines, Hong Kong, Nagasaki, and Yokohama, he returned home, happy to focus on daily tasks rather than unfamiliar sights, cultures, and environments.

In the following years, Muir guided the increasingly popular Sierra Club's annual summer camping trips and also introduced the backcountry to his grown daughters. In contrast to some of his Alpine predecessors, he enthusiastically welcomed women mountaineers, exclaiming: "Many of these young mountaineers were girls, in parties of ten or fifteen, making bright pictures as they tramped merrily along through the forest aisles, with the sparkle and exhilaration of the mountains in their eyes."[44] With Jeanne Carr and other strong women as mentors, a smart, judicious wife, and two perceptive daughters, Muir readily acknowledged women's place in the wilderness, though he did not pay much attention to social pressures and greater contexts. Back in 1875, tellingly, after a letter detailing his own grand Shasta adventure, he grumbled to Carr on June 3, 1875, "Where are you? Lost in conventions, elections, women's rights and fights, and buried beneath many a load of musty granger hay. You always seem inaccessible to me" (*Letters*, 259), revealing both the solipsistic nature of his ramblings and his obliviousness to the political issues at hand. For better and worse, his nature worship demanding equal access for all paid little attention to discrimination by gender, class, and race, which unfortunately kept many from benefiting from Muir's promises.

In Muir's own life, female presence declined steadily. In December 1903, Jeanne Carr died. His wife's death followed, in August 1905, from an advancing tumor, leaving Muir devastated by her loss. His older daughter, Wanda, married a civil engineer in the summer of 1906 and moved out of the house. His younger daughter, Helen, suffered from pulmonary illnesses and moved to the desert Southwest, where the dry air soothed infections, pneumonia, and tuberculosis before the days of penicillin. Later she married a struggling businessman. Older and lonelier, Muir had trouble rousing himself to write, but with the encouragement of friends, he finally finished his memoir *The Story of My Boyhood and Youth*, published first serially in the *Atlantic Monthly* and then in book form by Houghton Mifflin.

Political Battles and Material Celebrations

Meanwhile Muir's political battles intensified. Influential businessmen in San Francisco such as James Phelan, one of the city's wealthiest men, were keen on damming the Hetch Hetchy Valley to create a reservoir for the city's water supply. They argued that Hetch Hetchy offered exceptionally clean water that was, amazingly, free of charge, since it did not come from privately owned land. Whereas Muir hoped to appeal to the wealthy for his cause in setting aside wilderness areas that would help to better people as a whole—he had published essays heralding the beauty and therapeutic effects of the place—Phelan dismissed Muir's pleas as obstructing prosperity. In an exhausting struggle extending over several years, Muir spent much of his remaining energies and often became disappointed with former allies. Torn by various interest groups applying pressure on his administration, Roosevelt remained ambivalent about protection, and Muir also had difficulties winning Burroughs over to his cause. The Sierra Club was divided about the dam, and the newspapers caricatured Muir as an effeminate "nature lover." Finally the Roosevelt administration decided that the dam could be built only if approved by a two-thirds majority of San Francisco voters, and only after the water of another reservoir at Lake Eleanor had been depleted. Though unhappy, Muir accepted these terms with his usual willingness to compromise, trusting that Hetch Hetchy would not become an issue in his or his children's lifetimes. However, the debate was reopened much sooner after a new administration under President William Taft faced considerable pressure from Phelan and his lobby. After Muir gave a tour of the valley to the new president himself and secretary of the interior Richard Ballinger, all looked better again, especially since Muir had agreed to a proposal that would include development for tourism—hotels, stables, trails, even roads for cars.

With peace of mind, Muir, at seventy-three, embarked on his last great journey. In April 1911, he set off for the East Coast, meeting with Houghton Mifflin, which published *The Mountains of California* in a new edition and *My First Summer in the Sierra* in June. At Yale University, Muir attended graduation to receive an honorary degree. Afterward he departed on an ambitious trip, sailing to Brazil in August to finally see the lands that Humboldt had explored. Like Humboldt traveling upriver, Muir followed the Amazon to the Rio Negro along dense forests. Through the foothills of Argentina and Chile, he went as far south as Santiago before sailing north again to the Canary Islands and then boarding a steamer heading south, straight to Cape Town, South Africa. Muir passed Nairobi, Kilimanjaro, Lake Victoria, and the headwaters of the Nile before reaching the Italian port of Naples and heading home to America. While Muir referred in letters to a "most fruitful time of my life on this pair of hot continents," he never published anything related to this journey, as had been the case with his previous dizzying trip around the world.[45]

Meanwhile, back home, the fate of Hetch Hetchy was decided with unexpected swiftness when Woodrow Wilson won the general election and promptly appointed Phelan's friend Franklin Lane as secretary of the interior. As the tide turned against the absent Muir, and as even some former friends, including representative William Kent, who had named Muir Woods in Marin County in Muir's honor, rallied against him, Congress approved the Hetch Hetchy bill, and on December 19, President Wilson signed it into law. Although the dam construction did not begin until 1919, after Muir's death, he was heartbroken by the decision to sacrifice his beloved valley for political and economic gains. This course of history also put into question Muir's tendency to compromise and make alliances with wealthy businessmen and political bigwigs, who, like Roosevelt, Kent, and Gifford Pinchot (a lumber merchant and conservationist who had accompanied Muir in Alaska), often bent under political pressure. In his final year, Muir frantically sought to finish his Alaska book while battling influenza and pneumonia. Marion Randall Parsons, the widow of a friend and ally in the Hetch Hetchy campaign, helped Muir organize and type the manuscript, which lay in disarray. With the beginning of the rainy season in November, Muir felt worse again and, at the Sierra Club's invitation, took off for an annual Christmas holiday in Southern California. This did not lead to improvement, however. Sent to a Los Angeles hospital by his worried daughter Helen, Muir died there on December 23, 1914. The unfinished Alaska manuscript was completed by Parsons and published posthumously in 1915, as were three additional books assembled by William Badè (who in 1928 completed a two-volume *Life and Letters*): *A Thousand-Mile Walk to the Gulf* (1916), *The Cruise of the Corwin* (1917), and *Steep Trails* (1918).

With its nostalgic framework, immediate and simple language, seemingly spontaneous amazement at nature's wonders, and the affectionate tone in which Muir enjoyed the company of his Saint Bernard dog, Carlos, *My First Summer in the Sierra* remained Muir's most successful book, appealing to a wide range of audiences, young and old. Here Muir recalled (with sparse references to his previous life in Scotland and Wisconsin) the childlike enthusiasm of his youth, when, having no money but plenty of free time, "I was in the mood to accept work of any kind that would take me into the mountains" (153). Rejoicing in a wilderness he sees teeming with life, Muir sings its highest praise in exalted language; his favorite word, "glorious," is repeated no less than forty times in the text.

Beyond the overstated celebration, the text offers three important strands of Muir's nature philosophy. Foregrounding his distaste for the noisy, dusty, and destructive sheep ("A sheep can hardly be called an animal" [218]), sheepherder Muir hints at an exploitative capitalist mind-set that leads to the depletion of resources and environmental destruction. He warns that California's ideal climate and landscape lend themselves to exploitation, since "large flocks may be kept at slight expense, and large profits realized," so that "this quickly acquired wealth usually creates desire for more" (164). Under the mantle of an apolitical nature lover, Muir here offers some astute critique of capitalist expansion at the cost of environmental degradation. At the same time, he remains oblivious to other forms of degradation when claiming, "All the Western mountains are still rich in wildness, and by means of good roads are being brought nearer civilization every year."[46]

Thanking God for the "Divine beauty" (164) in this ode to nature, Muir incorporated his religious beliefs into the text. More so than his other books, *My First Summer* divulges Muir's beliefs in nature's holiness, where mountains become particular objects of worship: a cubical block of granite in a creek becomes an "altar" (180), and his (still impressive) climb of Cathedral Peak on September 7, 1869, famously turns into "the first time I have been at church in California" (301). By revering a clean and pure landscape, Muir departed from Humboldt's encompassing approach of fusing anthropology, geography, and geology. Muir, rather, advocated a wilderness park, carefully cleansed and tended, available for touristic consumption, but not an actual living space: "No words will ever describe the exquisite beauty and charm of this mountain park—Nature's landscape garden at once tenderly beautiful and sublime. No wonder it draws nature-lovers from all the world" (275).

At odds with the concept of a wilderness park for human consumption, Muir painted himself as part of nature rather than a separate human entity. This physical rather than spiritual celebration becomes a fascinating, if overlooked, dimension of Muir's oeuvre: "We are now in the mountains and they are in us, kindling enthusiasm, making every nerve quiver, filling every pore and cell of us" (161). Recalling the Alpine climbing tradition, Muir here expands Stephen's philosophy of modern climbing when the subject, rather than seeking the glory of ascents, experiences his faculties in interaction with the mountain. Going further, Muir turns the relationship around, depicting his body as an entity that, by its own accord, advances forward without paying attention to the interferences of the mind. "But in the face of Yosemite scenery cautious remonstrance is vain; under its spell one's body seems to go where it likes with a will over which we seem to have scarce any control" (220). Muir seeks to immerse himself in the land, but instead of selecting a particular peak, his rambles are often a goal in themselves, as he seeks to become one with the land: "But the vast mountains in the distance, shall I ever know them, shall I be allowed to enter into their midst and dwell with them?" (223). In this significant expansion of climbing philosophy, Muir defines mountaineering as a never-ceasing quest for nameless peaks, peaks he does not seek to conquer. Rather, mountaineering becomes an act of reading as Muir, harking back to Forbes quoting Goethe, compares geology to learning a foreign language. "From a point about half a mile from our camp we can see into the lower end of the famous valley, with its wonderful cliffs and groves, a grand page of mountain manuscript that I would gladly give my life to be able to read" (211).

John O'Grady has called Muir's involvement a "para-human love affair," and the immediate and physical aspects of Muir's passion indeed resemble and replace love relationships with humans, notably absent from the first half of his life.[47] In ecstatic engagement with his environment, a highly sensual experience, Muir closes *My First Summer* with a grand gesture of connection and flow:

> Contemplating the lace-like fabric of streams outspread over the mountains, we are reminded that everything is flowing—going somewhere, animals and so-called lifeless rocks as well as water. Thus the snow flows fast or slow in grand beauty-making glaciers and avalanches; the air in majestic floods carrying minerals, plant leaves, seeds, spores, with streams of music and fragrance; water streams carrying rocks both in solution and in the form of mud particles, sand, pebbles, and boulders. Rocks flow from volcanoes like water from springs, and animals flock together and flow in currents modified by stepping, leaping, gliding, flying, swimming, etc. While the stars go streaming through space pulsed on and on forever like blood globules in Nature's warm heart. (292)

This material emphasis, connecting rocks, volcanoes, and glaciers with rivers, trees, animals, and even the stars, makes Muir's writings surprisingly contemporary, perhaps precisely because of our desire to rejoice in a landscape imagined as untouched. Synthesizing, expanding, and concluding the mountaineering attempts of his nineteenth-century predecessors, for Muir the human love affair ultimately ends in humans' death, a fitting concept for our contemporary age of the Anthropocene. As such, he claims,

"Species develop and die like individuals, animal as well as plant. Man himself will as surely become extinct as sequoia or mastodon, and be at length known only as a fossil."[48] In appropriate conclusion, the human race will, sooner or later, become a fossil layer in earth's geologic history, quite possibly forming the mountains of the future.

EPILOGUE

Coming of age in West Berlin, Germany, during the heyday of punk and political activism in the years before the Wall fell, I found myself on my first (unintended) trip to the United States in 1991 and chanced upon a couple of rock climbers at Joshua Tree National Park. Awed by the desert, the rock formations, and the swanky climbing gear, I got to embark on my first rock scrambles and climbs that same trip. The West proved such a pull that I swapped all career prospects back in Germany to enroll in an English course at San Francisco State University instead—and began rock climbing on Yosemite's sheer walls. Through graduate study, moves, jobs, boyfriends, a marriage, divorce, remarriage, and a daughter, climbing has persisted, providing exercise and relaxation, a challenge and a task, an escape and a refuge. There is something so intensively satisfying and compelling about the simple act of placing one's hands and feet onto sun-drenched rock and moving upward. Reading the rock by looking for minuscule holds, a slightly larger area of contact, a side pull, a bulge, a crack that can provide a line of ascent, becomes an all-encompassing endeavor engaging body and mind under the influence of a host of brain-made chemicals, an addictive rush. Forced to focus on what is right under your hands and feet, you accomplish moves that previously seemed impossible, perhaps a meaningless feat, but one that provides immense pride and pleasure. This must be what Maurice Merleau-Ponty calls "motricity" [*motricité*], defined as "a space of movement and action rather than contemplation and knowledge. It is organized around my own body, and it orients my movements and perceptions. Things have meanings in this space, not in terms of their objective positions, but in terms of my bodily 'I can.'"[1]

What is more, rock climbing places you in magnificent positions, with swallows flying below, open sky above, a breeze buffeting your balance, and views not afforded to tourists. I understand why climbing has become exceedingly popular in the past decades. And yet, as demonstrated by the ever increasing hordes of climbers driving to the cliffs in SUVs or Sprinter vans, trampling the brush, chalking holds, drilling holes, leaving feces and trash, and doing it all over again the next day, we are destroying the very thing we love. These days, I often frequent the artificially created, climate-controlled climbing gym instead. How I used to scoff, when the first climbing gyms sprang up in the early 1990s, at climbers who pulled on plastic holds rather than daring to venture onto real rock. Jamming one's body onto and into Yosemite's granite walls while temporarily stuffing its cracks with chunks of metal and camming devices until finding the way back down deep in the night, bruised and exhilarated, was the proper and clean way to climb. It came, however, with the privilege of a stable climate, an intact ecosystem, and relatively few crowds. In our century, gym climbing might well be the more environmentally responsible thing to do.

Of course, simply retreating from outdoor recreation does not help people or the environment. As the historian William Cronon and others have pointed out, such beliefs stem from the erroneous assumption that we are separate from nature, and therefore nature is better off without us. Ironically, such dualism in part originated in the nineteenth century with the very stewards who were attempting to protect the natural environment. By demarcating national parks, for instance, the government officially set a space of privileged "wilderness" apart from the perceived vices of civilization. In the western United States, such policies acquired particularly vicious hypocrisy when creating "pristine nature" went hand in hand with the violent expulsion of Indian populations. The historian Patrick Kupper adds, "Likewise, it long remained little noticed that the seemingly pristine wilderness of America's national parks was subsequently and constantly renewed by media depictions of the parks and their exploration of millions of visitors."[2] Even in our century, imagery of nature continues to feed into such fantasies, with the majority of advertisements, posters, and screen savers promising an untouched landscape of snowcapped mountains, lakes, rivers, and trees. Compressing wilderness into easily recognizable icons and symbols, these images shortchange the value and range of wildernesses in the plural, discouraging us from finding wild nature in and around our backyards. Perpetuating the dualistic mind-set of humans versus nature therefore neglects responsibility by preventing us from exploring workable strategies for how to live in and with natural resources.

In the Anthropocene, keeping up the distinctions between nature and culture becomes increasingly tenuous. Moreover, our world in the Anthropocene eschews rules and predictability. Anthropogenic changes have had many unintended and unforeseen consequences. For instance, John Muir's beloved Hetch Hetchy Valley, largely submerged underwater with the help of the massive 430-foot-high O'Shaughnessy Dam, has turned into Yosemite's least visited area and arguably provides a more undisturbed ecosystem for birds, fish, and mammals than any other area in the national park. One hundred years later, Muir's greatest conservation failure turned into a thriving nature reserve: certainly a changed and man-made environment, but no less natural than the traffic-choked and amenity-rich Yosemite Valley a few miles to the southeast. Meanwhile calls are growing to restore Hetch Hetchy by removing the dam and re-creating another, "superior" valley for flora, fauna, and human visitors, but without cars and amenities.[3]

To the east of the Sierra Nevada Crest, the Owens Valley, where much of this book has been written, was turned into a desert by the Los Angeles Department of Water and Power (LADWP), which bought up most of the valley floor from ranchers and farmers to divert the water via an aqueduct to fuel the sprawling megalopolis 250 miles to the south. While the aqueduct continues to suck the area dry to satisfy the increasing water needs of the Los Angeles area, many small towns in the Owens Valley struggle economically, since they do not own the rights for development. Yet the fact that much of the land belongs to the city of Los Angeles has largely preserved the rugged character of the valley. Fittingly, this environment, which Robert V. Hine and John Mack Faragher in *The American West* call "frozen in time by the construction of the Los Angeles aqueduct," became a popular and cheap location for film reenactments of the American West, from traditional westerns to contemporary blockbusters to car commercials.[4] Like Hetch Hetchy, the Owens Valley is nowadays advertised as a way of circumventing the masses of national park tourists—Death Valley to the east and Yosemite to the west—and has turned into a premier climbing destination in California. Here, too, deep-seated anthropogenic changes have destroyed existing ecosystems and created new ones while preventing large-scale touristic development in what seems like an environmental paradox.

In the face of climate change, more unpredictabilities have arrived, and long-held assumptions are turned topsy-turvy, for instance, when a mountain's west face, traditionally considered easiest because of the least amount of snow, now hosts the most unstable routes because of melting ice. The entire sport of climbing and mountaineering has been deeply affected by the dramatic effects of global warming: mountaineering in the Alps, Andes, and Himalaya has become riskier and more dangerous as the weather has become less predictable. Formerly firm slopes and passes have turned looser, leading to increased rock and ice fall, as well as avalanches. These recent changes are often not reflected in guidebooks or route descriptions. What will happen in the coming decades is unpredictable but surely threatens the sport as we know it. In the Anthropocene, foreseeing environmental changes becomes increasingly challenging, the only certainty being that changes will occur at an accelerated pace. In this precarious time, navigating our place and time on earth becomes an urgent necessity. If an escape from the modern world into untouched nature becomes impossible, how can mountain climbing be integrated into a modern existence? What do we gain from putting our bodies in contact with mountains? How does time spent in the mountains help develop environmental awareness, and how does it contribute to environmental degradation? Which answers does climbing provide, and which ones does it reject?

While not delivering solutions to these dilemmas, looking at mountain climbers in the long nineteenth century helps to bring such questions into sharper focus. My analysis has provided a cultural and historical framework by showing how European mountaineering cultures emerged in a transnational context, connected through Alexander von Humboldt to American landscapes and histories of colonialism. If Saussure had imbued scientific endeavors with aesthetic investment while dwelling on his physical condition experienced in the Alps, influencing Humboldt's approach along his voyage, the Andean landscapes and populations that Humboldt encountered informed, differentiated, and sometimes contested the demarcations of mountaineering in the Alps. Sublime appreciation, scientific interests, as well as gendered and imperialist ideologies influenced prevailing concepts of mountaineering, mountain nature, and mountain dwellers, promoting an aesthetics that assigned recreational value to Alpine peaks, glaciers, and valleys. These Alpine discourses, in turn, shaped North American mountaineering and notions of wilderness, proving that the transnational character of this development was not one-directional. A post-colonial perspective, as Felix Driver and Luciana Martins fittingly observe, "must also bring into question not just the representation of Europe's others but also the production of 'Europe' itself—in our case, Europe as a space of temperate culture and nature."[5] Rather than reading mountaineering mainly in the context of the British Empire, as many excellent studies have done, I have attempted to elucidate the origins of mountaineering in the Alps as a scientific, aesthetic, and material quest, from the pursuits of Humboldt in South America to those of Clarence King and John Muir in North America.

While I hope to have teased out some transnational perspectives and influences, the diverse mix of mountaineers cannot be approached within a single category or interpreted in any one-sided cultural critique. Humboldt and Muir shared a complex relationship to both their parents and their home countries, and Albert Smith and Edward Whymper promoted national glory, foreshadowing the nationalistic tinge of twentieth-century Himalayan climbing. Whereas the British Alpine Club primarily accommodated upper-middle-class men such as Alfred Wills and Leslie Stephen, other mountaineers such as John Tyndall and Whymper did not fit this social profile. Moreover, as a site of lived experience and transcorporeal interchange, mountains cannot be reduced to a screen onto which ideologies were projected but acquired agency and constitutive meaning. While addressing scientific questions of the day and complementing prevailing theories of the sublime, European and North American explorers and naturalists thus adapted the vernacular of mountaineering as a testament to physical elation and exhaustion in unfamiliar lands, including promising aspirations, misguided bias, and the experience of failure. These connections between the body, emotion, and intellect in the pursuit of peaks had a profound effect on the political, social, and scientific rationale of mountaineering.

Humboldt's illustrations, scientific reports, and adventurous tales contributed to a growing European fascination with scaling heights previously thought inaccessible and sparked the imagination of contemporary and future scientists, artists, travelers, and laymen alike, but his failed ascents acquire renewed relevance in their subtle rejection of the summit position. In Humboldt's self-reflexive and ironic narratives, not reaching a mountain's summit becomes an integral experience of the shifting and ambiguous concept of mountaineering. Rather than viewing the ascent to the top as a symbol of progress, Humboldt questioned the very value of mountaineering, along with the entire trajectory of modern civilization. This, too, was motivated by the actual experience and encounter with alpine landscapes: rather than searching for a sense of omniscience and dominion from a bird's-eye summit view, Humboldt found himself drawn to sinister and frightening depths in the interiors of volcanic craters, enthralled by a post-apocalyptic world seemingly turned upside down. As Aaron Sachs recognizes in the *Humboldt Current:* "Humboldt's invocations of nature's sublimity are often not uplifting. Ultimately, they force his readers to experience a radical reversal of human dominance over the natural environment."[6] Even if Humboldt and his contemporaries in the Alps reached the summits they strived for, moments of triumph and celebrations of masculine strength mixed with disappointment and disillusionment resulting from the experience of physical and mental limitations, the limited research value, and a view often less grand than imagined owing to clouds or fog.

The summit position, therefore, became as much an experience of celebratory sovereignty as one of humbling entanglement with the mountainous surroundings. As the narratives of scientists who came to climb mountains teem with conflicting desires of mountain conquest, scientific triumph, Romantic undertaking, and public recognition, an evolving language of mountaineering negotiated gender and identity in ways neither straightforward nor predictable. In the performative and transcorporeal act of mountaineering, heterogeneous masculinities emerged as sometimes dominant, sometimes playful, but always contingent and fluid performances. While much of twentieth-century mountaineering became overshadowed by nationalism and imperialist drives to claim peaks, Humboldt's questioning of the meaning and value of mountaineering and his insistence on the shifting, multifaceted, and often contradictory motivations for the enterprise itself have gained that much more ground.

Not surprisingly, the ambivalences of nineteenth-century mountaineering led to contradictory ethical positions. From an experience of humbleness, naturalists such as Humboldt and Muir began to outline a position of embeddedness that situated humans as part of natural processes and ecosystems and laid the foundation of modern ecology. Conversely, the pursuits of Andean, Alpine, and North American peaks were also related to quests involving measurement, obsession, and conquest that excited scientific research and imperialist discovery in the nineteenth and twentieth centuries and eventually extended to the polar regions, similarly described in a language of the sublime. Perceived as blank and untouched places, both environments rendered scientific curiosity, aesthetic projections, and negotiations of masculinities, as well as physical disruptions and discomfort, anxieties, and competitiveness. Considering a wide historical and cultural framework, we can thus connect Alpine mountaineering with the exploration of faraway places, such as the Arctic and Africa, seen in distinct contrast to the temperate regions of central Europe. Peter H. Hansen observes that "mountain climbing helped to legitimize exploration and the broader imperial expansion by transforming imperialism from an abstraction into something tangible and readily accessible to ambitious professional men."[7] In the British Empire, exploration of the Arctic became mythologized— and thwarted—in ways similar to mountaineering by feeding into the discourse of discovery, the testing of one's limits, and the conquest of so-called virgin territory. In turn, narratives of mountaineering prompted desires for further "discoveries" and conquests around the world, thereby contributing to and upholding the imperialist hegemony.

At the same time, as Hansen concedes, mountaineering differed from imperial conquest in that the Alps were reachable by middle-class Victorian men within a couple days of travel and a few weeks of holidays. As a temporary mountaineering respite, travel to the Alps encouraged escapism and elitism when Britons enjoyed the luxuries of home while on vacation, expecting accommodations to adhere to British standards and locals to cater to British tastes, all the while seeking to preserve the exclusionary status of class, gender, and race. Unsurprisingly, this not only led to diminished awareness of and responsibility for the environment but created and upheld restrictions still in place today. Nowadays, national park passes, camping permits, climbing restrictions, and bolting rules try to constrain the amount of environmental damage done by climbers and other outdoor recreationists, but the biggest barrier limiting access to wilderness areas in climbing and outdoor recreation in general has been white privilege. The elitist and exclusionary parameters that Wills, Tyndall, Whymper, Stephen, and Muir (unwillingly) helped establish are still largely in place.

As has become evident, the early explorers and mountaineers in the Alps and North America in many ways contributed to the environmental challenges we face today: by seeking higher or faraway places, they often neglected the home environment, advocating the protection of certain natures over others. By promoting recreation in the mountains, they supported the development of mass tourism along with its destructive impact, all the while attempting to uphold privileges bestowed on gender, race, and class. A sublime aesthetics undergirded these advances, by heralding exceptional landscapes distinct from ordinary life and thus furthering the worship of wilderness or rugged nature in diametrical contrast to culture and civilization. Tragically, such thinking helped erase Native American cultures in the process. In the context of colonial imperialism, mountaineering justified the conquest of untrodden (and already trodden) peaks and imperialist expansion. In the Anthropocene age of a radically altered planet, we can no longer follow in these mountaineers' footsteps or look at their writings as feasible answers to our own dilemmas. Yet being caught in the tensions between scientific quest, conquest, and awe, the mountaineers featured in this book found imaginative and highly individualized responses to justify and characterize their pursuits. During a time when we will need to preserve our remaining mountain landscapes as well as create artificial environments for recreation, their texts remain exemplary and relevant. By grappling with the experience of failure and reflecting, if not conceding, a summit position, their texts acknowledge a multiplicity of forces at play, which Aldo Leopold articulated in his seminal essay "Thinking like a Mountain" (1949), and Hansen recently adapted to the premises of modern mountaineering: "Thinking like a mountain marks the summit as a limit point and renders visible perspectives that otherwise eludes the all-encompassing view claimed by the autonomy of the self or the legibility of the state."[8]

Taking this point even further, this book is concerned not only with a multiplicity of views and perspectives but also with a variety of embodied experiences. In this way, the early mountaineers exemplify ways of being *in* and *with* the mountains. They model a sometimes celebratory, sometimes humbling, sometimes painful, but always ambivalent and sensual engagement with nature. While their narratives may not reveal answers to our predicaments and may not even promote a greater environmental consciousness, they highlight—along with a host of other things—the satisfaction gained from seeing, smelling, and sensing different natures. Such experience and attachment remain crucial for us, even at the brink of ecological disaster. In his recent outdoor magazine article provocatively titled "Your Stoke Won't Save Us: The Idea That Outdoor Recreation Leads to Meaningful Conservation Rests on a Big 'If,'" Ethan Linck concludes: "In fact, there's evidence from a diversity of studies (in the U.S., Japan, Europe and elsewhere) that place attachment may be the only thing that cuts across socioeconomic divides to predict environmentally friendly behavior. At least some of this research has also found that dedicated, regular participation in outdoor recreation can help us develop this connection. This gives me hope that a different outdoor recreation culture, one that emphasized the pleasure of knowing the wild nearby, could be a powerful force in building these links."[9] Place attachment as a means of fostering environmental awareness also relates to the theories of Merleau-Ponty, who posed that our sense of orientation develops in relationship to our surroundings.[10] That is, perception always involves movement in the world, as it is embedded in the bodily motor capacities of our senses. Even cognitive functioning, therefore, is bodily realized.

Reading about the intersections of scientific, aesthetic, economic, and material interests in early mountain climbing across nations and continents furthers our understanding of the development of sensual, place-based attachments, but our encounters and experiences in a twenty-first-century recreation culture are fundamentally different from those of the nineteenth century. A new environmental culture would have to renegotiate concepts such as autonomy and freedom. In *The Shock of the Anthropocene: The Earth, History and Us,* Christophe Bonneuil and Jean-Baptiste Fressoz elaborate: "One of the major tasks of contemporary philosophy is undoubtedly to rethink freedom in a different way than this wrenching away from natural determinations, to explore what may be infinitely enriching and emancipatory in those attachments that link us with other beings on a finite Earth."[11] If the early mountaineers came to experience an environment that at times left them helpless, fearful, stranded, sick, or even injured, such experiences become amplified in the Anthropocene, when in the face of climate change's destructive floods, devastating fires, and droughts, we also become victims rather than masters of nature—with the crucial difference that these are changes of our own making. In a profoundly paradoxical situation, we are now, despite all our technological advances, more vulnerable than ever on our home planet because of human ignorance, greed, hubris, and conceit. All the more important it becomes to find creative responses to the challenges at hand, that is, to formulate and practice environmentalism, sustainability, adaptation, and resilience. The narratives of nineteenth-century mountaineers, poised at the threshold of scientific inquiry, aesthetic philosophy, resource extraction, and leisure pursuits, can bear much relevance here.

The time for solitude, the imperialist search for terra incognita, has irrevocably passed. But the time has come to share the mountains' resources, opportunities, and wonders while securing their protection, acknowledging their resistance, and celebrating the human creativity that comes with such entanglement. If Muir famously claimed, "I have a low opinion of books; they are but piles of stones set up to show coming travelers where other minds have been, or at best signal smokes to call attention," he was perhaps referring to mountains as piles of stones and the same smoke issuing from volcanoes that had already fascinated Humboldt.[12] Nowadays, the mixed metaphor takes on renewed urgency when we may read piles of stone as demonstrative gestures of human presence and power, and smoke as the carbon emissions rising from industry, transportation, and deforestation. It is up to us to head out to discover the piles of stones and read the smoke signals of the world in and around us before it is too late.

NOTES

Introduction

1. Alexander von Humboldt, *Reise durch Venezuela: Auswahl aus den amerikanischen Reisetagebüchern,* ed. Margot Faak (Berlin: Akademie, 2000), 81; hereafter cited as *Reise Venezuela.* All translations from this book are my own. As Hanno Beck illustrates, as early as 1793, Humboldt indicated in his letters plans for a major trip to West India, which in contemporary definitions—still following Columbus's error—included the South American tropics. Hanno Beck, *Alexander von Humboldt: Amerikanische Reise* (Wiesbaden: Erdmann, 2009), 30–33. To ascertain whether the English had blocked Tenerife's harbor, the ship made a previous brief stopover at the small island of Graciosa.

2. Humboldt, *Reise Venezuela,* 81. Also online at Edition Humboldt Digital, https://edition-humboldt.de/reisetagebuecher/detail.xql?id=H0016412&l=de diary page 15 r (recto)/27.

3. In 1664 the German geographer Bernhard Varenius listed the highest mountains of the world as follows: (1) Peak of Tenerife (Pico de Teide), (2) Peak of the Azores, (3) Andes (no specification), (4) Aetna on Sicily, (5) Hekla on Iceland, (6) the Adamsberg in Ceylon. Only La Condamine's expedition confirmed Chimborazo's height as the highest peak on earth. See Jon Mathieu, "Gesucht: Der höchste Berg," in *Die dritte Dimension: Eine vergleichende Geschichte der Berge in der Neuzeit* (Basel: Schwabe, 2011), 38–42.

4. Letter 7, in Alexander von Humboldt, *Briefe aus Amerika, 1799–1804*, ed. Ulrike Moheit (Berlin: Akademie, 1993), 36. All translations from this work are my own.

5. Letter 7 in Humboldt, *Briefe*, 36.

6. Alexander von Humboldt, *Personal Narrative of Travels to the Equinoctial Regions of America, During the Years 1799–1804*, vol. 1, trans. and ed. Thomasina Ross (London: Henry G. Bohn, 1852), 79–80.

7. Christophe Bonneuil and Jean-Baptiste Fressoz, *The Shock of the Anthropocene: The Earth, History, and Us* (London: Verso, 2016), 40.

8. Jonathan Franzen, "What If We Stopped Pretending?" *New Yorker*, September 8, 2019, https://www.newyorker.com/culture/cultural-comment/what-if-we-stopped-pretending.

9. See Serpil Oppermann, "Ecological Postmodernism to Material Ecocriticism," in *Material Ecocriticism*, ed. Serenella Iovino and Serpil Oppermann (Bloomington: Indiana University Press, 2014), 25.

10. Maurice Merleau-Ponty, *Phenomenology of Perception*, trans. Colin Smith (London: Routledge, 2002), 525.

11. Conrad Anker, "Climate and Climbers," *Rock and Ice* 251 (July 2018), https://rockandice.com/snowball/climate-and-climbers.

12. See Martin Guntau, "The Natural History of the Earth," in *Cultures of Natural History*, ed. N. Jardine, J. A. Secord, and E. C. Spary (Cambridge: Cambridge University Press, 1996), 211–29.

13. Thomas Burnet, *The Sacred Theory of the Earth* (London: Centaur Press, 1965), 110. Further references in the text refer to this edition. See also Simon Schama, *Landscape and Memory* (New York: Knopf, 1995), 451.

14. Edmund Burke, *A Philosophical Enquiry into the Origin of Our Ideas of the Sublime and Beautiful* (Oxford: Oxford University Press, 1990), 67. Further references in the text refer to this edition.

15. See Brad Prager, *Aesthetic Vision and German Romanticism: Writing Images* (Rochester, N.Y.: Camden House, 2007), 113–17.

16. "Das Erhabene verschafft uns also einen Ausgang aus der sinnlichen Welt, worin uns das Schöne gern immer gefangen halten möchte." Literal translation mine. Friedrich Schiller, "Über das Erhabene," in *Sämtliche Werke*, vol. 12 (Stuttgart: Cotta'sche Buchhandlung, 1836), 357. Translation from Project Gutenberg, "Aesthetical Essays," by Friedrich Schiller, http://www.gutenberg.org/files/6798/6798-h/6798-h.htm#link2H_4_0033.

17. Maurice Merleau-Ponty, *The Visible and the Invisible* (Chicago: Northwestern University Press, 1969), 38–39.

18. See Alan McNee, "The Haptic Sublime," in *The New Mountaineer in Late Victorian Britain: Materiality, Modernity, and the Haptic Sublime* (London: Palgrave Macmillan, 2016), 149–88.

19. Horace-Bénédict de Saussure, *Voyages dans les Alpes, précédés d'un essai sur l'histoire*

naturelle des environs de Genève, vol. 1 (Geneva: Chez Barde, Manget & Compagnie, 1779), xiv. Translated in Douglas William Freshfield, *The Life of Horace Benedict de Saussure* (London: Edward Arnold, 1920), 288.

20. The German cultural historian Martin Scharfe examines these theories in his *Berg-Sucht: Eine Kulturgeschichte des frühen Alpinismus, 1750–1850* (Vienna: Böhlau, 2007), 128–35.

21. In literature most famously by Johann Wolfgang von Goethe (1749–1832) in "Classical Walpurgis Night," act 2 of his *Faust II.* Goethe espoused water and sedimentary processes as the source of life and furthermore ridiculed volcanic eruptions as the devil's "cough and fart" in act 4.

22. For further detail, see Tobias Kraft, "Die Geburt der Gebirge: Alexander von Humboldts Erforschung des mexikanischen Vulkans Jorullo," *Arsprototo* 1 (2014): 33–36.

23. For more detail on the Royal Geographical Society in London, the largest scientific community in the Victorian era, see Felix Driver, *Geography Militant: Cultures of Exploration and Empire* (Oxford: Blackwell, 2001), 24–48.

24. Charlotte Bigg, David Aubin, and Philipp Felsch, "Introduction: The Laboratory of Nature—Science in the Mountains," *Science in Context* 22, no. 3 (2009): 317.

25. Bigg et al., "Introduction," 314.

26. For a discussion of sublime aesthetics, see, e.g., Jacek Wózniakowski, *Die Wildnis: Zur Deutungsgeschichte des Berges in der europäischen Neuzeit* (Frankfurt: Suhrkamp, 1987); Scharfe, *Berg-Sucht;* Anthony Ozturk, "Interlude: Geo-Poetics: The Alpine Sublime in Art and Literature, 1779–1860," in *Heights of Reflection: Mountains in the German Imagination from the Middle Ages to the Twenty-First Century,* ed. Sean Ireton and Caroline Schaumann (Rochester, N.Y.: Camden House, 2012), 77–97; Schama, *Landscape and Memory.* For science in the mountains, see Richard Olson, *Science and Scientism in Nineteenth-Century Europe* (Urbana: University of Illinois Press, 2008). For Alpine touristic development, see Alan Sillitoe, *Leading the Blind: A Century of Guidebook Travel, 1815–1914* (London: Macmillan, 1995); and Lynne Withey, *Grand Tours and Cook's Tours: A History of Leisure Travel, 1750 to 1915* (New York: William Morrow, 1997). Only few studies (Bigg, Felsch, Speich, Haley) consider the intersections of these areas. Daniel Speich, for instance, uses Swiss cartography as an example to analyze the intersections of scientific, aesthetic, economic, and political concerns by arguing that nineteenth-century cartographic discourses irreversibly and lastingly shaped the representation and consumption of Swiss mountains. See Speich, "Mountains Made in Switzerland: Facts and Concerns in Nineteenth-Century Cartography," *Science in Context* 22, no. 3 (2009): 287–408.

27. See, e.g., Mary Louise Pratt, *Imperial Eyes: Travel Writing and Transculturation* (New York: Routledge, 1992); Suanne Zantop, *Colonial Fantasies: Conquest, Family, and Nation in Precolonial Germany, 1770–1870* (Durham, N.C.: Duke University Press, 1997); Peter L. Bayers, *Imperial Ascent: Masculinity, Mountaineering, and Empire* (Boulder:

University Press of Colorado, 2003); Susan Schrepfer, *Nature's Altars: Mountains, Gender, and American Environmentalism* (Lawrence: University Press of Kansas, 2005).

28. Peter H. Hansen, *The Summits of Modern Man: Mountaineering After the Enlightenment* (Cambridge, Mass.: Harvard University Press, 2013), 11.

29. For an excellent and up-to-date overview of scholarship, see Thomas Simpson, "Historiographical Review: Modern Mountains from the Enlightenment to the Anthropocene," *Historical Journal* 62, no. 2 (2019): 1–29. Simpson calls for nuanced scholarship that acknowledges the inherent complexities of early and recent mountaineering, but also calls for work on global mountain imaginaries.

30. Richard White, "Discovering Nature in North America," *Journal of American History* 79, no. 3 (1992): 874.

31. Andrea Wulf, *The Invention of Nature: Alexander von Humboldt's New World* (London: A. Knopf, 2015), 5.

32. John Muir, letter to Jeanne Carr, September 13, 1865, quoted in Donald Worster, *A Passion for Nature: The Life of John Muir* (New York: Oxford University Press, 2008), 98.

33. With respect to text, see Claudia Albes, "Getreues Abbild oder dichterische Komposition? Zur Darstellung der Natur bei Alexander von Humboldt," in *Darstellbarkeit: Zu einem ästhetisch-philosophischen Problem um 1800,* ed. Claudia Albes and Christiane Frey (Würzburg: Königshausen and Neumann, 2003), 209–33; with respect to painting, Chunglin Kwa, "Alexander von Humboldt's Invention of the Natural Landscape," *European Legacy* 10, no. 2 (2005): 149–62; and with respect to photography, Hanno Beck, "Alexander von Humboldt (1769–1859), Förderer der frühen Photographie," in *Silber und Salz: Zur Frühzeit der Photographie im deutschen Sprachraum, 1839–1860* (Cologne: Braus, 1989), 40–59.

34. Alexander von Humboldt, "Meine Bekenntnisse (Autobiographische Skizze, 1769–1805)," in *Aus meinem Leben: Autobiographische Bekenntnisse,* ed. Kurt-R. Biermann (Munich: Beck, 1989), 60. Translation is my own.

35. Quoted in Schama, *Landscape and Memory,* 490.

36. Philipp Felsch, *Laborlandschaften: Physiologische Alpenreisen im 19. Jahrhundert* (Göttingen: Wallstein, 2007), 139.

37. Roland Jackson, "John Tyndall: Founder of Climate Science?" *Climate Lab Book,* April 26, 2018, www.climate-lab-book.ac.uk/2018/john-tyndall-founder-of-climate-science, accessed February 2020.

38. Withey, *Grand Tours and Cook's Tours,* 300.

39. In his classic article "Sport, Hegemony, and the Middle Class: The Victorian Mountaineers," the late David Robbins recognized, "It was precisely this fusion of the disparate themes of competition, reward for effort, innovation and masculinity with those of aesthetic improvement and mystical enlightenment that enabled the sport to appeal to and bring together such diverse sections of the Victorian middle and upper classes." *Theory, Culture and Society* 4 (1987): 596.

40. For further information, see Martin Hultman and Paul M. Pulé, *Ecological Masculinities: Theoretical Foundations and Practical Guidance* (London: Routledge, 2018).

1. The Vicissitudes of Humboldt's Mountain Moments

1. In German, the words "mountain" (*Berg*) and "mining" (*Bergbau*) etymologically have the same root, originating in the verb *bergen* (to recover or salvage). This is likely because mountains since the Middle Ages were thought to hold interior riches, and mining, or the extraction of materials from the surface layer of the earth, in part occurred on mountains. Significantly, the renowned mining academy in Freiberg in the hilly country of Saxony was named the Mountain Academy (*Bergakademie*), rather than the mining academy. Today the connection has again become more obvious with the preeminence of mountaintop removal mining taking place in the Adirondacks and elsewhere in the United States.

2. Humboldt, *Cosmos: A Sketch of a Physical Description of the Universe*, trans. E. C. Otté, vol. 2 (London: George Bell and Sons, 1900), 436.

3. For more information on the expedition, see Neil Safier, *Measuring the New World: Enlightenment Science and South America* (Chicago: University of Chicago Press, 2008).

4. See Anita McConnell, "La Condamine's Scientific Journey down the River Amazon, 1743–1744," *Annals of Science* 48 (1991): 1–19.

5. Johann Gottfried Herder, *Outlines of a Philosophy of the History of Man*, trans. T. Churchill, vol. 1 (London: Luke Hanford, 1803), 44 (punctuation modified); see also 40–44.

6. The Italian scientist Luigi Galvani had suggested that animal nerves transmit electricity, and at the time, galvanism sparked discussions about what constitutes life and inspired fantasies about galvanizing inanimate bodies to life via electricity, as in *Frankenstein*. Humboldt continued the experiments on himself, thus questioning long-held beliefs by both Descartes and Newton, who had conceptualized the animate and nonanimate world in strict dichotomies: Descartes with the theory that animals were essentially machines, and Newton with the idea that only an omnipresent God imbued the inert material world with qualities. While galvanism was eventually superseded by the Italian physicist Alessandro Volta, who proved that animal convulsions were caused by the contact of metals, Humboldt's conception of the world as a set of dynamic and interacting forces remains ever more relevant and timely.

7. Humboldt wrote to a Swiss friend a year before his trip: "Tell the esteemed Saussure, that this winter I reread all of his works, word for word" (my translation). Quoted in Hanno Beck, "Kommentar," in *Die Forschungsreise in den Tropen Amerikas*, by Alexander von Humboldt, vol. 3, ed. Hanno Beck (Darmstadt: Wissenschaftliche Buchgesellschaft, 2008), 443–44.

8. Alexander von Humboldt, "An Carl Freiesleben, Tegel, June 5, 1792," in *Aus meinem Leben: Autobiographische Bekenntnisse*, ed. Kurt-R. Biermann (Munich: Beck, 1989), 142.

9. Alexander von Humboldt, "Ich über mich selbst (mein Weg zum Naturwissenschaftler und Forschungsreisenden, 1769–1790)," in *Aus meinem Leben*, 38–40.

10. Alexander von Humboldt, *Personal Narrative of Travels to the Equinoctial Regions of America, During the Years 1799–1804*, vol. 1, trans. and ed. Thomasina Ross (London: Henry G. Bohn, 1852), ix; hereafter cited in the text. I have used the Ross translation rather than the earlier translation by Helen Maria Williams, which was published in collaboration with Humboldt between 1814 and 1829. While the Williams translation was Humboldt's choice and also has the advantage of translating all scientific digressions from the French original, I have found the more literal rather than lyrical Ross translation better suited for my purpose of close analysis. Punctuation modified.

11. Oliver Lubrich and Ottmar Ette, for instance, compiled Humboldt's pertinent Chimborazo texts and published them along with a detailed analysis in Alexander von Humboldt, *Ueber einen Versuch, den Gipfel des Chimborazo zu ersteigen* (Berlin: Eichborn, 2006). Aaron Sachs's *The Humboldt Current* concludes with an epilogue titled "Humboldt on Chimborazo," in which Sachs offers short excerpts of the diary translated into English. Sachs, *The Humboldt Current: Nineteenth-Century Exploration and the Roots of American Environmentalism* (New York: Penguin, 2006), 355–58.

12. To date no English translation of the diaries is available, which may have contributed to American scholars' reluctance to tackle Humboldt's mountain ascents.

13. Scholars have often assumed that Humboldt was unsuccessful in his first attempt of Pichincha. The Humboldt expert Hanno Beck claims, "On April 14, 1802, a first attempt to climb Pichincha failed" (my translation). Beck, *Amerikanische Reise*, 231. Humboldt, however, actually reached the higher Guagua Pichincha peak during this attempt. Conversely, scholars sometimes credit Humboldt with first ascents that he did not accomplish. Reinhard Andress erroneously credits Humboldt with ascending to the top of Antisana and three times to the summit of Pichincha: "Although Humboldt reached the summits of Teide on Tenerife, Silla de Caracas, Antisana, Pichincha—even three times—, Nevado de Toluca, Cofre de Perote, and Jorullo in Mexico, he remains inextricably linked to the failed attempt of Chimborazo" (my translation). In "Humboldt und Montúfar als Reisegefährten: Ein Vergleich ihrer Tagebücher," *Alexander von Humboldt im Netz. Internationale Zeitschrift für Humboldt-Studies (HiN)*, no. 22 (2011): 14. Andrea Wulf claims, "He discovered that they were barely 1,000 feet below the peak [of Chimborazo]," failing to mention that Humboldt was likely more than two thousand feet short of the summit when he turned around. Andrea Wulf, *The Invention of Nature: Alexander von Humboldt's New World* (New York: Knopf, 2015). On that ascent, she also misidentifies the fourth companion on Chimborazo as José de la Cruz, the mestizo

who had accompanied the group for the past two years. According to Humboldt, however, a "farmer from San Juan" accompanied them on Chimborazo. See Wulf, 60, 90, versus Alexander von Humboldt, *Reise auf dem Río Magdalena, durch die Anden und Mexico,* vol. 2 (Berlin: Akademie, 2003), 106. On Pichincha, Wulf mixes up Humboldt's companions when claiming that José de la Cruz broke through a snow bridge and Humboldt pressed on to the summit (83), when in fact it was the Indio Philipp Aldas who broke through the snow, with Humboldt deciding to turn around afterward (*Reise Magdalena,* 86–87; see also my depiction of the three Pichincha climbs in this book).

14. Mary Louise Pratt, *Imperial Eyes: Travel Writing and Transculturation* (New York: Routledge, 1992), 118.

15. Carolyn Dean, *A Culture of Stone: Inka Perspectives on Rock* (Durham, N.C.: Duke University Press, 2010), 1.

16. See Humboldt's comments to plate 5 in Alexander von Humboldt, *Views of the Cordilleras and Monuments of the Indigenous Peoples of the Americas,* trans. Vera M. Kutzinski and Ottmar Ette (Chicago: University of Chicago Press, 2012), 31, 33.

17. For a recent discussion, see "Humboldt's Legacy," in *Humboldt's Mexico: In the Footsteps of the Illustrious German Scientific Traveller,* by Myron Echenberg (Montreal: McGill-Queen's University Press, 2017), 198–208.

18. Sachs, "The Ultimate 'Other,'" 118.

19. Christiana Borchart de Moreno and Segundo E. Moreno Yánez, "From *País* to Nation: Alexander von Humboldt and the Formation of Ecuadorian Identity," in *Alexander von Humboldt and the Americas,* ed. Vera M. Kutzinski, Ottmar Ette, and Laura Dassow Walls (Berlin: Walter Frey, 2012), 117–43.

20. Jorge Cañizares-Esguerra, "The Problem with Andrea Wulf's Biography of Humboldt," *Time to Eat the Dogs* (podcast), September 24, 2019, http://timetoeat thedogs.libsyn.com/replay-the-problem-with-andrea-wulfs-biography-of-hum boldt. With many thanks to Karen Stolley for pointing me to this resource. See also Jorge Cañizares-Esguerra, *How to Write the History of the New World: Histories, Epistemologies, and Identities in the Eighteenth-Century Atlantic World* (Stanford, Calif.: Stanford University Press, 2001), 55–58, 124–29, for his own work on the issue.

21. See, e.g., Humboldt's letter to Carl Ludwig Willdenow sent from Havana on February 21, 1801: "It is very uncertain, almost improbable, that we both, Bonpland and I, return alive circumnavigating the Philippines and the Cape of Good Hope" (my translation). *Aus meinem Leben,* 171.

22. From 2014 to 2017, the German Federal Ministry of Education and Research funded a major research project on Humboldt's travel diaries, which comprised a full digitalization of the original diaries, as well as integrative research by a team of five doctoral students and postdocs led by Professor Ottmar Ette at the University of Potsdam. One of the resulting publications is devoted to Humboldt's drawings in the diaries: Ottmar Ette and Julia Maier, *Alexander von Humboldt: The*

Complete Drawings from the American Travel Journals (Munich: Prestel, 2018). While I have used and referenced excerpts from the diaries already published in Germany, I have compared the particular wording to the recently digitized artifacts, where appropriate. See Staatsbibliothek zu Berlin, Alexander von Humboldt Portal, http://humboldt.staatsbibliothek-berlin.de/werk.

23. See Margot Faak, "Einleitung," in *Alexander von Humboldt, Reise durch Venezuela: Auswahl aus den amerikanischen Reisetagebüchern*, ed. Margot Faak (Berlin: Akademie, 2000), 18; hereafter cited as *Reise Venezuela*. All translations from this book are my own.

24. See Julia Bayerl, "Gezeichnete Bewegung—bewegte Zeichnung," in *Landschaften und Kartographien der Humboldt'schen Wissenschaft*, ed. Ottmar Ette and Julian Drews (Hildesheim: Olms, 2017), 281–306; and Ottmar Ette, "Begegnungen aus der Bewegung," in *Das Buch der Begegnungen* (hereafter *Begegnungen*), by Alexander von Humboldt, ed. Ottmar Ette (Munich: Manesse, 2018), v–vii.

25. Alexander von Humboldt, *Views of Nature*, ed. Stephen T. Jackson and Laura Dassow Walls, trans. Mark W. Person (Chicago: University of Chicago Press, 2014), 25.

26. Later editors, however, seem to have disagreed with this reasoning: the latest German edition of *Views of Nature*, edited in Enzensberger's *Andere Bibliothek*, contains six colorful double-page images that were taken mostly from *Vues des Cordillères*.

27. Humboldt, *Views of Nature*, 257.

28. Humboldt, *Views of Nature*, 256.

29. Scholars have different ways of numbering the oeuvre; Hanno Beck counts thirty-four volumes, since he includes other works that document the American journey, such as *Views of Nature*. Beck, "Kommentar," in Humboldt, *Die Forschungsreise in den Tropen Amerikas*, vol. 3, 372. See also Ette, *Begegnungen*, 340.

30. The contemporary German translation by Hermann Hauff, *Reise in die Aequinoctial-Gegenden des neuen Continents* (1859–60), already concluded with Humboldt's trip to Cuba.

31. Kurt-R. Biermann estimates that all thirty volumes cost about 2,553 thalers, or, in today's purchasing power, 20,000 euros, though Humboldt liberally handed out free copies, contributing to his publishers' ruin. See "Einleitende Studie von Kurt-R. Biermann," in Humboldt, *Reise Magdalena*, 10, 12.

32. See Biermann, "Einleitende Studie," 13–15. According to Sachs, Humboldt also possibly had worked on a fourth volume but decided to destroy it, although Biermann disproves this theory. Sachs, *The Humboldt Current*, 71.

33. See also Anne Marie Claire Godlewska, "From Enlightenment Vision to Modern Science? Humboldt's Visual Thinking," in *Geography and Enlightenment*, ed. David N. Livingstone and Charles W. J. Withers (Chicago: University of Chicago Press, 1999), 236–75.

34. Humboldt, *Reise Venezuela*, 81. Also online at Edition Humboldt Digital,

https://edition-humboldt.de/reisetagebuecher/detail.xql?id=H0016412&l=de
diary page 15r (recto)/27.

35. Sean Franzel delineates the narrative structure of the sublime in "Time and Narrative in the Mountain Sublime Around 1800," in *Heights of Reflection: Mountains in the German Imagination from the Middle Ages to the Twenty-First Century*, ed. Sean Ireton and Caroline Schaumann (Rochester, N.Y.: Camden House, 2012), 98–115.

36. Although this clarification may seem insignificant today, European sailors since the fifteenth century had claimed that one could see the mountain from as far as sixty miles away, and that it equally rose sixty miles from the horizon. See Jon Mathieu, *Die dritte Dimension: Eine vergleichende Geschichte der Berge in der Neuzeit* (Basel: Schwabe, 2011), 39. Humboldt also included observations on the distance from which mountains can be seen in his diary entry on Silla de Caracas and the Chimborazo profile in *Géographie des Plantes Equinoxiales—Tableau physique des Andes et pays voisins*.

37. See Faak's note in Humboldt, *Reise Venezuela*, 86–87.

38. See letters 7–12 (35–46), letter 15 (47–60), in Alexander von Humboldt, *Briefe aus Amerika, 1799–1804*, ed. Ulrike Moheit (Berlin: Akademie, 1993).

39. See also Cettina Rapisarda's insightful analysis in "Blick ins Kraterinnere des Pic de Teyde und vulkanische Landschaften der Kanarischen Inseln bei Alexander von Humboldt," in Ette and Drews, *Landschaften und Kartographien*, 233–60.

40. See Oliver Lubrich and Ottmar Ette, "Die Reise durch eine andere Bibliothek: Nachwort," in *Ansichten der Kordilleren und Monumente der eingeborenen Völker Amerikas*, by Alexander von Humboldt, ed. Oliver Lubrich and Ottmar Ette (Berlin: Eichborn, 2004), 415–16.

41. With many thanks to Karen Stolley for her helpful comments on this section.

42. Humboldt, *Reise Venezuela*, 177.

43. Humboldt, *Reise Venezuela*, 181.

44. Humboldt, *Reise Venezuela*, 177. See also diary page 38r (front page), quoted in *Begegnungen*, 114. If available, I have chosen the more recently edited and translated *Begegnungen* volume.

45. Diary, 38v (back page), in *Begegnungen*, 115.

46. Diary, 39r, in *Begegnungen*, 116; Humboldt, *Reise Venezuela*, 180.

47. Humboldt, *Reise Venezuela*, 180–81.

48. Humboldt, *Reise Venezuela*, 181.

49. Humboldt, *Reise Venezuela*, 179; diary, 39r, in *Begegnungen*, 117.

50. Unlike Ottmar Ette, I read this passage not as a tribute to the sublime that, in the history of Petrarch's ascent of Mont Ventoux in 1336 and the tradition of Kant, celebrates the power of aesthetic thinking, but as a testament to altitude-induced fantasies, praising limitless human imagination. See Ottmar Ette, "Die Geburt der Landschaft aus dem Geiste der Theorie: Alexander von Humboldts wissenschaftlich-künstlerische *Amerikanische Reisetagebücher*," in Ette and Drews, *Landschaften und Kartographien*, 31.

51. See letters 23 (75–79), 26 (81–84), 27 (85–90), in Humboldt, *Briefe*.

52. Humboldt, *Views of the Cordilleras*, 368.

53. Oliver Lubrich has provided illustrations of the various measuring instruments in "Vom Guckkasten zum Erlebnisraum: Alexander von Humboldt und die Medien des Reisens," *Figurationen* 2 (2007): 51.

54. Compare the diary, 177–78, with the *Personal Narrative*, 419–20, 429–30.

55. Maurice Isserman and Stewart Weaver, *Fallen Giants: A History of Himalayan Mountaineering from the Age of Empire to the Age of Extremes* (New Haven, Conn.: Yale University Press, 2009), 14.

2. The Drama of Ascent

1. Alexander von Humboldt, *Reise auf dem Río Magdalena, durch die Anden und Mexiko*, vol. 2, trans. Margot Faak (Berlin: Akademie, 1990), 56; hereafter cited as *Reise Magdalena*. All translations from this volume are my own.

2. Humboldt, *Reise Magdalena*, 64.

3. Humboldt, *Reise Magdalena*, 56.

4. With the exception of Mount Chimborazo, which garnered two minor essays examined later in this chapter.

5. Bernard Debarbieux asserts: "One of the most original and least-noted aspects of Humboldt's method lies in his observations of the reactions of his own and his travelling companions' bodies to the influences of the environment. Generally speaking, in accordance with his holistic view of nature, he attributed a power to excite the senses and to develop one's sensitivity to immersion in the natural world." Bernard Debarbieux, "Mountains: Between Pure Reason and Embodied Experience; Philippe Buache and Alexander von Humboldt," in *High Places: Cultural Geographies of Mountains, Ice, and Sciences*, ed. Denis E. Cosgrove and Veronica Della Dora (New York: Palgrave, 2009), 101.

6. Humboldt, *Reise Magdalena*, 57.

7. Humboldt, *Reise Magdalena*, 57.

8. Humboldt, *Reise Magdalena*, 61.

9. Humboldt, *Reise Magdalena*, 66.

10. Later, the Swiss physician Conrad Meyer-Ahrens published a monograph titled *Die Bergkrankheit* (1854), summarizing all available material to date about altitude sickness. In the following decades, the "Father of Aviation Medicine," Paul Bert, conducted experiments in a pressurized chamber in his Parisian laboratory, the results of which he published as *La pression barométrique* (1878), an influential study on the physiological effects of air pressure that garnered the biennial prize from the French Academy of Sciences. See Philipp Felsch, *Laborlandschaften: Physiologische Alpenreisen im 19. Jahrhundert* (Göttingen: Wallstein, 2007), 58–66.

11. Humboldt, *Reise Magdalena*, 65.

12. For further elaboration, see Beck, *Amerikanische Reise*, 232–40. On the other hand, several scholars have pointed out Caldas's (and Mutis's) great influence on Humboldt's understanding of the Andean geography, and some have even charged Humboldt with copying Caldas's concepts. For more information, see Stephen T. Jackson, "Introduction: Humboldt, Ecology, and the Cosmos," in *Essay on the Geography of Plants*, by Alexander von Humboldt and Aimé Bonpland (Chicago: University of Chicago Press, 2009), 13.

13. Adolf Meyer-Abich, for instance, termed speculations about homosexuality "completely absurd" (*ganz abwegig*) and claimed that Humboldt considered marrying the widow of his friend Reinhard von Haeften. Adolf Meyer-Abich, *Alexander von Humboldt* (Hamburg: Rowohlt, 1967), 46–47. In a similar vein, in *Amerikanische Reise*, Hanno Beck proposed that Humboldt may have considered marrying Amalie Imhoff (40–41) and in Mexico may have fallen in love with a local beauty (266). The chapter "Outing Humboldt," in Nicolaas A. Rupke's *Alexander von Humboldt: A Metabiography* (Frankfurt am Main: Peter Lang, 2008), 196–202, offers a lucid and helpful introduction to the topic.

14. The renowned Humboldt biographer Hanno Beck, for instance, devotes one chapter each to Mutis and Caldas (and even includes a drawing of Caldas) but only mentions Montúfar in passing. When the novelist Daniel Kehlmann reworked the material into his novel *Die Vermessung der Welt* (2005, *Measuring the World*, 2006), he decided to omit Montúfar altogether.

15. See illustrations 313 and 338, "Cartographic practice drawing by Carlos Montúfar," which Humboldt complemented with the following note: "Sad memories cling to the simple lines (drawing attempts) that fill these pages. These lines are from the hand of the young Carlos Montúfar, son of the Marquis of Selvalegre, who accompanied us to Europe and whom the Spaniards shot to death. I taught him to draw maps in Quito. A. Humboldt, Sept. 1855." Alexander von Humboldt, *The Complete Drawings from the American Travel Diaries*, ed. Ottmar Ette and Julia Maier (Munich: Prestel, 2018), 294, 306.

16. Diary, 146v; Alexander von Humboldt, *Das Buch der Begegnungen*, ed. Ottmar Ette (Munich: Manesse, 2018), 224–25; hereafter cited as *Begegnungen*.

17. Humboldt, *Reise Magdalena*, 65.

18. Humboldt, *Reise Magdalena*, 64.

19. Humboldt, *Reise Magdalena*, 65.

20. Steven E. Fox and Kris Fulsass, eds., *Mountaineering: The Freedom of the Hills*, 7th ed. (Seattle: Mountaineers, 2003), 456.

21. Edward Whymper, *Travels Amongst the Great Andes* (London: Charles Knight, 1972), 112.

22. Humboldt, *Reise Magdalena*, 81.

23. Humboldt, *Reise Magdalena*, 84.

24. Humboldt, *Reise Magdalena*, 84.

25. Humboldt, *Views of the Cordilleras*, 64.

26. Humboldt, *Reise Magdalena*, 84.

27. Humboldt, *Reise Magdalena*, 73.

28. Humboldt, *Reise Magdalena*, 74.

29. Humboldt, *Reise Magdalena*, 75.

30. Humboldt, *Reise Magdalena*, 75.

31. Humboldt, *Reise Magdalena*, 85.

32. Humboldt, *Reise Magdalena*, 87.

33. Humboldt, *Reise Magdalena*, 88.

34. Humboldt, *Reise Magdalena*, 88.

35. Humboldt, *Reise Magdalena*, 88.

36. Humboldt, *Reise Magdalena*, 89.

37. Humboldt, *Reise Magdalena*, 90.

38. Based on the reports of subsequent climbers, scholars estimate that Humboldt reached a height of approximately 5,350 m/17,552 ft., rather than the 5,881 m/19,294 ft. he claimed. Humboldt, *Reise Magdalena*, 344, note 157.

39. Humboldt and Bonpland, *Essay on the Geography of Plants*, 61.

40. Stephen T. Jackson, "Introduction," 27.

41. All texts about Chimborazo have been compiled, edited, and newly translated in Oliver Lubrich and Ottmar Ette's excellent collection *Alexander von Humboldt: Ueber einen Versuch den Gipfel des Chimborazo zu ersteigen* (Berlin: Eichborn, 2006). Thus all references to Chimborazo follow this newer edition. All translations from this book into English are my own.

42. This essay has been translated by Vera M. Kutzinski as "About an Attempt to Climb to the Top of Chimborazo," *Atlantic Studies* 7, no. 2 (2010): 191–211.

43. Lubrich and Ette extensively commented on the differences between letters, diary, and published essays and carefully analyzed the descriptions of the ascent.

44. Lubrich and Ette, *Ueber einen Versuch*, 58 (my translation).

45. Lubrich and Ette, *Ueber einen Versuch*, 98.

46. Lubrich and Ette, *Ueber einen Versuch*, 99.

47. Lubrich and Ette, *Ueber einen Versuch*, 85.

48. See Daniel Kehlmann, *Measuring the World*, trans. Carol Brown Janeway (New York: Pantheon, 2006); and my article comparing novel and diary, "Who Measures the World? Alexander von Humboldt's Chimborazo Climb in the Literary Imagination," *German Quarterly* 82, no. 4 (2009): 447–68.

49. Lubrich and Ette, *Ueber einen Versuch*, 85.

50. Lubrich and Ette, *Ueber einen Versuch*, 98.

51. Lubrich and Ette, *Ueber einen Versuch*, 99.

52. Humboldt, *Views of the Cordilleras*, 224.

53. Humboldt, *Views of the Cordilleras*, 224.

54. Humboldt, *Views of the Cordilleras*, 126.

55. Humboldt, *Views of the Cordilleras*, 224.

56. Humboldt, *Views of the Cordilleras*, 226–27.

57. Lubrich and Ette, *Ueber einen Versuch*, 132.

58. Lubrich and Ette, *Ueber einen Versuch*, 132.

59. Lubrich and Ette, *Ueber einen Versuch*, 86.

60. Lubrich and Ette, *Ueber einen Versuch*, 97.

61. Lubrich and Ette, *Ueber einen Versuch*, 97.

62. Naia Morueta-Holme et al., "Strong Upslope Shifts in Chimborazo's Vegetation over Two Centuries Since Humboldt," *Proceedings of the National Academy of Sciences of the United States of America* 112, no. 41 (2015): 1–5.

63. For more detail on both the volcano's eruption and Humboldt's ascent, see Tobias Kraft, "Die Geburt der Gebirge: Alexander von Humboldts Erforschung des mexikanischen Vulkans Jorullo," *Arsprototo* 1 (2014): 33–36.

64. According to Beck, Montúfar also accompanied the team. Beck, *Amerikanische Reise*, 273.

65. Humboldt, *Reise Magdalena*, 282.

66. Humboldt, *Reise Magdalena*, 282.

67. Humboldt, *Reise Magdalena*, 283.

68. Humboldt, *Reise Magdalena*, 283.

69. Humboldt, *Reise Magdalena*, 284.

70. Humboldt, *Reise Magdalena*, 284.

71. Humboldt, *Views of the Cordilleras*, 288.

72. For the ascent of Toluca, see Humboldt, *Reise Magdalena*, 286–87. For Cofre the Perote, see Ulrike Leitner, ed., *Alexander von Humboldt: Von Mexiko-Stadt nach Veracruz; Tagebuch* (Berlin: Akademie, 2005), 115–18.

3. The Alps

1. This is a broad generalization, and important work has recently pointed to enduring mountain fascination in premodern times and antiquity. See Dawn L. Hollis, "*Mountain Gloom and Mountain Glory:* The Genealogy of an Idea," *ISLE: Interdisciplinary Studies in Literature and Environment*, isz044 (May 2019), https://doi.org/10.1093/isle/isz044; as well as the forthcoming anthology by Dawn Hollis and Jason König.

2. See Ötzi the Iceman, South Tyrol Museum of Archeology, http://www.iceman.it/en/the-iceman.

3. Johann Jakob Scheuchzer, *Natur-Geschichte des Schweizerlandes, samt seinen Reisen über die Schweizerische Gebürge*, vol. 2 (Zurich: David Gessner, 1746), 219 (my translation), https://www.e-rara.ch/zut/content/structure/2270007.

4. For further information on the Grand Tour, see Lynne Withey's excellent *Grand Tours and Cook's Tours: A History of Leisure Travel, 1750 to 1915* (New York: William Morrow, 1997).

5. Jean-Jacques Rousseau, *Julie, or The New Heloise: Letters of Two Lovers Who Live in a Small Town at the Foot of the Alps*, trans. Philip Stewart and Jean Vaché (Hanover, N.H.: Dartmouth College Press, 1997), 64. For a close analysis of Saint-Preux's mountain ascents, see Mary Ellen Birkett, "Rousseau and the Poetry of Mountaineering," in *Essays on the Literature of Mountaineering*, ed. Armand E. Singer (Morgantown: West Virginia University Press, 1982), 1–10.

6. See also Petra Raymond, *Von der Landschaft im Kopf zur Landschaft aus Sprache: Die Romantisierung der Alpen in den Reiseschilderungen und die Literarisierung des Gebirges in der Erzählprosa der Goethezeit* (Tübingen: Niemeyer, 1993).

7. Withey, *Grand Tours and Cook's Tours*, 62.

8. Richard Hill's Hawkstone estate, for instance, was constructed with a hundred-meter-high hill with "sublime views" and a cave complex in which a hermit was paid to live. Andrew Beattie, *The Alps: A Cultural History* (Oxford: Signal Books, 2006), 124.

9. See Jim Ring, *How the English Made the Alps* (London: Murray, 2000).

10. John Murray, *A Hand-Book for Travellers on the Continent* (London, 1836), iii.

11. For further detail, see Alan Sillitoe, *Leading the Blind: A Century of Guidebook Travel, 1815–1914* (London: Macmillan, 1995).

12. For more on the accident and the Compagnie, see Peter H. Hansen, *The Summits of Modern Man: Mountaineering After the Enlightenment* (Cambridge, Mass.: Harvard University Press, 2013), 153–58.

13. Hansen, *The Summits of Modern Man*, 157–58.

14. For more on the rise of sports in Britain, see Bruce Haley, "The New Era: Victorian Sport and Training," in *The Healthy Body and Victorian Culture* (Cambridge, Mass.: Harvard University Press, 1978), 123–40.

15. See Fergus Fleming, *Killing Dragons: The Conquest of the Alps* (New York: Atlantic Monthly Press, 2000).

16. For more information on the social background of the club's members, see David Robbins, "Sport, Hegemony, and the Middle Class: The Victorian Mountaineers," *Theory, Culture and Society* 4 (1987): 584–86.

17. Ring, *How the English*, 94.

18. Jon Mathieu, *Geschichte der Alpen, 1500–1900: Umwelt, Entwicklung, Gesellschaft* (Vienna: Böhlau, 1998), 95.

19. For more information on the burgeoning sport of skiing, see Andrew Denning, *Skiing into Modernity: A Cultural and Environmental History* (Berkeley: University of California Press, 2014).

20. Mark Twain, *A Tramp Abroad*, vol. 2, chap. 13 (New York: Harper, 1879), 173.

21. Wolfgang Hackl, *Eingeborene im Paradies: Die literarische Wahrnehmung des alpinen Tourismus im 19. und 20. Jahrhundert* (Tübingen: Niemeyer, 2004), 78–84.

22. See, e.g., Luis Trenker, who in *Helden der Berge* mythologized mountain climbers and celebrated mountaineering in nationalistic terms. Caroline Schaumann, "Weiße Phantasien: Reinheit und Schmutz in Texten von Luis Trenker, Heinrich Harrer und Hans Ertl," *Literatur für Leser* 14, no. 2 (2014): 102–4.

23. See also Caroline Schaumann, "The Return of the *Bergfilm: Nordwand* (2008) and *Nanga Parbat* (2010)," *German Quarterly* 87, no. 4 (Fall 2014): 418–21; Harald Höbusch, *"Mountain of Destiny": Nanga Parbat and Its Path into the German Imagination* (Rochester, N.Y.: Camden House, 2016).

24. See "Swiss Tourism in Figures 2015," published annually by the Swiss Tourism Federation, https://www.bfs.admin.ch/bfsstatic/dam/assets/502977/master (accessed January 11, 2017).

25. Climate Change Post, "Switzerland: Tourism Switzerland," http://www.climatechangepost.com/switzerland/tourism (accessed January 14, 2017).

4. Horace-Bénédict de Saussure's Quest for Mont Blanc

1. Quotations come from Saussure's diary manuscript. Owned by Saussure's offspring, the diary was made available only to Douglas William Freshfield. The exception is the Mont Blanc sections, amounting to three weeks from July 7 to August 4, 1887, which were published in 1926 and republished in 2006 by Anne Fauche and Samuel Cordier as *Journal de l'ascension du Mont-Blanc* (Chamonix: Guérin, 2006). Freshfield's informative but dated work is still the only extensive biography of Saussure available and the only source that translates portions of the diary and Saussure's *Voyages* into English. Although I have tried to provide my own translations wherever needed and also consulted the German translation of the first part of *Voyages, Reisen durch die Alpen,* my chapter owes greatly to Freshfield's text. Freshfield, *The Life of Horace Benedict de Saussure* (London: Edward Arnold, 1920), 230.

2. Saussure's diary, quoted in Freshfield, *Life of Horace Benedict de Saussure,* 233; and in Fauche and Cordier, *Journal,* 186.

3. Horace-Bénédict de Saussure, *Voyages dans les Alpes, précédés d'un essai sur l'histoire naturelle des environs de Genève,* vol. 7 (Neuchâtel: Chez Louis Fauche-Borel, 1796), 235–36, translated in Freshfield, *Life of Horace Benedict de Saussure,* 232. The Mont Blanc chapters were also translated by John Pinkerton as "An Account of the Attempts That Have Been Made to Attain the Summit of Mont Blanc," in *A General Collection of the Best and Most Interesting Voyages and Travels in All Parts of the World* (London: Longman, 1809), 677–709. The chapter describing Saussure's actual ascent of Mont Blanc was translated by Edward Whymper and published as "Ascent of Mont Blanc by Horace Benedict de Saussure," in *Chamonix and the Range of Mont Blanc: A Guide by Edward Whymper* (London: John Murray, 1896), 28–35.

4. In this vein, Peter H. Hansen, elucidating on Kant's response, reads Saussure's ascent as the epitome of Enlightenment. Hansen, *The Summits of Modern Man:*

Mountaineering After the Enlightenment (Cambridge, Mass.: Harvard University Press, 2013), 11–113. Hansen provides an excellent documentation of Saussure's climb using all sources available but does not distinguish between the tone of the various sources; see also 99–103.

5. Saussure, *Voyages*, vol. 7, 236. Translated in Whymper, "Ascent of Mont Blanc," 34; and Pinkerton, "An Account," 691.

6. Saussure, *Voyages*, vol. 7, 283–84. Translated in Freshfield, *Life of Horace Benedict de Saussure*, 231–32; and Pinkerton, "An Account," 704.

7. Horace-Bénédict de Saussure, *Voyages dans les Alpes, précédés d'un essai sur l'histoire naturelle des environs de Genève*, vol. 2 (Neuchâtel: Chez Louis Fauche-Borel, 1780), 131 (my translation).

8. Horace-Bénédict de Saussure, "Discours Préliminaire," in *Voyages dans les Alpes, précédés d'un essai sur l'histoire naturelle des environs de Genève*, vol. 1 (Geneva: Chez Barde, Manget, 1779), vi. Translated in Freshfield, *Life of Horace Benedict de Saussure*, 286.

9. Even esteemed scholars such as Hans Haeberli, the president of the Albrecht-von-Haller-Stiftung, confuse some of the details of Saussure's ascent, such as claiming that Saussure accomplished the second ascent of Mont Blanc. Hans Haeberli, "Vorwort," in *The Correspondence Between Albrecht von Haller and Horace-Bénédict de Saussure*, ed. Otto Sonntag (Bern: Hans Huber, 1990), 8.

10. Freshfield, *Life of Horace Benedict de Saussure*, 23.

11. "I love to follow in the footsteps of a great man" (my translation). Quoted in Hanno Beck, "Kommentar," in *Die Forschungsreise in den Tropen Amerikas*, by Alexander von Humboldt, vol. 3, ed. Hanno Beck (Darmstadt: Wissenschaftliche Buchgesellschaft, 2008), 443–44. See Emma Sdegno, "The Alps," in *The Cambridge Companion to John Ruskin*, ed. Francis O'Gorman (Cambridge: Cambridge University Press, 2015), 36; James David Forbes, *Travels Through the Alps of Savoy, and Other Parts of the Pennine Chain with Observations on the Phenomena of Glaciers* (Edinburgh: Adam and Charles Black, 1843), 9.

12. Saussure, "Discours Préliminaire," in *Voyages*, vol. 1, xvii–xviii. Translated in Freshfield, *Life of Horace Benedict de Saussure*, 289.

13. Freshfield, *Life of Horace Benedict de Saussure*, 409.

14. The letter exchange began in 1760, when Saussure was just twenty, and ended in 1777, three months before Haller's death. Their correspondence comprises at least 410 letters, of which 331 are preserved and reprinted in Otto Sonntag, ed., *The Correspondence Between Albrecht von Haller and Horace-Bénédict de Saussure* (Bern: Hans Huber, 1990).

15. Saussure, *Voyages*, vol. 2, 233. Translated in Freshfield, *Life of Horace Benedict de Saussure*, 68. Subsequent references will include the volume and page number of the original French text in parentheses.

16. Albrecht von Haller, *Versuch Schweizerischer Gedichte*, 9th ed. (1762; reprint, Bern:

Herbert Lang, 1969), 55–56, translated by Stanley Mason as *The Alps: An English Translation* (Dübendorf, Switzerland: Walter Amstutz De Clivo Press, 1987), 77.

17. For more on Haller, see my article "From Meadows to Mountaintops: Albrecht von Haller's 'Die Alpen,'" in *Heights of Reflection: Mountains in the German Imagination from the Middle Ages to the Twenty-First Century*, ed. Sean Ireton and Caroline Schaumann (Rochester, N.Y.: Camden House, 2012), 57–76.

18. Saussure reportedly learned German in 1770 for the express purpose of reading Gruner's text. Albert V. Carozzi and John K. Newman, *Horace-Bénédict de Saussure: Forerunner in Glaciology* (Geneva: Editions Passé Présent, 1995), 60–62, 77–83.

19. As Wyttenbach himself admitted, unexpected business forced him to entrust the translation of parts of *Voyages* to "one of his friends" [einen meiner Freunde]. Horatius Benedictus von Saussure, "Vorrede des Uebersetzers," in *Reisen durch die Alpen, nebst einem Versuche über die Naturgeschichte der Gegenden von Genf*, trans. Jacob Samuel Wyttenbach, vol. 1 (Leipzig: Johann Friedrich Junius, 1781), iv.

20. Saussure, *Voyages*, vol. 2, 156–66.

21. Saussure, *Voyages*, vol. 2, 169 (my translation).

22. Saussure, *Voyages*, vol. 2, 191 (my translation).

23. Carozzi and Newman, *Horace-Bénédict de Saussure*, 68.

24. Saussure, "Des glaciers en général," in *Voyages*, vol. 2, 241–82.

25. For further assessment of Saussure's scientific work, see Freshfield's chapter "De Saussure in Science and Literature," 412–56.

26. Saussure, "Discours Préliminaire," in *Voyages*, vol. 1, xxxi. Translated in Freshfield, *Life of Horace Benedict de Saussure*, 291.

27. See also "Discours Préliminaire," in *Voyages*, vol. 1, xvii–xviii.

28. Saussure, *Voyages*, vol. 2, 233 (my translation).

29. Saussure, *Voyages*, vol. 3, 95.

30. Saussure, *Voyages*, vol. 2, 167 (my translation).

31. Saussure, *Voyages*, vol. 2, 283 (my translation).

32. Saussure, *Voyages*, vol. 2, 337, 209 (my translation).

33. Saussure, *Voyages*, vol. 3, 40 (my translation).

34. Saussure, *Voyages*, vol. 3, 74 (my translation).

35. Saussure, *Voyages*, vol. 2, 315 (my translation).

36. Saussure, *Voyages*, vol. 3, 346 (my translation). See also vol. 2, 302–5. These spiked shoes had already been described by Josias Simler, whose *De Alpibus commentarius* (1574) gave the first printed advice about travel above the snowline. See Ronald W. Clark, *Men, Myths, and Mountains* (New York: Thomas Y. Crowell, 1976), 6–7.

37. Saussure, *Voyages*, vol. 3, 42; vol. 2, 342 (my translation).

38. Saussure, *Voyages*, vol. 2, 316 (my translation).

39. Saussure, *Voyages*, vol. 2, 342 (my translation).

40. See Peter H. Hansen, "The Living Eye," in *The Summits of Modern Man*,

58–60. For a fascinating history of the growing popularity of such fish-eye views, see also Veronica della Dora, *Mountain* (London: Reaktion Books, 2016), 126–31.

41. Saussure, *Voyages,* vol. 2, 133 (my translation).

42. "Saussure, *Voyages,* vol. 2, 199–200 (my translation).

43. Horace-Bénédict de Saussure, *Voyages dans les Alpes, précédés d'un essai sur l'histoire naturelle des environs de Genève,* vol. 4 (Genève: Chez Barde, Manget & Compagnie, 1786), 389 (my translation).

44. Saussure, *Voyages,* vol. 4, 390–91 (my translation).

45. Saussure, *Voyages,* vol. 4, 405. Translated in Freshfield, *Life of Horace Benedict de Saussure,* 202.

46. Saussure, *Voyages,* vol. 4, 406. Translated in Freshfield, *Life of Horace Benedict de Saussure,* 202–3.

47. Apparently Marc-Theodore Bourrit, fueled by jealousy, tried to discredit Paccard's ascent by inventing in the first published account of the climb the rumor that Paccard had merely been dragged to the top by Balmat. This story, perpetuated by Balmat himself, as well as in Alexandre Dumas's writings on the ascent (*Impressions de voyage,* 1834), prevails in popular descriptions to this day. Dumas, like Bourrit before him, had only interviewed Balmat, while Paccard's side of the story was never published and only surfaced in his late diary in the 1900s. Why Saussure did not correct the biased account remains unclear. For more on this story, see Walt Unsworth, *Savage Storms: The Story of Mont Blanc* (London: Hodder and Stoughton, 1986), 19–36; and Francis Gribble, *The Early Mountaineers* (London: T. Fisher, 1899), 162–81. Peter H. Hansen offers a more up-to-date account of the controversy in *The Summits of Modern Man,* 90–117.

48. Saussure, *Voyages,* vol. 7, 231. Translated in Whymper, "Ascent of Mont Blanc," 31; Pinkerton, "An Account," 690.

49. Saussure, *Reisen durch die Alpen,* vol. 4, trans. Jacob Samuel Wyttenbach (Leipzig: Johann Friedrich Junius, 1788), 346 (my translation).

50. Hansen, *The Summits of Modern Man,* 102.

51. Saussure, "Discours Préliminaire," in *Voyages,* vol. 1, viii–ix. Translated in Freshfield, *Life of Horace Benedict de Saussure,* 287.

52. Hansen, *The Summits of Modern Man,* 110–11.

5. Icecapades

My spelling "Icecapades" seeks to distinguish Agassiz's and Forbes's forays on the glaciers from the theatrical skating performances called the Ice Capades, which began in 1940 and featured former professional ice skaters who had retired from competition.

1. The Aletsch is Europe's largest glacier and has receded greatly in the past decade as a result of climate change.

2. James D. Forbes, *Norway and Its Glaciers, Visited in 1861, Followed by Journals of Excursions in the High Alps of Dauphine, Berne, and Savoy* (Edinburgh: Adam and Charles Black, 1853), 316.

3. Forbes, *Norway*, 320.

4. Forbes, *Norway*, 322.

5. "To Miss Forbes," Brieg, August 29, 1841, in *The Life and Letters of James David Forbes, F.R.S.*, by John Campbell Shairp, Peter Guthrie Tait, and Anthony Adams-Reilly (London: Macmillan, 1873), 267.

6. "Forbes to Whewell," November 7, 1841, in Bruce Hevly, "The Heroic Science of Glacier Motion," *Osiris* 11 (1996): 70.

7. Forbes, *Norway*, 325.

8. In his account of the ascent, Desor, too, admitted: "We came to the agreement, that this ascent should, in the mean time, remain a matter of secondary importance to the crossing of the Glacier of Viesch, and that we should attempt it only in case of finding ourselves free from fatigue at the end of our journey." Édouard Desor, "Ascent of the Jungfrau, Accomplished on the 28th August 1841," *Edinburgh New Philosophical Journal* 32 (1841): 292.

9. In his publication of the letters between Agassiz and Humboldt, for instance, the historian Wilhelm Ziehr credits Agassiz with the first ascent of the Jungfrau. See Wilhelm Ziehr, "Aus der Frühzeit der Gletscherforschung: Ein unbekannter Briefwechsel zwischen König Friedrich Wilhelm IV., Alexander von Humboldt und Louis Agassiz," *Berliner Manuskripte zur Alexander-von-Humboldt-Forschung* 29 (2007): 10.

10. Humboldt to Friedrich Wilhelm IV of Prussia, February 22, 1842, in Ziehr, "Aus der Frühzeit," 8. My translation.

11. Desor, "Ascent of the Jungfrau," 320.

12. "Agassiz to Philip Egerton," September 10, 1839, in Elizabeth Cary Agassiz, *Louis Agassiz, His Life and Correspondence* (Boston: Houghton Mifflin, 1885), 294.

13. Desor, "Ascent of the Jungfrau," 320. Desor's account deviates from Forbes's in minor details, such as departure times and the moments when some members of the party halted their ascent.

14. Desor, "Ascent of the Jungfrau," 320.

15. Forbes, journal, quoted in *Life and Letters*, 23.

16. The young Darwin entered the college the same year as Forbes, in 1825, but left no mark at the institution, leaving in 1831 on a five-year journey around the world on H.M.S. *Beagle*.

17. Forbes, "My Dear Uncle," January 30, 1830, in *Life and Letters*, 55.

18. "Agassiz to Braun," December 3, 1829, quoted in Cary Agassiz, *Louis Agassiz*, 119.

19. "Braun to Agassiz," August 9, 1827, quoted in Cary Agassiz, *Louis Agassiz*, 44; "Autobiographical Sketch," in Cary Agassiz, *Louis Agassiz*, 150.

20. See Cary Agassiz, *Louis Agassiz*, 95.

21. Letters reprinted in Cary Agassiz, *Louis Agassiz,* 61–62, 65, 69.

22. "Letter to his mother," February 3, 1828, quoted in Cary Agassiz, *Louis Agassiz,* 63.

23. "Letter to his mother," February 3, 1828, quoted in Cary Agassiz, *Louis Agassiz,* 64.

24. Along with a group of Austrian naturalists, Spix and Martius traveled in Brazil from 1817 to 1820, exploring the area around Rio de Janeiro and São Paulo before parting with the Austrians and advancing farther into the continent via several river routes. On their journey, they described flora, fauna, indigenous tribes, and anything else of imperialist interest, and they collected plants, insects, fish, amphibians, and mammals that later formed the basis of the National Zoological Collection at Munich. Upon their return to Munich in 1820, they also brought home numerous cultural artifacts, as well as a boy and a girl from different tribes, who were consequently renamed and baptized but soon perished. The account of their journey, *Reise in Brasilien auf Befehl Sr. Majestät Maximilian Joseph I. König von Baiern in den Jahren 1817–1820,* was published in three volumes in 1823, 1828, and 1831.

25. "Braun to his father," February 15, 1829, quoted in Cary Agassiz, *Louis Agassiz,* 103.

26. "Letter from his mother," March 1832, quoted in Cary Agassiz, *Louis Agassiz,* 172.

27. "Humboldt to Agassiz," March 27, 1832, quoted in Cary Agassiz, *Louis Agassiz,* 187.

28. Johann Wolfgang von Goethe, *The Collected Works,* trans. Krishna Winston, ed. Jane K. Brown (Princeton, N.J.: Princeton University Press, 1989), 279. For the original German, see Johann Wolfgang von Goethe, *Wilhelm Meisters Wanderjahre, oder Die Entsagenden,* book 2, chap. 10, in *Goethes sämtliche Werke in vierzig Bänden,* vol. 18 (Stuttgart: Cotta'scher, 1856), 319.

29. See Dorothy Cameron, "Goethe—Discoverer of the Ice Age," *Journal of Glaciology* 5, no. 41 (1964): 751–54; Eric Wilson, *The Spiritual History of Ice: Romanticism, Science, and the Imagination* (New York: Palgrave, 2003), 72–73; and most recently Jason Groves, "Goethe's Petrofiction: Reading the *Wanderjahre* in the Anthropocene," *Goethe Yearbook* 22 (1015): 95–113.

30. Schimper had researched with Charpentier, Hugi, and Agassiz and presented some lectures titled "Worldsummer and Worldwinter" in 1835–36, but he never published his theories. Albert V. Carozzi, "Editor's Introduction," in *Studies on Glaciers, Preceded by the Discourse of Neuchâtel,* by Louis Agassiz, ed. and trans. Albert V. Carozzi (New York: Hafner, 1967), xvii.

31. It is important to note that Agassiz did not see glaciers as transporting rocks but rather theorized that boulders had rolled down on the ice surface.

32. While Humboldt cautioned, "I think you should concentrate your moral

and also your pecuniary strength upon this beautiful work on fossil fishes," von Buch was more direct: "I am expecting the numbers of your Fossil Fishes, which have not yet come. Humboldt often speaks of them to me. Ah! how much I prefer you in a field which is wholly your own than in one where you break in upon the measured and cautious tread, introduced by Saussure in geology." "Humboldt to Agassiz," December 2, 1837, 267, and "Leopold von Buch to Agassiz," December 22, 1837, in Cary Agassiz, *Louis Agassiz,* 273–74.

33. "Humboldt to Agassiz," March 2, 1842, quoted in Cary Agassiz, *Louis Agassiz,* 346.

34. The quote continues as follows: "He [Saussure] has looked at almost all the glaciers of Switzerland, and he visited the ice sheets of the Mont-Blanc, Monte Rosa, and Bernese Oberland. His tireless interest in the natural history of the Alps made him discover the paths to their highest summits at a time when even the lower valleys, at present so crowded, appeared barely accessible to town people. The incredible number of facts which he collected during his fieldtrips still represent today the most complete set of data available on glaciers because not a single of their phenomena escaped his attention." Agassiz, *Études sur les glaciers,* 7, translated by Carozzi in *Studies on Glaciers,* 3–4. On the research of the others, Agassiz claimed: "Therefore, in order to correctly appreciate all the works dealing with them [the glaciers], we should know more about the problems pertaining to them." Agassiz, *Études sur les glaciers,* 1, translated by Carozzi in *Studies on Glaciers,* 1.

35. Agassiz, *Études sur les glaciers,* 314, translated by Carozzi in *Studies on Glaciers,* 169.

36. Louis Agassiz, *Untersuchungen über die Gletscher,* trans. Karl Christoph Vogt (Solothurn: Jent & Gaßmann, 1841), xi. My translation.

37. Louis Agassiz, *Untersuchungen über die Gletscher,* vii–viii. My translation.

38. In contrast to Agassiz, Schimper remained impoverished and unrecognized; he died in 1867 after a mugging. City of Mannheim, "Naturforscher Karl Friedrich Schimper etabliert Eiszeitlehre und Blattstellungstheorie," https://mannheim .de/wirtschaft-entwickeln/naturforscher-karl-friedrich-schimper-etabliert -eiszeitlehre-und-blattstellung (my translation). For Charpentier, what aggravated the matter was that Agassiz decided to publish his work shortly before Charpentier's volume *Essai sur les glaciers* was completed in October 1840, whereas Charpentier felt that his student should have waited out of respect for his former mentor.

39. Cunningham's findings sharply contrast with the laudatory tone of Cary Agassiz's biography, which assesses: "No one before had drawn such vast conclusions from the local phenomena of the Alpine valleys." Cary Agassiz, *Louis Agassiz,* 296. Frank F. Cunningham, *James David Forbes: Pioneer Scottish Glaciologist* (Edinburgh: Scottish Academic Press, 1990), 53.

40. We find an example of this scholarly bias, for instance, in Ziehr, who claims: "Agassiz, who out of all his contemporaries recognized most clearly the importance

of the ice-age theory for the natural sciences, in his writings did not mention Schimper's work and impetus." "Aus der Frühzeit," 15 (my translation).

41. Jules Marcou, *Life, Letters and Works of Louis Agassiz* (New York: Macmillan, 1896), 199.

42. James D. Forbes, *Travels Through the Alps of Savoy, and Other Parts of the Pennine Chain with Observations on the Phenomena of Glaciers* (Edinburgh: Adam and Charles Black, 1843), 58–59; hereafter cited in the text as *TS*.

43. In his diary of August 9, 1841, Forbes remarked on the peculiar structure of the ice and also noted Agassiz's unimpressed response. See Ian Campbell and David Hutchinson, "A Question of Priorities: Forbes, Agassiz, and Their Disputes on Glacier Observations," *Isis* 69, no. 3 (September 1978): 390.

44. "Forbes to Agassiz," November 15, 1841, quoted in Cunningham, *James David Forbes*, 97.

45. Forbes, "On a Remarkable Structure Observed by the Author in the Ice of Glaciers," *Edinburgh New Philosophical Journal* 32 (October–April 1842): 86.

46. "Forbes to Agassiz," March 11, 1842, quoted in Cunningham, *James David Forbes*, 101.

47. "Agassiz to Murray," February 9, 1842, quoted in Cunningham, *James David Forbes*, 103.

48. Forbes, "The Glacier Theory," *Edinburgh Review, or Critical Journal* 75 (April–July 1842): 49–104.

49. Notes by Forbes and Agassiz, transmitted by messenger, June 12, 1842, quoted in Cunningham, *James David Forbes*, 113.

50. Forbes, *Norway*, 298.

51. See John Tyndall's measurements on the velocity of the Alps in *Hours of Exercise in the Alps* (New York: Appleton, 1897), 244.

52. See J. S. Rowlinson, "The Theory of Glaciers," *Notes and Records of the Royal Society of London* 26, no. 2 (December 1971): 199–200.

53. "George Biddell Airy to Mrs. Forbes," April 11, 1872, quoted in *Life and Letters*, 159.

54. My translation. Significantly, the German *Liebhaberei* implies *Liebhaber* = lover. Johann Wolfgang von Goethe, *Wilhelm Meisters Wanderjahre, oder Die Entsagenden*, book 1, chap. 3, in *Goethes sämtliche Werke in vierzig Bänden*, 34; Goethe, *The Collected Works*, 116.

55. Goethe, *The Collected Works*, 116. In German, Goethe, *Wilhelm Meister*, 34 and 35.

56. Agassiz, *Études sur les glaciers*, 46, translated by Carozzi in *Studies on Glaciers*, 25.

57. Hevly, "Heroic Science of Glacier Motion," 66.

58. "Forbes to his sister," October 9, 1842, quoted in *Life and Letters*, 294.

59. "Forbes to his sister," October 9, 1842, quoted in *Life and Letters*, 294–95.

60. Hevly, "Heroic Science of Glacier Motion," 68.

61. Letter to "one of his Alpine contemporaries," quoted in *Life and Letters*, 375.

62. "Forbes to A. Wills," quoted in *Life and Letters*, 378.

63. Ziehr, "Aus der Frühzeit," 30.

64. See, for instance, the rise and fall of Agassiz's student Henry James Clark, whose story forms a riveting chapter in Christoph Irmscher's biography of Agassiz. Christoph Irmscher, "Mr. Clark's Headache," in *Louis Agassiz: Creator of American Science* (Boston: Houghton Mifflin, 2013), 168–218. Even complimentary sources such as Edward Lurie contend that "when such people appeared capable of striking out on their own and either imitating or superseding Agassiz-styled institutions or scientific innovations, The Master quite often reacted with hostility" (58), citing Edward S. Morse and other examples. Lurie, *Nature and the American Mind: Louis Agassiz and the Culture of Science* (New York: Science History Publications, 1974).

65. As Irmscher has recently done an excellent job documenting Agassiz's racially prejudiced beliefs and research, I have kept this section short.

66. Nancy Leys Stepan, *Picturing Tropical Nature* (Ithaca, N.Y.: Cornell University Press, 2001), 89.

67. Such as a letter to his mother describing his repulsion when served by black servants. See Irmscher, "Mr. Clark's Headache," 221.

68. Edward Lurie, for instance, heralded Agassiz in *Nature and the American Mind: Louis Agassiz and the Culture of Science* as "an Emerson who joined thought and action, an Adams who enjoyed playing the game for the high stakes that winning it would bring, or a Whitman who could employ science to gain the affection, sympathy, and support of various publics" (16), and moreover emphasized his democratic viewpoints: "This [the latter years of Agassiz's life] saw him embrace a social democracy that witnessed his fierce defense of the Union cause, his criticism of European elitism, and a freely democratic friendship with fish vendors, lighthouse keepers, fishermen, and the armies of common folk who swarmed to his public lectures from East coast to West" (27).

69. Mark Carey, "The History of Ice: How Glaciers Became an Endangered Species," *Environmental History* 12, no. 3 (July 2007): 497–527.

6. The Selling of the Alps and the Beginning of the "Golden Age"

1. Ann C. Colley reveals that Smith had visited the Alps with his parents, read accounts of Alpine climbs, composed some verses titled "Ascents of Mont Blanc," and even devised a panoramic display, "Alps in a Box," for his little sister. Colley, *Victorians in the Mountains: Sinking the Sublime* (Burlington: Ashgate, 2010), 78.

2. Albert Richard Smith, *The Story of Mont Blanc* (London: David Bogue, 1853), 154; hereafter cited in the text as *SMB*.

3. John Ruskin, "Letter to His Father," August 16, 1851, in *The Works of John Ruskin*, vol. 36, *The Letters of John Ruskin*, ed. E. T. Cook and Alexander Wedderburn (London: George Allen, 1909), 117.

4. The speediness of publication led Simon Schama to speculate that the article was likely written before the ascent. Schama, *Landscape and Memory* (New York: Knopf, 1995), 500.

5. The Haslejungfrau summit (3,701 m), now known as the Wetterhorn, was first climbed by the Grindelwald guides Melchior Bannholzer and Hans Jaun from Rosenlaui on August 31, 1844, and by Agassiz, Adolf Vogt and P. Bovet from Grimsel on July 31, 1845. Additional ascents from Grindelwald were rumored but not confirmed. See Trevor Braham, *When the Alps Cast Their Spell: Mountaineers of the Alpine Golden Age* (Glasgow: The In Pinn, 2004), 38.

6. As Alan McNee points out, continental European climbers had made numerous recreational ascents of other mountains in the years before Wills. McNee, *The New Mountaineer in Late Victorian Britain: Materiality, Modernity, and the Haptic Sublime* (London: Palgrave Macmillan, 2016), 9–10. Hansen also offers illuminating analysis considering this dating of the "Golden Age" in *The Summits of Modern Man*, 180–81.

7. Peter H. Hansen, "Smith, Albert Richard (1816–1860)," in *Oxford Dictionary of National Biography* (Oxford University Press, 2004), http://www.oxforddnb.com/view/article/25768 (accessed June 7, 2014). See also Arnold Louis Mumm, "Obituary: Sir Alfred Wills," *Alpine Journal* 27 (1913): 47–54.

8. Darren Bevin, *Cultural Climbs: John Ruskin, Albert Smith, and the Alpine Aesthetic* (Saarbrücken: VDM Verlag Dr. Müller, 2010), 34.

9. Edmund Clark and Markham Sherwill, *Account of Dr. Clark and Captain Sherwill's Ascent of Mont Blanc, in August 1825* (Edinburgh: William Blackwood, 1826).

10. Since the details and aftermath of Smith's show have been well documented, I keep my remarks short here. For further information, see Colley, "Spectators, Telescopes, and Spectacle," in *Victorians in the Mountains,* 57–100; and Peter H. Hansen, "Albert Smith, the Alpine Club, and the Invention of Mountaineering in Mid-Victorian Britain," *Journal of British Studies* 34, no. 3 (1995): 300–324. See also Braham, *When the Alps Cast Their Spell;* and Fergus Fleming, *Killing Dragons: The Conquest of the Alps* (New York: Atlantic Monthly Press, 2000).

11. See also Peter H. Hansen, "Albert Smith's Panorama of Mont Blanc," in *The Summits of Modern Man: Mountaineering After the Enlightenment* (Cambridge, Mass.: Harvard University Press, 2013), 174–79.

12. Alfred Wills, *Wanderings Among the High Alps* (London: Bentley, 1856), 278; hereafter cited in the text.

13. George Gordon Lord Byron, *Manfred: A Broadview Anthology of British Literature Edition* (Ontario: Broadview Press, 2017), 19.

14. Quoted in Hansen, "Albert Smith," 304.

15. Alfred Wills, *The Eagle's Nest in the Valley of Sixt: A Summer Home Among the Alps, Together with Some Excursions Among the Great Glaciers* (London: Longman, 1860), 11.

16. Wills, *The Eagle's Nest*, 15.

17. Rather than using the 1850 translation of *Faust* by the English author and feminist Anna Swanwick that Forbes quotes, I am quoting here from the 2001 translation by Walter Arndt. Johann Wolfgang von Goethe, *Faust: A Tragedy*, trans. Walter Arndt, ed. Cyrus Hamlin (New York: Norton, 2001), 110.

18. Wills, *The Eagle's Nest*, 138.

19. See Martina Kopf, "Sophie La Roche: Diary of Journey Through Switzerland (1787)," in *Mountains and the German Mind: Translations from Gessner to Messner, 1541–2009*, ed. Sean Ireton and Caroline Schaumann (Rochester, N.Y.: Camden House, 2020).

20. Alfred Wills, *The Eagle's Nest*, 15.

7. Poetic Science and Competitive Vigor

1. John Tyndall, *Hours of Exercise in the Alps* (New York: Appleton, 1897), 165. Further references in the text refer to this edition.

2. The eighteen-year-old Hadow had visited the Alps the preceding summer but had only climbed Mont Buet, a popular and easily accessible peak above Chamonix.

3. Edward Whymper, *Scrambles Amongst the Alps* (Washington, D.C.: Geographic, 2002), 37. Further references in the text refer to this edition.

4. John Tyndall, *Hours of Exercise in the Alps*, 3rd ed. (London: Longmans, Green, 1873), 167.

5. Tyndall, *Hours of Exercise in the Alps*, 3rd ed., 167.

6. In *Fall of Heaven: Whymper's Tragic Matterhorn Climb* (Seattle: Mountaineers Books, 2017), the South Tyrolean alpinist Reinhold Messner recounts the Matterhorn attempts from the perspective of the guide Jean-Antoine Carrel, including the prominent Italian attempt. Messner clearly sympathizes and identifies with Carrel, depicting both Whymper and Tyndall as oblivious and ignorant townsmen while fashioning Carrel into a responsible local hero.

7. See Edward Whymper, "The Matterhorn Accident: To the Editor of the *Times*," in *Peaks, Passes, and Glaciers*, ed. E. H. Blakeney (Geneva: Heron, 1971), 327.

8. Older scholarship, his wife Louisa, and Tyndall himself gave 1820 as his year of birth, but Roland Jackson, historian at the Royal Institution and series editor of the *John Tyndall Correspondence Project*, in his recent extensive biography dates Tyndall's birth to 1822, explaining that during the Irish Civil War in 1922, the parish records were destroyed in a fire. Roland Jackson, *The Ascent of John Tyndall: Victorian Scientist, Mountaineer, and Public Intellectual* (Oxford: Oxford University Press, 2018), 3.

9. On May 24, 1851, Humboldt had written, "The astute and at the same time

thorough works of Mr. John Tyndall are well-known to me," inviting Tyndall to a meeting on May 26. After their meeting, however, Tyndall wrote to his friend Hirst on June 5–6, 1851: "I had an interview with Humboldt a few days ago—I intended to put him a few home questions and thus extract something from his experience—but was defeated—He spoke straight forward and left me no opportunity. n'importe—The same sky bends over him and me." In *The Correspondence of John Tyndall,* vol. 3, ed. Ruth Barton, Jeremiah Rankin, and Michael S. Reidy (Pittsburgh: University of Pittsburgh Press, 2017), 226, 238. See also remarks by Tyndall's contemporary Elbert Hubbard in *Little Journeys to Homes of Great Scientists* (New York: Roycrofters, 1905), 74.

10. Tyndall, "On the Study of Physics," in *Fragments of Science,* vol. 1 (New York: Appleton, 1897), 298.

11. See Edward Whymper, *The Apprenticeship of a Mountaineer: Edward Whymper's London Diary, 1855–1859* (London: Record Society, 2008), 139, 154.

12. Edward Whymper, diary of August 9, 1860, quoted in Ian Smith, *Shadow of the Matterhorn: The Life of Edward Whymper* (Hildersley: Carreg, 2011), 42.

13. On this trip, however, Tyndall ascended the Rigi Mountain and crossed several passes, such as the Gotthard, Furka, and Grimsel Pass, as well as visiting mountain villages (Gutannen, Grindelwald, Lauterbrunnen). Werner Sackmann, "John Tyndall (1820–1893) und seine Beziehungen zu den Alpen und zur Schweiz," *Gesnerus* 50 (1993): 68.

14. John Tyndall, letter to Thomas Archer Hirst, August 9, 1856, in *The Correspondence of John Tyndall,* vol. 5, ed. William H. Brock and Geoffrey Cantor (Pittsburgh: University of Pittsburgh Press, 2018), 401.

15. John Tyndall, letter to Michael Faraday, August 27, 1856, in *Correspondence,* vol. 5, 403.

16. Frank F. Cunningham, *James David Forbes: Pioneer Scottish Glaciologist* (Edinburgh: Scottish Academic Press, 1990), 256.

17. Ursula DeYoung, *A Vision of Modern Science: John Tyndall and the Role of the Scientist in Victorian Culture* (New York: Palgrave Macmillan, 2011), 116; Bernard Lightman, "Scientists as Materialists in the Periodical Press: Tyndall's Belfast Address," in *Science Serialized,* ed. Geoffrey Cantor and Sally Shuttleworth (Cambridge, Mass.: MIT Press, 2004), 199–237.

18. For more details, see Trevor Braham, *When the Alps Cast Their Spell: Mountaineers of the Alpine Golden Age* (Glasgow: The In Pinn, 2004), 78–79.

19. Quoted from the report of Tyndall's inquest and retold in DeYoung, *A Vision of Modern Science,* 171.

20. Quoted in DeYoung, *A Vision of Modern Science,* 48.

21. John Tyndall, *Heat: A Mode of Motion,* 3rd ed. (London: Longmans, Green, 1868), xiii–xiv.

22. Quoted in DeYoung, *A Vision of Modern Science,* 52.

23. Mike Hulme, "On the Origin of 'The Greenhouse Effect': John Tyndall's 1859 Interrogation of Nature," *Weather* 64, no. 5 (April 27, 2009): 121–23. Recently there has been an upsurge in interest and research, with the publication of Roland Jackson's extensive biography and the ambitious *John Tyndall Correspondence Project,* edited by James Elwick, Roland Jackson, Bernard Lightman, and Michael S. Reidy, which seeks to collect and publish Tyndall's correspondence in a total of nineteen volumes, beginning in 1840, which greatly aids research. Six volumes have been published thus far, though the majority of Tyndall's Alpine ascents regrettably fall into volumes not yet published by the time of the editing of this book.

24. In his letters, Tyndall frequently mentioned Goethe's impact, claiming "that [Goethe] was the greatest scoundrel that ever lived," to Thomas Archer Hirst, December 19, 1855, in *Correspondence,* vol. 5, ed. William H. Brock and Geoffrey Cantor (Pittsburgh: University of Pittsburgh Press, 2018), 263. In 1880 Tyndall wrote an elaborate essay on Goethe's *Theory of Colors,* in which he also quoted a poem by Goethe. See "Goethe's 'Farbenlehre,'" in *New Fragments* (Cambridge: Cambridge University Press, 2011), 47–77.

25. See, e.g., the response of the Reverend C. A. Row, as related in DeYoung, *A Vision of Modern Science,* 109.

26. John Tyndall, *The Glaciers of the Alps and Mountaineering in 1861* (London: J. M. Dent, 1906), 30; see also 26.

27. See letters to Michael Faraday, Julia Pollock, George Biddell Airy, and Joseph Dalton Hooker, in *The Correspondence of John Tyndall,* vol. 6, ed. Michael D. Barton, Janet Browne, Ken Corbett, and Norman McMillan (Pittsburgh: University of Pittsburgh Press, 2018), 203–10, 217–18.

28. Tyndall, *Mountaineering in 1861,* 198.

29. Colley, *Victorians in the Mountains,* 52.

30. Jackson elaborates on this in *The Ascent of John Tyndall,* 37.

31. See also his similar assessment in *Mountaineering in 1861:* "The glaciers and the mountains have an interest for me beyond their scientific ones. They have been to me well-springs of life and joy, they have given me royal pictures and memories which can never fade. They have made me feel in all fibres the blessedness of perfect manhood, causing mind, and soul, and body, to work together with a harmony and strength unqualified by infirmity or ennui" (249).

32. Michael S. Reidy, "Mountaineering, Masculinity, and the Male Body in Mid-Victorian Britain," *Osiris* 30 (2015): 159.

33. Colley, *Victorians in the Mountains,* 103.

34. Elaine Freegood, *Victorian Writing About Risk* (Cambridge: Cambridge University Press, 2000).

35. R. D. Eaton, "In the 'World of Death and Beauty': Risk, Control, and John Tyndall as Alpinist," *Victorian Literature and Culture* 41 (2013): 55.

36. Eaton, "World of Death and Beauty," 71.

37. Quoted in Michael S. Reidy, "Evolutionary Naturalism on High: The Victorians Sequester the Alps," in *Victorian Scientific Naturalism: Community, Identity, Continuity*, ed. Gowan Dawson and Bernard Lightman (Chicago: University of Chicago Press, 2014), 57. See also letter from Hirst to Tyndall, September 18, 1849, in *The Correspondence of John Tyndall*, vol. 2, ed. Melinda Baldwin and Janet Browne (London: Routledge, 2016), 331–33. Other letters, too, reveal the abiding affection between the two men.

38. Francis O'Gorman, " 'The Mightiest Evangel of the Alpine Club': Masculinity and Agnosticism in the Alpine Writing of John Tyndall," in *Masculinity and Spirituality in Victorian Culture*, ed. Andrew Bradstock, Sean Gill, Anne Hogan, and Sue Morgan (New York: St. Martin's, 2000), 138.

39. However, as Ian Smith says, Whymper's diary description of the same night during the ascent of the Barre des Ecrins does not even mention Croz, suggesting that Whymper perhaps fabricated this intimate memory after Croz's death.

40. Whymper, *Travels Amongst the Great Andes*, 41.

41. As Whymper elucidates, "He says that they left their highest point a little after 1 p.m., and a few minutes after 2 reached the place where they left their mules (at 15,600 feet), that is to say, he claims to have descended 3,686 feet *in one hour!*" *Travels Amongst the Great Andes*, 17.

42. John Muir, *John Muir's Last Journey: South to the Amazon and East to Africa: Unpublished Journals and Selected Correspondence*, ed. Michael P. Branch (Washington, D.C.: Island Press, 2001), 384.

8. The Making of Modern Climbing

1. Leslie Stephen, "The Dangers of Mountaineering," in *Peaks, Passes, and Glaciers*, ed. E. H. Blakeney (Geneva: Heron, 1971), 331–32.

2. Leslie Stephen, "Sunset on Mont Blanc," in *The Playground of Europe* (San Rafael: Archivum, 2007), 178. Further references in the text refer to this edition.

3. Stephen, *The Playground of Europe*, 2nd ed. (New York: Putnam, 1909), iii.

4. See the excellent detailed entry by Alan Bell on Sir Leslie Stephen in the *Oxford Dictionary of National Biography* (Oxford University Press, 2004), online edition, May 2012, http://www.oxforddnb.com/view/article/36271 (accessed July 18, 2014).

5. Virginia Woolf, "Leslie Stephen," in *Collected Essays*, vol. 4 (London: Hogarth Press, 1967), 76–80.

6. Douglas William Freshfield, review of F. W. Maitland, *The Life and Letters of Leslie Stephen*, *Alpine Journal* 23 (February 1906–November 1907): 493.

7. A detailed climbing resume can be found in the appendix of Catherine Hollis, *Leslie Stephen as Mountaineer* (London: Cecil Woolf, 2010), 57–60.

8. Stephen, "The Dangers of Mountaineering," 337.

9. Stephen, "The Dangers of Mountaineering," 337.

10. Leslie Stephen, "In Praise of Walking," in *Studies of a Biographer,* vol. 3 (London: Duckworth, 1902), 269.

11. As, for instance, Ruskin's phrase "the crest of a helmet." David D. Zink, *Leslie Stephen* (New York: Twayne, 1972), 65.

12. See Emma Sdegno, "The Alps," in *The Cambridge Companion to John Ruskin,* ed. Francis O'Gorman (Cambridge: Cambridge University Press, 2015), 32–48.

13. Stephen, "In Praise of Walking," 269–70. Stephen's relationship to materialism was complicated: while using the language of materialism, he denied being a materialist and instead insisted on David Hume's empirical methods, which declared any metaphysical system untenable. For more information, see Zink, *Leslie Stephen,* 50–51.

14. Stephen, "The Dangers of Mountaineering," 340.

15. Stephen, "The Dangers of Mountaineering," 341.

16. Stephen, "The Dangers of Mountaineering," 342.

17. William Wordsworth, "Song at the Feast of Brougham Castle," in *The Complete Poetical Works of William Wordsworth* (Philadelphia: James Kay, Jun. and Brother, 1837), 154.

18. One might notice that this is still a fairly quick pace, far from a casual ascent.

19. Stephen, "In Praise of Walking," 259.

20. David Abram, *Becoming Animal: An Earthly Cosmology* (New York: Pantheon, 2010), 21.

21. Karen Barad, *Meeting the Universe Halfway* (Durham, N.C.: Duke University Press, 2007), 33.

22. As Michael S. Reidy reveals, Stephen's words also trace back to Charles Dickens, who in 1865 had infamously divided Switzerland into three zones, one of "ladies, children, elderly gentlemen, and ordinary folk in general," a second that could be reached only by carriage, and a third upmost region reserved for members of the Alpine Club. Quoted in Michael S. Reidy, "Mountaineering, Masculinity, and the Male Body in Mid-Victorian Britain," *Osiris* 30 (2015): 158.

23. See Wilfried Wilms, "Eduard Pichl, Autobiographical Sketch (1914) and 'The Alpine Association and German Purity' (1923)," in *Mountains of the German Mind: Translations from Gessner to Messner,* ed. Sean Ireton and Caroline Schaumann (Rochester, N.Y.: Camden House, 2020).

24. Reidy, "Mountaineering, Masculinity," 179.

25. Hollis, *Leslie Stephen as Mountaineer,* 11.

26. Quoted in Hollis, *Leslie Stephen as Mountaineer,* 11.

27. Hollis, *Leslie Stephen as Mountaineer,* 11.

28. Leslie Stephen, "Round Mont Blanc," in *Men, Books, and Mountains* (London: Hogarth, 1956), 182.

29. Heinrich Heine, chap. 22 of *Reise von München nach Genua*, in *Reisebilder und Reisebriefe, Werke und Briefe in zehn Bänden*, vol. 3 (Berlin: Holzinger, 1972), 237, http://www.zeno.org/Literatur/M/Heine,+Heinrich/Reisebilder+und+Reisebriefe/Reisebilder.+Dritter+Teil/Reise+von+M%C3%BCnchen+nach+Genua/Kapitel+22. Quoted in Stephen, *Playground*, 134.

9. Transcontinental Shifts

1. See Patrick Kupper, *Creating Wilderness: A Transnational History of the Swiss National Park* (New York: Berghahn, 2014), 3–7.

2. According to Moore, by 1880, 600 million board feet of lumber had been stripped from the Sierra Nevada to be used for timbering the mines. James Gregory Moore, *King of the 40th Parallel: Discovery in the American West* (Stanford, Calif.: Stanford University Press, 2006), 172.

3. John O'Grady, *Pilgrims to the Wild* (Salt Lake City: University of Utah Press, 1993), 91.

4. Clarence King, *Mountaineering in the Sierra Nevada* (1872; Lincoln: University of Nebraska Press, 1997), 292. Further references in the text refer to this edition.

5. Mark Allister, "Introduction," in *Eco-Man: New Perspectives on Masculinity and Nature*, ed. Mark Allister (Charlottesville: University of Virginia Press, 2004), 1–2.

6. Gardner's name is also sometimes spelled Gardiner, as he resumed the original spelling of his family name in 1881.

7. Thurman Wilkins, *Clarence King: A Biography*, rev. ed. (Albuquerque: University of New Mexico Press, 1988), 448.

8. Brewer described King: "King is enthusiastic, is wonderfully tough, has the greatest endurance I have ever seen, and is withal very muscular. He is a most perfect specimen of health." Quoted in Zeese Papanikolas, *American Silence* (Lincoln: University of Nebraska Press, 2007), 36.

9. James D. Hague, ed., *Clarence King Memoirs* (New York: G. P. Putnam's Sons, 1905), 319.

10. Daniel Arnold, *Early Days in the Range of Light: Encounters with Legendary Mountaineers* (Berkeley, Calif.: Counterpoint, 2009), 58.

11. As Arnold points out, "This surprise must have been feigned," since the higher peaks, including Whitney, are visible from the Kern Valley, the pass that King and Cotter had crossed the day previously, and even Mount Brewer (73).

12. Muir, as quoted in Aaron Sachs, *The Humboldt Current: Nineteenth-Century Exploration and the Roots of American Environmentalism* (New York: Penguin, 2006), 200.

13. Arnold, *Early Days in the Range of Light*, 78.

14. See Moore, *King of the 40th Parallel*, 16. Moore, who was able to get access to some of Gardner's letters through a personal acquaintance with his grandson,

relied heavily on personal and public letters for his biography on King and made them accessible to a broader audience.

15. Quoted in Moore, *King of the 40th Parallel*, 168.

16. For an excellent summary, see Robert V. Hine and John Mack Faragher, "Myth of the West," in *The American West: A New Interpretive History* (New Haven, Conn.: Yale University Press, 2000), 472–511.

17. John Muir, "Mountain Thoughts," in *John of the Mountains: The Unpublished Journals of John Muir*, ed. Linnie Marsh Wolfe (Boston: Houghton Mifflin, 1938), 95.

18. For further elaboration, see Sachs's fascinating analysis of O'Sullivan's photographs in *Humboldt Current*, 185–228.

19. Brewer, quoted in Moore, *King of the 40th Parallel*, 153.

20. David Mazel, *American Literary Environmentalism* (Athens: University of Georgia Press, 2000), 118.

21. Sachs has an excellent exploration of humans in O'Sullivan's landscapes, *Humboldt Current*, 216–19. As Moore points out, mining accidents were commonplace, as miners fell to their death from the shafts, cables would break and drop the men in cages, or heavy equipment would fall down the shafts. *King of the 40th Parallel*, 174.

22. In 2010 the historian Glenn Willumson compared these and other photographs from the survey, concluding, "These photographs display a different sensibility from those of Timothy H. O'Sullivan, and research now indicates that it was Andrew J. Russell, not O'Sullivan, who made the negatives in the Uinta Mountains." Glenn Willumson, "'Photographing Under Difficulties': Andrew Russell's Photographs for the King Survey," in *Framing the West: The Survey Photographs of Timothy H. O'Sullivan*, ed. Toby Jurovics et al. (New Haven, Conn.: Yale University Press, 2010), 177.

23. Maurice Isserman, *Continental Divide: A History of American Mountaineering* (New York: Norton, 2016), 108.

24. Quoted in Moore, *King of the 40th Parallel*, 213.

25. The volumes published include *Mining Industry* (vol. 3, 1870), *Botany* (vol. 5, 1871), *Microscopical Petrography* (vol. 6, 1876), *Descriptive Geology* (vol. 2, 1877), *Ornithology and Paleontology* (vol. 4, 1877), and *Systematic Geology* (vol. 1, 1878), written by King, who presented a synthesis of the entire survey, with data on the age of sedimentary rocks, the composition of plutonic and volcanic igneous rocks, and the extent of glaciation. In addition, the *Geological and Topographical Atlas*, published in 1876, contained twenty large, colorful map sheets and additional geologic-topographic cross sections.

26. For the former, see David Wyatt, "King and Catastrophe," in *The Fall into Eden: Landscape and Imagination in California* (Cambridge: Cambridge University Press, 1986), 47–66; and Robert Wilson, *The Explorer King: Adventure, Science, and the*

Great Diamond Hoax—Clarence King in the Old West (Berkeley: Shoemaker and Hoard, 2007). For the latter, see Moore, *King of the 40th Parallel.*

10. The Solitary Mountaineer

1. John Muir, "A Near View of the High Sierra," in *The Mountains of California,* in *Nature Writings,* ed. William Cronon (New York: Penguin, 1997), 350; hereafter cited as *Mountains.*

2. Muir, "Ascent of Mount Whitney," letter to *Daily Evening Bulletin,* August 17, 1875, in *Summering in the Sierra,* ed. Robert Engberg (Madison: University of Wisconsin Press, 1984), 104.

3. Muir, "Ascent of Mount Whitney," 112, 105.

4. Muir, "Shasta in Winter," in *Summering in the Sierra,* 33.

5. Muir, "Shasta in Winter," 34.

6. Muir's description, titled "Snow-Storm on Mount Shasta," was published in *Harper's Monthly,* September 1877; reprinted in *Nature Writings,* 634–48.

7. John Muir to Jeanne Carr, December 9, 1874, in *Kindred and Related Spirits: The Letters of John Muir and Jeanne Carr,* ed. Bonnie Johanna Gisel (Salt Lake City: University of Utah Press, 2001), 253, 255; hereafter cited as *Letters.*

8. Jedediah Purdy, *After Nature: A Politics for the Anthropocene* (Cambridge, Mass.: Harvard University Press, 2015), 117.

9. See, e.g., his description of the camp in "Ascent of Mount Whitney," 108–9.

10. John Muir, *The Story of My Boyhood and Youth,* in *Nature Writings* (New York: Penguin, 1997), 7, 12, 15; hereafter cited as *Boyhood.*

11. Muir claims, "By the time I was eleven years of age I had about three fourths of the Old Testament and all of the New by heart and by sore flesh." *Boyhood,* 20.

12. *Boyhood,* 128.

13. *Letters,* 29.

14. Jeanne Carr's first letter to Muir, marking the beginning of their correspondence, is lost but is quoted in Muir's letter.

15. Muir, *A Thousand-Mile Walk to the Gulf,* vol. 1 of *The Writings of John Muir* (Boston: Houghton Mifflin, 1916), 277.

16. Muir, *A Thousand-Mile Walk,* 276.

17. Muir, *The Yosemite* (New York: Century, 1912), 4.

18. While the non-Indian population of California leaped from 14,000 to more than 300,000 inhabitants between 1846 and 1860, American Indians were barred from voting, and many Indian children were forced into white custody. Daniel Duane, "Goodbye, Yosemite. Hello, What?" *New York Times,* September 2, 2017.

19. Muir, *My First Summer in the Sierra,* 157, in *Nature Writings;* hereafter cited as *Summer.*

20. Muir to Carr, autumn 1870, in *Letters,* 120.

21. See, e.g., Timothy J. Lukes, *Politics and Beauty in America: The Liberal Aesthetics of P. T. Barnum, John Muir, and Harley Earl* (New York: Palgrave, 2016), 133–37.

22. Muir to Jeanne Carr, spring 1872, in *Letters,* 179.

23. Le Conte delivered a lecture "advancing many new and interesting theories" on glaciation in the Sierra Nevada in October 1872, using Muir's findings in lieu of his own field research, but failed to credit him. See *Letters,* 190; see also 163–64, 194–95.

24. Muir wrote to Carr: "I feel [Gray] to be a great, progressive, unlimited man like Darwin and Huxley and Tyndall." July 14, 1872, in *Letters,* 181, also quoted in Donald Worster, *A Passion for Nature: The Life of John Muir* (Oxford: Oxford University Press, 2008), 204. I disagree with Worster here that Gray and others were "displacing not only Agassiz but also the once much admired Alexander von Humboldt, whose popular natural history for all its brilliant descriptions and holistic vision, . . . never really explained anything."

25. William Cronon, "The Trouble with Wilderness; or, Getting Back to the Wrong Nature," in *Uncommon Ground: Rethinking the Human Place in Nature,* ed. William Cronon (New York: Norton, 1996), 75.

26. Muir to Carr, April 3, 1871, in *Letters,* 137.

27. Matthew Kaiser, "A Joy on the Precipice of Death: John Muir and Robert Louis Stevenson in California," in *Nineteenth-Century British Travelers in the New World,* ed. Christine Devine (Farnham: Ashgate, 2013), 23–47.

28. See also Louise Westling, ed., "Introduction," in *The Cambridge Companion to Literature and the Environment* (New York: Cambridge University Press, 2015), 4.

29. John Muir, "Mountain Thoughts," in *John of the Mountains: The Unpublished Journals of John Muir,* ed. Linnie Marsh Wolfe (Boston: Houghton Mifflin, 1938), 94.

30. Carolyn Merchant voiced such arguments in her visionary essay "Shades of Darkness: Race and Environmental History," *Environmental History* 8, no. 3 (July 2003): 380–94.

31. Eric Michael Johnson, "How John Muir's Brand of Conservation Led to the Decline of Yosemite," *Scientific American Blog Network,* August 13, 2014, https://blogs .scientificamerican.com/primate-diaries/how-john-muir-s-brand-of-conservation -led-to-the-decline-of-yosemite.

32. Muir, "God's First Temples: How Shall We Preserve Our Forests?" *Sacramento Record-Union,* February 5, 1876, reprinted in *Nature Writings,* 632.

33. Muir, "God's First Temples," 633.

34. John Muir, "Travels in Utah," May–July 1877, University of the Pacific University Libraries, Scholarly Commons, http://scholarlycommons.pacific.edu/jmj -all/1137. Worster provides an accurate transcription in *A Passion for Nature,* 231.

35. Quoted in Worster, *A Passion for Nature,* 241.

36. John Muir to Mr. and Mrs. Bidwell, June 19, 1879, John Muir Correspondence, University of the Pacific University Libraries, Scholarly Commons, http://scholarlycommons.pacific.edu/jmcl/11563.

37. None other than Theodore Roosevelt opined, "John Muir talked even better than he wrote." "John Muir: An Appreciation," *Outlook* 109 (1915): 128. See also Richard D. Besel and Bernard K. Duffy, "'I had been crying in the wilderness': John Muir's Shifting Sublime Response," in *Green Voices: Defending Nature and the Environment in American Civic Discourse*, ed. Richard D. Besel and Bernard K. Duffy (Albany: State University of New York Press, 2016), 29–47.

38. Tesla, born in the Austro-Hungarian Empire (today belonging to Croatia), became an electrical engineer in Budapest and had already developed prototypes of an induction motor before coming to New York in 1884 to work for Thomas Edison. Soon, however, Tesla quarreled with Edison, who insisted on using direct current and did not want to lose his empire, even though Tesla's design of using alternating current (since all energies were cyclic) proved much more efficient and was soon patented, bought by the industrialist George Westinghouse, and distributed worldwide today.

39. Muir, *Mountains*, in *Nature Writings,* 316.

40. Muir, "The Wild Parks and Forest Reservations of the West," in *Our National Parks,* in *Nature Writings,* 721.

41. Muir, "The Wild Parks and Forest Reservations of the West," 722.

42. See Colin Fisher, *Urban Green: Nature, Recreation, and the Working Place in Industrial Chicago* (Chapel Hill: University of North Carolina Press, 2015), 27. With many thanks to the author for this reference.

43. See also Worster's distinction of these terms and concepts in *A Passion for Nature,* 416–17.

44. "The National Parks and Forest Reservations: Proceedings of the Meeting of the Sierra Club Held November 23, 1895," *Sierra Club Bulletin* 1 (1896): 280.

45. According to Worster, Muir repeated this phrase in letters to his daughter Helen, the Hookers, and other friends. Worster, *A Passion for Nature,* 446.

46. Muir, "The Wild Parks and Forest Reservations of the West," 722.

47. John P. O'Grady, "John Muir's Parables of Desire," in *Pilgrims to the Wild* (Salt Lake City: University of Utah Press, 1993), 59.

48. Muir, "God's First Temples," 631.

Epilogue

1. Noah Moss Brender, "On the Nature of Space: Getting from Motricity to Reflection and Back Again," in *Perception and Its Development in Merleau-Ponty's Phenomenology,* ed. Kirsten Jacobson and John Russon (Toronto: University of Toronto Press, 2017), 143.

2. Patrick Kupper, *Creating Wilderness: A Transnational History of the Swiss National Park* (New York: Berghahn, 2014), 5.

3. See Restore Hetch Hetchy, "Our Plan for Restoration," https://www.hetch hetchy.org/our_plan_for_restoration.

4. Robert V. Hine and John Mack Faragher, *The American West: A New Interpretive History* (New Haven, Conn.: Yale University Press, 2000), 504.

5. Felix Driver and Luciana Martins, "Introduction," in *Tropical Visions in an Age of Empire,* ed. Felix Driver and Luciana Martins (Chicago: University of Chicago Press, 2005), 5.

6. Aaron Sachs, *The Humboldt Current: A European Explorer and His American Disciples* (Oxford: Oxford University Press, 2007), 43.

7. Peter H. Hansen, "Albert Smith, the Alpine Club, and the Invention of Mountaineering in Mid-Victorian Britain," *Journal of British Studies* 34, no. 3 (July 1995): 322. See also Peter Bayers, *Imperial Ascent: Mountaineering, Masculinity and Empire* (Boulder: University Press of Colorado, 2003); and Reuben Ellis, *Vertical Margins: Mountaineering and the Landscape of Neoimperialism* (Madison: University of Wisconsin Press, 2001).

8. Peter H. Hansen, *The Summits of Modern Man: Mountaineering After the Enlightenment* (Cambridge, Mass.: Harvard University Press, 2013), 28.

9. Ethan Linck, "Your Stoke Won't Save Us: The Idea That Outdoor Recreation Leads to Meaningful Conservation Rests on a Big 'If,'" *High Country News,* May 14, 2018, https://www.hcn.org/issues/50.8/recreation-your-stoke-wont-save -us?fbclid=IwARomnRmDptGlqO9v7I7a6nCg4V8tSIOJpgzP2ODQuivH8 wAv8bBX7t_Ck6s.

10. See Kirsten Jacobson, "Neglecting Space: Making Sense of a Partial Loss of One's World Through a Phenomenological Account of the Spatiality of Embodiment," in *Perception and Its Development in Merleau-Ponty's Phenomenology,* ed. Kirsten Jacobson and John Russon (Toronto: University of Toronto Press, 2017), 101.

11. Christophe Bonneuil and Jean-Baptiste Fressoz, *The Shock of the Anthropocene: The Earth, History, and Us* (London: Verso, 2016), 41–42.

12. John Muir, "Mountain Thoughts," in *John of the Mountains: The Unpublished Journals of John Muir,* ed. Linnie Marsh Wolfe (Boston: Houghton Mifflin, 1938), 94–95.

BIBLIOGRAPHY

Abram, David. *Becoming Animal: An Earthly Cosmology.* New York: Pantheon, 2010.

Agassiz, Louis. *Studies on Glaciers, Preceded by the Discourse of Neuchâtel.* Edited and translated by Albert V. Carozzi. New York: Hafner, 1967.

———. *Untersuchungen über die Gletscher.* Translated by Karl Christoph Vogt. Solothurn: Jent & Gaßmann, 1841.

Albes, Claudia, and Christiane Frey. *Darstellbarkeit: Zu einem ästhetisch-philosophischen Problem um 1800.* Würzburg: Königshausen & Neumann, 2003.

Allister, Mark, ed. *Eco-Man: New Perspectives on Masculinity and Nature.* Charlottesville: University of Virginia Press, 2004.

Andress, Reinhard. "Humboldt und Montúfar als Reisegefährten: Ein Vergleich ihrer Tagebücher." *Humboldt im Netz* 12, no. 22 (2011): 10–28.

Anker, Conrad. "Climate and Climbers." *Rock and Ice* 251 (July 2018). https://rockandice.com/snowball/climate-and-climbers.

Arnold, Daniel. *Early Days in the Range of Light: Encounters with Legendary Mountaineers.* Berkeley, Calif.: Counterpoint, 2009.

Barad, Karen. *Meeting the Universe Halfway.* Durham, N.C.: Duke University Press, 2007.

Bayers, Peter L. *Imperial Ascent: Masculinity, Mountaineering, and Empire.* Boulder: University Press of Colorado, 2003.

Beattie, Andrew. *The Alps: A Cultural History.* Oxford: Signal Books, 2006.

Beck, Hanno. *Alexander von Humboldt: Amerikanische Reise*. Wiesbaden: Erdmann, 2009.

———. "Alexander von Humboldt (1769–1859), Förderer der frühen Photographie." In *Silber und Salz: Zur Frühzeit der Photographie im deutschen Sprachraum, 1839–1860*, 40–59. Cologne: Braus, 1989.

Bell, Alan. "Sir Leslie Stephen." In *Oxford Dictionary of National Biography*. Oxford: Oxford University Press, 2004. Online edition, May 2012. http://www.oxford dnb.com/view/article/36271.

Besel, Richard D., and Bernard K. Duffy. "'I had been crying in the wilderness': John Muir's Shifting Sublime Response." In *Green Voices: Defending Nature and the Environment in American Civic Discourse*, edited by Richard D. Besel and Bernard K. Duffy, 29–47. Albany: State University of New York Press, 2016.

Bevin, Darren. *Cultural Climbs: John Ruskin, Albert Smith, and the Alpine Aesthetic*. Saarbrücken: VDM Verlag Dr. Müller, 2010.

Bigg, Charlotte, David Aubin, and Philipp Felsch. "Introduction: The Laboratory of Nature—Science in the Mountains." *Science in Context* 22, no. 3 (2009): 311–21.

Bonneuil, Christophe, and Jean-Baptiste Fressoz. *The Shock of the Anthropocene: The Earth, History, and Us*. London: Verso, 2016.

Braham, Trevor. *When the Alps Cast Their Spell: Mountaineers of the Alpine Golden Age*. Glasgow: The In Pinn, 2004.

Burke, Edmund. *A Philosophical Enquiry into the Origin of Our Ideas of the Sublime and Beautiful*. Oxford: Oxford University Press, 1990.

Burnet, Thomas. *The Sacred Theory of the Earth*. London: Centaur Press, 1965.

Byron, George Gordon. *Manfred: A Broadview Anthology of British Literature Edition*. Ontario: Broadview Press, 2017.

Cameron, Dorothy. "Goethe—Discoverer of the Ice Age." *Journal of Glaciology* 5, no. 41 (1964): 751–54.

Campbell, Ian, and David Hutchinson. "A Question of Priorities: Forbes, Agassiz, and Their Disputes on Glacier Observations." *Isis* 69, no. 3 (September 1978): 388–99.

Campbell Shairp, John, Peter Guthrie Tait, and Anthony Adams-Reilly. *The Life and Letters of James David Forbes, F.R.S.* London: Macmillan, 1873.

Cañizares-Esguerra, Jorge. *How to Write the History of the New World: Histories, Epistemologies, and Identities in the Eighteenth-Century Atlantic World*. Stanford, Calif.: Stanford University Press, 2001.

———. "The Problem with Andrea Wulf's Biography of Humboldt." *Time to Eat the Dogs* (podcast), September 24, 2019, http://timetoeatthedogs.libsyn.com /replay-the-problem-with-andrea-wulfs-biography-of-humboldt.

Carey, Mark. "The History of Ice: How Glaciers Became an Endangered Species." *Environmental History* 12, no. 3 (July 2007): 497–527.

Carozzi, Albert V., and John K. Newman. *Horace-Bénédict de Saussure: Forerunner in Glaciology.* Geneva: Editions Passé Présent, 1995.

Cary Agassiz, Elizabeth. *Louis Agassiz, His Life and Correspondence.* Boston: Houghton Mifflin, 1885.

Clark, Edmund, and Markham Sherwill. *Account of Dr. Clark and Captain Sherwill's Ascent of Mont Blanc, in August 1825.* Edinburgh: William Blackwood, 1826.

Clark, Ronald W. *Men, Myths, and Mountains.* New York: Thomas Y. Crowell, 1976.

Colley, Ann C. *Victorians in the Mountains: Sinking the Sublime.* Burlington: Ashgate, 2010.

Cosgrove, Denis E., and Veronica Della Dora, eds. *High Places: Cultural Geographies of Mountains, Ice, and Sciences.* New York: Palgrave, 2009.

Cronon, William. "The Trouble with Wilderness; or, Getting Back to the Wrong Nature." In *Uncommon Ground: Rethinking the Human Place in Nature,* edited by William Cronon, 69–90. New York: Norton, 1996.

Cunningham, Frank F. *James David Forbes: Pioneer Scottish Glaciologist.* Edinburgh: Scottish Academic Press, 1990.

Dean, Carolyn. *A Culture of Stone: Inka Perspectives on Rock.* Durham, N.C.: Duke University Press, 2010.

Della Dora, Veronica. *Mountain.* London: Reaktion Books, 2016.

Denning, Andrew. *Skiing into Modernity: A Cultural and Environmental History.* Berkeley: University of California Press, 2014.

Desor, Édouard. "Ascent of the Jungfrau, Accomplished on the 28th August 1841." *Edinburgh New Philosophical Journal* 32 (1841): 291–337.

DeYoung, Ursula. *A Vision of Modern Science: John Tyndall and the Role of the Scientist in Victorian Culture.* New York: Palgrave Macmillan, 2011.

Driver, Felix. *Geography Militant: Cultures of Exploration and Empire.* Oxford: Blackwell, 2001.

Driver, Felix, and Luciana Martins, eds. *Tropical Visions in an Age of Empire.* Chicago: University of Chicago Press, 2005.

Duane, Daniel. "Goodbye, Yosemite. Hello, What?" *New York Times,* September 2, 2017.

Eaton, R. D. "In the 'World of Death and Beauty': Risk, Control, and John Tyndall as Alpinist." *Victorian Literature and Culture* 41 (2013): 55–73.

Echenberg, Myron. *Humboldt's Mexico: In the Footsteps of the Illustrious German Scientific Traveller.* Montreal: McGill-Queen's University Press, 2017.

Ellis, Reuben. *Vertical Margins: Mountaineering and the Landscape of Neoimperialism.* Madison: University of Wisconsin Press, 2001.

Ette, Ottmar, ed. *Alexander von Humboldt Handbuch: Leben – Werk – Wirkung.* Stuttgart: J. B. Metzler, 2018.

Ette, Ottmar, and Julian Drews, eds. *Landschaften und Kartographien der Humboldt'schen Wissenschaft.* Hildesheim: Olms, 2017.

Felsch, Philipp. *Laborlandschaften: Physiologische Alpenreisen im 19. Jahrhundert*. Göttingen: Wallstein, 2007.

Fisher, Colin. *Urban Green: Nature, Recreation, and the Working Place in Industrial Chicago*. Chapel Hill: University of North Carolina Press, 2015.

Fleming, Fergus. *Killing Dragons: The Conquest of the Alps*. New York: Atlantic Monthly Press, 2000.

Forbes, James David. "The Glacier Theory." *Edinburgh Review, or Critical Journal* 75 (April–July 1842): 49–104.

———. *Norway and Its Glaciers, Visited in 1861, Followed by Journals of Excursions in the High Alps of Dauphine, Berne, and Savoy*. Edinburgh: Adam and Charles Black, 1853.

———. "On a Remarkable Structure Observed by the Author in the Ice of Glaciers." *Edinburgh New Philosophical Journal* 32 (October 1841–April 1842): 84–89.

———. *Travels Through the Alps of Savoy, and Other Parts of the Pennine Chain with Observations on the Phenomena of Glaciers*. Edinburgh: Adam and Charles Black, 1843.

Franzen, Jonathan. "What If We Stopped Pretending?" *New Yorker*, September 8, 2019. https://www.newyorker.com/culture/cultural-comment/what-if-we-stopped -pretending.

Freegood, Elaine. *Victorian Writing About Risk*. Cambridge: Cambridge University Press, 2000.

Freshfield, Douglas William. *The Life of Horace Benedict de Saussure*. London: Edward Arnold, 1920.

———. Review of F. W. Maitland, *The Life and Letters of Leslie Stephen*. *Alpine Journal* 23 (1906–7): 493.

Godlewska, Anne Marie Claire. "From Enlightenment Vision to Modern Science? Humboldt's Visual Thinking." In *Geography and Enlightenment*, edited by David N. Livingstone and Charles W. J. Withers, 236–75. Chicago: University of Chicago Press, 1999.

Goethe, Johann Wolfgang von. *The Collected Works*. Translated by Krishna Winston, edited by Jane K. Brown. Princeton, N.J.: Princeton University Press, 1989.

———. *Faust: A Tragedy*. Translated by Walter Arndt, edited by Cyrus Hamlin. New York: Norton, 2001.

———. *Wilhelm Meisters Wanderjahre, oder Die Entsagenden*. In *Goethes sämtliche Werke in vierzig Bänden*, vol. 18. Stuttgart: Cotta'scher, 1856.

Gribble, Francis. *The Early Mountaineers*. London: T. Fisher, 1899.

Groves, Jason. "Goethe's Petrofiction: Reading the *Wanderjahre* in the Anthropocene." *Goethe Yearbook* 22 (2015): 95–113.

Guntau, Martin. "The Natural History of the Earth." In *Cultures of Natural History*, edited by N. Jardine, J. A. Secord, and E. C. Spary, 211–29. Cambridge: Cambridge University Press, 1996.

Hackl, Wolfgang. *Eingeborene im Paradies: Die literarische Wahrnehmung des alpinen Tourismus im 19. und 20. Jahrhundert*. Tübingen: Niemeyer, 2004.

Hague, James D., ed. *Clarence King Memoirs*. New York: G. P. Putnam's Sons, 1905.

Haley, Bruce. *The Healthy Body and Victorian Culture*. Cambridge, Mass.: Harvard University Press, 1978.

Haller, Albrecht von. *The Alps: An English Translation*. Translated by Stanley Mason. Dübendorf, Switzerland: Walter Amstutz De Clivo Press, 1987.

———. *Versuch schweizerischer Gedichte*. 9th ed., 1762. Reprint, Bern: Herbert Lang, 1969.

Hansen, Peter H. "Albert Smith, the Alpine Club, and the Invention of Mountain-eering in Mid-Victorian Britain." *Journal of British Studies* 34, no. 3 (1995): 300–324.

———. "Smith, Albert Richard (1816–1860)." In *Oxford Dictionary of National Biography*. Oxford: Oxford University Press, 2004.

———. *The Summits of Modern Man: Mountaineering After the Enlightenment*. Cambridge, Mass.: Harvard University Press, 2013.

Heine, Heinrich. *Reisebilder und Reisebriefe*. Vol. 3 of *Werke und Briefe in zehn Bänden*. Berlin: Holzinger, 1972.

Herder, Johann Gottfried. *Outlines of a Philosophy of the History of Man*. Vol. 1. Translated by T. Churchill. London: Luke Hanford, 1803.

Hetch Hetchy Restoration. https://www.hetchhetchy.org/our_plan_for_restoration.

Hevly, Bruce. "The Heroic Science of Glacier Motion." *Osiris* 11 (1996): 66–86.

Hine, Robert V., and John Mack Faragher. *The American West: A New Interpretive History*. New Haven, Conn.: Yale University Press, 2000.

Höbusch, Harald. *"Mountain of Destiny": Nanga Parbat and Its Path into the German Imagination*. Rochester, N.Y.: Camden House, 2016.

Hollis, Catherine. *Leslie Stephen as Mountaineer*. London: Cecil Woolf, 2010.

Hollis, Dawn L. *"Mountain Gloom and Mountain Glory:* The Genealogy of an Idea." *ISLE: Interdisciplinary Studies in Literature and Environment*, isz044 (May 2019). https://doi.org/10.1093/isle/isz044.

Hubbard, Elbert. *Little Journeys to Homes of Great Scientists*. New York: Roycrofters, 1905.

Hulme, Mike. "On the Origin of 'the Greenhouse Effect': John Tyndall's 1859 Interrogation of Nature." *Weather* 64, no. 5 (April 27, 2009): 121–23.

Hultman, Martin, and Paul M. Pulé. *Ecological Masculinities: Theoretical Foundations and Practical Guidance*. London: Routledge, 2018.

Humboldt, Alexander von. "About an Attempt to Climb to the Top of Chimborazo." Translated by Vera M. Kutzinski. *Atlantic Studies* 7, no. 2 (2010): 191–211.

———. *Alexander von Humboldt: Von Mexiko-Stadt nach Veracruz; Tagebuch*. Edited by Ulrike Leitner. Berlin: Akademie, 2005.

———. *Aus meinem Leben: Autobiographische Bekenntnisse*. Edited by Kurt-R. Biermann. Munich: Beck, 1989.

———. *Briefe aus Amerika, 1799–1804*. Edited by Ulrike Moheit. Berlin: Akademie, 1993.

———. *Das Buch der Begegnungen*. Edited by Ottmar Ette. Munich: Manesse, 2018.

————. *The Complete Drawings from the American Travel Journals.* Edited by Ottmar Ette and Julia Maier. Munich: Prestel, 2018.

————. *Cosmos: A Sketch of a Physical Description of the Universe.* Vol. 2, translated by E. C. Otté. London: George Bell and Sons, 1900.

————. *Die Forschungsreise in den Tropen Amerikas.* Vol. 3, edited by Hanno Beck. Darmstadt: Wissenschaftliche Buchgesellschaft, 2008.

————. *Personal Narrative of Travels to the Equinoctial Regions of America, During the Years 1799–1804.* Vol. 1, edited and translated by Thomasina Ross. London: Henry G. Bohn, 1852.

————. *Reise auf dem Río Magdalena, durch die Anden und Mexico.* Edited by Margot Faak. Berlin: Akademie, 2003.

————. *Reise durch Venezuela: Auswahl aus den amerikanischen Reisetagebüchern.* Edited by Margot Faak. Berlin: Akademie, 2000.

————. *Ueber einen Versuch, den Gipfel des Chimborazo zu ersteigen.* Edited by Oliver Lubrich and Ottmar Ette. Berlin: Eichborn, 2006.

————. *Views of the Cordilleras and Monuments of the Indigenous Peoples of the Americas.* Translated by Vera M. Kutzinski and Ottmar Ette. Chicago: University of Chicago Press, 2012.

————. *Views of Nature.* Translated by Mark W. Person, edited by Stephen T. Jackson and Laura Dassow Walls. Chicago: University of Chicago Press, 2014.

Humboldt, Alexander von, and Aimé Bonpland. *Essay on the Geography of Plants.* Chicago: University of Chicago Press, 2009.

Iovino, Serenella, and Serpil Oppermann, eds. *Material Ecocriticism.* Bloomington: Indiana University Press, 2014.

Ireton, Sean, and Caroline Schaumann, eds. *Heights of Reflection: Mountains in the German Imagination from the Middle Ages to the Twenty-First Century.* Rochester, N.Y.: Camden House, 2012.

————. *Mountains of the German Mind: Translations from Gessner to Messner.* Rochester, N.Y.: Camden House, 2020.

Irmscher, Christoph. *Louis Agassiz: Creator of American Science.* Boston: Houghton Mifflin, 2013.

Isserman, Maurice. *Continental Divide: A History of American Mountaineering.* New York: Norton, 2016.

Isserman, Maurice, and Stewart Weaver. *Fallen Giants: A History of Himalayan Mountaineering from the Age of Empire to the Age of Extremes.* New Haven, Conn.: Yale University Press, 2009.

Jackson, Roland. *The Ascent of John Tyndall: Victorian Scientist, Mountaineer, and Public Intellectual.* Oxford: Oxford University Press, 2018.

Jacobson, Kirsten, and John Russon. *Perception and Its Development in Merleau-Ponty's Phenomenology.* Toronto: University of Toronto Press, 2017.

Johnson, Eric Michael. "How John Muir's Brand of Conservation Led to the De-

cline of Yosemite." *Scientific American Blog Network,* August 13, 2014. https://blogs
.scientificamerican.com/primate-diaries/how-john-muir-s-brand-of-conservation
-led-to-the-decline-of-yosemite.

Jurovics, Toby, Carol M. Johnson, Glenn Willumson, and William F. Stapp. *Framing the West: The Survey Photographs of Timothy H. O'Sullivan.* New Haven, Conn.:
Yale University Press, 2010.

Kaiser, Matthew. "A Joy on the Precipice of Death: John Muir and Robert Louis
Stevenson in California." In *Nineteenth-Century British Travelers in the New World,*
edited by Christine Devine, 23–47. Farnham: Ashgate, 2013.

Kehlmann, Daniel. *Measuring the World.* Translated by Carol Brown Janeway. New
York: Pantheon, 2006.

King, Clarence. *Mountaineering in the Sierra Nevada.* 1872. Reprint, Lincoln: University of Nebraska Press, 1997.

Kopf, Martina. *Alpinismus–Andinismus: Gebirgslandschaften in europäischer und lateinamer-
ikanischer Literatur.* Stuttgart: Metzler, 2016.

Kraft, Tobias. "Die Geburt der Gebirge: Alexander von Humboldts Erforschung
des mexikanischen Vulkans Jorullo." *Arsprototo* 1 (2014): 33–36.

Kuklick, Henrika, and Robert E. Kohler, eds. "Introduction." In "Science in the
Field," special issue, *Osiris* 11 (1996): 1–14.

Kupper, Patrick. *Creating Wilderness: A Transnational History of the Swiss National Park.*
New York: Berghahn, 2014.

Kutzinski, Vera M., Ottmar Ette, and Laura Dassow Walls. *Alexander von Humboldt
and the Americas.* Berlin: Walter Frey, 2012.

Kwa, Chunglin. "Alexander von Humboldt's Invention of the Natural Landscape."
European Legacy 10, no. 2 (2005): 149–62.

Leys Stepan, Nancy. *Picturing Tropical Nature.* Ithaca, N.Y.: Cornell University Press,
2001.

Lightman, Bernard. "Scientists as Materialists in the Periodical Press: Tyndall's
Belfast Address." In *Science Serialized,* edited by Geoffrey Cantor and Sally Shuttleworth, 199–237. Cambridge, Mass.: MIT Press, 2004.

Linck, Ethan. "Your Stoke Won't Save Us: The Idea That Outdoor Recreation
Leads to Meaningful Conservation Rests on a Big 'If.'" *High Country News,* May
14, 2018. https://www.hcn.org/issues/50.8/recreation-your-stoke-wont-save-us
?fbclid=IwAR0mnRmDptGlqO9v7I7a6nCg4V8tSIOJpgzP2ODQu1vH8
wAv8bBX7t_Ck6s.

Lubrich, Oliver. "Vom Guckkasten zum Erlebnisraum: Alexander von Humboldt
und die Medien des Reisens." *Figurationen* 2 (2007): 47–66.

Lukes, Timothy J. *Politics and Beauty in America: The Liberal Aesthetics of P. T. Barnum,
John Muir, and Harley Earl.* New York: Palgrave, 2016.

Lurie, Edward. *Nature and the American Mind: Louis Agassiz and the Culture of Science.*
New York: Science History Publications, 1974.

Marcou, Jules. *Life, Letters and Works of Louis Agassiz*. New York: Macmillan, 1896.

Mathieu, Jon. *Die dritte Dimension: Eine vergleichende Geschichte der Berge in der Neuzeit*. Basel: Schwabe, 2011.

———. *Geschichte der Alpen, 1500–1900: Umwelt, Entwicklung, Gesellschaft*. Vienna: Böhlau, 1998.

Mazel, David. *American Literary Environmentalism*. Athens: University of Georgia Press, 2000.

McConnell, Anita. "La Condamine's Scientific Journey down the River Amazon, 1743–1744." *Annals of Science* 48 (1991): 1–19.

McNee, Alan. *The New Mountaineer in Late Victorian Britain: Materiality, Modernity, and the Haptic Sublime*. London: Palgrave Macmillan, 2016.

Merchant, Carolyn. "Shades of Darkness: Race and Environmental History." *Environmental History* 8, no. 3 (July 2003): 380–94.

Merleau-Ponty, Maurice. *Phenomenology of Perception*. Translated by Colin Smith. London: Routledge, 2002.

———. *The Visible and the Invisible*. Chicago: Northwestern University Press, 1969.

Messner, Reinhold. *Fall of Heaven: Whymper's Tragic Matterhorn Climb*. Seattle: Mountaineers Books, 2017.

Meyer-Abich, Adolf. *Alexander von Humboldt*. Hamburg: Rowohlt, 1967.

Moore, James Gregory. *King of the 40th Parallel: Discovery in the American West*. Stanford, Calif.: Stanford University Press, 2006.

Morueta-Holme, Naia, Kristine Engemann, Pablo Sandoval-Acuña, Jeremy D. Jonas, R. Max Segnitz, and Jens-Christian Svenning. "Strong Upslope Shifts in Chimborazo's Vegetation over Two Centuries Since Humboldt." *Proceedings of the National Academy of Sciences of the United States of America (PNAS)* 112, no. 41 (2015): 12741–45.

Muir, John. *Correspondence*. http://scholarlycommons.pacific.edu/jmcl/11563.

———. *John of the Mountains: The Unpublished Journals of John Muir*. Edited by Linnie Marsh Wolfe. Boston: Houghton Mifflin, 1938.

———. *John Muir's Last Journey: South to the Amazon and East to Africa; Unpublished Journals and Selected Correspondence*. Edited by Michael P. Branch. Washington, D.C.: Island Press, 2001.

———. *Nature Writings*. Edited by William Cronon. New York: Penguin, 1997.

———. *Summering in the Sierra*. Edited by Robert Engberg. Madison: University of Wisconsin Press, 1984.

———. *A Thousand-Mile Walk to the Gulf*. Vol. 1 of *The Writings of John Muir*. Boston: Houghton Mifflin, 1916.

———. "Travels in Utah." John Muir's journal, May–July 1877. http://scholarlycommons.pacific.edu/jmj-all/1137.

———. *The Yosemite*. New York: Century, 1912.

Muir, John, and Jeanne Carr. *Kindred and Related Spirits: The Letters of John Muir and*

Jeanne Carr. Edited by Bonnie Johanna Gisel. Salt Lake City: University of Utah Press, 2001.

Mumm, Arnold Louis. "Obituary: Sir Alfred Wills." *Alpine Journal* 27 (1913): 47–54.

Murray, John. *A Hand-Book for Travellers on the Continent.* London, 1836.

O'Gorman, Francis. "'The Mightiest Evangel of the Alpine Club': Masculinity and Agnosticism in the Alpine Writing of John Tyndall." In *Masculinity and Spirituality in Victorian Culture,* edited by Andrew Bradstock, Sean Gill, Anne Hogan, and Sue Morgan, 134–48. New York: St. Martin's, 2000.

O'Grady, John. *Pilgrims to the Wild.* Salt Lake City: University of Utah Press, 1993.

Olson, Richard. *Science and Scientism in Nineteenth-Century Europe.* Urbana: University of Illinois Press, 2008.

Ötzi the Iceman. South Tyrol Museum of Archeology. http://www.iceman.it/en /the-iceman.

Papanikolas, Zeese. *American Silence.* Lincoln: University of Nebraska Press, 2007.

Pinkerton, John. "An Account of the Attempts That Have Been Made to Attain the Summit of Mont Blanc." In *A General Collection of the Best and Most Interesting Voyages and Travels in All Parts of the World,* 677–709. London: Longman, 1809.

Prager, Brad. *Aesthetic Vision and German Romanticism: Writing Images.* Rochester, N.Y.: Camden House, 2007.

Pratt, Mary Louise. *Imperial Eyes: Travel Writing and Transculturation.* New York: Routledge, 1992.

Proctor, Robert N., and Londa Schiebinger, ed. *Agnotology: The Making and Unmaking of Ignorance.* Stanford, Calif.: Stanford University Press, 2008.

Purdy, Jedediah. *After Nature: A Politics for the Anthropocene.* Cambridge, Mass.: Harvard University Press, 2015.

Raymond, Petra. *Von der Landschaft im Kopf zur Landschaft aus Sprache: Die Romantisierung der Alpen in den Reiseschilderungen und die Literarisierung des Gebirges in der Erzählprosa der Goethezeit.* Tübingen: Niemeyer, 1993.

Reidy, Michael S. "Evolutionary Naturalism on High: The Victorians Sequester the Alps." In *Victorian Scientific Naturalism: Community, Identity, Continuity,* edited by Gowan Dawson and Bernard Lightman, 55–78. Chicago: University of Chicago Press, 2014.

———. "Mountaineering, Masculinity, and the Male Body in Mid-Victorian Britain." *Osiris* 30 (2015): 158–81.

Ring, Jim. *How the English Made the Alps.* London: Murray, 2000.

Robbins, David. "Sport, Hegemony, and the Middle Class: The Victorian Mountaineers." *Theory, Culture and Society* 4 (1987): 579–601.

Rousseau, Jean-Jacques. *Julie, or The New Heloise: Letters of Two Lovers Who Live in a Small Town at the Foot of the Alps.* Translated by Philip Stewart and Jean Vaché. Hanover, N.H.: Dartmouth College Press, 1997.

Rowlinson, J. S. "The Theory of Glaciers." *Notes and Records of the Royal Society of London* 26, no. 2 (December 1971): 189–204.

Rupke, Nicolaas A. *Alexander von Humboldt: A Metabiography.* Frankfurt am Main: Peter Lang, 2008.

Ruskin, John. *The Works of John Ruskin.* Vol. 36, *The Letters of John Ruskin,* edited by E. T. Cook and Alexander Wedderburn. London: George Allen, 1909.

Sachs, Aaron. *The Humboldt Current: Nineteenth-Century Exploration and the Roots of American Environmentalism.* New York: Penguin, 2006.

———. "The Ultimate 'Other': Post-Colonialism and Alexander von Humboldt's Ecological Relationship with Nature." *History and Theory* 42 (2003): 111–35.

Sackmann, Werner. "John Tyndall (1820–1893) und seine Beziehungen zu den Alpen und zur Schweiz." *Gesnerus* 50 (1993): 66–78.

Safier, Neil. *Measuring the New World: Enlightenment Science and South America.* Chicago: University of Chicago Press, 2008.

Saussure, Horace-Bénédict de. *Journal de l'ascension du Mont-Blanc.* Edited by Anne Fauche and Samuel Cordier. Chamonix: Guérin, 2006.

———. *Reisen durch die Alpen, nebst einem Versuche über die Naturgeschichte der Gegenden von Genf.* Translated by Jacob Samuel Wyttenbach. Vols. 1–4. Leipzig: Johann Friedrich Junius, 1781–88.

———. *Voyages dans les Alpes, précédés d'un essai sur l'histoire naturelle des environs de Genève.* Vol. 1. Geneva: Chez Barde, Manget & Compagnie, 1779.

———. *Voyages dans les Alpes, précédés d'un essai sur l'histoire naturelle des environs de Genève.* Vol. 2. Neuchâtel: Chez Louis Fauche-Borel, 1780.

———. *Voyages dans les Alpes, précédés d'un essai sur l'histoire naturelle des environs de Genève.* Vol. 4. Geneva: Chez Barde, Manget & Compagnie, 1786.

———. *Voyages dans les Alpes, précédés d'un essai sur l'histoire naturelle des environs de Genève.* Vol. 7. Neuchâtel: Chez Louis Fauche-Borel, 1796.

Schama, Simon. *Landscape and Memory.* New York: Knopf, 1995.

Scharfe, Martin. *Berg-Sucht: Eine Kulturgeschichte des frühen Alpinismus, 1750–1850.* Vienna: Böhlau, 2007.

Schaumann, Caroline. "The Return of the *Bergfilm: Nordwand* (2008) and *Nanga Parbat* (2010)." *German Quarterly* 87, no. 4 (Fall 2014): 416–39.

———. "Weiße Phantasien: Reinheit und Schmutz in Texten von Luis Trenker, Heinrich Harrer und Hans Ertl." *Literatur für Leser* 14, no. 2 (2014): 99–110.

———. "Who Measures the World? Alexander von Humboldt's Chimborazo Climb in the Literary Imagination." *German Quarterly* 82, no. 4 (2009): 447–68.

Scheuchzer, Johann Jakob. *Natur-Geschichte des Schweizerlandes, samt seinen Reisen über die Schweizerische Gebürge.* Vol. 2. Zurich: David Gessner, 1746. https://www.e-rara .ch/zut/content/structure/2270007.

Schiller, Friedrich. "Über das Erhabene." In *Sämtliche Werke,* vol. 12. Stuttgart: Cotta'sche Buchhandlung, 1836.

Schimper, Karl Friedrich. Biographical information provided by the city of Mann-

heim. https://mannheim.de/wirtschaft-entwickeln/naturforscher-karl-friedrich
-schimper-etabliert-eiszeitlehre-und-blattstellung.

Schrepfer, Susan. *Nature's Altars: Mountains, Gender, and American Environmentalism.* Lawrence: University Press of Kansas, 2005.

Sdegno, Emma. "The Alps." In *The Cambridge Companion to John Ruskin,* edited by Francis O'Gorman, 32–48. Cambridge: Cambridge University Press, 2015.

Sillitoe, Alan. *Leading the Blind: A Century of Guidebook Travel, 1815–1914.* London: Macmillan, 1995.

Simpson, Thomas. "Historiographical Review: Modern Mountains from the Enlightenment to the Anthropocene." *Historical Journal* 62, no. 2 (June 2019): 553–81.

Singer, Armand E., ed. *Essays on the Literature of Mountaineering.* Morgantown: West Virginia University Press, 1982.

Smith, Albert Richard. *The Story of Mont Blanc.* London: David Bogue, 1853.

Smith, Ian. *Shadow of the Matterhorn: The Life of Edward Whymper.* Hildersley: Carreg, 2011.

Sonntag, Otto. *The Correspondence between Albrecht von Haller and Horace-Bénédict de Saussure.* Bern: Hans Huber, 1990.

Speich, Daniel. "Mountains Made in Switzerland: Facts and Concerns in Nineteenth-Century Cartography." *Science in Context* 22, no. 3 (2009): 287–408.

Stephen, Leslie. "The Dangers of Mountaineering." In *Peaks, Passes, and Glaciers,* edited by E. H. Blakeney, 331–32. Geneva: Heron, 1971.

———. *The Playground of Europe.* 2nd ed. New York: Putnam, 1909.

———. *The Playground of Europe.* San Rafael, Calif.: Archivum, 2007.

———. "In Praise of Walking." In *Studies of a Biographer,* vol. 3, 254–85. London: Duckworth, 1902.

———. "Round Mont Blanc." In *Men, Books, and Mountains,* 182–202. London: Hogarth, 1956.

"Swiss Tourism in Figures 2015." https://www.bfs.admin.ch/bfsstatic/dam/assets/502977/master.

Taylor, Joseph E., III. *Pilgrims of the Vertical: Yosemite Rock Climbers and Nature at Risk.* Cambridge, Mass.: Harvard University Press, 2010.

Twain, Mark. *A Tramp Abroad.* Vol. 2. New York: Harper, 1879.

Tyndall, John. *The Correspondence of John Tyndall.* Vol. 1, edited by Geoffrey Cantor and Gowan Dawson. Pittsburgh: University of Pittsburgh Press, 2016.

———. *The Correspondence of John Tyndall.* Vol. 2, edited by Melinda Baldwin and Janet Browne. London: Routledge, 2016.

———. *The Correspondence of John Tyndall.* Vol. 3, edited by Ruth Barton, Jeremiah Rankin, and Michael S. Reidy. Pittsburgh: University of Pittsburgh Press, 2017.

———. *The Correspondence of John Tyndall.* Vol. 5, edited by William H. Brock and Geoffrey Cantor. Pittsburgh: University of Pittsburgh Press, 2018.

——. *The Correspondence of John Tyndall*. Vol. 6, edited by Michael D. Barton, Janet Browne, Ken Corbett, and Norman McMillan. Pittsburgh: University of Pittsburgh Press, 2018.

——. *The Glaciers of the Alps and Mountaineering in 1861*. London: J. M. Dent, 1906.

——. "Goethe's 'Farbenlehre.'" In *New Fragments*, 47–77. Cambridge: Cambridge University Press, 2011.

——. *Heat: A Mode of Motion*. 3rd ed. London: Longmans, Green, 1868.

——. *Hours of Exercise in the Alps*. New York: Appleton, 1897.

——. *Hours of Exercise in the Alps*. 3rd ed. London: Longmans, Green, 1873.

——. "On the Study of Physics." In *Fragments of Science*, vol. 1, 281–303. New York: Appleton, 1897.

Unsworth, Walt. *Savage Storms: The Story of Mont Blanc*. London: Hodder and Stoughton, 1986.

Westling, Louise, ed. *The Cambridge Companion to Literature and the Environment*. New York: Cambridge University Press, 2015.

White, Richard. "Discovering Nature in North America." *Journal of American History* 79, no. 3 (1992): 874–91.

Whymper, Edward. *The Apprenticeship of a Mountaineer: Edward Whymper's London Diary, 1855–1859*. London: Record Society, 2008.

——. *Chamonix and the Range of Mont Blanc: A Guide by Edward Whymper*. London: John Murray, 1896.

——. "The Matterhorn Accident: To the Editor of the Times." In *Peaks, Passes and Glaciers*, edited by E. H. Blakeney, 321–28. Geneva: Heron, 1971.

——. *Scrambles Amongst the Alps*. Washington, D.C.: Geographic, 2002.

——. *Travels Amongst the Great Andes*. London: Charles Knight, 1972.

Wilkins, Thurman. *Clarence King: A Biography*. Rev. ed. Albuquerque: University of New Mexico Press, 1988.

Wills, Alfred. *The Eagle's Nest in the Valley of Sixt: A Summer Home Among the Alps, Together with Some Excursions Among the Great Glaciers*. London: Longman, 1860.

——. *Wanderings Among the High Alps*. London: Bentley, 1856.

Wilson, Eric. *The Spiritual History of Ice: Romanticism, Science, and the Imagination*. New York: Palgrave, 2003.

Wilson, Robert. *The Explorer King: Adventure, Science, and the Great Diamond Hoax—Clarence King in the Old West*. Berkeley, Calif.: Shoemaker and Hoard, 2007.

Withey, Lynne. *Grand Tours and Cook's Tours: A History of Leisure Travel, 1750 to 1915*. New York: William Morrow, 1997.

Woolf, Virginia. "Leslie Stephen." In *Collected Essays*, vol. 4, 76–80. London: Hogarth Press, 1967.

Wordsworth, William. "Song at the Feast of Brougham Castle." In *The Complete Poetical Works of William Wordsworth*. Philadelphia: James Kay, Jun. and Brother, 1837.

Worster, Donald. *A Passion for Nature: The Life of John Muir.* New York: Oxford University Press, 2008.

Wózniakowski, Jacek. *Die Wildnis: Zur Deutungsgeschichte des Berges in der europäischen Neuzeit.* Frankfurt: Suhrkamp, 1987.

Wulf, Andrea. *The Invention of Nature: Alexander von Humboldt's New World.* London: Alfred A. Knopf, 2015.

Wyatt, David. *The Fall into Eden: Landscape and Imagination in California.* Cambridge: Cambridge University Press, 1986.

Zantop, Susanne. *Colonial Fantasies: Conquest, Family, and Nation in Precolonial Germany, 1770–1870.* Durham, N.C.: Duke University Press, 1997.

Ziehr, Wilhelm. "Aus der Frühzeit der Gletscherforschung: Ein unbekannter Briefwechsel zwischen König Friedrich Wilhelm IV., Alexander von Humboldt und Louis Agassiz." *Berliner Manuskripte zur Alexander-von-Humboldt-Forschung* 29 (2007): 5–23.

Zink, David D. *Leslie Stephen.* New York: Twayne, 1972.

INDEX